ORIGINAL MINDS

ORIGINAL MINDS

Conversations with CBC Radio's Eleanor Wachtel

with the initial collaboration of
Sandra Rabinovitch

HarperPerennialCanada

Original Minds: Conversations with CBC Radio's
Eleanor Wachtel
© 2003 by Eleanor Wachtel. All rights reserved.

Published by HarperPerennialCanada, an imprint of
HarperCollins Publishers Ltd

First published in hardcover by HarperFlamingo-
Canada, an imprint of HarperCollins Publishers Ltd,
2003. This paperback edition 2004.

HarperCollins books may be purchased for educational, business, or sales promotional use through
our Special Markets Department.

HarperCollins Publishers Ltd
2 Bloor Street East, 20th Floor
Toronto, Ontario, Canada
M4W 1A8

www.harpercanada.com

National Library of Canada Cataloguing in
Publication

Wachtel, Eleanor
Original minds : conversations with CBC Radio's
Eleanor Wachtel / foreword by Carol Shields. –
HarperPerennial Canada ed.

ISBN 0-00-639419-1

1. Interviews. I. Title.

D857.W33 2004   081   C2003-905656-2

HC 9 8 7 6 5 4 3 2 1

Printed and bound in the United States
Set in FF Quadraat

For S L S

and in loving memory of

Peter Dyson
1931–2002

Mary Meigs
1917–2002

and

Ray Reiter
1939–2002

Contents

Foreword by Carol Shields   ix

Introduction   1

Jonathan Miller   7

Jane Goodall   47

Bernardo Bertolucci   77

George Steiner   97

Desmond Tutu   128

Susan Sontag   143

Amartya Sen   170

Gloria Steinem   198

Jared Diamond   223

Oliver Sacks   250

Jane Jacobs   270

Umberto Eco   295

Mary Douglas   321

Noam Chomsky   350

Arthur C. Clarke 371
Harold Bloom 394

Acknowledgements 431

Foreword
Carol Shields

There's nothing quite like Eleanor Wachtel's "Writers & Company." It's like belonging to a private club that meets regularly at five o'clock—in my case on the west coast—on Sunday afternoons. You feel she's bringing you together with others who are listening and responding to the same ideas. There is a listenership that forms, a cohesive group interested in the very questions that you're interested in: how writers get ideas, how they run with them.

Eleanor's is one of the great radio voices though it doesn't sound like any other voice on the radio. There is no artifice, it's direct and real. It's not difficult to find "Writers & Company" on the dial. You immediately recognize the rhythm of the conversation, her intensity, concentration and warmth.

Her style is harder to describe. Eleanor is much more than an interviewer: she enters into conversations, opens debates, sketches in background. She interprets and suggests, but never imposes. She projects curiosity, spontaneity, humour and goodwill. Her sense of respect, her tact, her utter lack of obsequiousness, even with the famous, and her uncanny ability to ask difficult questions—don't I know it!—have endeared her to readers and listeners. And she does all this so economically. In the course of an hour-long interview, she often speaks relatively little. Just a word, a short response, will reveal her thorough knowledge of the author's work. A quick comment will clarify a possible misunderstanding. Each conversation has a shape and a direction, as if there were an arc of intent. But when an unexpected turn in the conversation occurs, she pursues it and we discover that the digression was essential.

Think of the moment when, instead of going on to another question, Eleanor pauses to consider the writer's last answer. "How so?" she asks and then the writer pauses too. The silence lingers. The listener wonders, what else is there to be said? And then comes the response: thoughtful, revealing. We sense the mind of the writer reaching into some zone of experience not before articulated. We admire the sweep of this mind, the way it connects ideas and feelings.

As a listener, I have the sense of being utterly present in the exchange. An intimate triangle is formed: the writer, Eleanor and me. I'm there when Roddy Doyle can't stop laughing, when J. M. Coetzee begins to relax, when Harold Bloom is moved to tears. I've known of friends who were listening on the car radio and who've had to pull over to the side of the road, to participate more fully. I've heard writers being interviewed who are unfamiliar with the show and who at first don't realize the skills of their host. As the interview progresses with the leisure of a whole hour, I've heard the penny drop. The careful responses fall away; the writers become open, excited. At interview's end, when they say they've enjoyed themselves, they speak with genuine pleasure.

I'm inspired by those people who've established what I call a writer's life. I hope to discover a little more about how one digs into the world with this writing mechanism. I like to know about their mothers and what their fathers did, whether they had siblings, how they feel about their families, what they believed was possible and what happened instead. I want to know when people developed their ideas: for example, when women became aware of feminism, where they were in the seventies. I'm interested in questions of how our lives synchronize or fail to synchronize. Eleanor understands how creative work is grounded in personal experience; she always tries to give us the emotional context for the work. She asks the questions that I really want to ask.

Eleanor is usually the first to interview me when I've finished a book, so I don't have my set speech ready; I'm probably a little fresher and more open, though not very polished. But I imagine that she wouldn't want her subjects to be polished. She wants them to be spontaneous. Writers produce books, but we're not necessarily analytical about how we arrive at our ideas or how we put them together. So being questioned holds us accountable for—in my case—narrative turnings, or certain qualities in my characters that seem to recur: Why do I keep going back to these particular subjects? That's what a good interview can do: catch in the net the things that seem to come randomly out of the writer's mind.

An interview with Eleanor is very like a conversation. Of course, because of my long familiarity with her voice, which comes out of our friendship, as well as from hearing her on the radio, I can forget for a moment that I'm being interviewed. I may become more conscious of rambling, but that's not necessarily bad—to ramble over the material to find new ways of looking at my writing. And I always know that she's going to catch me out where the fabric of my writing for some reason has gone weak and I've indulged in a kind of poetic fantasy that I haven't really figured out.

Like Eleanor's two previous volumes of interviews, *Original Minds* gives me a chance to enjoy these complex and rich conversations again. Here I meet people who've changed how we think, including the way we recreate our experience through imagination. These women and men tell me a great deal about the ways in which it is possible to understand our world, not only intellectually, but also symbolically and emotionally.

Take Susan Sontag. She is so articulate about what she wants to do, yet she still has her mind open and is ready to rethink everything in the light, for example, of her illness. She is an adventurous writer who has managed to handle conflict with her own culture quite gracefully. Or someone like Harold Bloom who is almost overwhelming in his love of literature; and that spills over to the reader or listener. He is perched on such a solid embankment of culture that it develops a reality for you. I admire people who are engaged but are willing to remain open and a little bit restless in their enquiries.

I've been thinking about what original means, and remember that famous quotation of Sir Isaac Newton. When he was praised, he said, "If I have seen further it is by standing on the shoulders of giants." Maybe there aren't very many original thinkers in the world, but there are certainly people who have questioned our overall system at historically important moments, or historically memorable moments—who think beyond their society but, more important, outside their time. These are the people we call original minds because what they have contributed has a sense of freshness, is utilitarian, is applicable.

I think one has to be courageous to be original. You have to blurt out ideas that are inconsistent with traditional thinking and do it at the risk of making a fool of yourself—to say something which is utterly obvious, for example, or just the opposite of obvious—utterly ridiculous. It's that flash of genius and you have to be brave enough to express it. You have to be devoted enough to pursue it and persist and make the ideas work. Both the radio series and now the book, *Original Minds*, have led me to many kinds of discoveries. I have come away with a sense of amplified humanity.

INTRODUCTION
ELEANOR WACHTEL

When I was eleven or twelve, my sister gave me German measles. It was quite a mild case, because I had received an inoculation; still, I was contagious, and wasn't allowed to go to school. In short, I had twelve days to stay (more or less) in bed and read.

I quickly ran out of books. From my bedroom window, I imagined I could see into the local children's library. Were there not a building or two in between, not to mention a brick wall, I probably could have. But I had to wait for my now-recovered sister to bring me books. What I remember best are the biographies—Madame Curie, Abraham Lincoln, Thomas Alva Edison (I savoured the exoticism of Alva). These were part of a series, the Signature books, that traced a whole life, from beginning to end, with all its courage, tenacity and ingenuity. They were exciting. Not that I necessarily imagined becoming a scientist or political leader or inventor, but I saw that these individuals had changed the world I lived in. Children are attracted to heroism, of course, but I was also drawn to the mix of the personal and the professional, the life and the work—stories that rivalled the fiction that was my usual reading.

And I wondered where that boldness, that singularity, that creativity had come from.

I was reminded of all this while putting together my *Original Minds* series for radio. As the new millennium approached, I wanted to interview people who had shaped the last century and whose influence would continue into the next. To be sure, the millennium, as a hinge, is an arbitrary point of perspective, but it seemed appropriate to seize such a moment to take a look around. Instead of basing a series on geography—as I'd done in South Africa, Berlin, Russia, India, and Israel—or on a timely theme, such as writers of the Muslim world, this would be portraits of individual thinkers and creators from the fields of art, science, economics, anthropology, and social policy. I hoped to have wide-ranging conversations with some of the most inspiring men and women of our time, people who've made a difference.

I began with my own wish list, people I had always admired, thinkers who were imaginative, who eluded the usual categories, who stood out on the horizon. In many cases I had followed their careers and was familiar with their ideas and their subjects—ranging from apes to angels—but now I welcomed the opportunity to find out how they gave shape to their own work. I suppose I wanted them to tell me the meaning of life, or at least to provide models of a fully engaged intellect.

As the interviews progressed, I realized that what I was trying to get at was something closer to a sensibility. One of the meanings of sensibility is "emotional consciousness," echoing the double meaning of the Latin *sensus*—both feeling and understanding. This area where thinking connects with feelings and with life events, where ideas merge with temperament was what I wanted to explore more deeply. I wanted to know what kept these thinkers so passionate.

For an original mind is above all a passionate mind. Though the backgrounds and styles of the people in this book are very divergent, they all share the drive and commitment of the perpetually curious—a quality also found in many of the best writers of fiction. They have an appetite for the world and for the present moment, and this openness is combined with discipline, with conviction, and with a readiness to take risks.

They also have in common a desire to be read by a wide public. This is not something to be taken for granted. Today, with increasingly specialized academic vocabularies, and a certain disdain for the popularizer, there is considerable reward for those who stick to their small, high-powered worlds—the genius lost in a cloud. By contrast, the thinkers gathered in this book all wish to make their ideas accessible. Whether activists, academics or artists, they direct their enthusiasm and energy towards a broad audience. There is generosity in this impulse, but also faith that a community of concerns unites us all. And although these thinkers neither share the same views nor agree with one another on many fundamental assumptions, they all insist on being citizens of our world. They are in daily conversation with us.

Each interviews maps out a different conceptual geography. We follow these innovators as they cross from one territory to another or—more often—expand the contours of their disciplines, so that after them the landscape is no longer the same: linguistics after Chomsky, anthropology after Mary Douglas, city planning after Jane Jacobs, semiotics after Umberto Eco, economics after Amartya Sen, neurology after Oliver Sacks. Or they envision wholly new ground from which to view the world: Desmond Tutu's South Africa or Gloria Steinem's feminism.

Given such different sensibilities, it is rare to find all these people—and all these fields—collected under one roof. For me, that is one of the particular pleasures of this enterprise, though it prevents me from proposing too many generalizations. These figures don't emerge from similar backgrounds or psychologies. Some had difficult or elusive mothers, or hard-to-please fathers; others credit enormously supportive mothers, or express ambivalence about deeply influential fathers. Some come from an environment of scholarly or professional achievement; others were the first in their family to attain higher education. Some knew from a very young age exactly what they wanted to do, others discovered their ambitions later, and some persist even now in exploring different areas of interest. In a way, I find this diversity reassuring, democratic: anyone, it seems, can do anything, given enough determination and inventiveness. To quote Einstein, "Imagination is more important than knowledge."

And this very determination is inspiring. Not long ago, when I was called upon to speak to a roomful of graduates, I found myself invoking a number of these extraordinary people: Jonathan Miller for his relentless curiosity in examining the ordinary, the overlooked, the undervalued—all that we take for granted; George Steiner for his faith in human adaptability; Arthur C. Clarke for anticipating communications satellites, spending the next half century conjuring fantastic and realistic futures, and still being fascinated by the possibility of life on Mars. Then there is the primatologist Jane Goodall, who studies chimpanzees in Tanzania. Without training, she first went there simply because of her love of animals. She'd read Dr. Dolittle as a child, and also Tarzan, and says she thought she would have made a much better Jane. Less wimpy. Besides, she was already called Jane.

Like the others in this book, Goodall is inspiring in more than one way. First, she followed her dream, her passion. She went to Africa to visit a school friend, and she figured out a way to stay and study what she loved. Then, after getting to know a marvellous community of chimps in an idyllic corner of the continent and establishing herself as a world authority, she left paradise and dedicated herself to saving chimps around the world: fighting for better conditions in captivity and decent treatment in laboratories. For more than twenty years now, she's never stayed anywhere for longer than three weeks. And the third way in which I find her inspiring is that, on the one hand, she believes that an individual can make a difference—and she herself is certainly evidence of this—and, on the other, that as a species we're evolving morally. She talks about seeing evidence of our physical evolution firsthand when she dug up the fossils at Olduvai Gorge with Louis Leakey. Then came our cultural evolution with the advent of language. And now—despite all the destruction and evil, which she's certainly aware of—she perceives a moral evolution occurring at a far greater pace than our physical one, although she acknowledges we're still in a race against time. She even titled one of her books Reason for Hope.

Perhaps because I myself spent time in Africa in the early 1970s, I've always been drawn to the continent, with its richness of animal species,

its troubling politics, and the extremes of response both of these produce. I remember South African novelist Nadine Gordimer telling me
how wonderful it was to live in a place where there were still heroes.
And when my interview with the former archbishop Desmond Tutu was
recently rebroadcast, a listener phoned to say he would happily trade
whatever knowledge or wisdom he possessed for just some of Tutu's
optimism. "Optimism is true moral courage," said a man of a very different time and place, the early-twentieth-century Antarctic explorer Sir
Ernest Shackleton. Again, this is not to say that everyone included here
is optimistic, but I do believe an implicit optimism fuels their continuing dedication.

George Steiner talks about the "debt of love" he feels towards the
great work of others, the sense of immense privilege he has in knowing
it. Invoking those fascinating nature films in which a tiny bird sits atop
a massive rhinoceros in the tall grasslands, he describes how the bird
helps clean the rhinoceros and warns it of imminent danger. "More
interestingly," he says, "the bird tells others that rhino is coming." It
chirps away and says, "Rhino is coming."

It has been my good luck to feel at times like that little bird, sitting
atop greatness. This book could be called Rhino Is Coming.

Jonathan Miller

I decided to begin with Jonathan Miller because he embraces so many subjects with fervent wit, curiosity and a capacious intelligence. His enthusiasms are so diverse that many people think there are two Jonathan Millers—or even three. My first exposure to him was through the antic comedy of *Beyond the Fringe*, a satirical revue that goes back to 1960 at the Edinburgh Festival, and went on to be a hit in London and New York. There were *Beyond the Fringe* recordings, and I can still remember many of those sketches.

Jonathan Miller was already a medical doctor when he became a performer, but that didn't really surface publicly until his thirteen-part television series on the history of medicine, *The Body in Question*, which also became a book (1978). It took a while for me to realize this was the same Jonathan Miller who'd performed with Peter Cook, Dudley Moore and Alan Bennett in *Beyond the Fringe*.

The third Jonathan Miller is the international director of theatre and opera, from the BBC Shakespeare series of the 1980s and working for London's National Theatre and the Old Vic, to directing more than fifty opera productions in London, New York, Paris,

Florence, Berlin and Zurich. Along the way, he wrote a book about theatre called The Afterlife of Plays (1992) and edited books about Freud, Don Giovanni, and humour.

Miller is famous for his innovative stage productions, often drawing on paintings or photographs for inspiration. When I went to see him, he was directing Rossini's Ermione for the Santa Fe Opera. The story takes place just after the Trojan War, but Miller decided to set it in nineteenth-century America, in the aftermath of the Civil War, creating a charcoal-toned set designed to look like a period daguerreotype. "It's another long fratricidal war," he explained to me. "And it gets rid of those damn Greek tunics."

In the last few years, Jonathan Miller has produced two books of visual art—one, On Reflection (1998), is based on a show about perception that he curated for the National Gallery in London. The other is a selection of his own colour photographs and notebook entries, going back thirty years, a striking book called Nowhere in Particular (1999).

While he was in Santa Fe, between rehearsals of Ermione, he had found a welder and was working on a sculpture, using rusty bits of odds and ends, a rather large and attractive construction. Of course, Miller's father was a philosopher who became interested in anthropology, who studied medicine and became a psychiatrist interested in criminology, who also painted and sculpted in his spare time.

Jonathan Miller is still something of a physical comic, with an expressive, mobile face. His conversation ranges from anthropology and art to neuroscience, psychology and theatre, but he doesn't hesitate to reproduce his imitations of clucking hens or a railway train, sketches that saved him from being bullied at school when he was eight years old. As we headed for one of the rehearsal rooms of the Santa Fe Opera, he mooched a cigarette from a cast member. "It's OK," he said, "I'm a doctor."

WACHTEL You've said that even as a child you were interested in the functioning of the brain. Do you know where such an unusual preoccupation for a child came from? What sparked it?

MILLER I don't really know where original curiosities arise. I can remember the first moment—at least my father tells me it was the first moment—when I seemed to show some interest in it. I suppose I must have been about six or seven, perhaps younger. He was opening his copy of Gray's *Anatomy* and came to the section where there were coloured illustrations of the brain. I asked him where the mind was, and I think he was stopped short in his tracks that someone should actually see that there might be a difference between "brain" and "mind," albeit with a connection. I don't think I showed any particular interest in it after that, but I think that from the outset of studying biology I was interested in what it was that made creatures behave and why it was that they didn't behave like rocks and puddles, why they seemed to have minds of their own, why they went in the opposite direction to the direction in which stones rolled on slopes. This seemed to me to be a rather puzzling and interesting thing, particularly when it was executed by something as small as an ant, which didn't seem to have much room for the sort of apparatus necessary to enable it or provoke it to go uphill, against gravity. From then on, I began to show an interest in these things.

WACHTEL Do you have any idea why you knew that the mind and the brain were connected?

MILLER I'm not really certain that I did know they were connected. Why I should, at the age of six, have said, "Where is the mind?" when shown a cross-section of the brain, remains a mystery to me. But I seemed to have had some sort of intimation that there was something about the head that seemed to be responsible for what I called the mind. I suppose a lot of people feel that the mind is in the head for the simple reason that the most important sense organ, the eyes, which deliver most of the content of consciousness—in other words, the visual world—are in the head, and I felt therefore that I saw the world from my head. Now, whether I really understood at that time that I saw the world with my head because of something in addition to the eyes is quite doubtful. I don't think I really understood that the eyes were really not much more than a portal through which things gained access to the inside of the head and that the inside of the head was what executed the extraordinarily complicated business of enabling me to see trees rather than just moving greenness.

WACHTEL You once described the first time you went to the cinema, when you were about seven years old, and saw *The Reluctant Dragon*. Even there it wasn't just the plot or the drama that you responded to; there was another dimension that you seemed to be aware of.

MILLER I was aware of the fact that I saw pictures that moved on a screen and that when I turned my head there was this fluttering, fluted beam made visible by the smoke—smoking was allowed in the cinema in those days—that seemed to issue from the chamber where the projector was. I saw then that there was a relationship between what could be seen and some source of visual information that was carried by this fluttering beam because I couldn't see a picture until the beam was intercepted by a screen. This seemed to me, at that time, to be a model of what perception was like, that perhaps the eye was like a projector and there was some sort of neurological equivalent of a beam which projected it to a screen in the head. I didn't realize at that time that such a model would have set up an infinite regress. If there was a screen inside my head, what was there looking at the screen? One had to set up the idea that there was another projector and another screen, and therefore an infinite regress of spectators. This, of course, is what one philosopher has described as the Cartesian theatre, the idea that there is a phantom spectator seated in a viewing room. It can't work like that, of course, for lots of reasons. I suppose as I became more and more acquainted with the brain, I realized that it is not something that accommodates a spectator, wherein that individual sits and looks at something projected, but that something about the brain, by virtue of its organization, gives rise to a subjective experience on the part of the owner of the brain.

I think now that there is perhaps an impenetrable mystery about why it is that something material and physical, the brain, can give rise to a subjective sensation, what the philosophers call *qualia*, or raw feelings. You can design a machine that behaves as if it distinguishes between red and green. With instructions, it can be trained to pick up red blocks and distinguish them from green blocks. But it's very unlikely that machines have a feeling of what it's like to see a red block. The mystery is how brains can give rise to something that is quite clearly *not* an observable phenomenon, the consciousness of redness. I think this will probably remain forever a mystery, although there are what we call radical eliminativists, who would like to take out of the system anything that might be non-material. I'm not saying that there is anything non-material which enables one to have pain, consciousness of redness and anger. I'm absolutely committed to a fundamentally materialist view of the brain. I don't think there's anything other than brain, that something else sneaks in. I don't think there's a cat flap in the back of the brain into which the spirit somehow gains access because, once again, that returns you to the Cartesian theatre. I'm a materialist, anyway—I'm what one of my friends, Colin McGinn, who's a philosopher at Rutgers, calls an agnostic materialist. I'm an absolutely dyed-in-the-wool materialist about brains and consciousness, but I think it may well be that we'll never find out how it is that brains can give rise to feelings of redness on the part of their owner.

WACHTEL I want to talk more about consciousness in a few minutes, but, as a kid, you had what I would think of as pretty precocious kinds of perceptions, and yet you've described yourself as not clever as a schoolboy. You say that "It wasn't until I was fourteen that I actually discovered I had a thoughtful mind." How did you make that discovery?

MILLER I was pretty wretched as a child. I knew I wasn't good at formal lessons. I couldn't do math or straightforward grammar or anything that would make me pass as a student. I was restless as a child, for the simple reason that my family travelled a great deal during the war, from one post to another, following my father, who was a military psychiatrist. So I never settled down, and I felt ill at ease at school, frightened and inadequate. And then, when I was ten or eleven, my father gave me an old brass microscope, and I began looking at what we call infusions, like hay being stewed up in water, and saw for the first time animalcules, infusoria. I was intrigued, once again, as I suppose I must have been when I was a very small child, by the idea of the spontaneity and mobility of these unpromising, small things that I could see down this brass tube. I became committed to the idea of zoology, so I gave up classics and switched to the science side of school. This was much against the will and wishes of my headmaster, who said, "I know you would like to be a doctor." At that time I didn't particularly want to be a doctor, but he said, "If you give up classics, what do you think will happen when you discover a new disease and can't name it because you don't know any Latin?" That seemed to me an implausible objection. So I made the jump into the biology side, as we called it at school, and became an enthusiastic Darwinian biologist. I was exposed to Darwinian ideas by my teacher, who was very inspired and rather charismatic. With a number of friends, including Oliver Sacks and others, we became students of zoology and botany and living forms because of our great interest. I discovered that I was good at dissecting and that I was good at thinking about how these things worked. I became fascinated by animal physiology and also by the classification of animals, why it was that they were so different from one another, why they became more and more complicated as they seemed to ascend the evolutionary scale. And then I discovered that curiosity was what I had, and that my curiosity made me smart.

WACHTEL You grew up in an intellectual, cultured family. Your father, as well as being one of the inaugurators of forensic psychiatry, child guidance and child psychiatry, was also qualified in neurology and the law. He was twenty years older than your mother, who was a novelist and literary biographer. What was the atmosphere like in your home?

MILLER Well, it wasn't conspicuously or even noticeably intellectual or literary when I was a child. My father was away a lot of the time because he was moving around the country—and even though we followed him, he was very busy. My mother was a rather hermetic and withdrawn writer. She would go to her study and type and write, and I don't think she ever talked very much about the act of writing or, indeed, encouraged me to be a reader. I was a reader. I read Mowgli [a character in Kipling's *The Jungle Book*]—that sort of thing—when I was a small boy. But I wasn't aware of there being intellectual discourse in the house until I was fourteen or fifteen and began talking to my father about his study of zoology and philosophy. He'd been a student of people like Bertrand Russell and John McTaggart, who was an English philosophical idealist. But, nevertheless, the bookshelves were lined with these volumes and I gradually began to dip into them. I remember at the age of fifteen reading Russell's *Analysis of Mind* and, once again, the notion of mentality began to interest me. There are all sorts of things that Russell invoked which I now don't believe in—sense data, for example. Sense data sounds as if there are things given to a mind to look at, and I don't think it works like that. But nevertheless, I was introduced to the notion that there was a problem about mentality and consciousness and perception and so forth, and also about action and what we mean by action, how we distinguish actions from mere events. And so by the time I was sixteen or seventeen, a philosophical mode of thought had begun to infiltrate my purely zoological interests and I began to think philosophically about what it was to be an organism and how organisms differed from things like stones and puddles.

WACHTEL You were also sent to psychiatrists as a child. Was that interesting or invasive?

MILLER I don't think it was invasive. It was boring, because it got in the way of playing cricket. I never quite understood why I was going to them. I was a rather miserable child, and I used to wet myself a lot when I was younger. I think that was simply the anxiety of travelling a great deal and the insecurities and darkness of the surrounding war. All those things made life uneasy for me. I probably had difficulties and tantrums, which I can't remember, that led to my being sent, one after another, to people like Susan Isaacs and even to D. W. Winnicott. So I was analyzed and brought up in the purple of British analysis, but I don't think it made any difference to my life at all. Not that I can remember.

WACHTEL You talked once about how you thought your parents may have found it harder to deal with their own family than with strangers. Do you know why that was?

MILLER I don't know. I think that my father was a characteristically Victorian figure, rather detached from his children, as many Victorian parents were. My mother was largely preoccupied with her work. She wasn't really interested in domesticity. She felt as a dutiful wife that she was required to do things like cooking, but that, for her, consisted of from time to time tipping the carcass of a chicken into some boiling water and coming back half an hour later in the hope that one could eat what had resulted. She wasn't physically affectionate and neither was my father, but I don't think it was a defect of theirs. My father was born, after all, in 1893 and my mother was born in 1910, and overt affection and the sort of sloppy, dishevelled comforts of modern families never occurred to them.

WACHTEL How do you think they influenced you? Or inspired you?

MILLER By the time I was sixteen or seventeen and could talk to both of them, I began to pride myself on accurate physical descriptions of what was to be seen, making discriminating judgements about how things looked and what they looked like. The use of metaphor, for example. I remember, when I was quite young actually, pleasing and startling my mother after I'd walked across a lawn where the grass was heavily covered with hoarfrost and saying to her that it looked like lavender because of that white hair of hoarfrost. She stopped dead in her tracks, pleased that I had somehow drawn a comparison. She encouraged me by her appreciation of accurate metaphors and characterizations.

My father introduced me to ideas that were later very important to me. When I was a medical student, he talked a lot about a particular teacher who had had a great influence on him, the anthropologist and physiologist W. H. Rivers, who started life as a doctor and who'd written a great long chapter in Schaeffer's *Textbook of Physiology*. Rivers was also one of the founding fathers of British anthropology and was interested in the significance of symbolic thought in social structures, as well as in physiology. I would have conversations with my father about the structure of the mind as the brain imposed structure upon it, and then he would invoke John Hughlings Jackson, the man who set such store in an evolutionary view of the nervous system as something that was hierarchically organized in a succession of levels that had been acquired, stage by stage, in the evolution of the human nervous system. That had a profound influence on me. I remember the two volumes of Jackson's *Selected Writings* which I began to dip into when I was seventeen or eighteen. So between Russell's analysis of mind, on the one hand, and Jackson's view of the nervous system on the other, I was already fixed on a particular approach to brains and mentalities. But I was also affected by my mother, who was interested in what it was like to have a mind and how having a mind gives one the ability to do something that animals don't do, which is to be metaphorical about experiences.

WACHTEL W. H. Rivers, of course, has become better known since Pat Barker wrote about him in her World War I novel *Regeneration*.

MILLER Indeed, and I think people became interested in Rivers's wartime study of shell shock. Shortly after Rivers qualified in 1917, he went to France and began to see injuries to the brain and spinal chord. He worked with a great English neurologist rather fittingly called Henry Head and another man called Gordon Holmes. They became interested in the fact that there were a significant number of men coming out of the trenches with serious disorders for which there wasn't a corresponding injury. They were paralyzed or they were blind or they were disabled in some way, and there was no shrapnel wound, nothing, to account for it. I think gradually my father drifted further and further towards the psychiatric interpretation of certain sorts of disability. But it was always backed by his neurological interest and by both Henry Head, who was deeply influenced by Hughlings Jackson, and by Hughlings Jackson himself, who in turn had been influenced by Herbert Spencer, a now largely forgotten English philosopher who was proto-Darwinian and a great supporter of Darwin. It was probably Spencer who was responsible for Darwin's use of the phrase "the survival of the fittest," which Darwin didn't really like. My father had all of Spencer's writing in his library. I never became a Spencerian, but I was, as it were, a Spencerian derivatively through the work of Hughlings Jackson.

WACHTEL You've described your father as a polymath because of his interests in philosophy, anthropology, medicine and forensic psychiatry, and because he painted and sculpted in his spare time. Do you think that influenced your own polymathic inclinations?

MILLER I don't think that anyone of that period ever thought in terms of being a polymath. That, I think, is a phrase that is characteristic of modern times. To have interests and achievements in more than one field is seen as being what vulgar journalism refers to as a Renaissance man, which I think is a most appalling way of describing simply catholic curiosities. I think that a large number of civilized and cultivated Victorians, people like Leslie Stephen, for example, and his offspring, felt it quite natural to have an interest in things that seemed connected to one another. Of course you read the classics and were familiar with Jane Austen and Wordsworth, but that didn't show you were a polymath. It simply showed that you had an accommodating curiosity about everything around you. There were obviously limits for each person. My limits were particularly that I couldn't do maths. I still can't, and I deeply regret it and feel disabled by it. I don't think of myself as a polymath, nor do I think of my father as one. He was absolutely characteristic of the highly educated Victorian intellectual for whom it was natural to go from one thing to another. How could they be disconnected, these things?

WACHTEL And for you?

MILLER I felt exactly the same way. I suppose I was brought up to believe the same thing as my parents believed: that curiosity was what made life worth living, that there were answers to things that were intriguing and interesting and interconnected, and what made them interesting was the fact that they *were* interconnected. They didn't follow the lines of university faculties.

WACHTEL Having made the leap into biology, as you said, was medicine an obvious choice for you?

MILLER I don't know at what point I made up my mind that I was going to be a physician rather than a zoologist. I suppose that my interest in the nervous system had begun to predominate by that time, and it seemed that the best way of getting to the most interesting nervous system there was—which is ours—was to have a medical qualification that licensed me to ask questions that would have seemed rude if one weren't a doctor. Like who's the prime minister and what day is it today. I think that those sorts of questions, asked by anyone other than a doctor, would be seen as rude and impudent, and particularly the more intimate questions, like how often do you have to pee and do you have difficulty peeing. Do you know that you've just shit yourself? Having a medical degree gives you a ringside seat at things that normally have to be seen at a distance by unqualified people. So I thought that it was going to be useful in that way.

WACHTEL Did studying and then practising medicine satisfy you?

MILLER Oh, the study of medicine was deeply interesting. It was simply zoology carried on by other methods, but it was more interesting than zoology in one sense, in that the animal I was studying was able to tell me things. As the American philosopher Tom Nagel has said, there must be something it's like to be a bat, but the bat's not telling—even under close questioning. Whereas a great deal of what it's like to be a person is communicable by language. We also now know, as a result of what is called the cognitive revolution, that a great deal of what enables us to be persons and do all the things that we regard as second nature— like speaking without having to look up words in a dictionary and identifying objects without having to look at an inventory to see what their name is—is due to operations and processes inside our heads to which we don't have conscious access. Perhaps the most important form of the unconscious is not the one that Freud described—what I call the "custodial unconscious," the unconscious in which shameful feelings are kept under lock and key—but the "enabling unconscious," which allows us to do things without having to plunge into deep structures that aren't accessible to us anyway.

WACHTEL Another thing that drew you into medicine was your interest in what you've described as the minutiae of human behaviour—

small gestures, inflections, body language. What truths about the mind did you hope to discover through these things?

MILLER I don't think I ever wanted to find out truths about the mind. It's just that I was naturally curious about these things, which very often were left undescribed because they were regarded as rubbish. What was really important was how we pursued virtue, how we behaved courageously, how morality was sustained, what the higher levels of intelligence consisted of. A lot of things went unobserved because they were thought to be trivial, like the hand movements that accompany speech, the non-verbal gestures that we constantly use to express things that can't be put into language, and how we would like other people to take us. In that respect, I was deeply influenced later—although I'd already had a curiosity about these things—by the writing of the American social anthropologist Erving Goffman. He rather successfully explained things that were otherwise impenetrable, and drew attention to aspects of behaviour that had been neglected because they were thought to be unimportant—the noise in the system, the idiosyncrasies. I think in a way it's comparable, though not entirely, to Freud's ability to see that slips of the tongue are revealing. I don't think he was right about slips of the tongue—other people wrote more interestingly later about what slips of the tongue told us about the structure of language than what Freud thought slips of the tongue told us about the unconscious. Victoria Fromkin at UCLA studied slips of the tongue very carefully and discovered that if you look at the incidence and the statistics of slips of the tongue, you actually find out something about how we organize speech. These slips of the tongue aren't necessarily guides to deeper thought, but they do give us fracture lines that enable us to see something about the way in which sentences are planned by the brain.

WACHTEL It was your observation of tiny things that people do that made you such a good comic performer and led you off in another direction entirely while you were at Cambridge. You were studying history and later the philosophy of science when you began performing in theatricals, and then later, while specializing, you performed in various London cabarets. What was the appeal for you of performing?

MILLER Oh, showing off, I suppose. As a small child I won the attention or approval—or diminished the disapproval—of my peers by imitating clucking hens or making sounds that were convincingly like railway trains. It isn't an enormously useful achievement now, but it actually served me quite well in the days when I might otherwise have been bullied or disparaged by my peers in school for being such an incompetent decliner of nouns and conjugator of verbs and an absolute incompetent in mathematics. Clucking like a hen may not have been a good substitute for conjugating irregular verbs, but nevertheless it was an achievement of some sort amongst schoolboys.

When I was about sixteen, I found that I could collaborate with colleagues and invent comic sketches. It was nice making people laugh, discovering stuff that makes people laugh. If it makes you laugh, chances are that it can make other people laugh. I didn't think I was ever going to do it professionally, but I went on doing it in Cambridge, though not very much. I was mostly too busy dissecting the human body and washing the rancid human fat off my hands at the end of the day. I was an enthusiastic scientific scholar, but I did these other things from time to time and became quite well known for doing them. After I did my clinical work, I was invited, along with the other three—Alan Bennett, Peter Cook and Dudley Moore—to participate in a late-night show at the Edinburgh Festival which became famous as *Beyond the Fringe*. It was downhill all the way from there.

WACHTEL Was it as much fun to do as it was for the audience?

MILLER I don't think it would have been as much fun for the audience if it hadn't been such fun for us. What was fresh about it was that we were drawing attention to stuff that wasn't show biz. Most of the earlier revues' approach had been, Wouldn't it be funny if . . . ?, while our approach was, Isn't it funny that . . . ? We drew attention to things that were ludicrous and interesting and comic about ordinary life. Often, again, trivialities. This has continued to be my policy as a director. People often ask me what being a director is, and it's very much the same as being a good comic performer. You're drawing attention to things that people have known all along but have forgotten. And one of the most exciting things about humour is, in fact, bringing to the surface things that have been forgotten, not because, as Freud might have said, they've been repressed, but simply because they've become second nature.

WACHTEL It isn't just that you brought our attention to things that were forgotten. There was a spin on what you did.

MILLER I can't see from inside what the spin was. I can sometimes see it when I look back, but they are almost all absurdities that are currently in our daily lives anyway. That is what makes people laugh.

WACHTEL You performed for three years in *Beyond the Fringe* and you say you used to stand open-mouthed with wonder at the relationship between the performance and the laughter that it provoked. You've co-edited a book on humour. You've written an essay about jokes and joking. What have you come to understand about humour? You've said it's unclassifiable and, of course, the deadly thing in talking about humour is that it becomes unfunny.

MILLER A good analysis of humour should never be unfunny. Whatever I have learned about humour comes from looking at it and seeing what various things have in common. But I think I've always managed to be funny about humour, and that means I understand it from the inside.

WACHTEL Can you say what it is, or how it works?

MILLER A lot of it, I think, is recognition, bringing to an explicit level of consciousness something that you implicitly knew without being able to put it into words. This is humour—not jokes. Jokes, I think, are different things altogether. Jokes are rather soiled currency, passed from one person to another and not belonging to the person who utters them. Jokes don't belong to you. They're just a part of the gift relationship that people pass around in return for other jokes that they're going to be told. It's like the circulation of cowrie shells in Micronesia. But there's a fundamental difference, I think, between jokes and what is genuinely funny. There are some genuinely funny jokes, but on the whole they're not. Jokes have a sort of formal structure, often with three parts. There was an Englishman, an Irishman and a Jewish chap . . . There were three priests who . . . It's a sort of formal device that obeys certain simple folkloric structures. Jokes are not, on the whole, very funny. Sometimes they can be, but they are usually devices for maintaining conviviality amongst people who don't know each other very well. Humour is a very different thing altogether. When you are in the presence of someone who can create funny material, you can start to see something about how it works. I used to watch Peter Cook's monologues with admiring delight and interest. The more I saw them every night, the more I learned about how humour worked and what it was that provoked laughter. Sometimes it's what the philosophers would call very serious category mistakes. It draws attention, once again, to the categories that we use unconsciously and inappropriately. There was a wonderful moment when Peter Cook was talking about being a miner who could have been a judge, but he never had the Latin. That in itself is a wonderful category mistake—as if, in fact, all that lay between miners being able to enter the law courts was a shortage of Latin.

WACHTEL So, after touring with *Beyond the Fringe*, in 1965 you returned to London to begin a career in television with the BBC. More than ten years later, you produced the series *The Body in Question*, a look at the growth in our understanding of what the body is made of and how it works. It was a new approach, and in the book that came out with the series, you said, "to some extent I have put questions about the human body in order to ask further questions about the nature of human thought, especially about the difficulty man has had in setting aside the notion that his body is worked by conscious mental process. It is the story of the identification of the machine in the ghost." Obviously you're playing with the idea of the ghost in the machine, but can you talk about that? Why is that shift in awareness so important?

MILLER I think that it's part and parcel of what one great philosopher and historian of science, Dyksterhuis, has called the mechanization of the world picture, that one of the things which created the great change in knowledge and introduced what we loosely call the scientific revolution—which probably took longer than most people acknowledge—was the willingness to see that events were not like actions. Events were not caused by intentions but rather by something for which there were mechanical, or at least material, explanations. Clouds, for example, don't move because they want to get from one side of the sky to the other; they move because of certain meteorological processes that don't leave any room for mental processes. So we have gradually learned to shrink the domain of the mental to ourselves. This also necessitates the ability to eliminate mental processes in describing physiological actions. So we gradually learned to mechanize the picture of the heart, the lungs, blood vessels, glands and so forth. It looks as if we're on the edge of doing exactly the same thing to mental processes themselves, now that mental processes are, in many respects, reproducible by machines. We've got machines that can play very creditable games of chess, probably better even than grand masters. But nevertheless there are obviously differences, and they're not differences which, I think, New Age people would like to see as the proverbial cat flap that lets in the spiritual. It's just that we don't know how mental processes work. There may be, as I have said, certain areas that will remain forever closed to us, but this closure doesn't mean that it's a cat flap into which the spirit gains access to the head. I think it's utterly material, but I'm mystified—and many of my colleagues are mystified—by how it is that brain processes can result in their owners seeing red and feeling sad.

WACHTEL So there's still a ghost, but the machine has a bigger role. Do you want to play with that?

MILLER Well, I still don't think there is a ghost, you see. Once you make this accommodation to the notion of ghostliness, or of a translucent phantom which is immaterial, I think you have all sorts of pseudo-explanations. Philosophers such as Descartes, who was a radical mechanist in some respects, referred to animals as "brute machines" and thought that they were mechanical. Well, that's as self-contradictory as the idea that we've failed to discover triangular circles because we haven't worked hard enough.

WACHTEL So is it ironic that something so essential to the way we function is so elusive? In other words, consciousness itself?

MILLER Yes, I think it's extremely puzzling. A few fundamental eliminativists want to get rid of mind altogether or want to get rid of mental talk in the belief that it's what they call folk psychology, but most serious philosophers really do accommodate themselves to the fact that there's something mysterious about being conscious. While acknowledging this mystery, they nevertheless rule out the possibility that what enables consciousness to occur is something otherworldly.

WACHTEL In a different sort of way, the unconscious seems unprovable.

MILLER No, I don't think the unconscious is unprovable. The Freudian unconscious perhaps is less provable than the unconscious that has returned to become a central preoccupation of modern psychology—the cognitive unconscious, which I call the enabling unconscious. But the unconscious of which we are by definition unaware, and to which we don't have access, allows us to do things that cannot be explained unless there is some sort of quasi-mental process going on which enables us to speak grammatically without having to look up grammar books. Now, someone as simple-minded as B. F. Skinner actually thought it was simply conditioning, that we talk grammatically because we were rewarded for speaking grammatically and punished for speaking ungrammatically—that, like Pavlov's dogs, we were conditioned to speak grammatically. I just don't think it's like that. One of the great achievements of Noam Chomsky was to see that it all happened in too short a space of time to be accounted for by a process of laborious and painful conditioning.

WACHTEL But this is a different unconscious from the one that fuels dreams or memory.

MILLER Yes, but then of course you might want to say that by definition dreams are not unconscious. I'm aware of my dreams and therefore they aren't something that has to be fuelled any more than speaking has to be fuelled. It's just simply something that happens. It's no more mysterious than seeing red when your eyes are open and you're confronted by a red tablecloth. The fact that you have very rich and complicated dreams when your eyes are closed and you're not confronted by anything is perhaps a bit more mysterious. But I've seen a lot of things. I've had my eyes open in front of red tablecloths and green trees and lots of very complicated human scenes, and my brain has computed these experiences, condensed them and simplified them and complicated them. It's hardly surprising that I don't switch off when I'm asleep. It would be rather odd if I did, if I had to have a life-support system when I was asleep. It would be rather odd if I had to have a thought-support system as well. It just keeps going, and it produces dreams of which I am aware. I may forget them, but then I forget lots of things of which I was aware during the day. People somehow seem more mystified by dreams than they are by the experiences they have with their eyes open.

WACHTEL But that might be the reason—

MILLER Well, I think it is, but it's not that mysterious. It's only mysterious if you think that being conscious is, in fact, only kicked into action by having the sense organs teased and tickled and stimulated. People forget that they've had many years of previous ticklings that have been stored and recorded. We're not mystified by tape recorders or by hard drives. There must be something that is the equivalent of a hard drive, which goes on wobbling around while you're asleep and delivers things that we call dreams. What is so interesting about dreams is their extraordinary combinant versatility, the fact that they can bring into existence experiences that are absolutely unlike any you've actually had, but are nevertheless derived from, and composed of, things that you have experienced. They're combined in the most extraordinary ways that make you feel, Where did that come from? Well, we haven't the faintest idea.

WACHTEL You once edited a book about Freud, who has come under a lot of attack lately. How do you feel about him now?

MILLER My attitude to Freud is that he was not the scientist he thought he was and that he wasn't really a scientific explorer or a conquistador, as one person called him, of the mind. I think he drew attention to things that we had previously not been consciously aware of, such as the fact that one could have wishes of which one was unaware. But I think probably most moralists understood that, in any case. It's called hypocrisy, and people can be hypocrites without being consciously aware that they're contradicting themselves by their actions and are actually going against what they know to be true. There are very few self-conscious hypocrites who say they will do this while feeling that. Most of the great literary figures have known that we are conflicted creatures. I actually don't think that Freud was right about the sources of it, that it works in quite the way he thought it did. But he belonged to what Philip Rieff originally called "the moral tradition," not a scientific tradition, and I think he was a wonderfully vivid describer of neurotic behaviour and of the oddness and peculiarity of neurotic behaviour. I'm not certain he was right about it. It's very, very ambiguous. He provided some useful language for talking about what it is to be unhappy. He also provided vocabulary and an idiom for talking about your own previously unacknowledged desires and wishes. That was a great achievement. And some of his essays are great literary works. His essay on mourning and melancholia—the essay on the three caskets—is probably wrong, but it's extremely invigorating and exciting. He is a great literary figure, but his science is absolutely cockeyed.

He, too, was deeply influenced by John Hughlings Jackson. Jackson's idea that there were deep primitive levels of the nervous system which had been held in check by more recently acquired levels of the nervous system obviously led Freud to produce the idea of the id and the ego. These are Jacksonian concepts, although rather indirectly; they're also Spencerian concepts, and we know that Spencer was an interesting, fascinating old gasbag like Freud, in some respects. What Freud didn't do, of course, was to actually look at the children about whose mental life he was so confident. We're doing much more interesting work about children now. People like Piaget have looked at them and even the Piagetian revolution has itself undergone fantastic revisions.

I think the analytic thing is much less interesting than what we're doing regarding cognition. I wouldn't want to say that it's all computational, as so many of the cognitivists think, because that leaves out the really fruitful and extremely productive ways that we have of talking about ourselves. I don't think that the language Shakespeare used to talk about what it's like to have a brother or a sister or someone of whom you're fearful or resentful is going to be replaced by neural talk. The Shakespeare of the future will not consist of nerve fibre printouts.

WACHTEL You've continued your investigation of the mind in more recent television documentaries—on language, on madness, "Museums of Madness." You even talked about writing a book on insanity. What interests you about insanity?

MILLER If you're interested in how things work, one of the best ways is to find out what happens when they don't work, or when they partly work. We learn a great deal about what physiology is by looking at disordered physiology. In exactly the same way we find out a great deal about how thought works by seeing disordered thought. Schizophrenia is an extremely good route into thinking because we have a disordered thought system in which people think that their thoughts are thought by other people and that their thoughts can be understood and recognized and felt and experienced by other people without having to talk to them.

Disordered systems are very good ways of finding out how things don't work—that's why physiologists damage things. Some people think that we have no right to damage other living things in order to find out how they work, and therefore how we work. But damaging things or looking at things that have been damaged—not by us but by nature—is one of the best ways of finding out how things happen. We discovered something about language when Broca, in the 1860s, discovered a man with a scar and an abscess on the left pre-frontal convolution. He couldn't speak except to say tan-tan-tan-tan. By looking at a damaged brain, which Broca himself had not inflicted upon the man, we began to see that language must be in some way implemented, and by looking at one aspect—a very crude example of damage—one began to see that the implementation was complicated and distributed and that one part of the brain could be damaged without influencing language, and another part of the brain could be damaged and cause profound disorders of language.

WACHTEL The stage has been a kind of laboratory for you in your study of the mind; you once referred to it as a "place of psychological and even physiological experimentation." You talked about going to the theatre as a child, and being captivated by this other world on stage beyond the darkness. What made it so compelling?

MILLER When I was a child the theatre was vivid, bright, garish, with the stage illuminated in ways that it is no longer lit—by footlights and limelight. People wore very bright makeup, with strongly outlined eyes and red cheeks. The actors were like living toys—very large, animated, living toys. It was another world, an alternative world, what the philosopher Saul Kripke called a possible world—a possible world that was also rather an improbable world. When I returned to the ordinary world, accommodating my eyes to the evening, I found that the buses were not as brightly coloured as the people on the stage had been. This was very interesting. I didn't particularly want to do what they were doing, but I longed to go and see these things happening. Then I became more interested in the art of pretending, or pretending to be other people, and I saw that it was connected with the very elaborate process of pretending that one experiences as a child—for instance, pretending that a matchbox is a car and going brrrr while you push it across the table. Now, a child doesn't think it's a car in the sense that if you say, "That's not a car," they'd say, "Well, it is." They know that pretending is rather different from doing something in earnest. But the process of pretending gives tremendous insight into the actual process of doing things for real. Again, you go back to this idea of things going wrong; pretending is a form of things being wrong. It falls short of being actual. By discovering the difference, and by analyzing the shortfall between the pretense and the actual, we learn something about the actual.

WACHTEL I was wondering how these early impressions have remained with you or influenced you in your work as a director—that magic of the other world, the other side of the lights.

MILLER Only in the sense that I take great delight in people pretending to be other people and in the fact that they can give the impression to an audience of being enraged or resentful or horrified or grief-struck, and so forth. I know perfectly well they'll go off the stage and perhaps pick up a cellphone and talk to their stockbroker with no residue of the grief that they've just shown on the stage.

WACHTEL You've said that your work in theatre has "always been informed by moral psychology, the psychology of motive, dynamic psychology." What does it mean to take a psychological approach to directing actors?

MILLER It simply means common sense, most of the time. What would someone be feeling under these circumstances? You can call it psychology, if you like. It only becomes technical psychology if you start to be laboriously Freudian about it, and I actually think that's really uninteresting on the stage. Most things can be released and facilitated by just thinking intelligently and imaginatively about the conscious thoughts that people have. You can say to them that behind this might lie ideas and motives of which you are unaware, not because they're kept under lock and key in the custodial unconscious of Freud but because you're simply not aware of the fact that you think otherwise than the way you're acting. There are all sorts of interesting things when people act other than the way they think they're acting, or are motivated by feelings which are not, in fact, available to them. I think most of it is simply moral common sense. Jane Austen did it all the time. When she distinguished between pride and prejudice and sense and sensibility, she was actually making distinctions that some might dismiss as folk psychology. I don't think this is psychology at all; this is moral imaginativeness.

WACHTEL You don't necessarily make a distinction between interpretation and creation. You talked about creation and interpretation being a symmetrical partnership, rather than distinct activities, but I was thinking about the idea of the director as a relatively new phenomenon.

MILLER Oh yes, I've written about this in a rather long article for the *New York Review of Books* about directing opera. I pointed out that there are directors now because when operas are revived from the distant past, interpretation becomes a problem. There was no problem about how to do an eighteenth-century opera in the eighteenth century, because new operas were done according to the standards of the time. They were largely dictated by the current idioms and styles of mounting a performance. But when you take something from the remote past, it's already a residue, something which I've described in another book as being in its afterlife. It no longer has the function that it had when it was done for the first time, and therefore it requires interpretation, resuscitation and all sorts of acts of transformation. Many traditionalists would say that an opera should be done as it was originally done, but there's a technical difficulty in restoring the original because we don't really know how it *was* done. We have vague intimations but very little in the way of records. If, by some magic, you were to do an opera as it had originally been done, it would have an intriguing archival quality, but we wouldn't actually be engaged by it as we would be when a work is transformed in a way that couldn't have been anticipated by the author or maker.

All sorts of things happen in the visual arts as well. Hundreds of things drop into our era like meteorites from another part of the universe, and we use and cherish them for reasons that are quite different from the reasons they were cherished and valued when they were created. We, for example, would probably find Greek statues rather vulgar if painted in the way they originally were. We actually like them in plain stone without their colour or, at the most, we like faded polychrome, the residue of the colouring. We also rather like statuary to be knocked about a bit, ruined objects bearing witness to their antiquity. In analogous ways, the texts that we inherit may not have been knocked about, but what they mean is different because we have different ideas about what constitutes meaning—not simply because of Freud but because we've passed into a different world of discriminations about the motives that we have for doing things. We're subtler, we're more complicated, and we are also perhaps cruder and more clodhopping than some of our predecessors. Nevertheless we use texts for different purposes, and we have to acknowledge that and allow it to occur.

WACHTEL It's not only operas—you also got into theatre just around the time of the ascendancy of the director.

MILLER The appearance of the director in theatre was itself relatively new. There weren't any directors until about the 1880s, and it was not a function that was fully developed until the early part of the twentieth century. That, again, was because most plays were new. So the interpretive problem is exactly the same for plays as it is for operas: we've inherited works that are in their afterlife and are therefore cherished and valued and used and exploited and resuscitated for reasons that are different from their original reasons. It's not because we've corrupted or abused them; it's just what we do all the time. There are all sorts of people living in sixteenth-century dovecotes that have been renovated as country houses. That doesn't mean that we've somehow abused the intentions of the dovecote maker, who would be appalled to see his dovecote used as a residence. We take these works from the past. They hang around as fragments and ruins and residues and are cannibalized and reused for very different purposes. That seems perfectly all right. That's how we develop.

WACHTEL Your theatre and opera productions are always highly original, often rich with allusion, metaphor, visual references, references specifically to works of art. You use different settings, different perspectives. How far do you feel you can go?

MILLER I don't think going too far is a dimensional issue. It's a question of whether you're smart enough to choose the right direction, not how far you go in that direction. I don't think it's a question of limits. Sometimes what seems to be going too far turns out, when you actually put it on the stage, to have been perfectly right for a modern audience. The text survives for someone to do something else with it, to cast light on something which people thought they understood and then discover, to their delight, that it might also mean something else, perhaps a meaning which was not even unconsciously thought by the maker. And that doesn't matter. We're endlessly using dovecotes as residences.

WACHTEL Is part of this just to make it interesting for yourself?

MILLER It's a very curious and interesting thing to do, to be a renovator. To take antiquities and reuse them and recycle them and make them do things that are different is an extremely interesting form of creativity. It's a second order of creativity. It's much more satisfying to make something for the first time, but it's still interesting to remake a thing that already exists. It's another form of art.

WACHTEL Your *Merchant of Venice* featured nineteenth-century bankers. You shifted the action of *Rigoletto* to the world of New York mobsters in the 1950s. Your *Tosca* was set in the fascist forties and the world of Rossellini's *Open City*. You staged *La Bohème* in 1930, based on period photos by Brassaï and Kertesz. How did you arrive at these transpositions?

MILLER My mother encouraged me to think metaphorically. You see in one work of art a curious similarity to another form of art and you then think how interesting it would be to transpose it, to try and see whether it worked in terms of that form of art which it so closely and strikingly and unexpectedly resembles. One is delighted by a disclosure that seems to cast a new light on what a work of art looks like. I said earlier that what often happens with a metaphor is that two things which you thought you understood, you now understand much more clearly by seeing what they have in common. In other words, your attention has been drawn to aspects of both which you had previously overlooked.

WACHTEL Do you know how you find them?

MILLER I haven't the faintest idea. I go into a rehearsal without knowing what I'm going to do that morning, but within about thirty seconds of starting the scene I am immediately struck by hearing someone talk in a certain way. I know what that really means, now that I hear them say it. I know what they *might* mean, which doesn't seem to correspond to the meanings that have previously been given to the scene. Obviously, long before I start rehearsing, I've already had ideas, because I would have commissioned a set or designed a set myself which was a departure from the tradition. But I don't know how I came by those ideas. What happens is that you have an experience of something which remains dormant for many years and then you get asked to do a play or an opera and suddenly one of these dormant experiences—a photograph by Kertesz or a Cartier-Bresson picture of Seville—leads you to say, hang on, that's what *Carmen* really ought to be like. A lot of what one's doing, of course, is eliminating kitsch. I can't bear the thought of *Carmen* done with flounced dresses and castanets and all that folkloric Spanish imagery. I suddenly find that I remember pictures which I had once seen of Seville in the 1930s and I think, Well, there's a Spain that doesn't necessitate having all this ridiculous flamenco drivel. Suddenly the opera becomes visible again. There's a quote that I often cite from Chesterton—I think it's in his novel *The Man Who Was Thursday*: "It isn't until you've seen something for the thousandth time that you see it for the first." That is what often happens. Seeing something for the first time is often the result of seeing how much what you saw for the nine hundred and ninety-ninth time has features that resemble something else that you've *also* seen nine hundred and ninety-nine times. When you put together each of these experiences which you've had many times before, you suddenly see both of them for the first time.

WACHTEL You managed to take the feathers off Papageno in *The Magic Flute.*

MILLER I can't stand this cute Tweety Pie figure who comes onto the stage looking like a bird. He catches birds; he doesn't have to resemble them.

WACHTEL How did Laurence Olivier react to playing Shylock as a nineteenth-century banker?

MILLER He leapt at the opportunity. I would have thought that he, as a great actor, with a long history of being a traditional performer, would have rebuked me and said, "No, no, my dear fellow, we can't do that!" But when you come up with a good idea, an interesting performer usually says yes. I always think that what happens when you come up with a glaringly simple idea that no one has seen is very like what happened when Thomas Henry Huxley read Darwin's *On the Origin of Species*. He closed the book and said, "How stupid not to have thought of that." When you have a really good idea, people suddenly recognize the metaphor, the resemblance. Let's see what happens if we go with that resemblance; let's try it in that period and see how the work can renew itself. There's no point in conscientious repetition of what has gone before. You could always assign a production to a low-level custodian who follows a book that tells you how to do it. Then it becomes rather like a religious service. But no one expects religious services to be criticized; adherents wouldn't say that for them the elevation of the Host basically "didn't work."

WACHTEL You've said that you don't listen to opera or go to it. Or not much, anyway. What's the appeal of opera for you?

MILLER The appeal of opera is in being an investigator, a mechanic. I think of myself as an Indianapolis racetrack mechanic. I'm in the pit, retuning the car and seeing if I can get it to move in an interesting and more versatile way. The race itself is of little interest to me. I often find it very hard to watch my own productions after I've done most of the rehearsals. I can sit through the dress rehearsal, and after that I've done with it. I go in to see the performers because I feel I owe it to them, but the experience of watching it is really pretty uninteresting. And certainly I don't see other productions very much. That's not because I'm filled with envy or contempt. It doesn't interest me in the way that pictures or science interest me. I find that I can approach the theatre more by thinking about things that have no apparent connection with the theatre and discovering that they do have more to do with the theatre than one might otherwise have thought.

WACHTEL You hardly ever go to the theatre either. Is there a relationship between directing theatre and directing opera for you? Does one influence the way you approach the other?

MILLER For me, they're one and the same thing. It just happens that people sing in opera, that's all. It's slightly odd that they're not talking, but then, it's rather odd the way people talk in a lot of plays. People don't talk the way Shakespeare has them talk, so that's as artificial as opera is. Ultimately, what you're doing is getting people to give you a sense that you have seen human conduct in a way that refreshes your knowledge of it. It's often a great advantage to have worked in the theatre. Opera has, until recently, been a primitive theatrical art form because it hasn't been directed by people who have spent their time directing unsung utterances.

WACHTEL You can't read music. Do you ever feel hindered by that, or is it an advantage?

MILLER I think it's both an advantage and a disadvantage. It's a great disadvantage when you're trying to point out a particular point where you would like someone to do something. What I have to do is say,

"Stop at that bit where you go *da-da-dee-dee-um-pa*—here's the way I want you to do it." That's a disadvantage. The great advantage is that it means my head isn't in the score. It means I'm looking at what they're doing. Some of the more primitive musical critics claim that my opera productions are bad because I can't read music and therefore I'm not musical. Well, I think I'm probably as musical as many people are because I listen to it, I hear it, I hear what it means. I don't have to read it. If that was true, then all dyslexic people would be completely deprived of any sort of literary sensibility, and that ain't necessarily so. If I listen to music, I know what is being said by the music as well as what is being said by the words.

WACHTEL You've written, "When I talk about the afterlife of plays, I'm talking also about the afterlife of productions. I suppose in an autobiographical and melancholy sense, I am talking about my own autobiography." Is it ultimately a source of frustration for you that your own work for the stage cannot endure as a painting would, or a book?

MILLER Yes, I'm very proud of some of the things I've done, and it is sad to think that what is sometimes an extremely complicated and often rather wonderful artwork can simply disappear. I have no idea what it would be like if they did endure. Some of them do endure in the form of videotapes, of course, but that's not what I did. I did something on the stage that was not intended to be seen on the screen. There are many works of performing art that do become old and derelict and are not liked, but the same thing happens to paintings. Who really likes Guido Reni now in the way that the Victorians were so passionate about him? And we now like Vermeer, though people didn't have a passion for him in the eighteenth century. But, yes, I'm sad that the things I've made have disappeared. I think some of them would probably continue to be of lasting value. There are films which were thought to be wonderful at one time and then disappeared, but there are also films that go on being absolutely luminous for fifty or sixty years. I can still watch *The Third Man* and think that it is a great work.

It's sad that my work will vanish, leaving only the genetic instructions for some future performance that will be someone else's, not mine. It's not like being what I was trained to be, a scientist, who could have left behind something of permanent value.

WACHTEL Novels and plays, especially by Shakespeare, are constantly being made into movies and television productions. Do you think that's a bad idea?

MILLER Yes, I do. It sounds very elitist to complain about popularizing what might otherwise not be read, but it's a shame that they're not read, and I think that when they are read as a result of having seen them, they're being read in a different frame of mind to the one which they require. I think that the literary embodiment of ideas is of a different order, and that description is not, as it were, a disabled form of depiction. There are things that can be expressed in sentences which simply cannot be expressed in performances. A writer is able to leave out a lot when describing something. Jane Austen doesn't describe what anything looked like at all. As soon as you start having things look like something, you're not dealing with Miss Austen's enterprise, which is the careful and scrupulous description of people's states of mind about their own actions. She is a great moralist, and most of the moral considerations are dealt with by people having thoughts about what they have just said or thoughts about what they will say or do. Internal thoughts are not expressible in a film; someone must say what they think and what they have felt. This is one of the great achievements of literature. There are many forms of representation that occur in literature—metaphorical descriptions, for example—which are not possible in film. You can do as Dickens did and refer to someone's mouth as looking like a letterbox so that he not so much ate his food as posted it. How can you convey that witty description? There again, what's funny about that is the category mistake, the idea of posting food. It's not what we do to food. What we do is eat it, and therefore the idea that someone might post their food and collect it and then transmit it to someone else is extremely amusing and interesting. How do you convey that in a picture? What you can do, I suppose, is have a rigorous casting director who looks around for people whose mouths look like the entrances to postboxes, but they never look enough like it for people to think, Oh good heavens, how much like a mailbox his mouth looks. Oh yes, he must be posting his food rather than eating it. You have to have someone make the metaphorical description explicit, and that is something which literature can do. Literature also uses very subtle deployments of tense which are not possible in other genres. You can say that on Thursdays they tended to do this. Well, how do you show in a film what people did on Thursdays? All you can show on a film is what they did on Thursday.

WACHTEL Is seeing the characters, actually having a visual representation, also a spoiler?

MILLER I think there are very complicated reasons why seeing the character is a spoiling experience. The commonest objection, which I think is a trivial one, is that that's not my Mr. Darcy. That's relatively unimportant. The Darcy I have conjured up in my imagination, under the auspices of the description provided by Jane Austen, is different from the one I now see on the screen. What is interesting about Mr. Darcy is that he doesn't really have an appearance at all, and that he can actually thrive as a character without having to have an appearance. Now, the damnable thing about films is that he not only has an appearance, he has minutely detailed appearances; he can turn round and we can see his back. These are distractions. They have nothing whatever to do with Miss Austen's enterprise.

WACHTEL In 1983, after twenty-five years in the arts, you returned to medicine, your original career. You did a two-year fellowship in neuro-psychology at the University of Sussex in cognitive studies. What called you back?

MILLER I was called back because I had always felt remorseful about not pursuing my original interest. But by that time my moral fibre had rotted. I couldn't stick with it in the same way that I might have done earlier. The whole point about being a scientist is that you've got to get up in the morning very early and stay in the lab till very late at night, and you often have to perform very dreary routines in order to have any achievement of any sort at all. Well, spending time in rehearsals and dressing people in other people's clothes distracts you from that sort of regime. It's entertaining and amusing and picaresque, and you go to work at different times from normal people. You often travel against the rush hour, and you can go to bed late and get up late and do all sorts of things that serious professional people and scientists can't do. If you do it for long enough, after a while your moral fibre softens. But I do constantly regret it and try, often rather fruitlessly, to make a return. It doesn't work. I've become too frivolous and silly.

WACHTEL Do you really think that?

MILLER Well, I often think that. I wish I'd been able to maintain the rigour that I would have had to have observed if I had wanted to be a serious scientist. But I'm glad I've done the things that I've done, and I think I've enlightened people and made them think in a new way about what it's like to be alive. That, I think, is also important. Some of my more serious academic colleagues are very contemptuous of the life that I undertook, and say that the theatre was an enemy of promise. Why did he do it? Why did he do something so frivolous? But then I often think about the way in which people conjugate the verb to theatre-go. These serious academics say, "I go to the theatre, you are interested in drama, he is in show biz."

WACHTEL I get the sense sometimes that you get caught in the middle, that you get it coming and going, that you're mocked for being brainy and then you're disdained by the pure scientists.

MILLER I do feel caught between two fires. In theatre or in journalism, where you are criticized by people who, in fact, are not your peers, you are either envied or despised for being what they call "brainy." So I can read without moving my lips and make references to things that are outside my field of expertise, and I'm called a polymath, which is really another way of saying jack of all trades and master of none. But I'm usually accused of that by people who are barely jacks of one trade.

WACHTEL You said that to lay claim to being an intellectual is stating an occupation, but in England there's an uneasiness with intellectuals and it's regarded as a boast. Why do you think that is?

MILLER I don't know why there's such suspicion of organized and often difficult thought. One can become quite fascinated by things which actually defeat all analysis, like being able to speak fluently and grammatically. What goes into speech is much more complicated than it seems to us as performers. That's one of the things that Chomsky drew our attention to. Now, you start to invoke a name like Chomsky amongst English journalists and they say, "Yeah, yeah, Chomsky, Chimsky—just a blabbermouth." The people who say that are not clever enough to understand what Chomsky did, that he actually drew attention to the fact that we can do things which seem second nature, which seem dead simple, but are actually very complicated. That what allows us to do them is something that currently defeats analysis. We may be able to invent computers that can play games of chess, but we're not very smart at inventing computers which can see that this sentence might mean at least five things. If it's as difficult as it turns out to be, then it's worth being difficult about it. But that's thought to be pretentious and stuck-up in England, a way of just strutting around. A bit of strutting around is quite useful, really. A lot of interesting things have happened by strutting around.

WACHTEL Is there a place for public intellectuals?

MILLER In England, yes, but they have to have a certain sort of form. On the whole, people who cross boundaries and see connections between more than two things are thought to be pretentious. It's regrettable and it's rather sad. It's quite hard to live in a country where most journalists think it's acceptable to use the word *pseud*, from that ghastly magazine *Private Eye*. What do they mean if they call something *pseud*? What do they mean by pseudo-intellectual? Presumably they have some standard of what being intellectual is, by which you can judge whether something is pseudo-intellectual. Well, most of the people who invoke the notion of the pseud have a very marginal acquaintance with what it's like to be an intellectual at all, or they think it's just as simple as being able to read Anthony Trollope.

WACHTEL Is it any better in North America? Here we would probably think it's better in England.

MILLER In North America there's a much more generous accommodation to the idea of cross-disciplinary interests, to moving from one field to another and seeing that they are closely related to one another—that thoughtfulness, in fact, is valuable and interesting and productive. This is not necessarily because it's materially productive—producing laptops, for example—but because what goes into making laptops helps us to think about what it's like to have a mind. On the whole, North Americans are much more hospitable to these sorts of cross-references, and they don't think it's pretentious. They delight in it and they like to see people making smart moves. I like that. I think that it's one of the reasons why America has been as explosively successful intellectually and technically as it has been. If you're bending over backwards to appear reticent, modest and a decent English gent, the result of it is that you don't actually do anything.

WACHTEL You, on the other hand, do a lot of things. A couple of years ago you curated a major exhibition at London's National Gallery, *On Reflection*. You said at the time that you wanted to "jam together the psychology of perception with the study of pictures." Why reflection? Why did you use that?

MILLER I didn't start out with that idea, but I became rather fascinated by what seemed to me to be certain insoluble paradoxes about reflection, about what it was like to look in one direction and see in another. I'm struck by this strange capability we have to look simultaneously through the front window of a motorcar and through the driving mirror and not confuse the views from the two frames. What went into making that decision? I was also struck by the notion of lustre. For example, the fact that when you look at a perfectly reflective surface in which there's nothing to be seen except what is reflected in it, you see something that is actually invisible—the shiny surface itself. Now, the shiny surface is not there at all. It's shiny only by virtue of the fact that you know it to be a reflection, and that's something which had not previously been described or noticed. If you cover the thing of which it's a reflection, the shiny surface disappears. You have to know, by virtue of the fact that it duplicates something in its immediate vicinity, that it is a reflection of it; in the knowledge that the surface presents a reflection, you then see something over and above what it reflects. You see the surface that affords the reflection.

WACHTEL But how do you get interested in something like lustre?

MILLER By just keeping one's eyes open. Life is filled with curious paradoxes and problems, and you have to keep your eyes open and not let things just run by you. A lot of people like lustre merely because it's lustrous; they never ask themselves what it is to be lustrous as opposed to merely bright red. Almost everything that is interesting is a matter of applying your mind to something that had previously been overlooked because it was thought to be obvious. By and large, the really interesting things are the things that we think to be obvious, because they turn out to have a deep structure which is very complicated. The philistines and the pseud hunters would say, "Oh God, you do make a lot of fuss about nothing," but on the whole, the most interesting things have usually been dug up as a result of people making a fuss about what others think is nothing.

WACHTEL You look very closely at the representation of mirrors in art. Why are mirrors so compelling to artists?

MILLER Mirrors are important and interesting to artists for the same reasons that they're important and interesting to all of us. First of all, mirrors are useful utensils. They enable us to do things we can't otherwise do, like look in one direction and see in another. Driving mirrors, for example. They also enable us to understand something we wouldn't know anything about if they didn't exist, like see ourselves. Seeing ourselves is actually quite startling, because if you cannot see anything more than the tip of your nose without the aid of a mirror, you can only infer that you have a nose because most people who belong to the same species have got them, too. It's quite surprising when you actually confront your reflection to discover, Well, I've got a nose of that sort, have I? No wonder people talk about my big conk. I can't see how big my conk is. Having it is not enough to tell me what size it is.

Then a mirror becomes, of course, a metaphorical device for talking about vanity. People who spend too much time looking in mirrors are delighted by their own reflection, and therefore the mirror becomes the symbol of self-regard, of exorbitant self-regard. But it also becomes a metaphor for self-knowledge, and has thus acquired connotations in the iconography of art: both Vanitas and Prudence hold mirrors in their hands. Once again, it shows the extraordinary versatility of the metaphorical imagination that human beings are so distinctive in holding and exploiting.

WACHTEL You use pictures to demonstrate perception, and then perception as a clue to pictures. I'm interested in that interface between the psychology of perception and the world of art. Were there surprises for you in the way that they informed each other?

MILLER One is constantly being surprised by one's thoughts about things. That's what makes any investigation interesting. Oh, it works like that, does it? Is that what it's about? I've become very interested recently in another subject about which I'm writing a book, though I don't think I'll make an exhibition—I'm interested in "looking." I'm fascinated by something about looking which seems to be self-evident. Why is it that eyes are so indicative? Why is it that, for example, we talk about the eyes in a portrait following you around the room? Actually, the rest of the face does so, too, because it's a flat configuration. But the nose is not indicative. We don't say that a really good portrait's nose follows you around the room. What is it about the eyes? They're just a pair of rather mobile blobs on either side of the bridge of the nose. When you start asking questions like that, you're actually asking interesting questions about what it's like to perceive faces, what it's like to experience vision.

WACHTEL Why do eyes in paintings follow you around?

MILLER Oh, I think it's perfectly simple, and it has nothing to do with the quality of the portrait. There are good, bad and indifferent portraits, and they all do that. It's the result of two things: the way someone was looking when they were painted, and the fact that in order to paint a subject you have to look at that person from one point of view. If it's on a flat surface, it can't be anything other than what it is: a picture of someone looking at you. And no matter where you look at it, it will go on being a picture of someone looking at you. You can't get round the side of it. No one ever talks about the eyes of a statue following them around the room. That would be very uncanny. A statue's eyes don't follow you around the room because there's only one position in which you can catch its eye. When you go around the side, it goes on looking in the other direction. I don't know why people haven't seen that. But why we're so intrigued by eyes that follow you around the room is a deeply interesting question.

WACHTEL Aren't eyes supposed to be the windows of the soul?

MILLER Yes, and it raises all sorts of questions about why we think the eyes are the windows of the soul. Why is it that we attach such importance to eyes? It looks as if very, very young infants are interested in eyes before they know that they're the windows of the soul. We know from watching children looking at their mother's face that they spend much longer looking at their mother's eyes than at any other part of her face. A six-week-old child hasn't any idea that those blobs on either side of her own head are affording her the experience of seeing. Once you start asking these questions, it becomes very problematic. Of course eyes are important to us, but we think they're important long before we know *why* they're important. And therefore you have to ask why we are wired up to take such an interest in eyes. Well, it's obvious: eyes give us some sort of insight, not into people's souls but into the fact that they're having an experience of you.

WACHTEL We're back to talking about the eyes as portals.

MILLER Yes, but I don't use the word *portals*. What they are is sense organs that afford us the richest and most complicated experience of something not in immediate contact with our own bodies. They're what another teacher of great importance to me, Charles Sherrington, called "distance receptors." They give us information about something we are not necessarily in physical contact with. Eyes give us minutely detailed topographical instructions as to where things are, that something is just to the left of our vision. Hearing is another distance receptor, but it doesn't tell you that something is just to the left of something else; neither does smell. So it's hardly surprising that the part of our face that affords such detailed knowledge of what the world at large is like, is credited with this thing we call "looking." You have to ask why it is that we're so aware of things, and of other people looking at things. Eyes are merely tiny little bobbles, and yet we see them as projecting something beyond themselves in the way that we don't see the chin or the nose projecting something beyond itself. Now, it's of course partly by analogy with our own eyes, but how do I know that the part of my head affording me vision corresponds to the part of someone else's head that I see on either side of their nose? I don't see with something on either side of my nose. That's not my subjective experience of vision. What happens is that I open what I have subsequently learned to be my eyes and am aware of a totally panoramic experience that extends beyond what I feel to be the size of my own head. How do I know that that part of my face is what does it?

WACHTEL In your exhibition and book *On Reflection*, you use photographs alongside reproductions of Old Masters, and your work for the stage has often drawn on photography. Recently you published *Nowhere in Particular*, a book of your own photographs taken over the past thirty-odd years. I thought this book demonstrated yet greater versatility and yet more imagination. You describe the book as "pictures of bits," alongside jottings or meditations. You say this is a recognizable genre, going back to 1820.

MILLER Yes, there was a time when people thought that the bits were simply what artists did in the expectation of actually composing a whole picture. They would address themselves to some sort of detail of a tree or a rooftop in order to be able to make a complete picture, of which a rooftop or the edge of a tree was a part. But as the art historian Peter Galassi, of the Museum of Modern Art, pointed out, there came a moment at the beginning of the nineteenth century when people began to offer pictures of bits as something more than merely bits of pictures. There were artists such as Thomas Jones and Pierre-Henri de Valenciennes who did, in fact, do pictures of bits and pieces that would previously have been thought to be studies of, for example, a complete picture of a house. They were then offered as works of art in their own right. I realized when reading Galassi's catalogue to the exhibition called *Painting before Photography* that I'd been doing this all along myself, that I had spent thirty years carrying a cheap portable camera around taking snaps of bits and pieces of things because I found them attractive and interesting. I never thought I was going to exhibit them. I just collected volume after volume of these bits. They weren't studies with a view to something that would ultimately be composed of them. I began to look at them, after several years, and saw that they were actually rather intriguing configurations. They don't, as it were, have to win approval by being components of some larger composition, because they are themselves composite and interesting. So I thought perhaps I ought to show them. There are lots of people who've taken photographs of this sort, but I thought that mine were rather nice.

WACHTEL They are, but it also seems that the haphazardness of it was important to you. I mean, using a cheap camera, using twenty-four-hour processing, the colours come out with different intensities.

MILLER I found that very interesting. Since there was a haphazardness about the process that had brought the actual artifact itself into existence—these torn posters and bits of concrete slabs lying in builders' yards—I thought that I could be, surely, as haphazard in the processing. I don't want to make art out of them. Then I discovered that the process of choosing to frame something and taking pleasure in the particular, and then having it printed by a twenty-four-hour developing service actually produced something which is a form of art. Yes, I think it is. In order to deflect and pre-empt any criticism, I was going to call the whole book *Absolute Rubbish*, knowing perfectly well that the British would say, "Oh God, absolute rubbish." Well, absolute rubbish is sometimes very interesting. It goes back to something else that I was saying. On the whole, many of the most interesting things are done by paying attention to the negligible. The overlooked is very often the underestimated and the undervalued, and may be the clue to something else. Now, I don't think these are clues to something else, but they draw attention to something that had previously been thought to be rubbish and turns out to be interesting. Lots of other people have done that before. Kurt Schwitters put together rubbish and made art out of it. I now make collages out of rubbish and bits and pieces. I don't claim any originality for doing that, but I think that the ones I've done within the domain I've chosen are quite original in their own right. But again, I'm called a pretentious pseud for doing that.

WACHTEL When I talk to you, you seem pleased with so much that you've done and at the same time regretful for so much that you haven't done.

MILLER Yes. Very often you do things that people value very highly, and you ought to be satisfied with creating productions that came as a revelation or changed people's minds about things. But you see, I was brought up to be a scientist. I lived in the rather priggish, otherworldly domain of Cambridge and was conditioned to think that certain things were achievements and other things were just frivolous pastimes.

WACHTEL You described how you went to see your father when you were forty and he asked when you were going to figure out what you were going to do.

MILLER I once went to visit him on a Saturday morning. He was sitting behind his consulting room desk, and he asked me if I had made up my mind about what I was going to do. I had to say that I hadn't made up my mind but that I seemed to be doing what I probably would go on doing. He looked rather glum about that.

WACHTEL So it's still a matter of winning parental approval or disappointing one's parents.

MILLER I think it's partly to do with that. My parents set very high standards about what they thought was interesting or a worthy achievement, and my father himself had been deeply influenced by the people he'd been in contact with at Cambridge. It's no accident that Cambridge was the Puritan university and Oxford the royalist one. But on the other hand, Cambridge did produce all sorts of rather interestingly frivolous figures who were closely associated with the serious ones. The Bloomsbury group included a lot of people who would have been thought to be frivolous by a lot of the scientists to whom they were closely related. Perhaps the Darwins at Cambridge, for example, would have thought little of the Stracheys.

WACHTEL You're more or less comfortable living with this ambivalence, or is remorse in the ascendance?

MILLER Remorse is constantly there. There's no way in which I'm going to discover anything fundamental about the nervous system, and I'm sad I won't. But I think I've discovered lots of things that are not scientific about the nervous system by watching what we do with it. So I live in a state of tolerable discomfort. I put up with the discomfort that I've committed myself to. I can't change now.

                                                                    July 2000

JANE GOODALL

As an enthusiast, a scientist and now an advocate, primatologist Jane Goodall has always been a woman of extraordinary character and dedication. Her revolutionary study of the chimpanzees in Tanzania's Gombe Reserve has transformed our understanding of what it means to be human.

Goodall was born in London in 1934. When she was five, the family moved to Bournemouth, on the English coast. Thoroughly outdoorsy and an animal lover virtually since birth, she rode horses and enjoyed the natural world around her, from scrutinizing the life habits of earthworms to wondering why, as she put it, "our human ancestors did not take to the trees, like the other apes." She says she can't remember a time when she didn't dream about going to Africa to study animals.

Her mother advised her that secretarial skills were portable, so Goodall went to secretarial school, worked as a waitress to save up the passage and travelled to Kenya. She sought out the renowned paleontologist Louis Leakey, who was then curator of the Natural History Museum in Nairobi. Goodall became his personal secretary. She went on the annual archaeological digs to Olduvai Gorge, and then was recruited to undertake her own study of chimpanzees on the eastern shore of Lake Tanganyika. She was twenty-five. She got to know our closest relatives by observing birth and death, sex and love, power and war.

A few years later, encouraged by Leakey and in danger of being dismissed as "a *National Geographic* cover girl"—Goodall is tall and blonde—she got a PhD in ethology from Cambridge University. Her classic, *In the Shadow of Man* (1971), recounted her first ten years at what became Gombe National Park. She followed it with *The Chimpanzees of Gombe: Patterns of Behaviour* (1986) and *Through a Window: My Thirty Years with the Chimpanzees of Gombe* (1990). As Stephen Jay Gould once wrote, "Jane Goodall's work with the chimpanzees represents one of the Western world's great scientific achievements."

In recent years, Goodall has devoted herself to saving the dwindling population of chimps. This is how she dedicated one of her books: "To the chimpanzees of the world, those still living free in the wild and those held captive and enslaved by humans. For all that they have contributed to knowledge and understanding."

I talked to Jane Goodall when she was in Toronto with two new books: *Reason for Hope: A Spiritual Journey* (1999) and *Africa in My Blood: An Autobiography in Letters* (2000). She subsequently published *Beyond Innocence: An Autobiography in Letters, The Later Years* (2001) and starred in the Canadian-made Imax documentary *Jane Goodall's Wild Chimpanzees* (2002).

I had read how people hearing her lecture or meeting her might be moved to tears. She hates being compared to Mother Teresa, but there is an absolute selflessness about her, bordering on the ascetic—with little interest in food or material comforts—combined with terrific determination. But in case this sounds all too serious or humourless, there was the moment—unfortunately not capturable in print—when I asked if she could do a chimpanzee greeting for me. She threw back her head and let out a series of cries and whoops utterly incongruous with the demeanour of the gracious sexagenarian seated across from me.

In 2002, Jane Goodall was named a U.N. Messenger of Peace.

WACHTEL It's been forty years since you first arrived at Gombe National Park, which was then a game reserve on the shores of Lake Tanganyika. Can you describe what you found there? What were your first impressions?

GOODALL I can vividly remember going in a little boat—a tiny little boat, really—with my mother, and looking up at the mountains and the rugged hills and wondering how on earth I was going to find the chimpanzees. A sense of unreality gripped me at that time. This was my dream, and here I was setting off into this remote place—it was very remote in those days—and my job was to find and learn about the chimpanzees. It was what I'd dreamed about all my life, and now it was really happening. It was strange.

WACHTEL Why was it your dream?

GOODALL I don't know. Like many children, I just started my life loving animals, and I had a wonderfully supportive mother who encouraged both her daughters in their interests. When I was eighteen months old, my mother came up to my room and found I'd taken a whole lot of earthworms up and was apparently watching entranced as they wriggled around the pillow. Instead of getting cross because of the dirt, she just said, "Jane, if you leave them here, they'll die. They need the earth." And so I trotted back with them into the little bit of green that we had in London. A few years later, when I was four and a half, the same sort of thing happened. I was supposed to be helping collect hens' eggs from a farm where we were having a holiday. In those days there were no cruel battery farms, and so the hens clucked about in the farmyard and laid their eggs mostly in little wooden henhouses. I was collecting the eggs. I was apparently asking everyone where there was a hole big enough for the egg to come out. I couldn't see such a hole, and obviously they didn't tell me to my satisfaction, so I hid. I hid in the back of the hen-house and waited about four hours. The family called the police, because they didn't know where I was. My mother was searching and dusk was falling, and then she saw me rushing towards the house with straw all over me. How many mothers, from sheer fear, would grab a child and say, "How dare you go off without telling us. Don't you ever do that again!" But she didn't. She saw my shining eyes and sat down to hear this wonderful story. If I shut my eyes, I can see it happening as though it's yesterday.

WACHTEL What did you do for the four hours?

GOODALL Just waited.

WACHTEL You had the patience even at four and a half.

GOODALL Yes. And isn't it amazing: the curiosity, the asking of questions, which is a part of science, and then the patience that you must have to do anything with animals. And of course the "eureka!" feeling. I think this is a big danger for children today. They have too much virtual reality. Every discovery, even if it's something that's been seen thousands of times, has a huge impact when it's your discovery for the first time, with your own eyes and your own skills.

Anyway, I went on to read various books about animals. I met Doctor Dolittle. And then, when I was about ten, I met Tarzan from the Edgar Rice Burroughs books. And that was it. I fell passionately in love; I was madly jealous of his Jane. I thought she was a wimp and that I'd have been a much better mate for Tarzan. Don't you think so?

WACHTEL And the fact that you were named Jane. Surely that was significant.

GOODALL Yes. So that was when I started dreaming about going to Africa, living with animals and writing books about them. No dream of being a scientist at all.

WACHTEL Once you finally got to Gombe, you discovered that the chimps were hard to find. Can you tell me why this was?

GOODALL Chimps are very conservative. They'd never seen "white apes" before and so they just ran away, and they went on running away. Even if I was on the other side of a narrow ravine, they would take one look and silently disappear. But I loved being out in the forest—it was absolute magic! The whole experience was tempered with enormous anxiety, however: if I didn't see something really exciting, really interesting, if I didn't get some good data, then Louis Leakey, my mentor, wouldn't get money for me to continue and I'd be letting him down. At that time it had taken him a year to find money for the project—I didn't have any training, I hadn't been to university, I was more or less fresh from England. So who would give money? In the end, it came from a wealthy American businessman, Nathan Wilkie. And the thought of getting permission from the British authorities for a young girl to go into the bush on her own was preposterous. In the end, because Louis just persisted, they said, "All right, but she must have a companion." So that same remarkable mother came with me.

WACHTEL Louis Leakey was then curator of the National History Museum in Nairobi. You set out to meet him and, in fact, you were quite nervy about it. You wrote in a letter home that, when a promised introduction didn't come about, you just rang him up and told him how interested in animals you were, and left the rest to him. What are some of your most vivid memories of him?

GOODALL He was larger than life, a quite extraordinary man. He instantly became my hero. He knew so much about animals and the people of Africa. He was the sort of person you dream about meeting, who can answer so many of your questions and open such exciting doors. He was also very impatient with people. I remember when I got the job as his assistant—his secretary, really—that he'd get a letter from someone or read a scientific paper and if this person didn't happen to agree exactly with him, the whole document would be covered with *Rubbish! Bosh! Tosh!* He'd want to ring the person up instantly, because he was mad at them, and I learned to—well, lie, really—and say that the person wasn't in, that he should call back tomorrow, and by that time it was all tempered and the conversation was reasonable. He would get so wrapped up in what he was thinking about at the time that he often seemed really rude. He'd just walk past someone without saying hello, which upset people.

WACHTEL Leakey was famous for his interest in women and also for his belief that they make the best field researchers. Was it hard to get him to shift his attentions from the first to the second?

GOODALL Well, actually, he was attracted to me, as a lot of other men were at that time, and I think he behaved really, really well. He could have just thought, Why should I bother? She's not worth bothering with. But he didn't. He had a real conviction that I could work and do this thing for him. And he really wanted to know about the behaviour of the chimps, thinking it might help him to have a better feeling for how our own early ancestors might have behaved. So he never lost sight of what he wanted me to do through it all.

WACHTEL And he recognized your abilities and your sensitivity, obviously, even though you were young and untrained at that time.

GOODALL He obviously did. I had an opportunity to go with him, his wife, Mary, and one other young English girl, Gillian, to Olduvai, on the Serengeti, which is now very famous because that was where the Leakeys made some of their amazing discoveries—Homo habilis and Zinjanthropus.

WACHTEL That the earliest humans were found there.

GOODALL Yes. When I first went, no human remains had been discovered, just some tools. Mary Leakey insisted that these finds were tools, though, and other people said they weren't. But of course they were. So it was just wild, untouched Africa. Every evening, after chipping away looking for fossils, Gillian and I were allowed to walk out onto those plains. There we were, with giraffe, with antelope, zebra, ostriches, one evening a rhino. Once a young male lion—two years old, adult size, just sprouting his mane—followed us for five hundred yards, curious, never having seen anything like us before.

WACHTEL Were you scared?

GOODALL I was almost too excited to be scared, and I just felt that, if we did the right thing, which I seemed to understand instinctively, we'd be OK. I believed that animals wouldn't harm me.

WACHTEL It was Leakey who launched other women in their research. He supported Dian Fossey in 1963 in her work with mountain gorillas, and then Biruté Galdikas with orangutans. But you were one of the first; you were the first.

GOODALL Well, no. He worked with two young women who tried to study gorillas but failed. I was the first success.

He felt that women simply made better observers. I think there are various issues here. This was before the feminist movement, and in those days women weren't expected to make a living for themselves. You sat around and some white knight would come sweeping along and bear you off into matrimony and look after you for the rest of your days, so you could afford to be patient. Whereas at that time a young man, if he wanted to have a family, would have to get his PhD. So I think there was that sort of an undercurrent, although it was totally unconscious. But then if you think about women in an evolutionary sense—which you learn to do by watching the chimpanzees—to be a good mother in the old-fashioned sense of the word you had to have patience and you had to learn to understand the behaviour of a non-verbal being, which is our own kids before they speak. And also, women traditionally have been masters at dealing with strife within a family, mediating and monitoring the tensions. All of these characteristics are very, very helpful for field research.

WACHTEL Clearly, Leakey didn't care about academic credentials—in fact, he preferred the more open, untutored mind—but were you concerned about your lack of formal training?

GOODALL I was just amazed that he would choose me. This is a mark of his genius. He specifically wanted someone whose mind was uncluttered by the very reductionist, scientific beliefs of the people studying behaviour, the ethologists. At the same time, as soon as I began getting my results, he insisted that I get a PhD at Cambridge. Once I'd proved what he knew—and I think he knew I'd prove it—then I had to get the credentials in order to stand on my own two feet. He was thinking ahead when he said, "Jane, you won't be able to get money to go on with this study." This was at a time when winning support for even a one-year study was amazing. He was such a far-sighted person. Even then he was thinking in terms of ten years.

WACHTEL Although you thought three years. When he said ten, you thought three.

GOODALL Yes. Ten when you are twenty-six really does seem forever; it stretches on and you'll be old by the time it's finished.

WACHTEL So, now it's forty-plus years and it's still going on.

GOODALL It's still going on and we're still learning new things.

WACHTEL In setting off for Gombe, did you have any firm ideas of how you would approach the research, or how you would collect data?

GOODALL Well, I'd had a little bit of experience because I'd gone off on Leakey's fossil-hunting boat to a little uninhabited island on Lake Victoria where I watched vervet monkeys for about three weeks. So although it wasn't planned, I was able to work out some techniques there, like wearing the same-coloured clothes, not trying to get too close too quickly, making good use of binoculars, writing everything down and thinking about it later.

WACHTEL And you wore khaki-coloured clothes. Was that to keep you a monochrome?

GOODALL Just so you didn't stand out, so you seemed to blend in. I just think that's polite. I didn't want to go out into the natural world in garish clothes—although of course the flowers and the birds and the butterflies are all brilliantly coloured. I wanted to be a part of the background rather than something standing out from it.

WACHTEL How would you describe the young Jane Goodall who arrived at Gombe?

GOODALL Totally naive. Filled with enthusiasm. Intensely excited about where I was, even though I couldn't quite believe it was happening. And really, really concerned that I shouldn't let Louis down.

WACHTEL Do you know how you found the strength and determination to go into a place that was so demanding and possibly dangerous?

GOODALL I didn't think of it like that. For me it was a dream come true, the only thing I wanted and dreamed of doing. It felt like a natural thing to do, so I didn't need strength and determination; it was just something I wanted to do.

WACHTEL Your family has been supportive in so many ways, and not only your mother, but a whole constellation of vigorous, engaged women—your grandmother, your aunts. Were they models for you?

GOODALL Oh, I think they must have been. My father left during the war—he and my mother got divorced—so the male in my life—and he was a very strong influence, too—was my mother's brother, Uncle Eric. An amazing person! He was a surgeon in a very big hospital, but he would come down most weekends. He used to let me watch him operating, and so I learned very early on how amazing the human body is and what it can withstand, what skills a surgeon must have, and about the care and concern that should be a part of medicine. He was a really compassionate, wonderful human being, so he was definitely a role model.

Of course my mother was always a role model. And my grandmother had a Victorian stiff upper lip. You were never to give in; if you gave in to something, then you were just a wimpy little thing. And yet she had a heart of gold. So she could seem really stern, but she was really all compassion. Another amazing person!

WACHTEL How did you experience her compassion?

GOODALL She was always there for me. If I were upset, she would be there to comfort me. She did have a thing about not giving in. What a wonderful upbringing! It's fading away, that Victorian notion that you don't give in to human frailty, you overcome it. There isn't enough of that around today, I think; children lack that kind of upbringing—the iron hand in the velvet glove.

WACHTEL One of the most striking things about your writing through all the years at Gombe, and in all the images that have been captured on film and video, is your affection and empathy for the chimpanzees. Did you feel that immediately?

GOODALL No, actually I didn't, because they kept running away. But as soon as I got to know the chimpanzees as individuals, and as soon as darling David Greybeard, who lost his fear before all the others, let me come near him and eventually let me groom him, everything changed. I shouldn't have done what I did, but I would do it again. When a fully grown adult male overcomes his fear and builds up a relationship so trusting that you can actually touch him, it's amazing!

WACHTEL Why shouldn't you have done it? Too dangerous?

GOODALL It's just that the whole purpose of the study is to observe their natural behaviour, and if you start interacting, you get into their society, but then you're interfering with it. Of course it is dangerous, too. They're ever so much stronger than us, so if they lose their respect, it can be bad. But Flo and little Flint and Mike and Goliath—they were wonderful, wonderful personalities. I can never forget them.

WACHTEL Were you torn between the sort of rigours of scientific distance and your connection to these individuals?

GOODALL No, but I hadn't been trained as a scientist. If you're watching something and you're supposed to be writing a scientific report, you write down what you see as objectively as you can. The fact that in your heart you're feeling angry or sad or amused at what the chimpanzee is doing shouldn't colour what you're writing. It's a kind of self-discipline.

WACHTEL You've pointed out that when you began your study at Gombe in 1960, it was "not permissible—at least not in ethological circles—to talk about an animal's mind. Only humans had minds. Nor was it quite proper to talk about animal personality." Why was it so important for you to allow the chimps their individuality, to name them and to name their emotions?

GOODALL It wasn't anything I gave a second thought to. You know, I hadn't been educated in a university, but I had an amazing teacher all through my childhood: my dog Rusty. He taught me so much about animal behaviour. So even before I got to Gombe, I knew that animals had personalities, that they were capable of rational thought, and that they had emotions—happiness, sadness, despair and so forth. And of course we're animals, too. I think this is the reason that Louis specially wanted someone whose mind wasn't cluttered up in an academic way. It was natural to me to give them names rather than numbers, as I was told I should have, and to describe their personalities. There they were, these vivid, unique personalities! You couldn't deny it. And to watch them solving completely new problems, using tools, for example, it was obvious that they have minds. Of course it's fashionable now to study the animal mind. And then the emotions—well, you can't spend time with chimpanzees and not realize that they have very strong emotions, very similar to many of ours. It was just common sense. And science has changed.

WACHTEL You had to defend yourself against anthropomorphizing the chimps, which is a tricky business. In one of your letters you write, "I am not trying to attribute human motives to David [Greybeard, one of the chimps]. What I wanted to convey is the impression, purely subjectively, that his action had upon me." How were you able to find so-called objective understanding of chimpanzee behaviour through your own inevitably subjective response to it?

GOODALL Every scientist's work is coloured by who they are and how they were brought up, and that's going to colour the kind of interpretations they make, especially with something like animal behaviour. That letter was obviously written after I'd gone to university and learned the dangers of anthropomorphism. But if you actually think it through, a lot of this scientific thinking was very illogical. You can take a chimpanzee and you can use him in medical research, including research into the brain, because physiologically, biologically, genetically, chimps and humans are very close. That isn't questioned. But why isn't it logical to assume that because of the similarities in the brain and central nervous system there should be similar intellectual performances and similar expressions of emotion? You can't really accept the one without question and deny the other. I would like to turn it around and say to the people who question this: All right, you prove that it's not so; why must I always be the one to prove that it is?

WACHTEL There are some very colourful examples of anthropomorphizing in your letters from those early days at Gombe. You talk about watching a male chimp eating a piece of meat, and you say he looks "for all the world like a bloke with a pork pie in one hand and a stick of celery in the other." I guess it's inevitable that you're going to relate what you see to your experience of human behaviour.

GOODALL It's interesting. Sometimes when you talk to people from other cultures, such as Japan, who've also studied monkeys, the different interpretations are absolutely related to the culture. It's curious. But, yes, in the letters home I wrote what I saw, and then I learned.

I had a wonderful PhD supervisor at Cambridge, and he really taught me how to get this massive body of information into a form that was scientifically acceptable. It was a challenge. I enjoyed it. I really liked the discipline. I remember one discussion with him. I'd written something about Fifi being jealous because other infants were touching her baby brother, and Robert Hinde said, "You can't say that." I said, "Well, you know, she was jealous," and he said, "Yes, but you can't prove it." So I said, "Well, what can I do, then?" He said, "Why don't you write, 'Fifi behaved in such a way that had she been human we would have said she was jealous.'" Now, isn't that clever? That's a wonderful lesson.

WACHTEL The difficulty of interpreting chimpanzee behaviour is also apparent in some of your letters and anecdotes. In a letter from 1963 you write that you found out why the chimps chew cardboard, that you saw them pulling off dead wood, chewing it and spitting it out. So cardboard is a type of dead wood for them. Of course, it now remains, why do they chew dead wood? Were there things that baffled you?

GOODALL Oh yes, and still do. We haven't got answers to anything like the whole picture.

WACHTEL Are there particular things that intrigue you in that way?

GOODALL Well, the sad thing—and one of the most intriguing—is the fact that everywhere chimps have been studied, they have different traditions, different tool-using behaviours, which we think we can describe as cultures, because they seem to be behaviours passed from one generation to the next through observation and imitation. And now we'll never be able to discover the full extent of chimp diversity in this regard, because the chimps are disappearing and their cultures are going with them. So we'll never ever be able to find out the whole range of behaviour. That's very sad.

WACHTEL In your book *Reason for Hope*, you write that those early months at Gombe helped to shape the personality that you have today. In what way?

GOODALL In those early months I was completely on my own. I was out in the forest. I was patient anyway, but I learned to be more patient. When you're out there waiting for chimpanzees and becoming aware of all the little sounds and colours and smells of the forest around you, you also have time to think, and although I wasn't consciously thinking, questioning and being a philosopher, I think somehow that time must have had a very calming effect. People always say I look peaceful and ask if I meditate. Well, I don't, but I'm sure it has to be those hours and hours in the forest.

WACHTEL That you still carry so many years later, that have become part of you.

GOODALL Yes. If things are all bustling and wild outside, there's a little core of quiet within. It's not only that time in the forest, it's also my upbringing. It's also the way we were taught as children to remain calm. So it's a mixture of the forest and my upbringing and my amazing family, and I suppose, to some extent, my genes.

WACHTEL Was it inevitable that your connection to the natural world would also evoke a spiritual dimension?

GOODALL Probably not inevitable, but I feel the two are very close together. When you're out in nature, in the natural world, it is so exquisitely beautiful and so timeless that something of spirit seems to be strongly there. Coming into a redwood forest and looking up at the sky far above, or lying in a tropical forest, or on the top of a mountain, or in the wilds of the Serengeti surrounded by wildebeest—these things are very close to a spiritual power that I feel quite strongly.

WACHTEL From childhood you've attended church fairly regularly and assumed the existence of God and responded to nature. Did you think of yourself as religious?

GOODALL No, not at all. We never had religion rammed down our throats or anything. The time when I suppose I hoped I was religious was when, as a teenager, I fell in love with the local parson. It was totally platonic. I adored him, I worshipped him. Everyone had a lot of fun teasing me about it, but I enjoyed that, as well. I was going to church as many times as there were services, so that I could gaze at my beloved's head. You know how teenagers are when they get huge crushes. But that was obviously very, very good for me, because it made me, I think, a better person. I tried to do things that I thought he would approve of. I'm sure that certain things I did afterwards were because of him. It's all tied in together, all those experiences. And of course the war, the Holocaust, or the memories of that.

WACHTEL The memories of learning about the Holocaust when you were young?

GOODALL Yes. Hearing about what was happening, seeing the pictures of the survivors, the pictures of the liberated camps with the heaps of skeleton bodies. It was just so shocking. The war was bad enough— the bombs and knowing that people had been killed. But that this had been quietly going on was just horrifying. I'd already begun thinking about human nature in some childlike way and this showed me how evil we can be. I suppose it was also particularly profound because I had such a loving family and this was such a stark contrast.

WACHTEL At the time you began your research in Africa, what were your spiritual concerns—what questions preoccupied you?

GOODALL I don't think any spiritual concerns preoccupied me at all when I started at Gombe. It was purely a matter of, Can I do it, will I be good enough, can I get the chimps to trust me, how can I get stronger so I can spend longer out in the forest? These were my concerns. It was very physically challenging, and you also had to be mentally tough because there were so many disappointments to get over. When chimps you've struggled to get near all ran away, there was a temptation to burst into tears and say, "I can't do it again, I'm exhausted." But you have to somehow go on.

WACHTEL You start your book *Reason for Hope* with an experience that you had in Notre Dame Cathedral in Paris, a moment of eternity or ecstasy, while you were sitting under the rose window and the organist was playing Bach. Do you understand what happened to you there?

GOODALL Looking back on it, it was as though there was a message. I think it depends how we feel about life. If we think there's a purpose to our life on earth, then looking back on that moment it was like a message coming to me, one that I didn't understand at the time. The message was a very simple one: that whole experience—the cathedral, the music, the beautiful rose window, the thought of all the people who'd worshipped in that cathedral and their prayers and their different personalities and lives—I was able to understand the whole of this and the whole of evolution in a split second. It made me feel that there's more to life than mere chance, that there is a purpose, there is a plan, and I was a part of it.

WACHTEL And does plan imply a capital P plan? What does it mean?

GOODALL I don't pretend to understand what the plan for our life on earth is, but it does seem to me that we are very slowly moving into a new phase of our evolution. First comes the physical evolution—and I had the experience of holding some of those ancient fossils in my hands—and then starts the moral evolution. We gradually develop a mind that's capable of working out things like right and wrong and how we should behave, and so there's cultural evolution, which we leapt into with the development of language. I think we're on the path of moral evolution and spiritual evolution, but the trouble is, we have been so destructive and we've reproduced ourselves so oversuccessfully that I wonder if there is going to be time to complete this plan, if it is a plan.

WACHTEL If moral evolution takes as long as physical evolution, we could be talking millions of years.

GOODALL Well, it wouldn't, because cultural evolution has speeded everything up. In my lifetime, sixty-six years, the technological developments have been staggering. It's in the realm of pure magic to me. I can't even work out how 747s take off, let alone stay up there.

WACHTEL Or how rockets go to the moon!

GOODALL Yes! It's all magic. If you'd said somebody was going to the moon when I was a child, it would have been science fiction. And we've done it! And therein lies the hope for the future: what our brains are capable of. Now that we've admitted that we've harmed the environment, the natural world, terribly, can't we start putting it right? And we are putting it right; it is beginning to happen. Will it be quick enough? I don't know. Nature is amazingly forgiving: we damage her and blight her and poison her, and yet give her a chance or time and she'll recover. But is there time enough?

WACHTEL   And given all that you know and have seen in terms of physical destruction of the environment, as well as human destruction among other things, what convinces you that we're on this path of moral evolution?

GOODALL   If I think back to the Victorian days in England, there were the ladies and gentlemen riding around in their carriages and living luxurious lives while their servants were treated literally like slaves, with hardly any money or freedom. There were still children barefoot in the snow and the ladies would graciously throw them a penny. There were the poorhouses, and there were the women and children down in the mines with these ghastly hours and very little rest and hardly any food. You could go on and on about social injustices, but they are being redressed—every single one is being worked on by somebody. There's more social consciousness around and there's more volunteerism. Take the United States, for example. You can go back to a time when there was slavery, but there was a civil war and slavery was abolished. Now there's discrimination, yes, but people are fighting it. I just pray that Africa, which is going through such a terribly, terribly distressing time right now, will slowly move onto a different level. It's a question of time!

WACHTEL   And that's why you called your book *Reason for Hope*, because there is reason, in your mind.

GOODALL   Yes. We've also got this amazing thing that I call the indomitable human spirit: people who tackle impossible tasks and succeed, and people who overcome terrible physical disabilities and become inspirations to everyone around them. Finally, there is the enormous energy and commitment of young people, once they know what the problems are and once they're empowered to act. That's why

I'm putting most of my energy into the Roots and Shoots program for young people, which is spreading around the world and giving kids hope.

WACHTEL I'd like to return to some of the pivotal moments in your experience at Gombe. One of them was when the chimp that you named David Greybeard took a red palm nut from you. What happened? What made the event so remarkable?

GOODALL Oh, that was a wonderful event! I was following David. It was just after he'd actually allowed me to follow him. Until then, he would let me come up and then I would allow him to go off and have his space. He'd gone through a narrow tunnel and some thorny, viny stuff. I was struggling and the thorns were catching my clothes. I thought, Oh well, I've lost him—but it was almost as though he was waiting for me, sitting by a little stream, and there I saw this bright red palm nut and I held it out to him on the palm of my hand, and he turned his head away. I thought, Why doesn't he want it? They love palm nuts. So I held it closer still. And he looked directly into my eyes, he reached out, he took the nut and with one movement dropped it, but at the same time he held my hand with a very gentle pressure. That's how chimpanzees reassure each other and calm each other down. So it was like a communication that didn't need words, which we both inherited from a very ancient primate past. It was as if he were saying, "I'm not spurning you; I just don't want the nut." It was amazing!

WACHTEL David Greybeard was special to you and so were various other chimps at Gombe. You've introduced us to a whole cast of characters, three generations of a real-life family saga.

GOODALL There was Flo and then Fifi, and Fifi has now had her daughters and they've had children. So it's four generations.

WACHTEL And you name all the children within the families with the same letter. That's why you have Flo and Fifi and Freud, and the whole lot.

GOODALL And Fifi is the one individual who was alive in 1960 who's still alive and going strong today. It's amazing, isn't it, that she and I share memories going back forty years. And some of those memories in the early sixties are probably unique to us. Only we two can remember them now.

WACHTEL Did you imagine, when you started out, that life in chimpanzee society could be so richly textured?

GOODALL No, I don't think anyone could have imagined it would be quite so rich, though Wolfgang Köhler, the Austrian psychologist, had written an amazing book, *The Mentality of Apes*, about a captive colony in the Canary Islands. It was my bible at that time.

WACHTEL The matriarch Flo is one of your best-loved characters— you knew her for eleven years—and you describe her as "filled with purpose, vigour and love of life." In fact, after her death in 1972, there was even an obituary in the London *Sunday Times*. Tell me about Flo.

GOODALL Flo had been through a lot. She had raggedy ears—she'd obviously been in a number of conflicts. She was an absolutely marvellous mother—very protective, but not overprotective. She was incredibly affectionate. She watched her kids and if there was any sign of trouble, she was there. She was very, very supportive, so if they got into difficulties with other chimps or baboons, which sometimes happened, even though she was a female chimp, she would unhesitatingly throw herself against an adult male to rescue one of her children. And she was very successful reproductively; she was an absolute *wow* with the males. It was actually when Flo came into estrus, and became socially and sexually attractive to the males, that so many of the chimps began coming into my camp. David Greybeard had already come for bananas and had brought Flo, and then Flo just brought all her suitors. They were so compelled to be with her that they overcame their fear of me and trailed into the camp. They were terrified, really, but they couldn't let Flo go. She was a real Marilyn Monroe.

WACHTEL You've said that you've modelled your own mothering after Flo, that her maternal behaviour influenced you.

GOODALL Yes. I think it was a mixture of Flo and my own mother, and probably Dr. Spock too, but the thing I felt so strongly about after watching Flo and the other two mothers is, first of all, that having your own child should be an enormous amount of joy and fun, and I determined that when I had my child I was going to enjoy him and have fun with him. The other thing that gradually emerged over the years was the incredible importance of early experience, particularly the type of mothering, in determining the future character of the child and the way it behaves. It became very obvious that the chimpanzees with supportive, protective, affectionate, playful mothers grew up to be assertive, and that they would do pretty well reproductively and have good relationships with the other chimps. On the other hand, with the more punitive and above all less supportive mothers, their offspring were more likely to grow up to be much more tense and nervous in their relationships with other individuals and less successful reproductively. If you extrapolate that to some of the ways we bring up—or don't bring up—our children today, it's no surprise to see the tremendous problems that some teenagers are having.

WACHTEL It's interesting, and also how one would expect it to be. But were there surprising discoveries, things that were not as you would have imagined or expected?

GOODALL I think I was surprised that there were some behaviours shown by the infant—I remember Flint when he got one of those big biting ants stuck on his cheek and it was instantly, in a flash, obvious to me why he was whimpering and in pain. Flo did everything: she cuddled him, she cradled him, she kissed him, but somehow she didn't put two and two together, and that was very puzzling. People working with captive chimps have said the same, that suddenly the chimp can't solve what seems to us a terribly simple problem, and they get irritable and wonder why the chimp can't do it. And we don't know. This is why, if we could just get into the mind of a chimp for a few minutes . . . You know, I can sit and look into Fifi's eyes and there's a thinking being looking out at me. But what is she thinking? What is the thought process? We don't know.

WACHTEL Power relations are also fascinating, and the idea of the alpha male has become quite widely known, but some unlikely chimps have found their way to the top through ingenuity. What have you learned about the dynamics of power through observing chimpanzees?

GOODALL It's absolutely fascinating. Every male who's taken that top-ranking position—I think there have been seven or eight of them now—has used different techniques to get to the top. It does seem to be a position that's very helpful to the male's reproductive success. The chimps who seem less aggressive, smaller, have had to use their intelligence to get to the top. But they seem to stay at the top longer, which is interesting. Our big bully Humphrey lasted only one and a half years, whereas somebody like Mike, who used empty kerosene cans and incorporated them into his intimidation displays, reigned for six years.

WACHTEL He made a huge noise.

GOODALL He made a lot of noise and the others ran out of the way. But he also had to have the guts to stand up to coalitions of males who tried to challenge his newly won dominance. So we're still learning a lot about dominance—the way a chimp becomes dominant and exactly what it means. The most important thing is forming alliances; making it on your own is tough. Mike had kerosene cans, but he also had a brother.

WACHTEL I'd like to talk about another dramatic moment at Gombe, when you first watched a chimp performing a magnificent rain dance. You wrote in a letter to your family, "Can you begin to imagine how I felt? The only human ever to have witnessed such a display, in all its primitive, fantastic wonder?" What did you see?

GOODALL This was another of those moments that I can vividly recall. It was raining, and I was sitting on the opposite side of a very narrow ravine. On the other side, the grass was green and about two feet tall because it was the rainy season. There was a group of chimpanzees sitting on a relatively open slope with only a few trees. It had been drizzling, and suddenly the heavens opened and it was very dark. There was thunder, very loud and reverberating from side to side amidst the mountains and valleys. Suddenly the chimpanzee males started charging, one by one, sometimes two together, straight down the slope, grabbing at branches, tearing them off the trees and dragging them along, swaying from side to side and then climbing up into a tree. The females were watching them, and then the males would tear back up the slope and do it again. It was absolutely extraordinary; I've never seen anything quite like that again. Nothing that's been quite so dramatic, almost choreographed. Rain displays are not uncommon in themselves. At the start of a heavy rain there will almost always be one chimp who will sway rhythmically from foot to foot, swaying the vegetation, dragging it. You know, it's almost as though he's challenging the elements. They do the same sort of thing at a waterfall.

WACHTEL Do they like rain?

GOODALL No, not at all. They get very miserable.

WACHTEL They sit and get wet. They don't even go under shelter.

GOODALL They start taking shelter, but after a bit, when the heavy rain starts dripping through, they just go out and sit in the open. They get soggy and sit up at night. The water does run off their hair, but they get cold.

WACHTEL So the rain dance is not celebratory.

GOODALL I think it's more like a challenge. There's something really exciting, particularly with the waterfall display, where the chimpanzee will sway from foot to foot on the rocky riverbed and throw big rocks and sometimes make his *whoo-whoo-whoo* sound and climb the little vines and push out into the spray that's caused by the eighty-foot drop of the water. If only the chimpanzees had language, if they could talk to each other about whatever emotion it is that's driving these displays— what I call "elemental displays"—mightn't that turn into something like a primitive animistic religion, the early religions that worship water and sun and rain, the things that are out of our control?

WACHTEL Because you discern, as your professor might say, a response that, were they human, you would describe as awe.

GOODALL That's right. Awe and wonder.

WACHTEL Wonder?

GOODALL I think wonder. I think there's wonder. When you watch chimps looking at some little thing that they've noticed in the environment, it's like a small child who's crawling around and learning about life for the first time. There is wonder in a young human. When they're out in nature, I don't see any difference in the behaviour of a young chimp and a child. They reach out and they look and they touch.

WACHTEL You were the first to observe chimps killing other animals—bush pigs, baboons—and consuming their flesh, but you still thought that the chimps were a lot like us, only nicer, until what you called the "four-year war." What happened?

GOODALL That was shocking. The first episode in that four-year war was seen by one of my students, David Bygott. He came and reported on this, and we thought we couldn't believe him. I mean, this was a group of adult males, patrolling the boundaries of their territory, coming upon a female from a neighbouring community, brutally attacking her, seizing her infant, and then not really eating it but playing with it and perhaps taking the odd mouthful while different males dragged the body around. This was the first time we saw hatred of strangers.

What we called the four-year war was almost worse, because the main study community was large and it began to divide. Seven males and a few females began spending more and more time in the southern part of an area which they had shared before. Two years after the break began, we realized that this was now a separate community. There were no more friendly interactions. Groups of males in the larger community began systematically penetrating deep into the heart of the area that the breakaway group had claimed for itself, and if they found individuals from that community, they subjected them to brutal twenty-minute gang attacks and left the victims to die of their wounds. It was totally horrible, and it lasted four years.

WACHTEL And it wasn't that they needed the territory for food or for themselves necessarily?

GOODALL They might have. I think it was fought over territory. They did move back into that territory, but they shouldn't have needed it after the community divided. The area that was left should have been large enough. Perhaps those males just wanted to go back where they had always been; they resented the fact that it had been taken over.

It was horrifying! They were fighting individuals that they knew, that they had groomed with and fed with. It was like a civil war.

WACHTEL How did you make sense of the violence?

GOODALL I made sense of it by realizing that it was probably fought over territory. We fight over territory, too, and they're like us. And then we turn it around and say that these ancient aggressive tendencies, and our aggressive tendencies, are presumably derived from an ancient phylogenetic common past.

WACHTEL Do you see human violence as being genetically driven?

GOODALL I think our aggressive tendencies are definitely rooted in this ancient shared heritage, going back five million years to when there was a common ancestor to chimps and humans, because we show so much similarity in behaviour. But that doesn't mean that we should accept violence and war as inevitable because it's in our genes. I don't think it is. And we prove it every day of our lives: most of us don't go around giving free rein to our aggressive feelings about people. If we did, there'd be total anarchy. How often do we feel so mad at someone that we actually say, "I could kill him!" "I could commit murder!" We may think it, but we don't do it.

WACHTEL When you say you were shocked—especially as these were individuals that you knew—was there also a sense of disappointment, that you had hoped that they would be better than us?

GOODALL Yes, it was shocking. It was shocking that my chimps could behave like that—these gentle chimpanzees could suddenly turn into really brutal, aggressive killers.

WACHTEL And it wasn't just the male chimps. There was also cannibalism by females.

GOODALL That was something different. Some cannibalism resulted from these intercommunity conflicts. But even more shocking, I think, were Passion and Pom, mother and daughter, ganging up, working as a team, to attack and steal and eat the newborn babies of other females in their own community. Strangely, the following day the two killers could be sitting with the mother whose child had been taken and they'd be grooming each other. So something strange was going on. That, too, lasted for four years, during which time all but one of eleven infants died, and we know five of them were killed by Passion and Pom. It was awful. I thought it was aberrant: Passion has always been a rather queer, cold mother, so I thought it was just her bizarre behaviour. But more recently we've seen it again, and this time it was Fifi ganging up with her adult daughter on one occasion and with a childless female on another. Fortunately, both times the mother they were attacking got away. I say fortunately because she happens to be my favourite chimp, Gremlin, who'd just given birth to two beautiful little girl twins, Gold and Glitter. Fifi went for the twins. It was horrible.

WACHTEL But they survived.

GOODALL Yes. Gremlin is so smart. She was captured. Gremlin was sitting on a long, naked branch, with Fifi, who was two days from giving birth herself, on the far end, swaying the branch, looking like an evil witch with her hair sticking out. Her daughter Fanny sat on the other end of the branch with her infant, and Gremlin was in the middle. I think if she'd tried to escape, if she'd moved, they would quickly have seized one of the twins, which they'd already tried to do. But she just sat. She was brave and tough enough to sit and outlast this violence on either side of her. Then Fanny gave up and climbed down.

WACHTEL Why would they do that? You've known Fifi all your life and she's the daughter of Flo, who was an affectionate, ideal mother as Fifi herself is.

GOODALL It wouldn't surprise me if Flo had done it too, now that I know them better. Why do they do it? Is it the smell of birth blood? Is it because these babies are strangers they haven't seen before? The males don't show that kind of behaviour; they never have. The day following the attempted attack on Gremlin and the twins, Fifi and Gremlin were grooming each other and there was no attempt to go for the twins. This is a real puzzler. We can't begin to understand it. I'm glad it doesn't happen more often.

WACHTEL You make an important distinction between human and chimp violence in *Reason for Hope*, where you talk about finding violence in both but finding evil only in humans, not in chimpanzees. What distinction are you making there in terms of violence and evil?

GOODALL I think it's an important distinction. If you compare brutal gang attacks by chimps and humans, much of the pattern is similar if not identical. But when we come to physical and mental torture, this is planned, a deliberate attempt to inflict as much pain on a victim as you possibly can. Chimps understand to some extent what their victim is feeling—I think they can empathize to some extent—but their understanding doesn't extend to cold, deliberate planning. Chimpanzees are not able to plan something like the Holocaust. They don't have language; they haven't developed to the level where they could actually do that. But I'm not saying that they might not have, if they could.

WACHTEL You even say, if you gave them guns and taught the chimps how to use them, they would.

GOODALL I think they would. But at the moment we're the only beings, because of our superior intellect, who are capable of planning this very deliberate torture. That's evil. That's genuine evil.

WACHTEL In the intervening years since your first awareness of human evil—upon learning about the Holocaust—have you come to understand why humans behave this way?

GOODALL No, I don't think I have. But I think it's important that we remember that, just as we've inherited some of these aggressive, brutal tendencies from an ancient shared past, we've also inherited love and compassion and altruism. This is the other side of chimp nature, just as it's the other side of human nature. Chimpanzees can be so gentle, so nurturing. When an older brother or sister, especially the brother, adopts a little orphaned infant, it's so touching, so moving. I felt the same when an adolescent male, who wasn't even related, looked after a three-year-old orphan and saved his life.

WACHTEL It seems to be your nature to look at the bright side, to acknowledge or discern the dark side but to quickly return to what is positive.

GOODALL I think we must! Our human brain is well enough developed that we can make a conscious choice. We've inherited these two aspects of ourselves, the good and the bad, so it's up to us now to make the choice as to where we want to go. I think we've made the choice. We're just bungling. One of the big problems is the number of people living on the planet today. Resources aren't being shared the way they should. There's so much greed and so much corruption.

WACHTEL I know that you and your research team have intervened at times to protect the chimps from disease or injury—providing antibiotics, for example—but the violence at Gombe, the killings and cannibalism, must have really tested you. What do you do in situations where, as a scientist, you have to keep your distance, but your heart pulls you in the opposite direction? Were you tempted to intervene? Could you? Would you?

GOODALL Well, I did try to intervene once, but it was useless because it was all happening high in a tree. The field staff, the Tanzanians, on one occasion actually threw a rock at Passion. She was attacking a newborn infant. She didn't even feel it. And it's not until you've actually seen chimps when they're in a terribly aggressive mode, so violent and so much stronger than we are, that you realize there's actually nothing you can do. So giving medicine is one thing, but intervening in a conflict is almost impossible.

WACHTEL You've been injured once or twice. Frodo whacked you on the head and almost broke your neck. Have you been in much physical danger over the years?

GOODALL Really only from Frodo. He's a real bully. He bullies other chimps as well as people. He's the biggest chimp we've ever had. He's not actually trying to hurt, he's certainly not trying to kill, but because the ground is very uneven and rocky and there are precipices, he's dangerous. He really is dangerous.

WACHTEL Have you ever been scared?

GOODALL I've been scared by Frodo. Here's this tank charging at me and I didn't really have time to be afraid while it was happening. I just prayed, "Please, Frodo, don't!" When he finished with me, I felt a kind of fear, yes. I don't want him to do it again.

WACHTEL Can you describe Gombe today, the environment and the chimpanzee community?

GOODALL There are three chimpanzee communities living in the thirty square miles of forest, which, when I arrived, was part of a forest that went right along the shores of Lake Tanganyika for about three hundred miles. Today the ten miles of Gombe are as they were, and the little National Park goes inland only to the peaks of the rift escarpment. If you go to the north or the south, or you climb up to those peaks and look out eastward, away from the lake, the trees have gone. The one hundred and twenty chimps living inside the park probably don't represent a big enough gene pool for long-term sustainability, so they're doomed. For our fortieth anniversary here, we are making an attempt to buy up some farms and make a corridor to another tiny relict group, but I don't think we can do it. I don't think there's enough space. There are far more people living in this area than the land can support, and so the chimps have gone, the soil has lost its fertility, the people are beginning to face extreme hardship, and refugees have poured in from Burundi over the lake from what was eastern Zaire. And so the question is: How do you preserve these precious chimps, at least for as long as possible, and their little jewel of forest, when the people outside are suffering? So our solution, as with other conservation organizations, is to work with the local people, to help them improve their lives. We have an amazing program in thirty-three villages now. It's working, and the people are now beginning to help us save the chimps. Our first problem was the refugees coming from eastern Zaire, with their tradition of eating chimps and monkeys. We have extra patrols now, done by the National Parks and by our research staff, as well.

WACHTEL You spend little time now at Gombe, because your devotion to conservation work and education and the cause of chimpanzees in captivity keeps you on the road for so much of the year. Do you still feel involved with the research at Gombe?

GOODALL Yes, I do, actually. I try to keep up with what research is going on, and of course I'm trying to get the money to make sure it *does* go on, and to find the right people. We don't have very many expats, not very many people from America or Europe; it's mostly Tanzanians. Also, we have a wonderful videographer, so I can actually see what's happening. I love to watch the development of the twins, even if it's only on film; that fills in the gaps between the increasingly rare chances I get to actually be there.

WACHTEL Do you miss it?

GOODALL Oh, I miss it terribly. But I couldn't enjoy it now, because I know I'm supposed to be doing what I'm doing now.

WACHTEL So you've never regretted the decision you felt you had to make fifteen years ago, to leave Gombe.

GOODALL No. I haven't regretted that decision. I had to make it.

WACHTEL You've described those early years at Gombe as the happiest in your life.

GOODALL They were, but how amazingly lucky I was to have those years, to actually be living my dream all that time. Who could ask for more? You can't just selfishly go on doing that while everything falls to pieces around you. You couldn't. I couldn't—not and live with myself.

WACHTEL Forty years after the project began, do you think you could or should have done anything differently at Gombe?

GOODALL Well, the banana feeding clearly was a mistake.

WACHTEL That's when you put bananas out to attract the chimps to the camp.

GOODALL Yes. But on the other hand it turned out to be an amazing kind of unplanned field experiment. We learned a lot from it. Most things that I've made conscious decisions to do, as far as the research was concerned, were pretty good decisions.

WACHTEL You've become an inspiring figure yourself. Does that embarrass you at all?

GOODALL At the beginning it did. I couldn't take all those strange things that people would say, and then they'd start crying. I think I understand better now. When people get awestruck and they have tears in their eyes, it's because they're emotionally moved, and if we aren't emotionally moved, we won't act. People have to realize that every single individual, every one of us, matters, and every one of us can make a difference every single day of our lives. We all wait for change to be made by governments and by industry and by science; we just sit back and wait for it to happen, because we feel so useless as one person in six billion. What can I do? I know what I *should* do, but it's not going to make any difference. If we could turn that around, we'd have literally millions of socially and environmentally educated people who would be acting rather differently if they knew that everything they did was making an impact. Especially in affluent societies, individuals have an immense power, used collectively, to make ethical decisions as to what we buy and what we don't buy. If we have the money, we're not forced to buy products from environmentally unfriendly or socially irresponsible companies, and we don't have to buy cosmetics tested on animals, and we can search for organic food. People who have low incomes can't afford to make those choices, but if we make them, the time will come when they, too, will have the luxury of making ethical purchases, because the price will have come down. It's a consumer-driven society.

WACHTEL I think about you with your camouflage khaki blending into the background, and you now. Does it feel like you're going against your own nature, or has your temperament had to catch up with the work that you're so involved in now?

GOODALL Yes. I'm sort of two people. I've always felt that very strongly. I'm just me, the little girl who grew up in Bournemouth and climbed trees, and I still behave like a child often, as all my colleagues will tell you. But I'm also the Jane who's been put out there partly by *National Geographic*, with all their magazines and documentaries, partly by the books I've written myself, and partly by the fact that I'm travelling everywhere and meeting people, doing television and radio and lectures. The one who's out there is playing a really important role right now; I know that because people have told me so. The nicest thing I'm told after lectures is that I make people realize that their lives have more value. And thousands of children from all over the world have said,

"You taught me that because you did it, I can do it too." That's amazing. That makes it all—all this effort—really worthwhile.

April 2000

Canadian branch of the Jane Goodall Institute:

L'Institut Jane Goodall Institute
5165 Sherbrooke West
Montreal, Quebec H4A 1T6
Tel: (514) 369-3384 Fax: (514) 489-8748
www.janegoodall.ca

BERNARDO BERTOLUCCI

In a career that spans more than forty years, Bernardo Bertolucci is regarded by many as the pre-eminent Italian film director of his generation. From *The Conformist* (1971) to the controversial *Last Tango in Paris* (1973) to the epic Oscar-winner *The Last Emperor* (1987), Bertolucci has succeeded—as one critic put it—"like no other European director in uniting a radically experimental vision of film with a broad appeal to [North] American audiences."

Cinema is the art form of the twentieth century and Bertolucci is one of its younger sons. He started off as a poet. In fact, the same year that he won one of Italy's top poetry prizes, he made his first feature. He was scarcely twenty-one years old. He'd already worked for the writer and poet Pier Paolo Pasolini—a friend of his father's—on the set of his first feature, *Accattone*. Then Bertolucci made his own movie, *The Grim Reaper* (1962), based on a story by Pasolini. Two years later, Bertolucci made *Before the Revolution* (1964), an autobiographical film set in his hometown of Parma. It was hailed at Cannes, became a model for the young American director Martin Scorsese, and was a rallying cry in Paris during the social upheaval of 1968.

Then came *The Conformist*—a chilling treatment of fascism and identity. There are images from that movie—the dancehall scene, the murder in the woods—that remain some thirty years later. But Bertolucci became really famous with his next feature—his first in English (although part was in French)—*Last Tango in Paris* with Marlon Brando and Maria Schneider. Provocative, despairing and sexual, it was at once a cause célèbre and a landmark in film history. Bertolucci became a star and an outcast in his own country.

Since that time—1972—Bertolucci has worked frequently in English or with English-speaking actors, travelling the world to make his movies. His greatest Hollywood success, *The Last Emperor*, took place in mid-twentieth-century China, and won nine Oscars, including best film and best director. His most recent movie—a collaboration with his wife, Clare Peploe—is *Besieged* (1998).

When I first approached Bertolucci for an interview, he said he had "new gigantic doubts about cinema every day." When we met a few months later at his flat in Rome, his uncertainties were focused more on himself than on the medium. He said that the death of his father a year earlier had left him paralyzed, though he had a number of projects in the works, including a film about the sixteenth-century composer, Carlo Gesualdo.

Bertolucci is not only charming but also remarkably candid, open. We spoke in his large, airy dining room. Behind him was a painting with the word *Tango*.

WACHTEL When you were an adolescent, just fifteen or sixteen, you made your first films with a 16-mm camera you got from a cousin. One of those films was about the slaughter of a pig. Can you describe it?
BERTOLUCCI Yes, especially because the film doesn't exist any more. Both the little movies I did at sixteen have been lost, so I'll try to remem-

ber and invent what they were. The death of the pig was a kind of documentary about a day that kids anticipated every year with anxiety, in the middle of winter in the Po Valley, full of snow, when two or three bicycles arrived with what we call in Italy *noccini*, the people who kill the pigs. They arrived with capes and bags full of knives and strange instruments. The kids were very excited because it was a very special day. A gallows was put up, and the kids pretended not to know what was going on. Then these men would enter the pigsty, hiding their hands with the instruments behind them, in order not to show the pigs what they were holding. But in fact, the pigs, I think, recognized the smell from the clothes of these killers. They recognized it was the day of their death. They started screaming and crying. Because of the presence of this little cameraman, the professional pig killer made a mistake. He had this long needle which had to go into the heart of the pig, but he put it in the wrong place and the pig ran away, out of the pigsty, and started to escape the courtyard of the farm, leaving red marks of blood on the snow—while the killers and the farmers were following, trying to stop the pig. I remember shooting that. Now I think, thank God it was a black-and-white movie with no sound. Otherwise, it would have been a horror movie, unbearable.

WACHTEL Why did you choose this particular subject? Apparently you even put the butchers into costume. You had them wear cloaks.

BERTOLUCCI No, they were already dressed like that, in costume. It was a kind of Brueghel vision. Why did I choose that subject? Because I have always been fascinated by these kinds of pagan rites, barbarian rites. And meantime, the joy, the all-day joy on the farm, in the courtyard, because the pig was hanging on the gallows and was butchered. They used everything from the pig. Everything, everything, everything—the skin, the hair, and you eat everything else. So there was a huge pot on the fire, in the open air, and they were throwing into it things that were eaten immediately. The kids were jumping, singing. It was a great feast. It was a mixture of brutality but also of great peasant culture.

WACHTEL So is it too much for me to see the nascent themes in your work? When I hear you describe this, even the pig running away with the blood, I see the death of the teacher in *The Conformist*. There is something—when you describe this mixture of brutality and joy.

BERTOLUCCI Maybe there was some kind of fascination in what I just told you, but it wasn't a pure fascination with brutality. In fact, I have a great respect for animals. I was just witnessing the killing of an animal. I've never killed an animal myself, apart from, as you have seen at the beginning of the movie 1900, where little Olmo is catching frogs. This is what I used to do when I was eight, nine, ten, in the ditches of my grandfather's farm. But I have always had a great respect for animals.

WACHTEL You say you just witnessed the killing of an animal?

BERTOLUCCI Yes, I filmed it. I think in order to see and accept something so brutal, I had to have a camera in my hands. Maybe that explains why many times in my life a camera helped me to face things that might have been very difficult to face disarmed. When I say disarmed, I mean without a camera.

WACHTEL There is a killing of a pig in 1900. And then in *Tragedy of a Ridiculous Man*, although that, I think, might be because it's shot near Parma.

BERTOLUCCI It's shot where they do this fantastic Parmesan cheese, and of course they don't want to throw away all the cheese scraps, so big pig farms get them.

WACHTEL The prosciutto—

BERTOLUCCI So sometimes I have two essential Italian things—the Parmesan and the prosciutto.

WACHTEL You said that "from the moment I held a camera in my hands I felt like a professional movie director." Can you say why? Do you remember what you felt?

BERTOLUCCI I tried, you know, to imitate my father; when I started to write, I wrote poems. But the moment of my real identification, when I became myself, was when I stopped writing poems and started to be a filmmaker. I felt so intensely that it was my destiny. I didn't see anything outside that destiny. It was either that or nothing.

WACHTEL You believe in destiny?

BERTOLUCCI Not at all. I use "destiny" in the conventional way. I believe that destiny is more or less what, in Freudian analysis, you learn. You create your own destiny. You are the writer of the screenplay of your life—so, too, of your destiny. I don't believe that there is a book somewhere in heaven where all our destinies are written. In fact, when I did the movie on Tibetan Buddhism I was fascinated by Buddhist philosophy, and found there was a very strong similarity between the idea of karma and destiny. The way you have behaved in your previous lives determines your karma. So again, one is the author of one's own destiny.

WACHTEL The world of your childhood figures in your work, directly or indirectly. You once said, "I grew up in an earthly paradise where poetic and natural realities were one." Can you talk a little about Parma, the kind of landscape and the kind of home that you grew up in?

BERTOLUCCI I grew up in the countryside and I was a real country bumpkin in the sense that I loved the earth where I grew up. I loved the monotonous flatness of the Po Valley, and I loved the idea that not far, half an hour's bicycling, there was a big, big city called Parma, which had no more than 150,000 inhabitants. My childhood was very determined by my father's poetry, by my parents' presence and by a warm attitude to legend. Everything around us seemed to be in the process of becoming a legend, or maybe that was my way of living with my world. When I started to read, I read the poems of my father. They were all about the world surrounding our house or the world in the Apennines where we had our summer place in a little village where my father's family came from. When I was twelve, we moved to Rome and that was, I must confess, a big shock. I felt a kind of deracination, because I couldn't forget and give up the mythology of the countryside, to accept a new mythology, the mythology of Rome, which was much more conventional and banal.

WACHTEL You describe yourself as feeling like a country bumpkin, but your parents weren't farmers. They were very cultivated, educated.

BERTOLUCCI My grandfather was a farmer. My father was one of those miracles: a young teenager, thirteen or fourteen, taken by his parents—farmers—for the first time to Venice, who enters a bookshop in Venice and buys a first edition, which we still have, of À la recherche du temps perdu, by Proust, without knowing why. My father was a miracle, one in whom culture blossomed like a natural thing. That's why he was never, with me or with anybody—even his students when he was a teacher—an academic. He always talked about culture and he was incredibly well read, incredibly knowledgeable, about poetry and art. In fact, he was an art historian and teacher of art history in a lyceum, which is a high school. I don't remember a single time when my father talked too seriously about culture. He always spoke in a simple yet sophisticated way. I remember very well that he wrote a poem about my mother, which I read when I was seven or eight. It was called "The White Rose," and he wrote, "You are like the white rose in the bottom of the garden, the last bees of the summer have visited you," and it ends saying, "This rose is forgetful, like you will be when you'll be thirty." They must have been very young. And so I remember myself as a child going to the bottom of the garden and seeing the white rose there. Immediately it was clear to me that the material of poetry is something that is around us. You can find it everywhere, if you know how to look at things. That was for me the greatest lesson that he never taught me. I mean, I learned everything from him without him teaching. It was just his way of communicating.

You asked me about Parma. My father made of Parma a kind of petite capitale d'autrefois: a little capital of the past. He was very much in love with the art in the city, with the frescoes of Correggio and Parmigianino, with the fantastic Romanesque sculptures of the cathedral and the baptistry by Benedetto Antelami—very early, about twelfth century. He always wanted to be in that flow, that cultural flow. He was completely in love with his hometown, like he was in love with his family. It was something that I felt so intensely. The first movie I wrote—every young director has to do an autobiographical film—was called Before the Revolution, and it took place in Parma. It was very much about that city. I thought I'd do that in order to be free of Parma, to be free of my father. In fact, that was pure illusion, because for a long time I returned there to shoot films.

WACHTEL Your film 1900 is shot there. In terms of being free of your father, one of your great themes is the relationship between parents and children, but especially fathers and sons.

BERTOLUCCI Yes. In fact, I have been reminded many times that often in my movies there is a murder of the father.

WACHTEL A father or father figure, a teacher. So why did you have to kill off your father?

BERTOLUCCI As they say in New York, Oedipus Schmoedipus. What's the matter, as long you love your mom. My father, a few years before dying—he died last year—said to me, "Very clever. You killed me so many times without having to go to prison."

WACHTEL Do you understand that obsession?

BERTOLUCCI I've done many, many years in analysis, so I think that I've had time to understand it and to forget it and to understand and forget it again. I was able to go deeply into that, and in some ways it has helped me. I'm not sure about that, but that's my hope.

WACHTEL Was it hard for you to deal with his actual death?

BERTOLUCCI Not was. Is. Very hard. Very hard because I have no children. I think I have no children because I always considered myself as a son. So how could I be a father if I was a son? When my father died, I was already quite old, and I felt terribly deceived because he made us believe that he was immortal. Maybe he meant immortal in his poetry. It's a very hard subject.

WACHTEL Speaking of Oedipus Schmoedipus and Mom, your mother always seems more in the background. You described her once as the most mysterious person in your life. What was she like?

BERTOLUCCI Maybe I said mysterious as a bit of a euphemism. There was a moment when I found that my father and mother were a symbiotic unity. They were like one thing, so it was difficult to distinguish between the two of them. But my mother was more discreet. Sometimes I thought that my father tried, and succeeded, in fact, in being the third child. We are two brothers, myself and my brother Giuseppe, and then there was a third brother who was my father, in the sense that he wanted to steal our mother's passion and be the centre. It's something that happens, I think, very, very often, but I felt it strongly. I did not really understand these things till very late, when I started to lie down on Freud's sofa and talk to an invisible character behind me who sometimes had a voice and sometimes was silent.

WACHTEL One of the hazards of your starting so young and making films when you were barely twenty is that people think you're much older than you are now, because you've been making movies for forty years. But back then, you were working through these themes with the movies that you were making. These ideas would somehow work their way through you, and whether you understood them or not, they were a source of creativity.

BERTOLUCCI Yes, but then there is a moment when you'd better understand. It's fantastic to be creative in a total, unconscious trance, but then there comes a moment when you have to wake up and try to decipher—no, to detect—what is in that obscurity, what is the meaning of everything. I knew that one of the major reasons why I made movies is therapeutic. Doing a movie, if I'm in a bad moment, is the real way to banish demons and nightmares. Making a movie is a great form of therapy.

WACHTEL Some people are afraid to undertake therapy because they think they'll find out too much, that it will somehow kill the spontaneity or the creativity. What made you want to start therapy? It was before you made *The Spider's Stratagem* or *The Conformist*, in the late sixties. What made you decide to undertake it?

BERTOLUCCI I think it was time. I was so filled up with unconscious material, unconscious ghosts, that I thought I was exploding, and my cinema also was becoming more and more obscure. Before doing *The Spider's Stratagem* and *The Conformist*, which is exactly when I started my Freudian analysis, I'd done a movie called *Partner*, which was very, very obscure—not to me, but it was very obscure to everybody else, including critics, audience, friends, relatives. I started to feel really bad, and to feel that it was very sterile to go on making movies that had no feedback from anywhere. I wanted desperately for people to see my movies and to leave with something. This is the case for many other directors of my generation, directors who were the same age as me in the sixties, when we were making movies almost *against* an audience. At the end of that period I felt I wanted to have a dialogue, I wanted to stop doing those monologues. I wanted to stop talking about myself; I wanted to have a dialectic with somebody else.

I'm one of the first of my generation who started to throw away all the moralistic and puritanical attitudes that we had in the sixties and to accept the idea that somebody could just go to see movies—my movies. Also, I am one of the first who started to accept the idea of pleasure, because, you know, we were all very politicized in the sixties and—I don't think I'm saying anything new, but for extreme-left European and non-European filmmakers and artists in the sixties, the word *pleasure* was considered a right-wing word. I dove into the idea of pleasure, that a movie has to be a pleasure, not only for the one who is doing it but also for the people who are seeing it. Then I read these fantastic essays of Roland Barthes called *Le plaisir du texte*, which was exactly about that, the fact that he was dreaming of a moment where a writer could write something that was the complete annihilation of what in English is called consistency. To write something that was both poetry and prose, that was both political and not political, that was both psychological and apsychological. A kind of ideology of contradictions, an ideology of contrast. That, to me, was very important. I started to think that I would like my movies to tell the audience, I love you, I want to be yours—a very essential relationship between a movie and the audience. I think that this was always in my movies, but without me knowing it. When I started to be conscious of this, I started to enjoy what I was doing much more. That's why I joke about my camera moving a lot. My camera is very often dynamic. I've said that in love you have the positions of the *Kama Sutra*, but in cinema you have the positions of the Camera Sutra.

WACHTEL Your films, especially the early films but maybe even later, have that mix of politics and sex, the search for a political identity and a sexual identity. Did you have any conflict in yourself as a middle-class intellectual with a political awareness?

BERTOLUCCI I think I was a walking conflict. In my movies you always have these conflicts between doubt and certainty. That's why sometimes, if I look back at my more political movies, I can see that in some moments they were over-certain in order to overcome this terrible aggression of doubt. That's why I had to be so sure about certain political points—because I was completely besieged by doubts. But I think that as long as there are doubts there will be life.

WACHTEL You once described the cinema as the true poetic language and as the language of reality. I was wondering in what way poetic and real?

BERTOLUCCI I started to make my first film just when I stopped writing poetry, so I was just switching from one language to another. I needed to see that there was a continuity between writing poetry and shooting movies. It was for me vital and essential. I also thought that cinema was a kind of resumé of all other languages, and I felt that in the twentieth century we have the privilege of being born with cinema. Cinema is a bit older than me, but I love to think about cinema as something that, as a baby—like all newborn babies—couldn't speak. And, like a baby, the silent cinema was extremely visionary. Then cinema started to speak and it became more real, and more so when colour was invented because life is coloured, not black and white. In the early sixties, with the *nouvelle vague*, especially with Godard, cinema started to think, and to think about itself. This was the moment when I started to make movies. Godard was my real mentor—and tormentor.

WACHTEL Why mentor *and* tormentor?

BERTOLUCCI Because I was completely in love with everything he was doing with his movies. I was a very good friend of his, but in '68 we had a kind of falling-out because he became very pro-Chinese—Maoist—at exactly the same moment when I joined the Italian Communist Party. He accused me and all members of the Communist Party of being reformist, too weak and too frail. So I call him mentor-tormentor because he was also my new father, my third father. First there was my father and then Pasolini. With Pasolini I walked onto a movie set for the first time in my life. It was also his first time. It was the movie *Accattone*, which remains a masterpiece. It was extraordinary for me because of the experience—it wasn't just learning from a director. First of all, he wasn't a director. He was a writer who became a director. I was assisting the birth of a director while I was assisting the birth of cinema. He didn't have, as I already had, this kind of cinephilia, obsession.

WACHTEL You'd seen a lot more movies than he had.

BERTOLUCCI Yes, and so it was that he had to invent cinema. It was extraordinary. It was like being next to Griffith or the primitives, in fact, because Paolo always said that his mother, his reference, was not cinema but primitive painting, the Tuscan paintings of the Sienese, Simone Martini.

WACHTEL So Godard was your third father. The first is your father, then Pasolini and then Godard.

BERTOLUCCI Pasolini and then Godard. And for all these fathers, I felt incredible respect, love and, I guess, aggressiveness.

WACHTEL Cineastes like to point out that the address of the teacher in The Conformist was the actual address of Godard, the man that the Jean-Louis Trintignant character had to kill.

BERTOLUCCI That was a clear message for Jean-Luc. We both knew about that. It was 1970, the opening of The Conformist in Paris, and I remember calling him at the same phone number that in the movie is given to the teacher who has to die. I called him and said, "Jean-Luc, I know that we haven't been very close recently, but I would like you to see this film." He said he'd go to see it at ten o'clock and meet me at midnight at the Drugstore St. Germain. So at twelve o'clock, at midnight, I was there at the drugstore. It was a very rainy winter night.

There were all these young French raincoats entering, looking for news and friends, and finally Jean-Luc arrives. He looks at me. He doesn't say anything. He just gives me a note and I open it, and there was a portrait of Chairman Mao and written with red felt pen, "You have to struggle against individualism and capitalism." And then he left. He didn't say anything. That was his only reaction. It was a completely political message. I was so upset. I remember that I tore this note up in thousands of pieces and threw it on the floor. Too bad, because it would be very nice to find it now in my papers and send it to some fetishist cinematheque.

WACHTEL You were saying that cinema is the art of the twentieth century. After the French New Wave, were there any other influences? I know there's that line in your 1964 film, *Before the Revolution*, where this film enthusiast says, "How can you live without Rossellini?" Do you see other particular influences on your work?

BERTOLUCCI I love to think that cinema directors influence each other and that you can see traces of this influence in movies. When you don't see anything like that, it makes me very sad, because I like the idea of subterranean communication. I think that I've been more influenced by the past. The directors I really owe a lot to are—apart from Rossellini—Renoir, first of all, Mizoguchi and many, many others. The memory of a shot I loved in one of their movies comes back when I'm shooting. I welcome this. I love to feel that through my movies there is a kind of continuity of something which goes ahead. I must say that recently something is happening. I talked about the most important moment of change in cinema, from silent to sound, to the talkies, from black-and-white to colour and then the sixties. I would add Italian neo-realism, when Rossellini, followed by De Sica and Visconti, took the camera out of the studio into real life, into the streets. Then there was the *nouvelle vague*. I think the present is also a very interesting moment, a moment of great, great change. I would say a real mutation is going on. I don't know if every director of my generation, or even of a younger generation, is aware of that. I feel that with the new technologies it's not just a change of equipment or facility, of convenience in shooting. And to shoot in digital—I think it means there will be big changes in the dramaturgy, big changes in the structure of the story, in the approach that you have with the characters, with the meaning of the stories.

WACHTEL Why with meaning?

BERTOLUCCI Oh, because somebody said the medium is the message. So when Rossellini shot *Rome, Open City* or *Paisà*, or *Germany Year Zero*, it was a change of style, it was really cinema without makeup. It was cinema in real places, and that meant not only a change of style but a change in the structure of the movie. Have you seen the movies of a Taiwanese director called Tsai Ming-liang or of Wong Kar-Wai, who made In the Mood for Love? Or a very young American director called Harmonie Korine? You can see that what I say is not nonsense. There is a change of style, and there is also a big change in the way you tell the story.

WACHTEL You mentioned earlier that doubts are almost necessary, that doubts keep you alive. But you told me that you have new, gigantic doubts about cinema every day, and that didn't sound that good—why?

BERTOLUCCI Because I'm terribly fascinated by these new directors and by this different, alternative way of making movies. That's why, in my last movie, Besieged, made in 1998, you can feel that there is a kind of change. An example: After I've done big epic movies like Little Buddha or The Sheltering Sky, which are movies made with money, with luxurious decorations and design and many extras, made with a generous production schedule, I felt I had to do a movie in a few days with very little crew, using the minimal amount of light. When in 1995 Lars von Trier wrote me a letter saying that they were creating something called Dogma 95 and was I interested in that, I answered him that I was a bit reticent, being Italian, being born Catholic, to have another dogma. We have so much dogma in the Catholic Church.

WACHTEL And this dogma was to use only available light, to use handheld cameras, to make films with very low budgets.

BERTOLUCCI Yes, and so I didn't feel that I could be part of that movement. But I was very curious, because I was sure that Lars von Trier was creating this kind of impediment and these limitations in order to give more impact, more strength to young directors. And in fact I think, like every talented artist, von Trier is the first one to betray the dogma that he created.

WACHTEL Tell me about the doubts—

BERTOLUCCI Cinema is fascinating because it is changing, it is mutating. I just turned sixty. My doubt is, will I ever be able to catch this kind of mutation? I will try, but I don't know if my enthusiasm will be followed by talent, a gift for catching that special thing that is happening now in cinema. But you know, all my life I've liked to take risks. I like to put myself in a situation of risk. For example, moving from one kind of movie to a completely different one was for me a kind of inner rule. That's why, after *The Conformist*, which was a political and psychological film, I felt like doing *Last Tango in Paris*. At the time they said it was a political film because it's about the struggle between men and women, but it was a very private story. After that very intimate film I had to do 1900, which was a kind of historical epic, big and political again. And then after 1900, I did *La Luna*, which was again between two characters, a mother and her son. So there has always been a desire to turn pages and go ahead, as if none of my movies was a point of arrival. I always felt that my movies were stations, not destinations.

WACHTEL I remember when *Last Tango* came out, you said that somehow it meshed with the general consciousness. It was an extraordinary success in 1972, as well as getting you into a lot of trouble when it was banned in Italy. What chord do you think it struck?

BERTOLUCCI I did it in a state of complete innocence. I remember when the judges were interrogating me for having done an obscene movie. I told them I was innocent. I didn't know that this movie would have the impact it had. I swear when I saw the first rough cut with Franco Arcalli, my editor and co-writer, and the producer, at the end of the first screening the editor and I looked at each other and said, "Oh my God, nobody will go to see this film about an aging man, so desperate and the terrible ending—" Then the lights came up and we saw that the producer was dancing all alone with joy. So that's why I said I'm innocent. I really didn't know that I was doing something which would have that kind of impact. What I was saying was so intimate and yet so familiar to me. These fantasies were so normal for me.

WACHTEL The fantasy of anonymous sex?

BERTOLUCCI Yes. *Last Tango in Paris* was a very romantic movie. Two creatures decide to meet in a kind of neutral place, which is an empty flat, without knowing each other's names, addresses, phone numbers, without knowing anything of each other, being completely naked of social identity. There was a real need that I felt for a relationship, so impossible, but in fact very, very romantic. Of course, there was a kind of sincerity which was perhaps offensive at the time. Maybe the movie was a few years ahead of what society would have then accepted as a normal thing. I think today it doesn't have the incredible impact that it had at that moment. I even remember being a bit afraid. When I discovered that I had lost my civil rights in Italy, it was a very bad moment. Because of a movie, for five years I didn't have the right to vote, and in those days I was very politicized.

WACHTEL And yet the previous films—I'm thinking of The Conformist and even The Spider's Stratagem—were so imbued with Italian politics and anti-fascism.

BERTOLUCCI Yes, but if you look back at my movies, especially in those distant years, you see all the time a desire to find political identity and sexual identity and they're all mixed up.

WACHTEL It was surprising to me, when I went back to see Last Tango after almost thirty years, that what was so striking was not so much the sex but everything that surrounded these characters. So much impinged upon their lives in terms of family and other people: the Marlon Brando character's mother-in-law or his dead wife's ex-lover or Maria Schneider's boyfriend and her mother and her dead father. There were so many other people present—

BERTOLUCCI Yes, but what you remembered was just the two of them.

WACHTEL That's right.

BERTOLUCCI You know, I don't like to see my movies. A long time has to pass before I see my movies again. I saw Last Tango in Paris, made in '72, again only in '97, something like twenty-five years later in the Locarno festival. There is a huge square in Locarno where they show movies in the evening, at the beginning of August, in front of some nine thousand people. It's the biggest screen in Europe. That's where I decided to see Last Tango in Paris. Why don't I see my old movies? Because my movies are always so full of very personal, intimate little things that I blush when I see how much of my own life I have put into the movies. But twenty-five years later it's all right. I can stand all that, because after twenty, thirty years have passed, it's like going back to a previous life. It's as if today I am a reincarnation of the man who made that movie then.

WACHTEL What did you think of it when you saw it?

BERTOLUCCI I thought that it was very curious. For example, the character of Maria Schneider's boyfriend, played by Jean-Pierre Léaud, who was a parody of a cinephile—typical of a young filmmaker: I remember when I first saw the film that the audience and I wanted only to see Marlon and Maria. This time when I saw the film, I felt that the filmmaker-boyfriend was very necessary because the relationship between Marlon and Maria is so heavy that the film needed some moments where you could breathe, some less tense moments, lighter moments.

WACHTEL The tango that features in the title of that film is part of a recurrent dance motif in your work. There are dancehalls, dance sequences, from your very first feature. Even in The Grim Reaper there's a dancehall, and of course famously in The Conformist. In virtually every movie. What's that about?

BERTOLUCCI I think it is because I love the idea of dancing. I was never able to dance, so my revenge was to have a lot of dancing in my movies. I want to do a take on this shy attitude towards dancing, and also because the moments of dancing are special, magic moments in a movie where anything can happen, and it can be sad. And you are not a slave of psychological consistency. In my last movie, unfortunately, there's no dancing. In Stealing Beauty there is the girl dancing on the lawn.

WACHTEL And even when you say anything can happen, you don't have to be logical. In Tragedy of a Ridiculous Man, the son comes back from the dead and effectively is reborn in a dancehall. It seems like there's something in that.

BERTOLUCCI Right. But maybe it says a lot about my love for music and my love for the idea that cinema owes a lot to music. Very often, my camera movements are inexplicable if you don't see them as musical movements. It's rare for me to have a movie without music. There is one, La Luna, which is the story of a soprano and her troubled young son. Because there was a lot of Verdi's music, I didn't feel I could put in a score. I thought everything would look very pale next to Verdi. In general, during some moment of directing, if I find I am lost, that I don't know what to do, I listen to a piece of music with my actors and my collaborators and enter into a mood where all the big doubts and impediments and emptiness melt.

WACHTEL Sometimes the dancehall is not necessarily a happy place. In The Grim Reaper it's ominous, because we know that someone has been killed. And yet, again, when I went back to see The Conformist, the dance scene there was less ominous than I remembered. There was more joy there. But I noticed there was also a little picture of Laurel and Hardy in the corner of the dancehall and I thought something else was going on.

BERTOLUCCI Yes. But I think that the scene is more meaningful than what you think because we know there is a tragedy—somewhere a tragedy will happen. I wanted the tragedy to come out of a very happy scene. And also it's where you see the clash between Dominique Sanda and Stefania Sandrelli. The two girls dance, and there's something quite outrageous going on because you can see that Dominique dances as if she was in love with Stefania. That was very important to the story. At the end of the scene, the wife of the conformist, Stefania Sandrelli, is very drunk and happy, and then you cut to the killing, to the murder of the teacher. I like this kind of contrast—very dramatic.

I'm going to ask you a question. We're talking about these movies as if the people listening to us know them. Do you think this is so?

WACHTEL I hope they do. Certainly most of them are available on video.

BERTOLUCCI The young people I know understand so little about the past. I think that film should be a way of communicating with young people who seem to have a total loss of memory. Youth is a dead memory. It's not their fault. It's not at all an accusation or a judgement. Maybe they don't need memory. Maybe the world today doesn't need to remember. We come from a world that was based on memory, based on the past. The present must be so exciting to young people today, so alive and so fascinating, that the past is thrown aside.

WACHTEL If we were to trace your work through politics, sex, religion or spirituality, and the Eastern films, and then, more recently, love, would you see it as a thematic movement?

BERTOLUCCI I think these elements are mostly present together. Some very directly. Some very indirectly. That's why it's very difficult to think that all my movies are like separated blocks. For me it's much easier to think that all the titles are chapters, chapters of one movie, which is—

WACHTEL Which is you.

BERTOLUCCI Me.

WACHTEL What would you call the book?

BERTOLUCCI I would call it "You Are Not I"; it's the title of a short story by Paul Bowles.

WACHTEL For more than ten years you were in a kind of voluntary exile from Italy. Was that hard for you? It was when you were making the three movies you mentioned earlier—The Last Emperor, The Sheltering Sky, Little Buddha—what's sometimes been called your Oriental trilogy because it was set in the East and in North Africa. Was it hard for you to be away from home?

BERTOLUCCI I felt very uneasy in Italy in that period. I told myself it was impossible to shoot a movie in a country which I feel is terribly corrupt and one that has become so cynical that they can't recognize it. So I went as far away as possible, both geographically and culturally. I found out in an almost physical way that there are cultures that are so different from our culture, and every time, I fell in love with these new cultures, these very old cultures. I first discovered China. It was love at first sight. I took two years preparing The Last Emperor, travelling back and forth many times from Europe to China, and every time, the more I knew of it, the more obscure it became. It was fascinating. And then North Africa, the desert, and this agonizing couple who had to face the culture of the desert. That was a very painful thing to do.

WACHTEL The Sheltering Sky, based on the Paul Bowles novel.

BERTOLUCCI Yes, and then Little Buddha was another incredible experience because of Tibetan philosophy and Buddhism. So every time, being homesick was cured by these great discoveries.

WACHTEL Why did you go home to Italy in the mid-nineties?

BERTOLUCCI Because the atmosphere had changed, although there are very dark clouds over this country now, and I hope I won't be forced once more to go into a kind of voluntary exile.

WACHTEL What happened to your communism?

BERTOLUCCI Better to ask what happened to communism.

WACHTEL We know what happened to that.

BERTOLUCCI With the fall of the Berlin Wall, it was clear to everybody that something completely unexpected was happening, and probably something that was very right to happen. We knew, even if we didn't want to admit it, that millions of people were suffering. We knew that the experience wasn't a success. The contradiction was that, being communists in Italy, we didn't feel at all that we were responsible for the terrible things that had happened in the Soviet universe. We felt that Italian communism was something very important, very close to the people, but it had to change. The name of the party was changed, and the people had to give up the idea of a certain destiny. Of course, for a few years we were left with the feeling of losing the ground under our feet, especially me personally. One of the major problems was that I had once been allowed to have great utopian dreams. Now these dreams are not allowed, are not possible. That's all.

WACHTEL You can't be a utopian any more.

BERTOLUCCI No. Not in the way I used to be.

WACHTEL How would you describe yourself in political terms?

BERTOLUCCI I hope that something will happen in politics as it's happening in cinema. In fact, something is happening—the ecological movement, with all its tension, is, I think, very interesting. What in Italy is called il popolo di Seattle, the people of Seattle, means going forward. It's one of the most dynamic things going on today. Real politics today is being reborn with this movement.

WACHTEL This is in reaction to the World Trade Organization.

BERTOLUCCI Yes, but also to globalization and to the environment. The world is joyously, joyfully committing suicide. Should we assist in that suicide by doing nothing? There is a sleepy attitude in the world.

When you see what's going on, when you see that the U.S. is refusing to endorse the Kyoto Protocol, it is very worrying. If the deforestation of Amazonia goes on as it has been going on, in twenty-five or thirty years all Amazonia will be a kind of marsh, and that will have an impact on global warming. The quality of the atmosphere on our planet is threatened. How can we go on without doing something about this? It is a great worry for me.

WACHTEL And do you feel at home in Italy?

BERTOLUCCI Yes. Much more than when I left in the mid-eighties.

WACHTEL Do you still get back to Parma? Is it still the family home?

BERTOLUCCI Strange. Yes, I have been back, because they invited me to Parma a few years ago. They gave me a great celebration, and because every kind of celebration makes me feel guilty, I haven't been to Parma since.

WACHTEL Why does it make you feel guilty?

BERTOLUCCI You'd better ask my analyst.

WACHTEL I thought you'd stopped.

BERTOLUCCI I have started again.

May 2001

GEORGE STEINER

In the mid-1980s, when George Steiner spoke at the University of Toronto, Northrop Frye called the lecture a historic event. Steiner, known for his passionate lectures and grand theories, has a daunting reputation. His terrain isn't simply literature but the nature of humanity. Feisty and erudite, he can quote from literature in a dozen languages. Once, on British television, he apologized for his written Danish being slightly poorer than he would like.

He was born in Paris, to Austrian-Jewish parents. When he was eleven, in 1940, the family fled to the United States. He credits his father's wisdom for their survival. "He was a great teacher of uncertainty, and I owe him everything," Steiner said.

What I like about talking to George Steiner is that you get to ask big questions, impossible questions, because Steiner himself entertains them. For instance, he once said that central to everything he is and believes and has written is his "astonishment, naive as it seems to some people, that you can use human speech to bless, to live, to build, to forgive and also to torture, to hate, to destroy and annihilate."

I first spoke to Steiner in Paris in 1992. When I returned home, a writer friend asked, "What's it like to talk to the world's most intelligent human being?" Well, you listen a lot, but it's exciting. I was reminded of something Edward Said once wrote: Steiner "is that rare thing, a critic propelled by diverse enthusiasms, a man able to understand the implications of trends in different fields, an autodidact for whom no subject is too arcane. Yet Steiner is to be read for his quirks, rather than in spite of them. He does not peddle a system or a set of norms by which all things can be managed, every text decoded. He writes to be understood by nonspecialists, and his terms of reference come from his experience—which is trilingual, eccentric and highly urbane—not from something as stable as doctrine or authority."

A few years ago, Steiner published a short intellectual memoir, *Errata: An Examined Life* (1998). He credits his undergraduate years at the University of Chicago in the late forties with "what very probably decided my life and work . . . the sheer genius of intellectual exhilaration, the passionate electricity of spirit, that had made the U. of C. . . . the best there was." He went on to Harvard and then to Oxford on a Rhodes scholarship. Steiner has taught widely in the U.S. and the U.K., but primarily at Cambridge and in Geneva. In 1994, he became the first Lord Weidenfeld Professor of Comparative Literature at Oxford. In 2001, he reflected on language, creativity and Western culture in *Grammars of Creation*.

Most of what appears here is from a conversation we had in Toronto, but I am grateful to Richard Handler for first infecting me with his enthusiasm for George Steiner back in '92.

———————

WACHTEL In the opening sentence of your first book, *Tolstoy or Dostoyevsky*, published more than forty years ago, you defined true criticism, true reading, as a "debt of love." How did you come to acquire that sense of love?

STEINER I was struck already, as a very, very young person, by the notion that ours is not so much an age of anxiety—the very famous phrase of W. H. Auden—but an age of bottomless envy, that in the academic and literary worlds, what really characterizes our atmosphere is jealousy and envy of greatness, and a kind of awful little vengeance on what is great and universal. By the way, thirty-five, forty years later, this was the subject of Martin Amis's best-selling novel The Information, a study of literary jealousy and envy of success. I always felt that if you couldn't do the real thing, if you yourself couldn't create, if you were not inspired enough or lucky enough or brilliant enough or gifted enough to produce first-rate work, the next best thing, and an immense joy and privilege, was to help that work break through, get recognized, get read, get loved. While strictly of the second rank, strictly non-creative on that scale, I've always thought of myself as immensely privileged to be of some use to the great work. We've all seen those breathtaking nature films where on a rhinoceros there sits a tiny bird. The bird helps clean the rhinoceros, gives him warning of enemies but, more interestingly, tells others, "Rhino is coming." The really good teacher, the really good critic, the really good reader, chirps away and says, "Rhino is coming." The test of a major critic, of a major presence, is whether he has some rhinos, whether he's taken some gambles on what will be the classic of tomorrow. I've tried always to be of use to the new, but also to bring back the classic, which is always new. So in that sense, it's an act of love, of delight, of feeling privileged and honoured. And what has made it very difficult for me at times in what is called loosely "the academy," in the professional university circuit or as a professional critic, is that, quite naturally, the men and women around me do not like to think of themselves as marginal, as ancillary figures, as auxiliaries to the real thing. That first book was the beginning of the problems I've had in my long career; in it I said that, if you could write one paragraph of Dostoyevsky's novels, you wouldn't, for God's sakes, be writing a critical book on him. Dostoyevsky doesn't need to write about Steiner. Steiner has to write about Dostoyevsky. And that, the university does not like to hear.

WACHTEL In your 1992 critical book, *Real Presences*, you postulate a society without what you call "metatext"—criticism or discussion of art—and you say that art would not really be diminished much by that.

STEINER That is, of course, a deliberate paradox and overstatement, but in a very real sense I mean it. We could do without nine-tenths of our millions and millions of books about books, about other books about books, if we could get people back to the primary shock, the great wing stroke and blaze of light of coming up yourself against a great major text or a new artistic experience. That's why I always quote a true story which puts it so much better than any abstract words I can use. Schumann had played a difficult, difficult étude, and the younger people who were working with him and some of his friends who had heard it said, "Look, this is terribly difficult. Can you explain it?" And he said, "Oh yes, oh yes, I can." And he sat down and played it again. This is, to me, a very, very important story. The way an artist explains is to enact, possibly to repeat. And Pierre Boulez has made it a practice with a difficult piece—not necessarily only new pieces but difficult twentieth-century music—to play it once at the start of the concert and then again at the end. I think that is a major pedagogic idea, to say, "Look, it is difficult, look, it is new. I'm going to explain it to you by letting you hear it again." Which is another way of putting it when you face a difficult poem or a great play or a great text—try it again. Reread it. There are, God knows, magnificent critical acts and commentaries and explanations. I was overstating my case just to get people to think about the overwhelming presence in our intellectual lives of the parasitic, of that which feeds on, feeds on, feeds on. It's become almost ridiculous. The industry of bad theses, the industry of third-rate academic publication in order to survive and get a job at any price. What does one do? Weep? Laugh? Both? The six hundredth book of the year on the genius of Keats—yes, yes, Keats had genius. It's something we've suspected for some time. The notion that we need a hundred more theses to expound that fact, to live off that fact, I find more and more dismaying.

WACHTEL Obviously you are, by taking an extreme position, putting yourself out in the margins, too, with your colleagues—

STEINER And within my profession, but I've just finished twenty years in Geneva where the main liberty was to read together, to read around a table, as students, with very, very little secondary material. This is called the Geneva School. It's really quite a simple, unpompous way of returning to primary texts with the help you need.

It's not clear to me where this criticism industry is going to end. It is finally devouring itself. We have more and more texts in controversy with other critical texts. We're beginning to get a situation which has been put in a nutshell by—and it's very difficult to take seriously in some ways—a most influential movement known as "deconstruction." I don't want to go into that, except to repeat the formidable pun of its great leader, Monsieur Derrida, who says there are no texts; there are only pretexts. To me, that is a kind of inspired barbarism. In a sense, it has become hideously true, and we can almost date it. This is very fascinating: there is a letter of W. H. Auden's from the late forties. He was earning his living teaching in the United States before returning to England. In this letter he said, "Oh my God, I've begun to notice that my recent poems are written in the hope of being studied in a seminar and, God help me." He suddenly saw, this very great poet, that what he was aiming at was to be respectable in the graduate seminar, to have papers written on those poems. And a panic, a kind of great panic, came over him. Shakespeare doesn't need any of us. He's not a pretext. No poem is a pretext, and to regard literature as a kind of happy excuse for the analytic, the explanation, the monograph that will be written on it is, of course, to put the cart before the horse in a quite insane way. We live— again, a slightly pompous word but it doesn't matter—in a Byzantine time. It's also been called the Age of Alexandria, meaning those periods in antiquity when the energy had seeped out of great poetry and drama, and the scholars, the librarians, the critics were triumphant, had taken over. Deep down in every critic, there is a hatred of writers. Deep, deep down. You never know what those crazy people might do next. That fear and hatred, alas, infects some of the principal teachers and critics in our time. More people are turned off literature—far more—by the techniques of analytic pedagogy than are brought home to it.

WACHTEL I want to go back, if you will, to what books you first read, to how you first developed your own love, your own response, to literature.

STEINER I was unbelievably fortunate. It was very much in the shadow of the rise of Hitlerism in Europe, but I was brought up in France and had two formidable strokes of luck. Above all, my father began training me very, very early on by reading only major books. I never really read much children's literature. What he did was decisive. It marked my life. I can't have been more than five, perhaps a little less. He would take a passage in The Iliad of fantastic excitement, where somebody was throwing a spear at somebody or butchering somebody or lifting a sword, and he'd come to a critical point and then he'd say, "I'm awfully sorry. There's no translation of the lines that follow." I, of course, believed him implicitly. I was shaking with excitement. And he said, "Look, we've got to find out what's going to happen. Let's try it in Greek." And that was the beginning of my Greek and an absolute stroke of genius on his part. I just couldn't bear not to find out. He would not let me have the next book until I'd written a tiny précis of the one I had just read or read with him. That was another terrific piece of training.

WACHTEL Essentially, you were at Oxford when you were five years old.

STEINER Yes, I was having home tutorials. Second, the French lycée system in which I was brought up, with its terrific emphasis on literature, on articulacy, on poetry, on learning by heart, and with its splendid anti-democratic frankness, saying to us little boys, in our blue overalls, as we stood there—I shall never forget that—"One of you in this big class, standing to attention, one of you may, by miracle, make a tiny scratch on the wall of culture with your nail. We're not saying you'll be Victor Hugo. We're not saying you'll be Zola. But you might write a book worth reading or find a theorem in maths worth learning. One of you might have the lottery ticket to do something for which humanity has some right to be proud. It's the job of this hierarchic, elitist system to find that one, and we're going to damn well try and do it." It was a terrific incentive. It was something to strive for, to hope for. You see, if you walk, as a little boy, to school in the morning and home in the afternoon, through streets marked Victor Hugo, Descartes, Pascal, Racine, you're going to begin doing some thinking. Something's going to rub off. They're not called Maple or Pine or Broad or Lake. The difference is simply enormous. Again, no credit to me at all, no merit whatever. I had a very powerful training in memory, a very powerful training in exact reading as a matter of course. It never struck me as any kind of particular achievement. It still doesn't. The system aimed for and produced that life of the mind, that ambition of the mind, which is still, in many ways, the hallmark of a very tragically tired and divided Europe.

WACHTEL Almost thirty years ago, in the Massey Lectures on CBC Radio, you used an evocative and eloquent phrase: you talked about "the nostalgia for the absolute." What did you mean by that?

STEINER I meant that a great many human beings, men and women in every walk of life, in every culture, were filled with a sense of emptiness. The collapse of traditional religion, the collapse of most traditional philosophies—perhaps even more disturbing due to psychoanalysis and due to our new awareness of the black holes in the universe—a collapse of the old reassurances of who we were, where we were, what it was all about. My hunch was that in that nostalgia, in that hunger for something to hold on to, to grab on to, human beings would begin turning towards some rather alarming solutions: they want answers. That's what I meant at that time and now, of course, with the collapse of a certain kind of Marxism and communism—and I do underline "a certain kind"—with that collapse, the vacuum seems even more turbulent and alarming.

WACHTEL When do you date this emptiness from?

STEINER I think the world stops as we know it in August 1914. I'm old enough to have known human beings who lived then. As a child, I remember being overwhelmed by their saying, "You'll never know what the summers were like," by which they meant the peace, the stability, the notion that of course there were great problems but they would be solved; human beings would sit around tables and hammer out their hatreds and difficulties. Even if there were great industrial revolutions, economic inequalities, generally, the escalator was going upward for more and more human beings.

Once casualty lists of thirty thousand a day begin appearing on the walls of Europe in 1915—thirty thousand young men, killed, gassed, blown to smithereens every day, their bodies never recapturable—something goes out of our whole world: a possibility of thinking that we are on a gradual ascent towards human reason, human forgiveness and, to put it quite simply, those long, quiet summers which our politics has never known again.

WACHTEL It's a really haunting image to go back to a pre-war summer day. Reminds me of that line by Henry James—the two most beautiful words in the English language are a "summer afternoon."

STEINER But that summer day had behind it certain stabilities of religious, social, philosophic belief. Human beings, even if they didn't have very much of a notion of God except as a gentleman with a long beard—even the more sophisticated ones—felt that life had a meaning, a purpose, that they knew a bit about their own insides. And this is crucial—that they knew that other human beings—suppose they were angry, bitter, in a quarrel—were operating within certain limits. There were certain things that could not possibly happen: nobody would put six million people in gas ovens and nobody would carpet-bomb great ancient cities out of existence. No one would store, as we now do, vast amounts of food to keep up the market price, while not very far away millions, particularly children, are dropping dead of hunger. These things would have seemed the gothic horror movie fantasies of a few deranged minds.

WACHTEL What happened? I mean, you point to a particular week, a particular event: the Great War; you talk about 1915; you talk about the degree of slaughter just escalating—but what happened? I mean, what punctured humanity's moral fibre? What destroyed this?

STEINER You ask a tremendously difficult question. We still don't understand it. My wife is a professor of diplomatic history at Cambridge who writes books on the origin of that world war. It's still controversial: What went wrong? It could have been one of endless local little dynastic wars after which silly emperors with long moustaches would sit down and shake hands; it could have been something like some of the colonial wars, which were very bad but strictly professional. We still don't understand how the thing got completely out of hand. We still cannot conceive of the break in the basic rules of the game which made it possible at Verdun, in one battle, for half a million bodies to lie unburied—something which hadn't even been known in the Dark Ages.

Now, one of my guesses—only one—is that there were about a hundred years, after Waterloo, of boredom. I tried to write about this in a book called *In Bluebeard's Castle*. It may be that there is in men (men in particular—not women, who are far more sophisticated) an enormous weight of boredom if they don't every so often start slaughtering each other. I'm just guessing. When you see a great football mob pouring down a street; when you see the hatred which sport really inspires; when you see the loathing of violence in the street boy, in the unemployed, in the hopeless—put them in uniform and the hooligan of today is your hero of tomorrow. Give the same young man an enemy and he will show virtues of discipline, courage, leadership and sacrifice, which have been sleeping inside him.

That's one possible guess. Biology does suggest that there are animal species which need to explode from time to time, which need to attack. That's just a very pessimistic guess. Others would say—and that's a classic Marxist analysis—that the production line, mass production, twenty thousand Ford cars a week or whatever it was—the famous breakthrough to the anonymity of the industrial process, God help us, translated into human lives. What happened in those desperate massacre battles was a funny kind of transposition, a translation into human bodies, of piecework, assembly-line factory work, the anonymous turning out of enormous numbers of products, one like the other.

WACHTEL This very grim picture that you're giving me right now is in response to my question of when you date the beginning of the emptiness, of the "nostalgia for the absolute." So what you're saying is that the first sign of this huge destructiveness, or potential for destruction, was at the same time as when absolutes disappeared.

STEINER Let's be careful. Which causes which? We don't know. The argument is dangerous if it becomes circular. For example: There were in the Middle Ages some pretty dreadful moments, but something was called "the peace of God." You stopped on Saturday and Sunday; there were no battles on Saturdays and Sundays. Why? Because the great authority of the Church said, "If you don't have the peace of God, we'll excommunicate you." Once God is dead, once the churches have become the weak social organs they are, the great weapon of punishment, of threat from above, has lost all its force.

Second, Freud comes along (and of course I'm oversimplifying) and says, very roughly, something like this: the unconscious is turbulent, bestial and cruel, dangerous. Civilization is a thin crust on the volcano; it can crack. He had foreseen it in many ways. And, suddenly, man no longer felt inside himself the old confident moral sanctions saying, "Thou shalt and thou shalt not." And if you have bad dreams, well, you forget about them, you bottle them up—the great bottling up in the nineteenth century.

Now, I happen to detest psychoanalysis: I regard it as the Jewish version of Christian Science. That's my own particular problem. But once Freud identifies the wish to violently have sex with your mother and murder your father—the wish of the primal horde to kill the father figure, civilization—in his great study on civilization and its discontents; civilization is a kind of aspirin that doesn't work very many hours and your tooth starts aching very badly again—once this great statement has been made, a tremendous anchor is taken away from human conduct. So with the revolution of the psyche, the revolution of religious values, without a single admissible moral code any more, the old barriers were smashed down and we were now in the great bullring.

WACHTEL This perception of the world, the themes that you raised in the Massey Lectures—this "nostalgia for the absolute"—when did these concerns first emerge for you in your own life and reading?

STEINER Oh, immensely early. In Paris, where I was born and brought up, my father, who was a man of sombre wisdom, taught me from earliest childhood that we had to have our bags packed. He would never let that message not dominate my very young life—our beautiful home, very privileged, everything you could wish for; and his always saying, "This is totally temporary; Hitler is coming; we have our bags packed; you're going to learn a lot of languages, so that when we start moving you can study and earn a living."

From the beginning he was a great teacher of uncertainty and I owe him everything. If tomorrow I had to go to Jakarta to earn my living, I would not say to God, "How could you do this to me?" I would try and learn Javanese, which would do me a world of good—I've gotten lazy about languages—and God helping me, I think I could manage, and what a tremendous adventure it would be.

The notion that we should have roots fills me with absolute irony and even derision. Trees have roots and that's why lightning cuts them down; I have legs and that's why I can move and survive.

WACHTEL What did your father do?

STEINER My father had first written some very important books in economic history and then became an international banker and businessman, very largely so that his son could become a scholar. This is a great Jewish tradition: a generation earns the means for its children not to have to become businessmen. That's the dream. It doesn't always work, but it's a deep, underlying structure.

WACHTEL I can also imagine someone growing up in an environment with this feeling of impermanence responding in a completely opposite fashion. Rather than having skepticism and derision towards roots, one might say, "As soon as I get a chance I'm going to put roots down somewhere."

STEINER Simply impossible. We lived in a lovely house, but once we were able to escape, miraculously, in 1940, I never again invested any love or trust in a place. In time, yes; that's something quite different. The Jewish passport is not a passport of place. I collect passports, by the way, as others do stamps, simply because God knows when they might come in handy. One never knows. And a Jewish passport is a passport in time, in history, in his or her identity as a human being in a tradition of study and survival. I much prefer time to space.

WACHTEL Did you love that house you lived in?

STEINER Very deeply, and for a child to leave a house like that and to leave his fox terrier—oh God. Human beings are sentimental. I'm as sentimental as the next person, but I don't think I've ever again feared the notion that whatever I'd built up could collapse overnight. Not so very long ago, colleagues of mine were teaching in Sarajevo, in Dubrovnik, and had the most beautiful of homes, were envied for the climate, for the beauty of the setting, for the chance they seemed to have to enter a new Europe. A week later they were running for their lives.

My own theory is possibly a very sad one that has certainly evolved since the Massey Lectures—that God has decided to make Jews of everybody. By that, I mean very simply that He's going to teach everybody else what it's like to have to wander, what it's like not to have safety and protection. Millions in Eastern Europe will try to stream westward because there will be nothing left for them. The number from Africa cannot even be calculated. The movements of despair—it does look to me as if a lot of human beings are going to learn what it is like to be Jewish, to be refugees, hunted people, people who have to learn languages to survive, people who have to relearn jobs, ways of life. Well, it's pretty awful, but it's a lot of fun too.

WACHTEL I see even as you're saying this that there's a glint in your eye that perhaps suggests some satisfaction in this?

STEINER Not satisfaction, but pride in human adaptability. We're cats: we do tend to fall on our feet as they toss us off the balcony. We turn over and over and we give a big meow, and then we land on our feet and start hunting mice. Otherwise, humanity might as well pack it in. After Hiroshima, Nagasaki—more horrible still, after Pol Pot burying alive one hundred thousand people in the Killing Fields—after all that, there would have been a lemming-like case after Auschwitz for humanity to say, "Enough, stop the world and let me get off. Stop the world." The world doesn't stop; the train is moving too fast. We can't get off, and humanity is going to have to learn to jump and roll over.

WACHTEL So there's a kind of a grim optimism here.

STEINER Extreme, extreme.

WACHTEL When I was asking you when your first sense of this "nostalgia for the absolute" emerged, you said it was very, very early and you talked about your father. But in terms of your intellectual apprehension of the date, what's the history of it?

STEINER That certainly came later. I was very lucky: I had great masters. First, in the French lycée, then in New York, there were very, very great world figures who had fled other nations in 1940 and who, in order to earn their living, also taught silly little boys and girls until they got their university chairs, great philosophers like Etienne Gilson. Before the anthropologist Claude Lévi-Strauss became a world-famous name, I had him as a teacher.

So first of all, I was very lucky in getting the smell of what a real mind is; it's got a smell. A real mind cannot be faked; you pick it up the moment you are near it, a sense of someone who lives ideas, who lives intellectual and artistic and moral and scientific passions.

Then, at the University of Chicago, I was under a great absolutist called Robert Hutchins, one of the major figures in the history of educational reform, who at that time had made Chicago the top university in the West. There I came in contact with philosophers, with scholars, who also were living this obsessive sense of trying to argue and teach values.

And it seemed clear to me that, whereas if you sold stocks and bonds or looked for oil or sold toilet seats, this could bring you many millions, it seemed to me that that was utterly unacceptable in a brief human lifetime, that the animals that we are have developed these very, very strange, *very* strange powers—pure mathematics, philosophy, music, the great sciences—spinning out of ourselves the web of other worlds. And I was just desperate, even in a small way, at the edge of the web, to get in on it. I'm terribly lucky there was never any doubt in me about a vocation. And I would like to underline the word *vocation*. I detest the word *tenure*—tenure you can have on the stock market; vocation is a calling, the sense of the infinite, of privilege, of being called to make some tiny, tiny contribution in the bitterly difficult process of getting the mind to creep forward a little.

WACHTEL Very early on, you regarded literature as "essential humanity," that it existed in a context that was embedded in philosophy, religion, political concerns. What was it in you that, in fact, rebelled against the conventions of specialization or the fashions of the New Criticism? Why did you have to see things as interconnected?

STEINER Being polyglot, being actually brought up from birth with a number of languages—German, French and English to begin with, and Italian a little later—I could not be a specialist. It's as simple as that. A polyglot mind sees the world in a kaleidoscopic manner of shifting, multiple light. It looks out different windows on reality. It looks through different windows on its own perceptions and identity. Second, I had the great good luck of falling flat on my face, but *really* on my face, when I came to the University of Chicago very, very young. Those were the years, as I say, of Robert Hutchins, a very great educator, who had a system, quite wonderfully mad, whereby he said that if you think you're smart and think that the American university system is a waste of time—which it largely was—you can take as many final exams as you want on arrival. Whatever you get an A in, you don't need to take the course. I took all the fourteen final exams on arrival and failed magnificently—D-minus, F-double-minus in four of them. Being a product of the French-Greek-Latin-classical syllabus, I failed, of course, in math, physics, chemistry and something I'd never heard of, called social studies. I literally didn't know what it meant. It was incredibly thrilling. It was sociology and anthropology with people like Redfield and others. Fermi, the man who cracked the atom, was teaching idiots like me physics. And I just loved it. It was a revelation—this other universe. And when I had done my year—I was able to do a BA in a year because you could do four courses in a year—and done well in the exams, I ran like a little peacock to a creature called the graduate advisor, another thing Europe didn't have. Very fascinating to me, a graduate advisor. I said I'd like to go on in science, Chicago being at that time stuffed with Nobel-winners and one of the world's greatest science centres. He called for my papers and he said, "Please don't take it personally. You got a *summa cum laude*, but you're an idiot in a technical sense. That is to say, your European training meant you learned every damned formula by heart and you learned certain techniques, but there's not a spark of creative mathematical understanding in you."

So I was heartbroken, absolutely heartbroken. Swore vengeance, but we'll come back to that in a moment. Heartbroken, I went into literature and philosophy. Literature with a great American poet and critic, Allen Tate. Philosophy with a man very well known to Toronto, Richard McKeon, the great Aristotle scholar. This decided the rest of my life. But I did swear I wouldn't forget my disappointment. Years later— thirty-forty years later—I smuggled a little paper into *Nature*, the great magazine of science, on a tiny historical point in mathematics, and sent it off to this gentleman. By that time he had retired but was still in full vigour. I got a lovely letter back saying he had no regrets, having done so much for literature, which was a delightfully flattering and humorous answer. But it meant that my interest in the sciences—so far as any layman can keep up at all—prevented certain kinds of specialization. I just know that if we were living in Florence of the fifteenth century, you and I would hope to have breakfast from time to time with the painters. And I've been privileged at Princeton, at Cambridge, to have breakfast with the scientists, whose world is at the moment intellectually by far the most exciting, the most challenging, and philosophically one of the most interesting in the history of the West. This makes it impossible to be what so many in my profession reproach me for not being—the deep specialist, the master of one tiny area. Cows have fields. I'm not a cow, although I have deep respect for cows and what they produce. But you can't fake that one. Too many things have fascinated me.

WACHTEL One of your most ambitious interdisciplinary books, *After Babel*, explores some questions that I'd like to ask you about. One that I find very tantalizing is the idea that the existence of a future tense, or "if" proposition, empowers us to hope. As you put it, "We endure because we can speak tomorrow."

STEINER You know as well as I that we know next to nothing about the origins of human speech. There have been ambitious books in the last few years—there have been since the eighteenth century—trying to guess. There are some indications that it was a very slow, a very gradual process. That would make sense. Our larynx, our vocal cords changed and became adapted to the rich variety of speech sounds beyond those available to animals. Probably the brain had to reach a critical mass. Something very exciting seems to have happened around the end of the last ice age. It involved not consuming on the spot what you had hunted or planted, but rather putting it away. The notion of a future. Hebrew does not have our verb tenses. Hebrew has a single essential verb system where past, present and future are very curiously the same. And you have to show which you mean by inflections. Hebrew lives within a kind of eternity. Greek developed, as did many other languages, this complicated and fantastic idea that you can speak about the coming Monday morning, about your own death, perfectly coherently. Now you can speak about constellations or galaxies or black holes and what they're doing and where they will be a billion years after the extinction of our solar system, which is certain to come. That's a quite amazing feat. The second thing you can do is reinvent the world. You can say, "If Napoleon had been in charge of the American army at Vietnam" and so on. "If Hitler had been killed in '33 when there was an attempt" and so on. Quite fantastic that you can do that, and then coherently go on and create an alternative language world. My hunch is that the certainty of biological death, which most of us try to forget about our whole lives, the absolute, ineluctable certainty of extinction, might not have been bearable to us had we not developed these complicated and magical ways of thinking beyond ourselves and beyond brutal biological reality. Language is the way we do that. Animals don't. We can only guess whether animals have any consciousness of their own death. One thing they certainly don't have is a future tense or subjunctive forms of the verb.

WACHTEL But you put so much in the grammar itself. You say the utopian and the messianic are figures of syntax, but what comes first, the chicken or the egg? I mean, is language the egg from which emerges the chicken of hope?

STEINER There's no answer to that whatever. They might have come together. They might have come from a reciprocal need, from a dialectic of emotion looking for expressive forms. I take music to be much older and more universal than language. Music can give joy, hope, in many, many ways, but it does not have this peculiar power of future projection. How this arose, when, for the first time, a human being spoke about the time after his own death—not in some fantasy of the world of Elysium or the underworld or a myth but by actually saying something like, "This town is going to be in much worse shape a hundred years from now unless we do something"—we certainly can't identify. What has struck me so much is that cultures of deprivation, of hunger, of extremely marginal life, as in the Kalahari Desert, or among the Bushmen, have a wealth of future forms and conditionals, as if they were compensating linguistically for the grimness and the time-bound misery of their economic and social lives. This is a very striking contrast.

WACHTEL You also pose a question that I'm amazed no one has really been able to answer, or before you, perhaps even ask, which is why are there so many languages?

STEINER No one wants to tackle that one. No Chomskians have ever tried to answer the questions in *After Babel*. The book is taboo. Now, the notion of a single universal underlying grammar is unquestionably true in the sense in which it's true that we all need oxygen. Quite right. Or that all of us will die if we breathe too much carbon dioxide. Quite right. It's also terribly trivial and uninteresting. The really exciting and problematic question is why some twenty to twenty-five thousand tongues have been spoken on this tiny planet: why, within 114 or 120 languages in the Philippines, there should be two that have no connection with any other three kilometres away from their neighbour; why the French word *pain* is totally untranslatable into English *bread*, and so on. That's why I put forward the guess that, even as there are far too many species—a hundred and fifty thousand beetles of great beauty, of great intricacy, in one tiny corner of the Amazon—this richness, this overproduction, this prodigality of expressive means has something to do with the human need for freedom, for structuring as many worlds as possible, for reading the world in many, many different ways. And the corollary, of which I've no doubt whatever, is that the death of a language—and they're dying all around us—the death of a language is irretrievable, as are the deaths of fauna and flora. There, at least, they're trying to do something with frozen semen in zoos. You can't do that with language. You can never bring a language back to life, except in an academic experiment. In my own lifetime, so many important languages have died. The last native speaker of Manx, an ancient and important English language of the British Isles, died about thirty-forty years ago. There is a deeply intricate, fascinatingly complex and unique language spoken in the Pripet Marshes between Poland, Lithuania and what was the Soviet Union. It's called a Livonian language. Nine people now speak it. It is tape-recorded, and I know that's right and that scholars want to have that, at least. It's also unutterably sad. It's like putting Stradivari in air-conditioned glass cases and there they die in the great silence of not being used. So the death of a language is the death of a possibility of experiencing and understanding the world.

WACHTEL Something else you've talked about has continued to trouble me. I was pleased to note in one of your books that it continues to trouble you, that you confess to finding this an obsessive, almost maddening question: Does the cry in the tragic play muffle or even blot out the cry in the street? In other words, does art not only not humanize us, but desensitize us?

STEINER Pragmatically, it seems to me that this is the rather awful and paradoxical case. Again and again, in my own life, I've known emotions coming off a page, off a painting, off a piece of music in particular, of such overwhelming totality that they have blotted out the messy, sad, uncouth reality of daily needs in others. There is something inhuman in the cultivation of the imagination; where the imagination is made so receptive, so responsive to fiction, reality tends to pale—what Freud called the Reality Principle gets remoter and remoter. We know now it has reached a point of folly. People will go to museums. There will be a great work of art on one wall and on the other wall a television program on that work, and they look at the television only. So that even within art, unrealities of impact, of communication, are becoming a real problem. The example I always gave is if you've been reading Lear all day long or acting or reciting or learning Lear by heart, and telling your students about the agony of Cordelia, if somebody yells out there, you're going to get very mad. You're going to tell them to shut up, that you're trying to understand one of the summits of human speech and perception and insight. They yell again, and you don't go to the window and you certainly don't rush downstairs to be of help. There is an isolation in the emotions of great art, generated by great thought and art, which often cuts human beings off from the unthinking immediacy of response and reflex, which should be that of our humaneness. I don't see my way out of that. I've wanted my whole life long to try and say, "Isn't there a way of teaching great literature which makes you politically and socially more responsive?" and certainly none has turned up. The academy is in many ways now more unreal to the problems on its doorstep, particularly in the inner city where it is often located, than it has ever been before.

WACHTEL But if you really believe that—and you quote Coleridge, "Poetry excites us to artificial feelings and makes us callous to real ones"—how could you devote so much of your life to teaching an appreciation of high art or an appreciation of the cry in the tragic play?

STEINER Because I have failed. It's not at all complicated. To be a Mother Teresa is given to very few. To be a Médecin sans frontières is given to few. The derived, the reflected image in great art and literature is not only an inexhaustible joy, it flatters one often with a sense of self-importance. If one is religious, if one is even ethically fully serious, the person who's in a geriatric ward all night, cleaning up the spilled-over excrement of old, dying and incontinent patients, presumably stands much higher on the scale of need and human value than does the greatest explicator of Lear or Coleridge. I've never doubted that. These human beings, who don't like to be talked about and don't like to talk about themselves, will somewhere, if there is a last judgement, be very far ahead of you and me in the queue. Otherwise, what's it all about? The lectures I've given in Toronto in part arise from the crucial and paradoxical fact that neither Socrates nor Jesus, the two fountainheads of our ethics, together with the Mosaic law behind Jesus, chose to write. There is a wonderful, penetrating joke on all this. You may remember, when the tenure craziness began, when people began butchering each other for a chance at tenure, Harvard produced one of its greatest jokes: A group of rabbis is standing along the edge of the road to Golgotha. And Jesus comes by under the cross on his way to the crucifixion. A young rabbi timidly says out loud, "What a pity. What a pity." And the old rabbi asks, "Why?" And he says, "Because he was such a great teacher." "So what? He didn't publish." That famous Harvard joke puts it in an awful nutshell.

In terms of moral seriousness, you and I are not out there on the ward. We're not in the Rwandan camps. This comes home to us because there was a time when great causes enlisted intellectual risk and support: what was called *engagement*, commitment, after the war. In Cambridge itself, I knew people—they're now very old or gone—who dropped their tutorials and examination papers to fight and die in Spain, in the Spanish Civil War. It was a movement that drew tremendous risk and participation. One of the horrors today is for what cause would one drop everything and go out and risk it? There is the premature irony and cynicism of our young. I can almost date it. I was supervising at the time of one of the most cruel butcheries, the El Salvador civil war. I dropped some remark, some silly, unguarded remark, to my Cambridge students: "I imagine none of you will be doing what your grandfathers or fathers did, leaving me a note: Sorry, no essay next week. I'm off to San Salvador." They got together and wrote me a letter and said, "Look, if we go to fight for the left, we know it will end up as a Stalinist horror of communist concentration camps if they win. If we go for the right, it's a farce of American-supported CIA fascism. Why? We won't. We're not going to be caught again. We're not going to be taken in." It's one of the saddest documents. I've kept it, of course. Utterly right. Utterly insightful. It's awful if at nineteen or twenty you know that much. It's awful if you can no longer commit the great mistakes of hope and passionate idealism. Our crime against the young is the extent to which we have bequeathed to them an insight of detached, ironic savvy, that cruel English word *knowingness*. They know it's no use on either side. Their fathers and grandfathers were still ready to make very big mistakes, and he who has not made some big mistakes when he's young is probably going to be a very boring person when he grows up.

WACHTEL You enjoy the contradictions of human nature and, for instance, with respect to the great Marxist critic Lukács, you ask, "What enables a man to illuminate Goethe and Balzac in the morning and be an outrider to Stalinism in the afternoon?" Or, with respect to the famous spy and art historian Anthony Blount, you ask, "What enables a man in the morning to teach students that a false attribution of a Watteau drawing or an inaccurate transcription of a fourteenth-century epigraph is a sin against the spirit and in the afternoon to transmit to the agents of Soviet intelligence classified information?" How do you answer these questions?

STEINER If my work is to have any little echo after me, it will be that I was one of the first to ask this question in an even sharper form: You play Schubert and then go and torture people. We can document this. The easy way out, of course, is to say you play him badly. The hell you do. You play him very beautifully, with deep insight and love. And this question, which rings through everything I've written, which is at the centre as I come after the Shoah, after the Holocaust and so on, and the massacres of today, and Stalinism, seems to me finally the most important of all. There have been a lot of answers. Arthur Koestler, whom I had the privilege of knowing, said it's perfectly obvious, and he's written about this. "We are in a stage of evolution where our animal and sadistic back brain, the big part identified with the back of the head, the thalamus, is still too strong to be overcome by the small, evolving front lobes of the brain which are the seat of moral feeling, of reasoning, of self-control." At the slightest possibility of provocation, the back of us takes over and the bestiality has its fun—which doesn't mean that the front doesn't have its fun also. We are basically a schizophrenic creature, part bestial, part profoundly artistic, cultivated, loving, responsive and so on. I gather this has never found favour with neurophysiologists and with people who work on these brain and behaviour patterns. Others have said that there is something peculiar in German high civilization, where the love of poetry and music was a sentimental veneer over a profound political brutality and bestiality. It's endemic in German history. It's there, right from the start. It's in Luther's terrible pamphlets about burning Jews. It's there in Nietzsche and Wagner. The famous classical argument: they've just never grown up into the perception of a balanced humanity. I don't buy that one, because I remain surprised to this day that it happened in Germany and not in France or Austria or a whole number of other places. But there are cultural historians convinced that it was just incredible bad luck.

There have been many answers. I have none. I keep asking the question. It presses upon me continually because massacres can start again at any time. I have no answer. The only thing that is clear are the facts. Great art does not protect us against barbarism. Very often, as you know, it plays with it. It collaborates with it. Plato—there is no greater mind in the history of Western man—is an anxious and willing advisor to a very cruel despot; indeed, he wants to be his Kissinger. Heidegger and Nazism. Sartre unspeakably defending the Russian camps and Mao's Cultural Revolution, right to the end of his own great and eminent life as a moralist. All I am trying to do is get us to be clear-sighted about the facts, and even that has become very, very difficult. As the media sanitize, make unreal, the daily bestiality and violence, they, too, are collaborating with that violence. They are not making it less possible or less attractive. It is said that genocide is being fuelled, encouraged, organized by previous pictures of genocide. One of the most frightening things I've heard recently is there was a United States Information Service travelling exhibition, beautifully done, against genocide. In certain countries of Asia, this exhibition had to be rapidly closed when it emerged that the crowds pressing in wanted to see how the damn thing was done. They were extremely excited, saying, "Look, it's been done before, so we can do it, too." It was dynamite, dynamite in hot oil.

So the power of the imagination to be buttressed by great documentary expositions of horror, even in the case of the Vietnam War, remains extremely ambiguous. But I'm not a genius. I'm not an angel of the Lord God. I know no answer as to how this operates in a human being. Wherever you look at great lives, you will find areas of almost unspeakable darkness. Not in all, but in the majority. I know no way out of that labyrinth. Proust, in his private bordello, the one he partially owned, tortured animals and had young women perform certain acts which he wished to describe exactly in his novel. You and I are forever and overwhelmingly in his debt. I couldn't imagine my life without *The Remembrance of Things Past*, without Proust's work. Next question: Was that price too high? That really is a religious question.

WACHTEL I want to ask you about something that you recently said troubles you, in a response to a book of essays in your honour, a sort of festschrift. It has to do with a shift in your aesthetic response that you describe as Christianizing. This surprised me, and, as you say in your remark, it surprised you.

STEINER Yes, I don't accept it. I know what it's based on. It is based on the fact—as I'm arguing, and arguing very vehemently—that the ultimate underwriting, the ultimate reassurance for a belief in language, for a belief in meaning, for a belief in form and communication, cannot be formal. It cannot just be technical. Deconstruction has shown that. You cannot refute, on a formal or technical level, the assertion that all of us are talking nonsense, or that the meaning of what we say changes even as we say it, or that no text contains any correspondence to the intention of its author. My image is a very simple one. About twenty-five years ago, there were tremendous floods in New England. Lloyds of London, which at that time was still a very great world power, couldn't cover the insurance. Then I found out—most laymen didn't know this—that there are re-insurers, almost always unnamed Swiss and other final wall companies that can hold Lloyds and make it possible to pay for this vast damage.

That image stuck with me very deeply, and I began asking myself, What is the re-insurance behind my belief in the survival of art, of language, of intelligence, of communication? It turned out to be theological, a kind of wager on the possibility that human creativity has some kind of distant analogy with what we metaphorize as divine creativity. An old idea—nothing original, nothing new. When you deal with that material, you're going to have to deal with certain great Christian insights into it, from Thomas Aquinas to our own time. And you're going to have to deal with the peculiar Christian mystery or doctrine of something being made incarnate, being made flesh. That something earthly has shining through it the light of a possible other presence, a real presence, as I call it. So in that sense, yes, I'm drawing also on Christian material as any serious person dealing with art in the Western tradition has to, as he would have to deal with Buddhism if writing about art in China and Japan and the interior of Asia.

On the other hand, my sense of the possible collapse of Christianity, because of its profound dishonesty in the face of its own responsibilities for the genocide of the Jews in Europe, is getting sharper and sharper. My hunch is it's in unbelievable trouble. The mediocrity of Christian theological thought today—let's not go into that. On the comic level, the breaking apart of Anglicanism, of the Church of England, feeds the humour columns of the daily papers in Britain where I live. It has reached proportions of farce. The churches are empty. And I believe this decline is inevitable unless the Church, through some great act of honesty towards itself, begins saying out loud what it knows to be the truth: that Auschwitz grew out of its own teachings and out of two thousand years of Jew hatred imbedded in the canonic books of Christianity. So in that sense, I also have to involve myself with Christian theology just because I feel it is so irresponsible in the face of our present situation.

WACHTEL So it's another one of those contradictions where the notion of transcendence or mysticism or mystery enables you to apprehend certain artistic experiences—

STEINER And certain doctrines about how we create something. A lot of scientists are thinking along these lines, too. You take the world's all-time best-seller in science, Mr. Hawking's *A Brief History of Time*, which passed eight million copies recently, of which I'm convinced only five thousand copies have actually been read. But the other

7,995,000 are out there. I believe there are eleven mentions of God in this short book—which is a great deal. It ends with a sentence which has become significant in the language: if we can solve certain field equations, we shall then know the mind of God. Right. Now, there are three possible hypotheses. First, which most of the fellows at Cambridge, my companions in these great colleges, hold, that it's a joke. He's having us on. That this deeply special, very private mind whose bodily condition is, as you know, tragic beyond words, has the right to a joke. That's the first hypothesis. Second hypothesis: he's not quite sure, and there's no harm at all in courteously allowing the possibility. Third hypothesis: in this outwardly agnostic or atheist or positivist genius and sensibility, there is a believer and when he says we shall then know the mind of God, that's exactly what he means, whatever that may mean. It's fun to think about that situation and to think about why, in the 1990s, we should have to argue about a man who subscribes to such a cosmology, which still has the great ghost that will not quite be put to rest. My hunch is—I may be totally wrong—is that Malraux, the great French writer and critic and political man and war hero, had it right when he said that the next centuries would be religious or they would not be at all. This very startling assertion is instinctively convincing to me. My worry is what form this will take. It could be one of fundamentalist intolerance, hatred, brutality. It could be that which is on the march, not only in Islam but in American fundamentalism, a most awful form of religious intolerance, despotism and obscurantism. That is distinctly possible.

WACHTEL I would like to go back for a moment to your 1992 novella, *Proofs*. It's about trying to come to terms with great dreams and the terrible consequences of those dreams. Your main character is a proofreader in Italy and a former communist, who has to deal with the failure of his great dream, which was a belief in communism. How is it possible that so many others like him could hold onto those dreams, even when the evidence started to become clear—at least from our perspective—that there were as many as twenty-five million dead just from Stalin alone?

STEINER I've asked myself how it was possible for any Christians to stick with their faith a week after the alleged resurrection, when absolutely nothing changed or happened, when absolutely no messiah in glory walked around—so they then, you remember, postponed it. They said it will be in the year 100; 100 came, then it was going to be the year 200—it's never stopped. Faith is precisely that which does not even run its head against proof. In a very, very strange way, faith is a thing that grows even stronger from things that go wrong.

I remember in the early nineties, a batch of overseas journalists asked Fidel Castro, "Now, come on, no sugar left, no oil, no nothing, one cigar on the whole island and it's yours. Won't you finally realize it hasn't worked?" And Castro found a tremendous answer: "When was Christianity truly strong? In the catacombs." Exactly correct. The greatest hour perhaps of the Christian faith was with the lions waiting upstairs and the Christians in the catacombs downstairs.

Let's take that in a deeper sense. First of all, no Western leader could even have had the culture to give that answer. Why does a Marxist have that culture? Because Marxism is rooted in a knowledge of history and is rooted in a vision of things mattering more than material circumstance—that somehow we're on this earth in a messianic sense in order to get justice going, in order to get the economy distributively going, and so on.

Tell a real believer like that that it's all gone to hell; if he's very intelligent, he doesn't need to deny it. What he then asks is, "Can you please imagine human beings for whom a McDonald's or Disney World are the supreme goal of history?" He will challenge you. He'll say, "If I've got it wrong, what have you got to put in its place?" And that's what my little novella is about. That's when things get much, much trickier.

WACHTEL But it's interesting because you're saying that Marxism is a question of faith rather than materialism—no?

STEINER Remember, there are two great heresies of Judaism: Christianity and Marxism, both invented by Jews—Jesus and Marx. Both are visions of getting it right on this earth first, of having love, justice, pardon, to each according to his wants, et cetera—this great Utopia. Of course, this is a Utopia of material liberation for Marxism, which says, it's no use dreaming about justice if you're hungry—but the getting your stomach full has always been for Marxism a step towards this crazily, crazily high vision of human justice, which is a vision of the great prophets.

On the last page of a quite amazing little book by Leon Trotsky, called *Literature and Revolution*—which he wrote in an armoured train while running five armies during the Soviet civil war—on the last page (I think I know the sentence by heart; if I'm slightly misquoting it, forgive me, but it won't be much of a misquotation) he says: The day will come when ordinary men and women (the two of us, here at this table), ordinary men and women, will think of Leonardo, Shakespeare and Goethe as the foothills in front of the mountains which they will climb.

Now, you may say that's lunatic. Fine. I prefer that lunacy infinitely to the day when there will be a McDonald's at every street corner, when there will be a Disney World for every single human being to take his holiday in. The really difficult question is one the socialists have always asked: Isn't there a third way? Isn't there? And there, I must confess, I'm very, very skeptical.

WACHTEL Surely that's something that you have put your mind to try to uncover, because the first way and the second way haven't worked very well, as you elaborate very clearly in this book.

STEINER The first way ended us in the Gulag; the second, it seems to me, is ending us in a vast culture of sub-literacy. The second way says to human beings: Reach your mean average. And I'm playing on the word *mean*: it's pretty mean, that average. What these messianic visions said was: Be better than yourselves, try to stretch yourself by gripping your fingers onto the ledge and pulling yourself upward.

WACHTEL At the centre of your novella *Proofs* is a debate that articulates some of these issues that you're talking about now. There's a debate between the Italian proofreader and a politically engaged priest, and it's really an argument about capitalism and communism. It seems to be about which is better, but in fact it ends up being about which is relatively less destructive, and the balance is pretty devastating on both sides. The starting points are different. The argument is that for Marx, as you put it, "Every beggar is a prince of possibility," and that's where you're talking about the overestimation of humankind, in the communist dream or ideal. The American way, as you put it, "views man as a pack snarling for luxuries and grunting at the trough." If you do a body count—well, is that the way to do a final evaluation?

STEINER No, no, and I'm not a fool. I know the price, the unacceptable cost in human lives and suffering of the great totalitarian visions. The other cost is immense, too. I mean, saying to human beings that when you get your second car or your better television, you have reached the summit of your potentialities; or if you get the raise or if your shares go up. I mean, when hope becomes a market product, when it can be packaged and when there is a ceiling.

If I'm wrong, I have to be wrong because I'm a teacher. All my writing, my whole life, everything I do—and this is radically Jewish— grows out of teaching. And what does a teacher do? He crams down the throats of other people things they don't want to swallow. That's the very definition of a teacher. If he's successful, a tiny number of them, instead of spitting it out as soon as they get out of the room, like when the dentist cleans your teeth, will swallow it and it'll start growing inside them, and they'll say, "It didn't taste awfully good and it was very hard to get down, but I'm beginning to grow." So that's a miracle, and it doesn't happen very often. Teachers, if they're tremendously lucky, in a long lifetime, will have given to half a dozen other people this mysterious cancer of hope, this devouring addiction to thinking we can do better.

I have no illusions about that, but let's be very careful. We believed that with the collapse of absolutism, of tyranny, such things as censorship and suppression would grow less menacing in our liberal world. But there is a censorship of the market, which is now stronger than ever: money talks. Money doesn't only talk, it screams.

But Hegel, the great German philosopher, somewhere has a wonderful remark, an aside about given the choice between salvation and paradise and the morning newspaper, he'd choose the morning newspaper.

Now, the depth of that remark is the fascination of the world and the fascination of being alive in the morning and finding out what's going on. That's very, very powerful. It really does counterbalance despair. It's just so enormously interesting to try to be alive. Oh no, that's definitely upbeat, but upbeat of a very strange kind. We all know that disasters excite us just no end; they also sell newspapers.

WACHTEL You seem increasingly drawn to music, and it's much too big a subject to plumb now, but there's something you say that I do have to ask you about. You write that "Addicts of language and of reading often turn to music *in their decline*." Now, I'm putting "in their decline" in italics because surely you don't see yourself as in decline.

STEINER Of course I do. This is an entirely familiar phenomenon. Many people of my age turn to music more and more, and it's interesting why this should be. Psychologists are very much agreed on it. I also find myself rereading constantly and perhaps reading new things less than I ought to. Courtesy bids one say that's my own fault, but I'm not so sure. The state of fiction at the moment—and I do say this with deep respect in the country of Alice Munro, of Robertson Davies, of Margaret Atwood and many others—nevertheless, I pick up new novels and after five pages I drop them because of their infantilism, their cliché-ridden monotony. In England it's whether you should commit adultery in Hampstead or in Westminster and so on. I was recently at Gallimard, my own great French publisher, and they say there isn't a novel worth reading. That is the house which in Europe had all the great novelists. There's wonderful poetry being written, which I do try to keep up with, but we are in a major period of music. There are ten or twelve world-class composers at the moment. Difficult music, avant-garde music, music which often first puts you off and you keep having to work at it. But I have absolutely no doubt that this is one of the great periods of musical creation. I try to keep up. I go to concerts. I collect recordings. I try to hear, to hear, to hear what is new in music, and I find it immensely exciting and challenging. I don't find literature very exciting at the moment. What are the best-sellers? Biographies and political documents and documentation. Not all periods have major literary genius.

That happens. It's a very curious, complicated, cyclical process. So I find immense refreshment in trying to stay a little young by keeping up with what is going on in music. And music, if you have deep personal relations, which I'm lucky enough to have, is the only thing in the world which you hear alone with someone else. We don't have a good word for that. Both human beings are alone and both are together. Reading out loud to each other isn't done any more. It's an enormous loss. With music, you can be next to the human being you need and care for most in the world or the group of human beings you want to be closest to, and each one of them is sharing a unique aloneness. That, later in one's life, proves to be a very important experience.

WACHTEL With all respect, you don't speak like a man in decline. A word that I keep coming across in your work is "remembrancer"—

STEINER It's a legal word. I've stolen it from seventeenth- and eighteenth-century law books and you will find it in the *Oxford Dictionary* as a legal term. I use it to mean someone who tries to make other people responsible to their own memories. As you may know, I regard the end of learning by heart in schools to be the end of a classical discipline of language, of history. What we have now is planned amnesia. Our young are being brought up with no past. For students even from the best schools, the Korean War doesn't exist; the Vietnam War is now gone; the Gulf War will be forgotten. There is simply no remembering whatever. A remembrancer is a human being who knows that to be a human being is to carry within yourself a responsibility, not only to your own present but to the past from which you have come. A remembrancer is a kind of witness through memory. In a specific sense, I've always had a deep conviction that comes from having been perhaps too often to the sites of the unspeakable in Eastern Europe, with their millions of names on walls, the unnameables who were made ash. My proposal, made many, many years ago, is not at all an apocalyptic or tragic proposal. It's almost—strangely—a joyous proposal: that each of us learn by heart the names of ten people on one of those walls of hundreds of thousands or on the immensely moving Vietnam War Memorial in Washington, designed by a young woman. Pick ten, learn them by heart, and once a month recite them to yourself or to anyone you love or who is near you so that someone on this earth remembers. That tiny proposal encapsulates almost everything I tried to do in my work.

April 1995/May 1992

DESMOND TUTU

The former Archbishop Desmond Tutu is one of the most honoured and beloved of men, a hero of South Africa's liberation struggle.

A couple of years ago when I was in South Africa to interview writers, Desmond Tutu was in Toronto to receive an honorary doctorate. At the time, he was living in Atlanta, as a visiting professor at Emory University, while receiving treatment for prostate cancer. But everywhere I went in South Africa, his presence was felt—from people pointing out where he lived in Cape Town, to analyzing his role as co-chair of the groundbreaking Truth and Reconciliation Commission (TRC). For all those years that Nelson Mandela was imprisoned, Desmond Tutu was one of the most outspoken and internationally recognized critics of apartheid.

Now, Desmond Tutu is back in South Africa, retired as Archbishop, finished as co-chair of the TRC, and ostensibly withdrawn from public life. But in fact, he's still active and busy, a man of remarkable modesty, infectious good humour and enduring optimism.

Desmond Tutu was born in 1932 in Klerksdorp, in what was the western Transvaal, in South Africa. His father was a schoolteacher, his mother a domestic servant. Tutu got a teacher's diploma from the Bantu Normal College in Pretoria, and then studied at the University of South Africa in Johannesburg. After teaching for a few years in Krugersdorp, he studied at St. Peter's Theological College and was ordained as a priest when he was thirty. He lived in England for a time in the mid-sixties and again in the seventies. In 1975, he became the first black Dean at the Cathedral in Johannesburg. A year later, he was consecrated Bishop of Lesotho, one of the government-designated black "homelands." At the same time, he was becoming more and more involved in the anti-apartheid movement. On the one hand, he met with activists and tried to discourage violence; on the other, he wrote to Prime Minister John Vorster warning him of the explosive situation in Soweto. A few months later, on June 16, 1976, six hundred black demonstrators were killed by white security forces.

From that point until the election of Nelson Mandela almost twenty years later (in 1994), Desmond Tutu campaigned for freedom. In one instance, his passport was confiscated because of his call for an international boycott of South African coal. In 1984, he was awarded the Nobel Peace Prize. Tutu used the money to establish the South African Refugee Scholarship Fund. And he became even more fervent, even more dedicated to liberation.

When it came, he was at the forefront in creating a new country out of what he called "the Rainbow People of God." Through the Truth and Reconciliation Commission, he brought a spiritual dimension to the painful process of healing—which he described in his book *No Future Without Forgiveness* (1999).

WACHTEL The Bible has been one of your greatest influences. Are there particular books of the Bible, or stories from it, that you return to?

TUTU I have found the first few chapters of Genesis particularly help-ful. In South Africa, as you know, people were frequently told that they didn't count because of a biological irrelevance, and it is good to be able to return to those chapters and show just how subversive they were of views such as that.

WACHTEL In what way subversive?

TUTU Subversive in terms of oppression and injustice, because they were saying that every single person is created in the image of God and that this divine image is intrinsic; it is what constitutes us as human beings, and it doesn't depend on externals, biological or otherwise. I mean, it doesn't depend on your status: educational status, social sta-tus, economic status. It's fantastic to be able to tell people who have so frequently had their noses rubbed in the dust, "Hey, do you know what you are? You are God's representative, you are God's viceroy, because you have been created in the image of God."

WACHTEL And are there others?

TUTU I'm also drawn very much to the prophet Jeremiah. He's fre-quently misunderstood. People say, "Oh, this is a Jeremiah," meaning this is someone who always sees the dark side of things, and he's always making predictions about dire things that are going to happen. In fact, Jeremiah is one of the most hopeful of people, and it is only because he feels the plight of his people so deeply that he is constantly weeping. At some point he engages with God quite toughly and says, "God, you misled me; you made me a prophet and all I do is pronounce doom and judgement to these people. You know that if I say I'm not going to speak on your behalf, God, your word burns inside me like a fire and I can't hold it in." And Jeremiah is quite fantastic, because right in the beginning, when God calls him to be a prophet, he says to God, "Sorry, no, I can't, I'm too young." And God says something quite extraordinary to him: "You know, Jeremiah, before I formed you in the womb, I knew you." Which is an incredible assertion about each one of us, that none of us is an afterthought, that each one of us is an indispen-sable part of God's plan for all eternity. Isn't that fantastic?

WACHTEL Yes, and when I hear you speak of the way Jeremiah feels so deeply about his people, I can hear you identify with him at that level, too.

TUTU Yes, yes, yes. To give you just one other example of his hopefulness: Jerusalem is about to be destroyed. The surrounding countryside is already devastated and Jeremiah goes, on God's suggestion, to his ancestral home, amidst all the devastation by the foreign invader. He buys land as a token of the fact that, in the future, the Jews, the Israelites, are going to reclaim this land. They will own the land which has been confiscated by the invader. Is that not remarkable?

WACHTEL What was your first exposure to the Bible? Did you hear Bible stories at home when you were a child?

TUTU At Sunday school, mainly. You know, the usual stories—David and Goliath, and Joseph the dreamer, Moses in the bullrushes, and Noah. And of course the New Testament, as well. I heard those stories and they did become part of the warp and woof of life without my being aware that I was absorbing them, taking them in, as it were, almost with my mother's milk.

WACHTEL Would you describe the household you grew up in as religious? *Was* it in your mother's milk?

TUTU Well, yes, my parents were both Christians. My father was headmaster of a church school. My mother was not highly educated—she was a domestic worker—but she was very devout, a very gentle, caring and compassionate person. I resemble her physically. She was short and had a large nose like I have, and I often say I hope that I resemble her too in her caring, in her compassion, in her concern for the underdog.

WACHTEL She died the year you got the Nobel Prize. Was she able to see you win?

TUTU When we got the Nobel Peace Prize, we flew back to South Africa (from New York) because it belonged not to us but to our people. I was able to meet my mother, but I don't know that she took it all in, because it looks as if she was at the beginning stages of Alzheimer's. So I'm not sure—but I'm glad that I was able to come back and tell her that her son had been named representatively.

WACHTEL Your father, you were saying, was the headmaster of a church school. Did that give your family some social status?

TUTU Oh yes, I think so. Schoolmasters and mistresses, as well as ministers of religion, were people who were held in fairly high regard and were thought to be people of some standing in communities that didn't have a great deal materially. Our people were not allowed into many professions, and so quite a few became teachers and ministers of religion. Women would become teachers or nurses, and sometimes you'd get a brilliant person becoming a physician, or, very infrequently, a lawyer. So there were not too many openings. The educated elite in the community would usually be teachers or pastors.

WACHTEL You were born and spent your childhood in the western Transvaal, in the mining town of Klerksdorp. What was it like there? What are your earliest memories of that place?

TUTU I didn't live there for very long, but what I do recall is my father being fond of fishing, and I would sometimes go with him and we would sit quietly together as he fished. I recall, too, that he had a musical bent. There was a piano in the house, and he sometimes tickled the ivories, as they say. I also have a very distinct memory of the day bugles and drums and kettledrums arrived for the Pathfinders. South Africa was crazy: Scouts were for whites; blacks could not be Scouts but they could be Pathfinders. The troop that belonged to my father's school had been given the instruments that they needed for their marching band. I have a very clear memory of that.

We lived in a segregated township and I can still, in my mind's eye, see where we lived, in what was called a "native location." And just between us and the white town I can see the row of eucalyptus trees that grew there. We didn't go about, as it were, heavily burdened by the fact that there was segregation, discrimination, oppression, even though we were occasionally roughed up by whites. It seemed as if this was how things were ordered, a divine decree, and you didn't keep kicking against the gods, you know. This was in Klerksdorp. But then we moved to Ventersdorp, a town close to Klerksdorp that has become notorious as the headquarters of the Afrikaner Weerstand Beweging, the Afrikaans resistance movement of Eugene Terreblanche, which is a neo-Nazi organization. Sometimes I say that Ventersdorp produced E.T. and D.T.: Eugene Terreblanche and Desmond Tutu. Not the other E.T.

In Ventersdorp I recall instances of what would probably be racist incidents. I would sometimes be sent to town by my father to buy newspapers. I was probably the only black boy who had his own bicycle, and I would run the gauntlet of white kids who would taunt me. They called out, "Pik, pik!" Now pik has two meanings: one is a pick, the thing with which you dig. When I was at a safe distance, I would call back at them, "Graaf, graaf!" Now, graaf is a spade. It was only later that I discovered they were really speaking about an intensive form of black, pikswart—pitch black. And so one had that kind of experience. Also, we had our own school in the township, and at the time Indians and those we call "coloureds" in South Africa attended our school, although Indians in fact lived in town, which was just one of those aberrations and anomalies of South Africa. Often you went past the white school and you would see black kids scavenging in the bins of the school, because in the crazy logic that we had in this country, the government was giving school lunches to whites, who could afford them, and was not giving any to black children. Many of the white children would bring their own school lunches, and what they got as government supply—perfectly good apples and sandwiches—they would just throw away. At the time, these things were impressing themselves on my mind. You just looked and you thought, Oh well, this is how things are ordered.

But there was a very odd thing that also happened in Ventersdorp, which shows another side of this picture. As I was saying, my father used to send me to buy newspapers, and before going back home I would spread the newspaper on the pavement, outside the shop in the white town, and kneel to read the newspaper. Now, that is very strange, because you would have thought then, in a racist town such as Ventersdorp was, that white people would either harass me or they would walk across the pages of the newspaper. Now, do you know, they didn't.

They almost always walked around me. I still look back at that and say that human beings are really very odd creatures. I mean, it is very difficult to put them into categories and say this is how racists behave, because that behaviour was an aberration, really: they should either have shooed me away or just walked across the pages of the newspaper. They didn't do any of that!

WACHTEL Maybe they were impressed that you were reading the paper.

TUTU But that should have annoyed them, especially as I was reading an English newspaper, and most of those white people in that town were Afrikaners and they tended to feel hot under the collar about the English. They still do in many ways, actually. They haven't worked out the consequences, as it were, of the Anglo-Boer War. This is something we keep telling them about the value of the Truth and Reconciliation Commission, that you do actually need to come to terms with your past. The English and the Afrikaners frequently pretend that relationships between them are OK, when they aren't really. Just below the surface, the Afrikaner still resents the fact that so many Afrikaner women and children were ill-treated and many died in the concentration camps. You know, concentration camps are a South African invention; they happened here long before they happened in Nazi Germany. The Afrikaners and the English are still going to have to come to terms with what they did to each other at the turn of the last century.

WACHTEL When you were in your early teens and your family was in Johannesburg, you spent nearly two years in hospital with tuberculosis, which is a very long time at such a young age. How were you shaped by that experience?

TUTU I was very fortunate that one of the people who showed incredible compassion and caring was Trevor Huddleston. Although he was very, very busy—and I knew just how busy he was in Sophiatown—he tried, when he was in town, to visit me at least once a week.

WACHTEL He was an Anglican priest who was working with people in Sophiatown. How did he know you?

TUTU Well, I was at a high school that had been founded by the community of the Resurrection Fathers, to which Trevor Huddleston belonged. And then I went to live in a hostel in Sophiatown that had been started by the Resurrection Fathers, where Huddleston at the time was the prior. And he, in fact, is the one who took me to hospital in what was called Coronationville, which is very near Sophiatown. When they found that I had T.B., I was transferred to a T.B. isolation hospital near Alexandra Township. And Trevor Huddleston in particular brought me books and helped develop my voracious reading. I enjoyed reading enormously. But I was in fact quite sick; at one time I was hemorrhaging. I would cough and then I'd cough up blood. I was in a general ward and had seen that many of those who coughed up blood didn't survive. In fact, almost all of those who got to the stage where they were coughing up blood ended up in the mortuary.

I was maybe thirteen or fourteen. I recall on one occasion going to the rest room and coughing up quite a bit of blood. I said to God, "Well, if this means I am going to die, OK; I probably want to live, but if what is going to happen to me is that I'm going to die, that's OK by me." It sounds like bravado, but at the time I think I meant it, and I had a very deep sense of peace come over me. It was only much, much later—I was already a bishop and Trevor Huddleston was an archbishop—that he told me about one occasion when he came to visit me and the doctor who was looking after us told him, "I am very sorry, but your young friend is dying." Well, that was in 1947–48. I've had a reprieve. I've had a reprieve of some fifty years, and you know I am deeply thankful to the people who looked after me. At one time we were looked after by white nurses. It was quite crazy to have white nurses looking after all the sorts of intimate things that happen in a ward and yet be in a country where the most normal intercourse and relationship between a black person and white people would almost always be at a level of master-servant, mistress-maid, and here they were serving us and they didn't seem to see the anomaly in that. But this country has always been crazy.

WACHTEL What effect do you think that had on you?

TUTU I don't know that it particularly struck me at the time; in retrospect you might ask how they justified it to their friends. It didn't, in fact, last a very long time; they may have been there for a year when I was there and then we had black nurses. But we'd had them, and so far as I can make out, the sky didn't fall, you know. Perhaps it was an indication of what would ultimately happen when we became more normal, that you would be looked after by whoever was available and race would really be the irrelevance that we are striving to make it be.

WACHTEL Your first love was medicine. You wanted to be a doctor and then later switched to teaching, but you became disillusioned with the education system and took yet another direction. You said once that you felt as if God had grabbed you by the scruff of the neck and sent you off to spread His word. What happened? What made this such a natural and necessary move for you?

TUTU As you say, my first love was medicine, and I was admitted to medical school at the University of the Witwatersrand in Johannesburg, but my family was unable to pay fees, so I could not take up my place. And I have to say, I still have a small hankering for stethoscopes and white coats and things of that sort. Then I went into teaching—which I love very much—but I found that I couldn't possibly be part of this conspiracy to fob our children off with something that was deliberately inferior. I didn't have too many options and so I didn't have highfalutin reasons for becoming a priest. I went because it was about the only alternative available to me. It wasn't, as it were, a deliberate decision, cold-blooded, carefully worked out. I had, unbeknown to me, been influenced not only by Huddleston but by the first Anglican priest I encountered, a black priest, who was a remarkable person. We used to go with him as altar boys, and when we went to rural areas, the priest was treated very much like a big chief and they laid out food for him while we lesser mortals stayed outside. Now, this priest—and this is something I've never forgotten—this priest never sat down to his meal before coming outside to check out whether we were looked after. I've always remembered that there was this person who could care for utter nonentities—us—and maybe somewhere in my psyche these things took root. And yes, I went to college, studied, went to King's College, studied, came back and taught at seminary. But when I was then called to the See of Johannesburg, it wasn't as a deliberate career move. I was there, and most of our leaders were away, either in jail or in exile, and being the first black to hold this position, I got a platform that was not readily available to others, but it wasn't deliberate manoeuvering. It seemed as if God had put His finger on me. I recall, too, at one of the retreats we had, that I wrote a letter to the then prime minister. It's hard to describe, but it was a kind of divine pressure, because I sat down and the words of that letter just came, you know; they flowed from my pen. I warned the prime minister that unless they did something dramatic, we would have an explosion. He rejected this contemptuously. This was in May of 1976—two weeks later, the Soweto uprising happened. I can't pretend that I know what it means to be given a divine injunction, but I seem to have moments when I can do no other.

Sometimes it seems to be the height of arrogance to say that God says I should. But it has happened on one or two other occasions. When things got rough here in Cape Town, I broke down and wept in my chapel after being told that when people tried to protest against the racist elections, many had been killed and children had been shot at, even when they were standing in their own yards. Well, you see, Jeremiah—

WACHTEL I was just thinking about Jeremiah, yes.

TUTU And then it just seemed to come, you know, not as a voice from heaven, but it said, "You must march." And so I said to people, "Well, we will march." And it does sound almost arrogant, because I don't have any organization and some of the people said, "But we haven't consulted, we haven't—" I said, "Tough luck! This is what I think we must do. We're going to go on such-and-such a date." And so we had a march in September of 1989, when most of Cape Town came out to protest the violence that was happening. I said I was not the real leader; I was an interim leader; I had been taken by the scruff of the neck and I could do no other.

WACHTEL I was interested to read that you said you really can't stand confrontation and strife, even though you've had to take on so much of it, and you say you have a "very big weakness of wanting to be loved." How has that weakness affected your behaviour?

TUTU There were many, many occasions when I wanted to avoid a confrontation and where I should have stood up, but I shilly-shallied. I can't bear not to be loved, you know. It was one of the greatest burdens I had to bear in the time of the struggle, when I was regarded as the most obnoxious ogre by many white people in this country. Whenever I walked onto a plane, you could almost cut the atmosphere, it was so thick. If looks could kill, I have been murdered many times over. That was awful.

I am aware that there were times in my life when I should have said no and I said yes, because I thought that somehow that would avoid confrontation or perhaps curry favour. And so, temperamentally, I wasn't cut out for what happened, and that reminded me of a reflection of Jeremiah: "God, I love these people and would love to have said soothing, nice things. I love this country, but all you make me say to them is 'you have had it!' You know, God, that if I keep quiet, your word is a burden; it is fire in my breast." I think there were people who thought that I must be deriving a kind of pleasure in constantly standing up and saying, "This thing is easy." I wish that they understood—many don't believe me to this day—that it was going so utterly against the grain for me. Of course, now it is an odd place to be when you can walk in a shopping mall and white people come up and they say, "How is your health?" And they are really very concerned, people who would probably in the past have wished that the cancer had really done its job thoroughly well and dispatched me. To get messages of support and assurances of prayer and cards and things from the most unlikely sources is almost disorientating. You wonder what's happened to your reputation now. We have a wonderful humorist here in South Africa who says, "Love your enemy: it will ruin his reputation."

WACHTEL During all those years of struggle, your faith must have been challenged. Did you have doubts? In your conversations with God, how were you able to reconcile the awfulness of apartheid with God's goodness?

TUTU I don't think that I had too many concerns about the goodness of God. What I did wonder was why it seemed to be a goodness that was biased in one direction. Why was it that suffering seemed to seek out black people especially? We never doubted the goodness of God or the almightiness of God, we just wondered: God, for goodness' sake, on whose side are you? In fact, the burden of the scriptures was that this is a God who has been notoriously biased in favour of the oppressed. The doctrine of the church came alive for us in a way that it probably doesn't for people who are not. I think that the scriptures themselves come alive because most of them seem to be written with sufferers in mind—I mean people who are being oppressed, people who are having a rough time. And that was what upset those in power. There was no way in which they could ultimately succeed.

We also realized just how much we owed to other people. The international community, this church to which we belonged, this catholic church with a small c, the church worldwide, it was real! Do you remember when Peter goes to our Lord and says, "Well, what about us, who have left all of this to follow you? What are we going to have?" and our Lord's promise was, "You are going to have sisters and brothers more than you can number." It became real for us, knowing that we had sisters and brothers, many of whom we were never going to meet this side of death, praying for us. I tell so frequently the story of the nun whom I met on one occasion in New York and I said, "Please, can you tell me a little bit about yourself?" She said, "I live in the woods in California" — which is where she was at the time— "and my day begins at two in the morning and do you know what, Bishop Tutu? I pray for you." I said to myself, "Hey, here I am, being prayed for at two in the morning, in the woods in California. What chance does the South African government stand, the apartheid government?" And of course it stood not a snowball's chance in hell.

We are the beneficiaries of incredible loving and prayer. And of course, the anti-apartheid movement was a worldwide movement and we can never claim that our victory was the result of only our efforts. Without the support of the international community we would not have made first base, and we owe a debt of gratitude that we will probably never be able to discharge. People are amazed by the miracle that did, in fact, happen in South Africa, where, instead of the bloodbath that almost all of us were predicting or fearing, we had a relatively peaceful transition, and instead of the orgy of revenge when blacks came into governance, we have had the Truth and Reconciliation Commission. If we really believe in the power of prayer, why are we surprised that such a miracle should have taken place in South Africa? South Africa is probably the one place in the world which was most prayed for. I don't believe that any other country has had so much prayer so concentrated over such a period of time as we had. And I don't think that there is a movement today that grasps the imagination and the commitment of people to the same extent as the anti-apartheid movement engaged people. I want to say to everyone out there: "We owe a very great deal to you; we are enormously, enormously grateful for the love and the prayers and the support that you gave us over all those years. I myself believe very fervently in the efficacy of prayer. And you want proof that prayer works? Well, here we are! Here we are today, a democratic country."

WACHTEL You've been through so much, you've done so much. If you had to pick a single accomplishment or moment that you're most proud of, what would it be?

TUTU I'm not aware of what you would call a personal accomplishment, and that's not being falsely modest. I was extremely fortunate to have been around at a crucial time when the other leaders were not there, and I became a focal point. I think the most wonderful, wonderful moment was when Nelson Mandela walked out of jail. Actually, no. I mean, that was tremendous—it was unbelievable! But the most thrilling event was his inauguration. I was on the rostrum with three other religious leaders—a Muslim, a Jew, a Hindu and myself—and we were told we had to pray. Why then, precisely? Because airplanes were going to take off and we had to finish just in time. We couldn't tell the jets to slow down because Archbishop Tutu is still praying! I was standing facing north on the rostrum. I don't know what made me turn around—I was just about to pray. I turned round and saw these jets and helicopters coming over the amphitheatre of the Union buildings in Pretoria. Were we ever surprised! I wept, but this time it was tears of sheer, incredible joy and exhilaration. The planes came over us, trailing smoke in the colours of the new flag. It was as if someone had flicked a switch and at precisely the same moment an incredible sound rose from the throats of everyone, especially black people. It seemed to say: These things which, all of these years, have been used against us, belong to us. It seemed to be a realization that came to all of us at the same moment. It was an uncanny experience. I think it sums up everything that's happened.

WACHTEL Some people argue that the rainbow coalition is starting to fade, that whites have retained their privileged status and economic power, that the spirit of Mandela has been replaced by a less open-hearted atmosphere. Do you ever feel discouraged?

TUTU Sometimes I wish we could move a little more quickly, but perhaps we are unrealistic in our expectations in South Africa. Just look at Germany—East and West Germany. They are one ethnic group; they speak the same language; they had much the same history until the split in 1945. And yet, Germany today is two nations within one country. They've tried everything they could to weld these people who share one language, who share one homeland, one skin colour. We have eleven official languages! We have had a horrendous history for several hundred years, and we fondly imagined that in a matter of less than ten years we would have managed to bring together all of these disparate parts into one coherent whole. The remarkable thing is that we have the level of stability that we do have.

It would be totally dishonest to pretend that we don't have problems. We have *massive* problems! The world powers created the Marshall Plan to help Europe stand on its legs after World War II, and we could be helped by a similar program. South Africa, in fact southern Africa, has been devastated by apartheid. Now it is crucial that democracy succeeds in South Africa. Democracy will not succeed if the wide disparities—mainly between white and black, between the haves and the have-nots—are not removed, the gap between the rich and the poor. If that is not narrowed rapidly, dramatically, then we'll have to kiss reconciliation goodbye. I think it remains a marvel that people who are still living in hovels and shacks after seven years haven't yet gone on a rampage. It is crucial that people realize that clean water, electricity, paved streets, decent homes, schools and clinics are coming because of democracy, because of freedom. When we said we were a rainbow nation, we were not saying that we have accomplished all our goals. This is a dream, this is our hope, this is our vision. We are in a process. We have not reached our goal. We are en route. And all of you who have worked with us to overcome apartheid have done so to help us become all that we can be, for the sake of the world.

March 2001

SUSAN SONTAG

I've admired Susan Sontag for some thirty-five years—ever since I read her first collection of essays, *Against Interpretation* (1966), while still at university. Here was a writer—an intellectual but not an academic—who was making connections so imaginatively about everything from the moral philosophy of Simone Weil to her own groundbreaking ideas about the pop phenomenon known as "Camp." She cared about art, and wrote with ardour about how it affects our lives.

I continued to read and admire Sontag as she wrote distinctive books about photography, about fascism and about cancer—about the "image" of cancer in her book *Illness as Metaphor* (1978), and then later, *AIDS and Its Metaphors* (1989). Sontag wrote about her heroes—mostly European thinkers, such as Walter Benjamin, Roland Barthes and Elias Canetti, or filmmakers, such as Jean-Luc Godard, Ingmar Bergman and Hans-Jürgen Syberberg. At the same time, in addition to the essays, she wrote novels, film scripts and short stories. But it was into her essays that she put most of her energy; it wasn't unusual for her to spend six or nine months on a single piece, going through ten or fifteen drafts. The fiction comes easier, and lately fills her with enormous enthusiasm.

The Mexican writer Carlos Fuentes compares Sontag's mind to that of Erasmus, the great humanist of the Renaissance. "Erasmus," he says, "travelled with thirty-two volumes, which contained all the knowledge worth knowing. Susan Sontag carries it in her brain! I know of no other intellectual who is so clear-minded with a capacity to link, to relate. She is unique."

Susan Sontag was born in New York in 1933. She grew up in Arizona and California, but she's lived in New York—and Europe— for most of her professional life. I first spoke to her when she published *The Volcano Lover* (1992), an ambitious novel set in eighteenth-century Naples. It's something of a historical romance, involving a very famous triangle: the British envoy to Naples, Sir William Hamilton; his wife Emma, who was a renowned beauty; and the naval hero Lord Nelson. Although full of ideas and reflections on the nature of collecting or history or the role of women, the novel is a vivid evocation of a particular time and place.

More recently, Sontag has turned her focus to nineteenth-century America, inspired by an actual Polish actress who emigrated to the United States to found a utopian commune. The novel, *In America* (2000), won the National Book Award. A year later, she published another book of essays, *Where the Stress Falls*. Talking to Susan Sontag is surprising. For a formidable thinker and powerful presence, she can be remarkably friendly, personal, informal, forthcoming. There's an appetite, an enthusiasm, a large embrace for life— whether she's talking opera, politics, books or restaurants.

WACHTEL In your latest novel, *In America*, there's a young man, a writer full of ambition, who's described as one of those people who become writers because they cannot imagine a better use of their watchfulness, their sense of being different from others. Would you say that describes you, too?

SONTAG   Yes. I guess I think of being a writer as not just work, but as a way of being in the world, a way of living your life. It's a somewhat restrictive idea—it's a bit playful—but I suppose it describes one way in which I think of writing. When I create characters in novels, I am, in part, trying out different facets of my own identity, or my own fanta-sized identity. At the moment that I write those sentences, I believe in them. Of course, then I always think of something else or something entirely different. That's the great thing about writing novels: you can contradict yourself with the ideas or the notions or perceptions of different characters.

WACHTEL   What took me there, of course, is that he's also described as extremely intelligent and he says that his intelligence could also be a handicap. I wonder if it can, because one must believe in people to be a great writer, which means continually adjusting your expectations.

SONTAG   Well, we live in a time where anti-intellectual clichés are ram-pant. The most common thing is to put down intelligence. For instance, all the different movements teaching you how to be healthy often stress: don't think, just breathe, just get in touch with your inner whatever—your inner victim, your inner child, your inner innocent—as if the mind were the enemy of health or spontaneity. I think there's a very, very lim-ited sense in which that's true, of course. You can become very self-conscious and hesitant. In the old days that kind of psychology was attributed to Hamlet; he was somebody who thought too much. There's a line in Hamlet, something about being "sicklied over with the pale cast of thought." The idea that thinking or being intelligent is somehow a handicap is a very old idea. What we have now, of course, is a lot of peo-ple putting down intelligence. I don't think intelligence is a handicap at all. I think that it's an incredible source of strength. First of all, it's a way of feeling things—it gives you access to all kinds of feelings. And then it gives you real power. For instance, I've been seriously ill twice in the last twenty-five years, both times with cancer. I recently had an entirely new cancer; I've had surgery and I'm going through treatment. The fact that I could think about illness or think about other patients, or think about different ideas of illness or read medical books, or discuss things with doctors—this is a source of strength. If I just were hiding my head under a pillow and saying, "Let them do with me or for me what they can, I don't want to know about it, I'm too scared to know," I would be a weaker person than somebody who becomes an active patient. That's a completely different domain. I think whenever you can understand things, you're in a stronger position. I don't mean necessarily that truth will set you free—it doesn't go that far—but I think it's a tremendous source of strength to be able to understand where you are, what your situation is, what your alternatives are. For one thing, it can put you more in touch with other people. In that particular passage in *In America*, I'm talking more about a certain cliché about writers, that writers have to write from their feelings and they have to be spontaneous. Writing is a process that recapitulates every aspect of being aware. You do have to be spontaneous, and then you have to be very watchful. A lot of writers work this out by saving their spontaneity for the first draft and then being watchful in all those revisions. I'm a tremendous rewriter. I would never think that the first draft was enough; it's just a first step on the ladder. It isn't as if writing is one thing. Writing is a way of being intense, it's a way of being in connection with things outside yourself. You have no choice but to work with yourself as a lens through which to see the world. I think the great thing is to be connected with the rest of reality and not so focused on yourself. Along with the anti-intellectualism I've been talking about, there's a tremendous upsurge of approved vanity or egotism in this culture. It's now considered perfectly normal to be interested only in yourself and what you can do for yourself, what you can get for yourself, and the way you see things. I think you're just cut off from 99 percent of what's out there.

WACHTEL Where do you think that kind of approved narcissism comes from?

SONTAG I'm not sure, because I can only think about it in terms of things that seem as much symptoms as causes. It's such a large, complex phenomenon. I don't know how to get hold of what seems to be the causal part of it. Maybe it has something to do with a certain promotion of the way the economy works, where we're being encouraged to buy things all the time, and if we're going to be buying things all the time, most of which, of course, are not necessary—new models and replacements of things and so on—then maybe we have to be self-absorbed. Maybe this is the character type that's appropriate for consumer capitalism. The era of shopping.

WACHTEL But even here, I was thinking in terms of the encouragement of buying things. In the fifties, you were encouraged to buy things like expensive appliances, but then it was for the family. At least the consumer group was a bit larger. Whereas now it seems that you make your body perfect and then you attach all these things to the body and then . . .

SONTAG I have a very dim memory of that era, even though I left my teens and entered adulthood in the fifties. I just remember the cult of domesticity, of the home. You were encouraged to set up and furnish a nest, but as I dimly recall—I was no shopper or consumer; I was much too poor and marginal—the idea was that you were buying these things for life. You bought a refrigerator, let's say, but not with the idea that there would be some terribly chic Italian refrigerator with which you'd want to replace your old refrigerator in two years' time.

I don't know where it comes from, but the promotion of egotism and of egocentricity in this culture is very, very interesting. I don't think it's necessarily that people are behaving worse than they used to, but they certainly have a much more limited understanding of why they might behave well, almost as if that were simply an arbitrary, freakish decision. It's very hard to get people to acknowledge the existence of principles in their own lives. It seems stuffy and old-fashioned and weird that you would act on principle. You would act because you believe that in principle you ought to do this or that. So there's been a collapse of the older moral vocabularies.

WACHTEL I was thinking of what you said earlier, that intelligence helped you deal with cancer when you were first diagnosed. One of the ways you dealt with it was to write *Illness as Metaphor*, where you didn't write about yourself but instead analyzed the language in which disease has been articulated. With this recurrence, you haven't written about it. How have you dealt with it?

SONTAG I thought that I should, but I'm always contradicting myself—that's a principle of my temperament, so to speak. I think if I did write something now, it would probably be very autobiographical and personal, although it's extraordinary to me how different it is to be a cancer patient in the late nineties than it was to be a cancer patient in the late seventies. In the late seventies, when I had cancer for the first time, I was getting chemotherapy after surgery, first in a big cancer hospital in New York City and then in Paris. The other patients that I met in hospital, or sat with in a large chemotherapy room, didn't know anything about their treatment. We would be sitting in those chairs that were like being in a beauty parlour from hell—they tilt back a little bit while you have your intravenous infusion of chemotherapy—and you'd start chatting with people, when you're not vomiting. I would say, "What drugs are you getting?" and people would say, "Chemotherapy." And I'd say, "Yeah, but what drugs?" because I knew the name of my drugs.

WACHTEL And you were getting very powerful treatments—you were diagnosed to die, basically.

SONTAG I was in stage four and I was not given any chance at all of surviving. So much for that prognosis. Anyway, people didn't know the names of their drugs; they couldn't discuss their treatment; they didn't seem to want to; and they were still very much under the spell of these incredible clichés about cancer as some sort of scandalous disease. You barely could say the word *cancer*. You'd say "the big C" or "It" or "you know," and of course people died of cancer. Still in the 1970s you would read in obituaries, "died after a long illness." The word very often was not even used in obituaries.

Anyway, cut to a little over twenty years later: I'm again a cancer patient. An entirely different cancer. Not as advanced. It was caught earlier by accident, not in stage four, but it's a lethal cancer, uterine cancer.

And I'm in the chemo room in another major cancer hospital and I turn to patients who are also in the room getting their treatment and I say, "What drugs are you getting?" and everybody knows. Everyone knows the names of their drugs, and these are not doctors, lawyers, professors—they're quite ordinary people. And how do they know? They know from the Internet. They know because people now are much more skilled at getting information. That has largely to do with the information culture that has come via the computer. People who in the past would never think of going into a large metropolitan bookstore and asking for the medical books section think nothing about going on-line to find "onconet" or "American Cancer Society.org" or anything.

There are all sorts of informative cancer sites that will give you vast amounts of information and put you in touch with specialists all over the world. They'll tell you that a certain study for your rare cancer is being done in Karolinska Hospital in Stockholm or some hospital in Tokyo.

The doctors' phone and fax numbers will be listed and their e-mail addresses, and the doctors actually will answer you. There are digests of reports from medical journals. You can get a vast amount of information. So now, you sit in the cancer hospital talking to other patients and they're pulling out their computer printouts and exchanging information and giving each other hot tips about places you can go for more information on a new drug protocol—I think it's fabulous! So oddly enough, although we still have all these anti-intellectual clichés floating around, the computer has democratized access to useful information and strengthened the idea that knowing something could make you stronger and could make you a better advocate of your own interests.

WACHTEL You say that if you were to write about it now, you would probably write more autobiographically.

SONTAG Yes. You know, twenty years ago, when I wrote the first of the two illness books, my main idea was that it should be useful to other people. First of all, I was told I was going to die and I thought that was going to be my last writing. I was full of ideas and indignant perceptions of how cancer patients were psychologically punished for having cancer. To tell you just another anecdote: When I was a cancer patient the first time, in the late seventies, I used to get the bills from the Sloan-Kettering Memorial Cancer Center. I would get the bills from the hospital with just the address on the envelope. So I asked my doctor, "Is the reason I'm getting these bills with just a return address—as if I were getting pornographic materials in the mail—the reason I think it is?" And he said, "Yes, of course. There are sometimes family members who don't know that the patient has cancer, or neighbours, or people at your place of employment, so we don't want to violate anyone's privacy by putting the name of the hospital on anything that comes from the hospital." Now that's not true any more at all, because the stigma attached to cancer has, at least in North America, largely been lifted. But at that time I wanted to write something that would be useful to people. And it has been. It is. Almost twenty years later, there isn't a week that goes by that I don't have a couple of communications from people, and it might be just somebody stopping me in the street and saying, "I was going through my mother's cancer and it was very helpful to me," or "I gave it to my brother." I know it's been used in a lot of medical schools and nursing schools. So the idea that you would talk about the ideas and the mythology, the mystifications, that surround cancer seems a lot more useful than telling my story—how suddenly I found I had cancer and I cried and I was scared, and the treatment was horrible, but I survived. I didn't want to write something personal; I wanted to write something useful. I had the idea—it was very self-effacing—that my story was too banal and that what was important was to give people some ideas they could hang on to and use to defend themselves against being freaked out by the fact that they had this illness, which, as terrible as it is, is just an illness like any other illness. There's no special shame or stigma or scandal that should be attached to it.

If I write something—and the impulse is to write something—I think about writing essays because they perform some sort of ethical purpose. But I'm a little shy about the autobiographical impulse.

WACHTEL Has your sense of death, your view of death, changed in those years? Did that affect your reaction to being ill again?

SONTAG In the summer of '98, when I was diagnosed with a new cancer, my first thought was, Oh hell, I won't be able to finish *In America*. I was within thirty or forty pages of the end. It was July, and I was supposed to turn the novel in at the beginning of September. I knew that I would have to go into the hospital immediately, have surgery, start chemotherapy, and I thought, I won't finish the book. I cried for the book. Somebody once said, you can no more stare at your own death than you can stare at the sun for a long time. But if you are told that you are going to die, then you must. All those years ago I was told that I had only six months to live. I think there's a part of you that dies when you have that kind of news. There's a part of you that accepts it. There's a part of you, of course, that's utterly heartbroken. I was in my early forties; I had a beloved son on whom I didn't want to inflict such grief, and I loved being alive. I am somebody who loves the truth, so of course I did accept it in some way, but at the same time I'd decided to go for broke and seek out the most radical treatment possible. And it worked. When you accept the imminence of your own death and are then reprieved, I don't think you ever come back to the innocence with respect to death that you had before. Or, to put it a little bit melodramatically, you are from then on a little bit posthumous. You are a bit posthumous to your own life.

Of course I'm older now, obviously, so I've "had my life," although I would love to live to be a hundred and see just how badly it all turns out. But I feel armoured. I'm full of appetite for life and I'm so grateful to be alive; the day is never long enough, and I feel tremendous energies and desire to see and experience and do all sorts of things. I'm in no sense living the life of an elderly person. But I felt less of a shock when I was told this last time. I think it can never be as much of a shock as it is the very first time when you deal with the reality of your own mortality. I have incorporated that into my way of thinking. I've never been a person who's had a problem connecting with other people. I have a very large emotional life and I make friends quite easily and feel very connected to a fair number of people, but I would say that my illness experience, starting twenty years ago, has deepened my connections with other people and made me more attentive and more compassionate, more sensitive to other people's needs. I don't think it necessarily has that result on everybody. I think it can make you just more desperate to have your own life and to hell with others. But I feel—and it wasn't that I was closed before—more open to people and more open to the sufferings of people and more compelled to intervene when I can. I do whatever I can to connect with people and reduce a bit the incredible burden and suffering that most people labour under.

WACHTEL Does it amaze you sometimes that you're still alive?

SONTAG I'm very grateful to be alive. My first cancer was a metasta-sized breast cancer. I went through an extraordinary experience at that time, which brought me close to many people and deepened and strengthened me. The mutilation of a radical mastectomy is a very, very painful thing that can happen to you. Although I've lived with it for many years, it's still painful. It is something that one should not deny. But it was a great experience, because I think I've made something good out of it. Not only is there the question of the mastectomy that I carry forever on my body, but, more importantly, like everyone who is given that kind of prognosis, I have never completely come back. I'm grateful every morning I wake up. I really wanted to live and I'm very grateful that I have now had so much more time to live. But once you come to terms with death and you do accept your own mortality at a relatively early age, that's a knowledge you can never forget.

WACHTEL In what you've written about your childhood it seems as if you were a cuckoo in the nest, a resident alien within your own family, and that childhood felt like a kind of prison. You even said somewhere that you had a sense of the moral, or an interest in the moral, from the time you were three. How did that come about?

SONTAG I don't know where children get the idea of being different or develop a critical relation to their surroundings. It's so easy for us to explain people as the product of their environment—their problems or neglect or abuse or advantages and privileges. I think we always under-stand that after the fact; it's easy to say, "Oh yes, I read a lot when I was a child because I was alone or because I had asthma or because I was neglected." But there are lot of people who were alone and had asthma and were neglected and they didn't read. I somehow taught myself to read when I was very young, around three or so. When I started school at six, I was put in first grade, 1A on Monday, 1B on Tuesday and 2A on Wednesday, 2B on Thursday and 3A on Friday. And then when I came back the following Monday I was really astonished that I was still in 3A. I thought I would just keep on going. I also skipped another year later, so I graduated high school when I was fifteen. I can't tell you how many times I've been asked whether I was a well-adjusted child, or if I found this very difficult. It's only now that people would ask such questions that presume so many things that I think shouldn't be taken for granted. First of all, who am I to say whether I was well adjusted? Secondly, what's so good about being well adjusted? Third, and most important, what does well adjusted mean? I was certainly very grateful throughout my childhood that I didn't have to spend any longer in school than I did. Imagine if I had had to wait till seventeen or eighteen to graduate from high school instead of being sprung at fifteen!

As for having developed an interest in the moral at age three, from my earliest childhood I could see that people were unhappy or didn't have the privileges or comforts that I had. I didn't have an extraordinarily privileged childhood, but I wasn't starving and I wasn't standing on a street holding out a begging bowl. You can be struck to the heart by images of how unfortunate and unjust the lot of most people is. That's something I think I always knew. That's as close as I can come to explaining it.

I want to return to the question about difference. I remember Jasper Johns told me once that he knew he was going to become a painter when he was six years old, growing up in a tiny community in South Carolina. His family was poor, uneducated. There wasn't any idea of education, of culture, of art. I asked him how he would even have known what a painter was, and he said, "I don't know, maybe I went to Woolworth's and saw a picture of a sunset in a plastic frame. Or maybe I looked through an issue of Life magazine with some article about a painter and thought I would like to do that." I think all over the world children have these ideas, but then, of course, most people give up. They don't follow what they feel, what they dream of.

WACHTEL You once said, "I've been a demon reader from earliest childhood" and then added, "To read was to drive a knife into their lives." Why this fierceness?

SONTAG I just wanted people to be more intense. I love intensity. I don't see why it shouldn't always be wonderful. And I felt very restless when I was a child. I didn't understand when people would be diffident about what they were having for dinner or what they were going to do, or see, or listen to. People seemed to be, as we say vulgarly, pissing their lives away. It seemed so wonderful to be alive. I felt as if I had another metabolism. I wanted to jump out of my skin and everyone else was just bumping along, being rather depressed. I used to get so excited seeing a sunset, and I couldn't understand why people weren't more excited by everything. I still feel that.

WACHTEL You talk about passion and intensity and also melancholy. Do these three go together? I always think of a melancholic as someone who doesn't embrace passion and intensity or isn't fuelled by it.

SONTAG That's very interesting. I do a lot of generalization. Or, I do a lot of generalizing at the invitation of intelligent and friendly people when I would never do it on my own. Most of the things I think about are in reaction to what other people have thought. Otherwise, most of the time I'm just dreaming, and watching and listening in a totally concrete, sensory way. I have learned in response to dialogue with what I read and dialogue with other people to acknowledge a certain idea of the melancholic or saturnine temperament as the one out of which I write. And yet, that's more a learned idea, because the real way I feel about myself is that I've spent a lot of my life in a state of euphoria. That, too, is perhaps not very fashionable—you're supposed to have higher standards in order to have euphoric experiences. But I can get really happy about very ordinary things, like being back in Toronto after two years or going to a terrific Chinese restaurant on Spadina. Everything is very, very vivid for me all the time. Is that in contradiction to melancholia? I don't know. It fascinates me that you think it might be.

I'll tell you another story that came out of a conversation. William Gass, who's a writer I particularly admire, asked me once, "What emotion do you write out of, Susan?" And I thought, Oh, what an interesting question. And he said, without missing a beat, because obviously it's something he'd thought and felt a lot, that he wrote out of rage. I said for me it was grief. And I was so surprised to hear myself say that. I wouldn't have suspected it. And then I thought, is that true? And how awful it seemed to me that he said rage.

WACHTEL What do you have to feel grief about?

SONTAG Well, one has griefs. But the question is more, why do you identify? My father died when I was five. Let's say that is official—you know, a tragedy that marks you and defines you. And it's not only that he died when I was five, he died in a foreign country. I didn't know that he had died. I didn't find out until months later; the circumstances of his death were concealed from me and so on. I wasn't able to mourn properly. One learns to understand this as an adult. Comparable sadnesses happen to many children. Do they, at some much later point in their lives, say that the principal activity they perform comes from grief? No, not necessarily. There have been a lot of things that have happened to me about which I have every reason and right to feel extremely angry. Great injustice has been done to me, as to many other people. I don't define myself as an angry person. So it isn't so much what's really happened as the way you think of yourself and what is given to you by your temperament. I hate cruelty and I hate injustice and I love it when people do reconcile and forgive and are merciful to each other—William Gass cherishes his rage or his anger; I don't cherish mine. You might also say, of course, that's a typical male–female split: women are taught to repress their anger or not to acknowledge it. But I'm unwilling to think that I'm somehow determined by the gender codes. I am, obviously, to some extent influenced by them, but I'm also capable, as are many other women, of transcending them or criticizing them. So where do these come from? I do know it's very liberating to think about these questions, because as soon as you see, as it were, the dimensions of the room, you feel as if you can step outside and move on to other emotions. I think perhaps I've never felt so locked within grief as the moment that I said this or that I heard myself say it—that immediately I wanted to contradict myself, I wanted to be able to move on to other emotions.

That's why I like making up stories and inventing characters, imagining worlds, in which then I might lend some detail of myself, some fantasy about myself, some alternate life, which I don't lead but that's very real to me imaginatively. I'm interested in expanding the way I write and the kinds of things that I can write about, which I think I'm finally able to do, after all these years of writing and rewriting, with these two novels—*The Volcano Lover* and *In America*.

WACHTEL You said very early on that what you really wanted to do was to have every kind of life, and the writer's life seemed the most inclusive. It's curious that even then it wasn't just the experience itself but the writing about it that seemed to promise a life of engagement and adventure.

SONTAG No, that's actually not true. It's more that the writer's life is a pretext for running around. When I went to Sarajevo for the first time, in April 1993, I went there because my son, who's a well-known journalist, had been there. I was scared to death when he went off to Bosnia, but when he came back, he said, "You really ought to see this." And then I had an opportunity to go on a field trip with a friend who was running a humanitarian organization there. It was a very, very terrifying place to visit, needless to say. You arrive on U.N. troop planes knowing you could be shot down by Serb anti-aircraft guns. It was very, very scary. But when I went—apart from the real reason, which is that I was curious and wanted to know where my son was risking his life—I thought to myself, Well, I have a right to go, I'm a writer. I might write about this. It's very childish in a way, but I've heard photographers talk that way: "Well, I have a right to go there, I might take the picture." In these vocations you designate yourself as a professional observer or watcher or witness.

As it turned out, my wonderful son, David Rieff, eventually wrote a book called *Slaughterhouse*, about the war in Bosnia. I don't think it's easy for David to be a writer and the son of a well-known writer. I vowed that I would never write about the siege of Sarajevo and the war in Bosnia, because I wouldn't for anything try to upstage him or take his story away from him. So then I was faced with the odd situation of deciding to go back to Sarajevo and spend a lot of time there, as I did during the siege, and not having my writer's justification any more. I couldn't say to myself, Well, one day I'm going to write about this—I knew I *wasn't* going to write about it. And yet, somehow, being a writer gave me permission to be there, even though I wasn't there as a writer. I was just there as a part-time volunteer, to do whatever people thought was useful, and to bring money in and make connections for people. So it isn't really that I'm saying to myself, I can do everything because I'm going to write about it; what I'm really saying is that I want to live as large a life as I can, as inclusive a life as I can, and being a writer gives me that permission. I actually think it's rather presumptuous, in a way, for people to write. A lot of writers I know, or know about, write on the basis of very little knowledge, and they think just because they're there, they can then dash something off. The only well-known writer besides myself who came more than once to Sarajevo, though he only came twice, did just that.

WACHTEL Who is he?

SONTAG I'll be rude and mention his name. He's somebody I love, but I think what he did was not good. He's a great Spanish novelist named Juan Goytisolo. I ran into Juan, who's an old friend, after my first time in Sarajevo, in April '93, and I told him that he really ought to see this. It's amazing, it's heartbreaking, it's just an extraordinary place. If there's anything that's like the Spanish Civil War in the late 1930s, it's this war in Bosnia. There really are the goodies and the baddies, which doesn't happen very often in wars. Unlike many other writers I made the same pitch to, he said, "Right, I'll go." So he got a commission from El Pais, the great newspaper in Madrid, and he went twice, the first time for a week and the second time for about four days, and he wrote two books on the basis of this. I call that typing, not writing.

I don't say he was wrong to do it—it may have been a useful thing to do—but from my point of view it's not a worthy thing. He was willing, because he's very fast and it was just something he could do, to turn out a little book about being in Sarajevo during the siege, on the basis of one week's residence. I can't do that. I don't want to do that. I think you have to know something really, really well; you have to hang out. But I probably use the identity of a writer, which is for me an ethical identity—I don't make a distinction between the ethical and the aesthetic— as a reason for putting myself in danger or going around just trying to understand the time in which I live. I would consider it a very unworthy life just to have lived in the reality that I was born into.

WACHTEL You've gone to war zones before. You went to Hanoi during the Vietnam War, you went to Israel, to the Sinai.

SONTAG That's right. Bosnia was my third war. I was in Vietnam twice during the war and I was in Israel during the war of '73. But Sarajevo was a different experience. Because I had a U.N. credential sponsored by a humanitarian organization, I could leave the city. It was very dangerous to come in and out. I was most scared when I was entering and leaving, but I did it nonetheless. I felt that the experience of living entirely in the present, in a situation of total danger, was absolutely extraordinary. You know, our consciousness becomes very slack when we live our privileged lives. We have the past always in our minds and we use it as a referent and then we have some idea of the future. Sarajevo was an incredibly intense experience—at any given moment you could be killed, your head could leave your shoulders. Dwelling on the past would just weaken you and sadden you, and of course the future was totally unreal. So you're absolutely living on that thin slice, that margin, of the present, as you negotiate your day in this shooting gallery. Several people have asked me if I wrote when I was in Sarajevo—never mind whether I wrote about it—but did I write at all. Of course, the idea was preposterous. Right after I finished *The Volcano Lover*, I started *In America*—that was in early 1993—and then four months later I was in Sarajevo for the first time. Essentially, I didn't do anything with the book for three years. When I went back to it, I thought I'd lost it. It was a novel that I had drafted in my head; I had only written the first drafts of the first two chapters. I knew what it was about, but I started it and then I didn't work on it for two and a half, almost three years. And it was scary. I thought maybe I couldn't go back to it. But I did go back and I worked and worked at it, and then, just before I was getting to the end, I was told I was ill. So this novel represents climbing several mountains, not just the usual Mount Everest of writing a novel, but coming through some very strong experiences that separated me from the book. I don't know if it deepened the book at all. I'm very tenacious and I thought, Well, this is the novel I want to write, this strange novel about immigration to the United States, about the discovery of America, about an actress. It's a theatre novel. It's something I needed to write and I knew what I was going to do. I knew the arc, the trajectory, of the book. I knew how it would end. And I liked writing something that was epic, that had lots of characters and created a world.

WACHTEL But in the extraordinary opening chapter of In America, your narrator—who you say is not Susan Sontag but who seems to share some aspects of your own experience—finds herself mysteriously present at a party in Russian-occupied Warsaw in 1876, eavesdropping on conversations in an unfamiliar language, eager to enter the story, casting about for her cast—

SONTAG That's right. I'm holding auditions for my novel.

WACHTEL But the narrator seems somewhat surprised, maybe even apologetic, that the story is not set in Sarajevo.

SONTAG Well, that was put in after, of course. I didn't write that at the beginning. But when I revised it, yes, I thought, Oh, I should be writing about Sarajevo; I should be writing a novel called The Siege. But I have to write from a deep place and it takes a long time for things to seep down. This novel, which is a deep reflection about my native country, of course, began when I first lived abroad. I think you only really understand your country when you go abroad and discover how other people see it, and—whatever your quarrel with your own country—you discover the parts of yourself that have incorporated an American way of being or thinking or prejudice. Being a citizen of the United States of America—I needn't emphasize this in Canada; it's so obvious to all

Canadians—is a very complex destiny, because the United States looms so large in the world and there is such enormous complacency about its identity. I've actually been approached by Americans abroad, sometimes on a plane going to Italy or in an airport in a European country, who are genuinely puzzled that people don't speak English and that they can't use the American dollar in these countries. It's very hard for a citizen of the United States—obviously I'm speaking for myself—with some idea of the rest of the world, not to feel somewhat ambivalent about the United States. We have the luxury, as American citizens, to be extremely critical of our own country, without feeling unpatriotic. And yet when I go abroad, I recognize—and I've lived long parts of my adult life in several European countries, notably in France and in Italy—that there are very American things about me. For instance, my belief that you can always make a new start, that you shouldn't feel imprisoned by your past. I didn't think of this as particularly American—I just thought this was the way you're supposed to be. But from years in both France and Italy, I've discovered that people don't feel that way at all. They feel very shaped and limited by their past, and they don't see themselves as being, as some people in America say, "born again." They don't understand that as a possibility, and I think the fact that I do shows, after all, that I am an American, although there are lots of things about America that I can't stand. Anyway, I've been thinking about that, and I wanted to write a novel about educated, complex Europeans coming to the United States and discovering America. These are people who've read de Tocqueville; these are not people coming across in steerage, refugees from economic disaster. They're people who chose to come to the United States for idealistic reasons, to make a new life from an ethical point of view. They're a group of Polish people who go to southern California, in the 1870s, to start a commune, a co-operative life on the land. There was even a word for it then: "simple lifers." They were simple lifers. So this didn't start in the sixties with hippie communes; it goes all the way back to the nineteenth century. The main character is a great actor; she's going to renounce her career in Poland and live the simple life. When that doesn't work out, for various reasons, she goes back on stage, so it becomes a theatre novel. It's an examination of the psychology of an actor. I spend a lot of my life with actors and directors and I think I understand that world very well. So these were things that I'd been thinking of for a long time: discovering America, the clichés about America, what it is to be an actor. I also like stories about foreigners. I realized that only after I'd written two novels about foreigners.

WACHTEL *The Volcano Lover* in Italy, the Polish in America. I hear your next book is about the French in Japan.

SONTAG That's right. And when that is done, I'm going to place the next one in the twenty-first century, in North America.

WACHTEL In this novel, *In America*, the Polish émigrés are coming in the late-nineteenth century, as your own grandparents did. What did you know of their Poland before you started writing this book? Did any of them talk about it?

SONTAG No. Absolutely nothing. Zero. My grandparents came as very small children. They did not speak with an accent. So, they were born in Poland, which, of course, wasn't even a country in the late nineteenth century. It was partitioned; the eastern part was Russia, the northwestern part was Prussia, and the southwestern part was in the Austrian empire. So for all practical purposes it's my great-grandparents who came to America, and I didn't know them. I didn't have much family life, but I do remember asking my paternal grandmother, who had not been born in the United States, "Grandma, where do you come from?" and she said, "Europe." Being a precocious child, I knew that Europe was not quite the right answer, that Europe had parts and that the parts were called countries. So I asked, "Where in Europe, Grandma?" and she said, "Europe." But I insisted, and finally she said, "Austria," which means that she was probably a poor Polish Jew from somewhere in Galicia, in southwestern Poland, which belonged to the Austrian empire. She was talking about her parents, not about her own life, because she didn't remember Poland. In other words, I had very little family history connected with Poland. I only know my great-grandparents were born there and emigrated to the United States with their tiny children, in the 1870s or 1880s. I know nothing about them. I grew up in a completely

different part of the United States, not in the northeast but in the southwest, with very little family life. So it's really entirely arbitrary. I discovered that there really was a Polish actress who came to America, and if it
had been a Hungarian actress or a Czech actress or a Norwegian actress,
I suppose I would have used that, and would have found out as much as I
could about the country.

WACHTEL Why do you like foreignness?

SONTAG I think foreignness is a wonderful vantage point, like being a
writer. It's a terrific place to experience the world, to see things in an
intense way. Now, obviously I'm talking about the privileged here, not a
poor immigrant who has to work in a restaurant for two dollars an hour
or something like that, or is here illegally and in hiding from the police.
I don't mean that kind of life, which of course is the life of most foreigners or economic refugees. What I'm talking about is the life of a
foreigner who has chosen to be a foreigner out of a desire to embrace
more of the world, out of other affinities, out of innate curiosity and
cosmopolitanism. That situation is a tremendous intensifier of experience: you can't take anything for granted; things are always odd and
striking; one thought or perception is always rubbing against another
one. We all admire and are attracted to the openness and curiosity and
innate poetic sense of small children. But then we see that, as children
grow up, they don't ask interesting questions any more and they settle
into routines and start limiting themselves and leading more and more
confined lives, accepting more and more limits on their imagination
and their daily lives. In a way that's understandable, of course. When
you're a child, your main business is just being a child; when you're a
grown-up, you have to care for other people, you have family obliga-
tions, you have to work, you have to pay the rent, you have to do all sorts
of things. But if you throw yourself over a cliff, so to speak, if you go
abroad, you change your life. I know this sounds very American, but it's
true: you break the grip of your own routine ways of thinking. I like
this—I'm attracted to these people as fictional subjects. It wasn't an
idea I had before I wrote these two novels, but after the fact I realized
that I'd given my characters something really interesting to do. My

English people in Italy, in *The Volcano Lover*, my Poles in *In America*, had something exciting to do, which is to understand where they are. Whereas if you just live your whole life where you are, you take a lot for granted. Foreigners can't take things for granted. And I like people who have active, emotional mental lives.

WACHTEL You've been identified with European culture and thought in your career, in your essay writing and your work on cinema. Yet in this novel, *In America*, you take such pleasure in America, in the image of it, the reality. Were you surprised by the passion for America, for the New World, that emerges in this book?

SONTAG Well, I'd wanted to write about America for a very long time. I'm always in arrears with myself, I feel. As much as I'm tempted to write essays because I like to support or promote things that I believe in, or that I think would be interesting or exciting to people, the greater pleasure of writing novels is that I feel I can catch up on a lot of passions and interests that I had to put aside because I didn't think they were "useful," or that I had anything particularly original to say.

In America is a theatre novel in part, and the main character is a woman who is the greatest star of the Polish theatre and who emigrates to America. This is a period of a most intense idolatry of Shakespeare in Europe and, above all, in the English-speaking world. More than half of all theatre productions in North America at this time were performances of Shakespeare plays. I love Shakespeare, of course—who doesn't?—and I got a chance to express my love of Shakespeare as my main character, Marina, plays in these Shakespeare productions. I have characters quoting Shakespeare to each other and knowing all the lines, as everybody did who went to the theatre and saw these plays.

I think I've become so associated with promoting certain kinds of very modern or difficult writing—"weird" is what most people would say—that people assume that's what I actually most like. In fact, what I most like are things that are very mainstream but great, like Shakespeare. So, no essay about Shakespeare. How could there be? But I could write a novel about people in love with Shakespeare, besotted with Shakespeare, and then all my love of Shakespeare could come out.

In that same vein, I have lots of ideas and feelings about what it is to be a mother, because that's been one of the main experiences of my life. Now I guess I'm a mother emerita, but we're still very close. We see each other all the time and regularly talk on the phone, but I can't imagine writing an essay about being a mother—that's not the kind of essay I write. But in these two novels, *The Volcano Lover* and *In America*, I have two portraits of mothers in which I put a lot of myself and a lot of what I object to in the way that certain people are mothers. In *The Volcano Lover* there's a monologue by a woman who worships her daughter—it's Emma Hamilton's mother—and I realized when I was writing the monologue that she's an illiterate woman who speaks a kind of folk-speak, and no one could be more remote from me than this eighteenth-century English peasant woman. But still, when she's talking about my daughter, my daughter, my wonderful daughter, I realized that somewhere I was thinking of my son. In the new novel, *In America*, Marina, the actress, has a little boy, and she's a lousy mother, as are most women who go on the stage. I've known a lot of actresses, some very famous ones, and they're usually bad mothers. They alternate between being incredibly, almost oppressively, affectionate and close to their children and then ignoring them for long periods of time, just exactly what you would expect. It seems to be a kind of *déformation professionelle*: it's very hard to be an actress and give very much time to maternal responsibilities.

I've known this, I've observed this, and I also had a mother who was a very inadequate and unmaternal mother. So I got to show something that I know about being a mother in the negative model in this novel. It's very exalting to have finally found the form I was always looking for, where, if I want to, I can have some essayistic digressions, as many nineteenth- and twentieth-century novelists have, but I can contradict myself—that's the great thing. Henry James said, "Nothing is my last word on anything." A wonderful, wonderful sentence of a true novelist, a great novelist, the greatest American novelist. And that's what I feel about these novels: it's not my last word. But at least I can play catch-up with myself and write about things that I have known and felt and wanted to depict for a very long time. And I can give pleasure. The pleasure of storytelling and the pleasure of moving people—that's a wonderful experience.

WACHTEL When you were talking about Shakespeare, I remembered a line in *In America* where someone says, "Shakespeare, there's everything in Shakespeare," and the response was, "Yes, it's like America. There's everything in America."

SONTAG Yes. The novel is a very capacious vessel. You can put everything in it, although that possibility gives me the idea that I would like to write something very lean, as well. Just the other day I came across a newspaper clipping that I'd cut out about two years ago, a *New York Times* obituary of a man who had befriended another man who had assaulted him when he was a teenager. He had been badly assaulted—robbed, tortured, mutilated—he was very scarred and he lost the sight in one eye. It wasn't a sexual crime, but it was very brutal and sadistic. Anyway, the assailant was caught. He served a certain sentence in jail; it was during the period when capital punishment was still outlawed in the United States—we were a more civilized country then. Anyway, in this obituary it said that when the man got out of prison, the younger man, who had been so injured—left for dead—befriended him. The criminal was a poor, illiterate guy; the victim was an educated, middle-class person, and he looked after this guy, who was by then quite elderly. He took care of him and visited him, and had no rancour at all, no hatred. He just felt sorry for him, and became a friend, a real friend. But it was the younger man, the man who was injured, who died, and I thought, Oh, I want to write about that. That was only days ago, and I don't know how to do it. I think maybe it's very lean, and maybe it all takes place in the head of the criminal or in the head of the young man. Or maybe it all takes place in the head of somebody else who can't understand this kind of forgiveness, this *caritas*, this *agape*. There are stories that just visit you, that haunt you. So I've been thinking about this for two days now, and I hope telling you about it won't kill it for me, because there are some things that you want to keep for yourself. But I think not, in this case. I think I'm going to write about it. These stories float in, just like discovering the story of the Polish actress when I was in a bookstore. I pulled a book down and read a paragraph about this story and thought, That would be a great novel. I could tell a story about discovering America and I could write about theatre.

WACHTEL Theatre used to figure in your own life. You used to act, you've written for the theatre, you were drawn to directing, and then, as a spectator, you were drawn to the formalism of ballet and later, as I think you once put it, "the ecstasy of opera." Can you talk about your evolving relationship with these performing arts?

SONTAG It's just passion. I shouldn't say just. It's a source of the most intense pleasure. It may have something to do with the fact that being a writer, for all that I talk—that we have talked, I think interestingly—about writing as a way of being in the world, and observing and noticing and having a more intense relationship to things outside yourself, for all that that's true, the actual process of writing is intensely solitary. You have to stay by yourself in a room for thousands of hours—I do, anyway—to produce anything that's any good, writing and rewriting and rewriting. It's the most intense and isolating experience. It's comparable to being in a spaceship, where you're the pilot and the only passenger. I have lots of mixed feelings about writing, too. I'm not a graphomaniac. I feel regret at having to pull myself away from all these other things that interest me so much. Theatre and the performing arts are such a pleasure because, first of all, they are collaborative, and it's enormous fun to work with other people and build something. And then instead of staying in, you go out, so it's a constant temptation and a great source of pleasure. And of course films, which are not a live performing art but are a narrative art, have been a passion my whole life. I've spent a huge amount of time in the movies, mostly seeing old films or foreign films. You made a point, Eleanor, about my affinity to Europe. The real truth is, I don't like most American culture. I just don't like it; I'm not drawn to it. I never was. I grew up in a very provincial part of the United States and I never felt very connected to American art or American music. Even American literature didn't matter as much to me as English literature did. Where I got these weird tastes I don't know. It certainly didn't come from my family; nobody told me what to read or what to think. There were nineteenth-century American writers I loved. I loved Hawthorne and Melville and, above all, Edgar Allan Poe, when I was a child. But I certainly loved the great English novels more, even as a young reader. And when I was in my early teens, it was the discovery of European authors—Dostoyevsky, Thomas Mann—that really mattered much, much more to me. So reading, above all reading. But classical music was also European in my mind. I wasn't interested in Aaron Copland; I was interested in Beethoven. I had the idea—and I don't think it was snobbish, it was just logical inference—that more good things came from Europe than from North America—more things that I admired, more things that were exalting to me. I didn't have any feeling that I should like American things because they were American. If somebody said I had to like Hemingway, because I'm an American, I'd say why? I prefer Thomas Mann, or Proust, or Chekhov. So my own discoveries predisposed me to think of a certain kind of seriousness and artistic ambition as being mainly located in Europe, and of course in the past.

WACHTEL You've said that we're living in a really debased time, in a period of vulgar vacuity. Do you really think it's as bad as all that?

SONTAG Yes, I do. I'll give you an immediate example: This morning J. K. Rowling is reading in the Skydome and two Canadian writers of children's books are preceding her. One is Kenneth Oppel, the author of a very popular book called Silverwing. There was a feature story about him, and I can't remember whether he said it or a journalist said it for him: that finding out that you were going to read with J. K. Rowling in the Skydome was like being a cellist and finding out you were going to be the opening act for Madonna, meaning, you had really hit the big time. If you're a classical musician, it seems to me—and I'm really old-fashioned here—you wouldn't want to be the opening act for Madonna. You would have long ago decided it was better to be a classical musician than to be the kind of musician who might be playing popular music before very large audiences. It's not as if people who make choices to write books that have a claim to being literature, or who play classical music, would secretly like to do something else, but *faute de mieux* found themselves doing this weird, very uncommercial thing and would spring for the other possibility if they ever had a chance. No, they engage in these things because they really think there's something else besides making money. They volunteer to do something that they honour, that they think is admirable, that they respect, that they think is valuable, that they think deepens the heart and the feelings and the conscience. That point of view, which I wholeheartedly and easily subscribe to, is, I think, really being lost now. I think it's harder and harder for people to understand why you wouldn't do anything for money and that the biggest audience may not be the best thing. I think the values of mass entertainment and celebrity culture have tremendously eroded our serious culture and our politics.

WACHTEL But isn't there still an appetite for seriousness? Wasn't it always a minority taste?

SONTAG I think there's less now. I think that seriousness was honoured, in part hypocritically, but no, I think it's really, really changed.

WACHTEL But there was always middle-brow culture—

SONTAG But I'm not talking about middle-brow culture, because there's middle-brow seriousness, too. I'm talking about all sorts of phenomena. For instance, in colleges and universities—particularly in the humanities—studiousness is much less valued.

WACHTEL But even when we were in school, we didn't admit that we were swatting.

SONTAG But we did it. We did. One of the things that was held against Al Gore was that he seemed to think he was smart and he seemed like a smarty-pants. But we have very, very low expectations for George W. Bush—if he gets through a sentence without mispronouncing three words, everybody thinks he's doing great—while Gore is thought to be this stiff, unappealing person because he knows a lot. People didn't have criteria like that in the past. Show-biz standards of being appealing, cute and money-minded have taken over this culture. I can give you countless examples. One of the reproaches that was made against Gore, besides the fact that he isn't charming in the right way or that he seems too smart, is that he has no stocks. When he entered public life in 1976—he does come from a prominent and well-to-do family and he inherited a certain stock portfolio—he entirely divested himself of all his stocks. He got rid of everything because he thought it was a conflict of interest, and ever since, he has kept all his money in a simple savings account, in a bank. Not even in a mutual fund—in a bank, where he gets 2 or 3 percent interest. He's been reproached for this now, for being a fool! Not only is he not being honoured for having those sorts of standards, he's being reproached, because how could he be the steward of America's fiscal policy if he doesn't know anything about investing? Whereas it seems perfectly normal that two oilmen from Texas are running and they're interested in money.

It's not just about seriousness, it's about principles, it's about public service. I don't think there's any culture without altruism and I think altruism is really under attack now.

WACHTEL And it's not just everybody saying everything's getting worse, that things were better thirty years ago because they were younger and the culture was richer?

SONTAG No. I think it's really changed. You're absolutely right to point out that everybody always says it was better before. But I'm not talking about it being better for me. My life is better now than it was before. What I see is pressure on young people to stifle their idealism, an absolute insistence that they care more about money than leading honourable lives, lives that involve some kind of social service.

WACHTEL I want to end with a line from your novel *In America* that makes me think of you, and that's when the narrator—who, of course, may or may not be you—reflects, "I could do whatever I set my mind to. Steadfastness and caring about what was important would take me wherever I wanted to go."

SONTAG Yes, I guess that's me.

October 2000/October 1992

Amartya Sen

When the Swedish Academy awarded Amartya Sen the Nobel Prize for Economics in 1998, they noted that he had "restored an ethical dimension to the discussion of vital economic problems." Another economics laureate described Sen as "the conscience of our profession." He's also been called the "Mother Teresa of Economics," for his compassion and concern with poverty. In India, a lentil dessert was named after him—"the Nobel Amartya."

Amartya Sen is an economist and a moral philosopher. Drawing on his own experience growing up in India, he brings a unique perspective to the complex issues of famine, inequality and development. He long ago determined that money is not necessarily the measure of all things. In fact, he helped establish the United Nations Human Development Index to evaluate societies. This is the one where Canada scores so high because it measures not only per capita income but also life expectancy—which means health care—and levels of literacy and education. Using this index, Sen came up with some surprising findings—for instance, that some

African Americans may have less chance of reaching the age of forty than people in Bangladesh.

Sen's humanist approach is evident in the titles of his books: *Collective Choice and Social Welfare* (1970), *On Ethics and Economics* (1987), *Inequality Re-examined* (1992) and most recently, *Development as Freedom* (1999). Sen maintains that the choice between economic growth and social opportunity is a "false dilemma." Growth should be "high and participatory." At the same time, he is critical of conservatives who are skeptical about human development. What they should rather worry about, he writes in *Development as Freedom*, "is the use of public resources for purposes where the social benefits are very far from clear, such as the massive expenditures that now go into the military in one poor country after another. . . . Financial conservatives should be the nightmare of the militarist, and not of the schoolteacher or the hospital nurse."

Amartya Sen was born in 1933 in Shantiniketan, a small town outside Calcutta, into a family of scholars and teachers. He studied in Calcutta and then at Trinity College, Cambridge, where he's now the Master of Trinity College—the first non-Brit to hold that position. He's also affiliated with Harvard, where he taught for more than a decade. Sen often writes for a general audience—for instance, about his fellow Bengali intellectuals, such as the Nobel Prize–winning poet Rabindranath Tagore and India's most famous filmmaker, Satyajit Ray.

I had already thought of Amartya Sen as one of the most inspiring thinkers of our time, but when I met him at Harvard, I was also struck by his warmth, openness, tact and modesty. He was surprised and a little curious when I told him he was discussed in Amit Chaudhuri's recent novel, *A New World*. Characters speculate on when he will get the Nobel Prize, on where he currently is—"Harvard, I think. Though he seems to be everywhere at once. . . . In Oxford, in Cambridge, tomorrow at Jadavpur." They even talk about his marriages and divorce. In real life, Sen is married to the economic historian and specialist on Adam Smith, Emma Rothschild—"from the poorer branch of the family," he assured me.

———————————

WACHTEL You were born in Shantiniketan, outside Calcutta, where the Nobel Prize–winning writer Rabindranath Tagore established his education centre. Can you tell me about growing up there?

SEN Yes. It's a small village. In my day the centre was a school, but it also had quite a distinguished set of higher studies departments. My maternal grandfather was a professor of Sanskrit there. They also had Chinese studies, Japanese studies and so on. It was very international, and different from many of the institutions in India, since "international" did not mean British only. It had some awareness of the rest of the world. I loved being schooled there. It was very progressive. I felt very lucky to be there.

WACHTEL What was the school like? I read that you had classes outdoors—

SEN That's right. Classes were always outdoors if the weather permitted, I mean, as long as it wasn't monsoon. The school was coeducational, and it never overemphasized academic performance. In fact, we were often quite ashamed to admit that we were doing well in exams— it was not thought the right thing to do. I remember one of my teachers once telling me that a classmate of mine was quite a deep thinker, even though her grades were very good. It was generally thought that those whose grades were good crammed for their courses. There's a lot of that in India, and in Bengal in particular. Tagore was against this practice. Some years we didn't even have exams. It's amazing that we actually managed to do some academic work. But it was quite exciting.

WACHTEL Your family wasn't from Calcutta but from Dhaka, which is now the capital of Bangladesh.

SEN Yes, my family came from Dhaka, which is a lovely place. I started school in Dhaka. But my father, who was a professor at the University of

Dhaka, was persuaded that the war with the Japanese and then in Burma would lead to the bombing of both Dhaka and Calcutta.

At the time of partition, Dhaka was the capital of East Pakistan and then later, when Bangladesh became independent, it became the capital of Bangladesh. That's where I'm from—the old city of Dhaka. In fact, I don't recognize most of Dhaka any more. They seem to have added on bits to the old city. We had a house right in the middle of the old city. My father thought that all that area would be bombed, so I was sent to Shantiniketan. I remember my father explaining to me that no Japanese bomber in his right mind would think about bombing Shantiniketan, so that was why I ended up there in '41.

WACHTEL And it was Tagore himself who gave you the name Amartya.

SEN That's right. My family, you know, was very close to him. My mother, who is still alive—she's close to ninety now—was a dancer, and she took the lead part in several of Tagore's dance dramas in Calcutta. She was a great favourite of Tagore's, so when I was born, Tagore, who thought it was very unimaginative that everyone ended up having one of twenty-five different names, gave me an invented name, Amartya.

WACHTEL Which means?

SEN Basically it means immortal. It's like a-mortal: Amartya. You can see the Indo-European roots in that. It has different interpretations. Martya is where people die. Amartya could be unearthly—it's a slightly derogatory version. The more refined version, which for some reason my parents loved, was to say "one who *deserves* to be immortal," not necessarily one who actually is immortal. That has always pleased me. I haven't encountered anyone with my name until very recently.

WACHTEL The Indian filmmaker Satyajit Ray was also a student at Shantiniketan. He said that the years he spent there were the most fruitful of his life, that they opened his eyes to Indian and Far Eastern art and that it was Shantiniketan that made him "the combined product of East and West." How do you think it shaped you?

SEN In many ways, our experience was similar. Ray had come to

Shantiniketan rather late, after having his early schooling in Calcutta. When he came to Shantiniketan he had a formed view; by that time he was very much into Western culture and Western music and literature. Shantiniketan opened him much more to the cultures of the East— Indian, Chinese, Japanese and so forth. I was much younger when I went there—I was eight—and so for me it was really my earliest acquaintance with the whole world. We had a tremendous internationalist presence in our education, but also, on top of that, there was a lot about ancient and medieval India. It was done in a kind of "know your country, know your civilization" way, but non-belligerently, not chauvinistically. Like many other civilizations, India's is not a pre-eminent civilization, but it's a good one. I think that idea was very strong in my mind and has to a great extent affected my outlook.

WACHTEL How would you describe your Bengali cultural inheritance? It seems so rich—

SEN Yes, it's very strong in me. I've got a clear identity. There is a Bengali identity, which, of course, unites me with Bangladesh, where I'm an honorary—and very proud—citizen. A part of Bengal is in India and a part forms Bangladesh. There's a strong Indian identity, a very strong Asian identity. I felt I had to really assert my identity as a human being, as well. The Bengali identity is particularly powerful in literature; the poetry, for example, is notoriously difficult to read and understand in translation. In fact, I was amazed that Rabindranath Tagore could get the Nobel Prize in Literature in English translation. I think the translations don't really carry as much of the original as one would have hoped. Some of the translations were done with the help of Yeats, who was entirely persuaded that they were good translations. When I did a piece in the *New York Review of Books* not long ago, I tried to argue that Yeats actually reinterpreted Tagore in a much more monolithic way, leading to a view of Tagore's mysticism which was, to some extent, closer to Yeats's own view of the East. Bengali culture goes back a long time, and Bengali poetry goes back to about the sixth century AD. It's an interesting literature, a daughter of Sanskrit. I've studied Sanskrit texts for a long time; between the ages of three and seventeen I did a lot of work on Sanskrit.

WACHTEL I understand that at one time you were thinking of becoming a Sanskrit scholar.

SEN I was, actually. I love Sanskrit, and since I began my studies of it at the age of three, before I knew any English, it made a big mark on me. My grandfather was very keen that I read some of the philosophical writings in Sanskrit, rather than in translation, like *Gita*, parts of *Upanishads*, and some of the Indian treatises on logic and epistemology.

WACHTEL Your grandfather was a scholar. He would ask you about your beliefs in life. How do you think he influenced you?

SEN He influenced me very strongly in three ways. One was his great interest in one's earlier culture and civilization, which is non-Western, of course. Later on, my grandfather became very involved in Muslim mystical poetry, the work of Sufis and the combined work of Hindu and Muslim poets. In the fourteenth and fifteenth centuries, such writing was very important. He was the first one to collect this poetry. He was a Muslim weaver who did one of the great sets of poems about God basically being the same in different religions. He is really in some ways the originator of Indian secularism, and he took pride in his culture and in the plurality of culture. Secondly, as a Sanskritist, he was exacting, so it would never do to say something which is a weasel statement. You had to be very fussy. The third one, which I'm not sure has served me so well, was his great passion for brevity. If I'd write anything with more than a few lines, he always thought it prolix. That's the way he wrote. Later on, Penguin asked him to do a book on Hinduism, which he did, and it's a very successful book. I think I'm right in saying that it's the most successful of the World Religions series of the Penguin books, still in print, even though it was written in the fifties. But it had the feature of being extraordinarily brief. He knew very little English and the original translation was dreadful, so I had to retranslate it. But when I was retranslating it, I was struck by the fact that the chapters were two or three pages long. One sentence makes a point. The next sentence makes another point. And I knew what it was like—it's like the Sanskrit logical *shloka*, where each sentence is numbered and number twenty-three is different from twenty-two because it's a different point. But that's not the way you can actually write in English, so I'm not sure that it was a very good training for me. Though insofar as one has a tendency to go in the other direction, it's been somewhat useful.

So my maternal grandfather, this professor of Sanskrit, had a great influence on me. My own father was actually a professor of chemistry at the University of Dhaka. His father, whom I knew only as a very tiny child, had been a lawyer. He was connected with the University of Dhaka, too, as its first treasurer.

WACHTEL How did you get from thinking of becoming a Sanskrit scholar to economics?

SEN Sanskrit was really in competition with mathematics in school. It was generally thought in Indian schools—and in this respect Shantiniketan wasn't an exception—that if you're interested in maths you're not likely to be a classicist, and if you're interested in classics, which is Sanskrit and to some extent Pali and Prakit, you will not be interested in mathematics. So they were competing streams, and as long as I could, I maintained both. The point came when I had to do one or the other. By that time, my interest in mathematics was so strong that I decided to take it as my main specialization in school. Sanskrit became a secondary interest then. At that time, I began my college education, studying physics. But I had always had a great interest in human beings, in how they act. I think human behaviour is a central issue for me. I found that physics, while exciting—and I was reasonably good at it—was nevertheless very dry, and I wanted to go to something that was more human. Given the fact that there was a lot of hardship and poverty around, in choosing between different social sciences, economics seemed to recommend itself rather strongly. I was unlucky in some respects and lucky in other ways in witnessing the Bengal famine of 1943. It happened when I was nine.

WACHTEL What do you remember from that?

SEN I remember three things particularly. First of all, the number of people who died. It was extraordinary. I'd never seen anything like that—people were dying everywhere. Shantiniketan was on the route from some of the very bad areas to Calcutta, and there was a belief that

Calcutta was where you could go to get some relief, where people would feed you. The government was giving no relief whatsoever; in fact, the British-Indian government took a very hard-nosed, dreadful view of it. They believed that Calcutta would provide private charity, which they did, but not adequately, of course.

Secondly, the suddenness of it was extraordinary. I remember still the time when somebody suddenly came into the school behaving very strangely. Some rather nasty kids were teasing him, so some of us tried to intervene. We were very small, of course, only nine, but with the help of the teacher, we tried to rescue him. It was quite clear that he was deranged; his conversation was deranged. Later on, when I studied famine and became to some extent a hunger-related worker, I recognized how often that kind of mental derangement is associated with long periods of starvation. So suddenly there was one and then two and then ten, then a hundred, then tens of thousands. And then what seemed to me like a million. It couldn't have been, because the total number of deaths in the famine was somewhere between two and three million. My estimate was about three million, but some later studies indicate that it might have been more like two and a half million.

The third feature was its class-based character. There were all these people dying, none of whom I knew; none of them came from my class. Not that I was particularly rich—my family was lower middle class. We were the children of teachers, not a highly paid occupation. But our lives were a quantum jump from the lives of landless rural labourers, who were dying in the largest numbers. So it was a class-based famine, which most famines are. Later, I would find out why rural labourers were hit so hard by the famine. It was frightening that I knew no one in school, among social acquaintances, anywhere—Calcutta, Dhaka, Shantiniketan—not a single person who had to starve, who had any kind of hardship through the period. It was a very unequal situation.

WACHTEL You were giving out food in cigarette tins—

SEN It's true, but it wasn't a big thing. My grandfather allowed us to give one tin of rice to anyone coming and begging, but no more. That was very hard. On the other hand, there was only so much that he could spare. So it gave me an involvement, and a sense of gratitude, sometimes from the surprise that came in the eyes of people. A few just said that they didn't know where to cook the rice; was there any way we could help them?

Later on I spent ten or fifteen years studying famines across the world, in Asia, in Africa and also the historical ones in places like Ireland and China. What I had seen gave me a kind of insight. It was very instructive for me to have seen a famine. I had a view as to the cause of the Bengal famine. What emerged later on, when I was much older—I was more than forty when I did that work—was not all that different from what I had thought when I was nine. It's a fact that rice prices shot up, partly connected with the boom in the war economy, with lots of people getting employment in urban areas. They were often quite poor, but they would have to buy food. That would make the prices shoot up. The government was very keen that there should be no unrest in the urban areas because that would hamper the war effort. So their instruction to local governments was that they would subsidize any amount of food purchased in the rural areas, at whatever price, to be sold cheap in Calcutta. So Calcutta had cheap food and higher incomes, and rural areas had higher prices and lower incomes because all the prices went up. Their money wages may not have changed, but their real purchasing power fell dramatically. That was really the beginning of the famine. Peasants who had some rice of their own, even sharecroppers, did not suffer so much, because their income came in the form of food itself. But the poor, who were paid in rupees, in cash wages, they were the ones who went to the wall.

WACHTEL One of the most astonishing discoveries you made, later on, when you came to study famines, was that famine isn't necessarily related to shortages of food. It's so counterintuitive. You think, There's not enough food, therefore there's famine; but in fact, in many instances—not just the Bengal famine in '43—there was enough food available.

SEN Absolutely. Later I would find other famines—for example, the Bangladesh famine of 1974—when not only was there no decline in food, but it was a year of peak food availability. The belief that there was enough food wasn't original to me. People knew that. That was the general criticism in the Bengali papers, but they were censored. They were not allowed to publish anything very much, on the grounds that it would hamper the war effort. Only the English-owned paper, the *Statesman*, coming out of Calcutta, was never censored. This is a very interesting story. Ian Stevens, who was the editor and, like the rest of the British community in India, part of the Raj, played along with the game of not reporting on the famine until he couldn't stand it any longer. Then in the middle of October 1943, in a very moving statement, he began a vitriolic attack on the government of British India for not recognizing the famine, for suppressing knowledge of it. Within a week it was being discussed in parliament and within another week the intervention began. Two weeks later the famine was over, which indicated how much negligence was involved. The general belief at that time was that there was plenty of food. The government believed this, too, and that's why they thought there wouldn't be a famine. Their facts were right; their theory was wrong. Oddly enough, such is the power of theory that when the famine inquiry commission reported on the famine two years later, they revised the facts but not the theory. They said, "Well, our facts must have been wrong. The stocks were low at home and therefore there was a famine." So it wasn't so much that people didn't know it. It was just that they found it so counterintuitive, as you mentioned, that it appeared to them not to be plausible. And the fact is, of course, that it's very plausible. Many famines have occurred without a decline in the availability of food. Not all—the Irish famine did have a potato blight, and with the Chinese famine following the Great Leap Forward, when thirty million people died, there was a decline in food availability. But with some famines this is not the case at all, and with those famines that did have a decline in food availability, you have no clue as to why some starve and others don't. You need a theory that discriminates between classes, occupation groups and so on.

WACHTEL So it wasn't so much the amount of food or the availability of food or even what we sometimes think—the distribution of food. All of these are factors, but they aren't the determining factors. You found the determining factors to be something else.

SEN Yes. It was purchasing power, but that's a natural thought for an economist to have. I can't really get any credit for it and I have to say that our great classical economists, at least those who have thought about this issue at all, wrote along the same lines. Adam Smith discussed it. David Ricardo, giving a speech in parliament about the Irish famine of about 1825—not the big famine, which was in 1840—discussed why it's perfectly possible that if people don't have money to buy food, they will die. It has nothing to do with the food supply. He says that quite clearly. So I don't think that I was original. To some extent, this is what happened: as long as an idea is put forth as an ad hoc thought, it's not integrated into the whole body of economic literature. You have to integrate it with economics. That's something which took me some time to work on, how even reasonably high-brow economic theory, like equilibrium theory, is perfectly consistent with people dying of hunger in large numbers. It's natural, I think, for an economist considering hunger to ask whether these people could buy the food, just as it's natural for a geographer to ask whether there was enough food available. I was taking the economist's position on that.

WACHTEL You also came up with another remarkable—if not so surprising—statement, which is that there has never been a major famine in a democracy.

SEN Yes. That came to me somewhat later, after I had published my first book about famine in 1981. The work had been done in the seventies, and at that time I noted this puzzling fact as I looked through the whole history of famine. I was fortunate to have a long table at that time, on which I had marked famines all across the globe. One of the striking things was that there wasn't a single democratic country on the list. At first I thought, Well, the democratic countries are richer—Europe and America. But not true. Poor democratic countries didn't have famines, either. In fact, even as I was writing, Ethiopia and Somalia were having famines with much more food availability than Botswana—or Zimbabwe, which was a democracy then, though somewhat less so now. I didn't theorize about that in the first book because I was dealing with the causation of purchasing power and trying to explain past famines. By the time the book came out, in 1981, I had written a paper that was published in the *New York Review of Books*. The article was called "How Is India Doing?" and I mentioned that despite all the bungling that had happened, famine disappeared with independence. The last famine was the one I observed in 1943, four years before independence in '47. Never again. China, which was in many ways more successful than India, continued to have famine, including the most gigantic famine in the history of the world, following the Great Leap Forward in 1958, with thirty million dead. I noted that democracy prevented famine because you can't win an election after a famine. A governing party doesn't like being criticized by opposition parties and open newspapers. I'd learned something from the British-owned *Statesman*'s role in stopping the Bengal famine after six months and two million dead. As long as India was cut off and didn't have its own parliament—and the British parliament wouldn't listen—there would be no protection. In China, of course, there was no protection. So as the Great Leap Forward failed, ten million died each year and policies went unchanged for about three years.

WACHTEL This was from '58 to '61.

SEN Fifty-eight to '61, breaking in '62. At that time, Mao Tse-tung made an interesting statement to seven thousand Communist Party cadres, one of the few instances where he praised democracy. In that context, he didn't claim that democracy was intrinsically valuable because it gives people power, but he said that we need the information for efficient centralism and for that, people should be fearless in reporting. But you need real democracy for the centre to have more information, and the people *were* fearful. There was, however, a kind of grudging acceptance on Mao's part that democracy had a role.

The interesting thing, for an economist, is that one always has to see whether the future is in line with what the past was. Otherwise, it's almost impossible for you to make sense of the past by thinking about it with the wisdom of hindsight. But, alas, that's the way it's gone. I say alas because even though it's a confirmed theory, it's at the cost of a great deal of human suffering, and famines continue to occur. As I was writing, there was the Cambodian famine. Then, of course, there was the famine in Sudan, the famine in Ethiopia continuing in the early eighties. Now there's been famine in North Korea for the last few years. All have the pattern of being non-democratic countries, or colonial regimes or military dictatorships like Ethiopia, Sudan, Somalia and so on. So that's a pattern that emerges, and it's not difficult to understand. Governments do have a political incentive to stop famine, but you need the economic and the political together. You need economics to understand what causes famines and how easy it is to stop a famine by just recreating income, even with the same amount of food. These people are dying because they are unusually deprived. You offer them jobs at a relatively low wage, which is self-selecting, because only people who really need such a job will take it. They get income. With the income they can buy food in the market and they compete with others. Food prices go up a little bit. That's what you need in order for others to tighten their belts and to share the total supply of food. This can stop famine dramatically and very quickly. The moment people get some income, they go and buy food. That's it. And that ease of prevention, the economic component, has to be married with the political incentive that a democratic government has to prevent famine. The two together means that you never have to have a famine in a democratic country.

WACHTEL So you really think famines could be prevented worldwide, along with poverty and natural disasters and food shortages?

SEN I see no reason whatsoever to have famine.

WACHTEL Overpopulation?

SEN Absolutely not. There are two different issues here. First of all, you have to be really very deprived to have a famine. It's not like hunger. India has quite a lot of hunger still, but it doesn't have famine. Hunger isn't so dramatic. It's very difficult to make a political case out of hunger. The journalists have to be very sophisticated in order to press for anti-hunger—as opposed to anti-starvation—policy. Famines are dreadful deprivation, but they're easy to prevent. Second, you mention overpopulation. The fact is that the food supply virtually everywhere in the world has been growing faster than the population, with the exception of Africa. But it's not just food production—it's just production per se. There are lots of areas where food production has fallen compared with population, but since other income has gone up, people can buy food from elsewhere. So it's mainly a matter of access—what I call entitlement to food, the ability to buy food—that you have to look at. That's an easy thing to deal with: policies, on the one hand, that generate economic growth, and on the other hand, policies that generate employment, which is very important. My famine study was done for the world employment program of the ILO—the International Labour Organization. That was the initial connection. An employment growth policy plus a little bit of social security is all you need, basically, to prevent famine altogether—along with democracy, of course.

WACHTEL This conversation about famine has grown out of, in a sense, your witnessing a famine when you were just nine years old. You've talked about how, when you were ten or so, in Dhaka, you encountered a Muslim labourer named Kader Mia, who had been stabbed to death while looking for work in your Hindu neighbourhood. Why did this experience affect you so profoundly?

SEN It affected me in three different ways. First of all, I had seen death in the form of famine just before that, and in overwhelming numbers. But I had not seen murder. I hadn't seen the nastiness of one human being to another. I was playing in the garden when this Kader Mia came in from a side door asking for help. I remember shouting for my father. Kader Mia was asking for water, so I was trying to shout for help and also get him some water. He was bleeding profusely from his belly, where he had been stabbed. I kept on asking what had happened to him, and he said he'd just been knifed by Hindu thugs. This was at the height of the communal riots, of course. Hindu thugs were killing Muslims wherever they could get hold of them. Very often the victims were poor people. And Muslim thugs were killing poor Hindus they found in their neighbourhoods. And so the sight of murder was one thing.

Secondly, it hadn't occurred to me how pernicious this identity issue could be. Identity had become such a big and great and loving word in communitarian philosophy and politics. Identity and community were good; the nation was a dreadful thing. There was an enormous amount of literature about that, but I was inoculated against that very early because of this Muslim labourer. He had done nothing—no harm—to these thugs, but just because he belonged to a different community, he was knifed dead. This also made me very interested in the issue of identity and the violence connected with it. It became quite clear that even people who six months earlier saw themselves broadly as Indians or human beings, suddenly saw themselves as narrowly Hindu or finely Muslim and distinguished themselves from each other. This change of identity was very closely connected with violence. So I remain, of course, very deeply skeptical of identity-based thinking. Not that identities are unimportant, but you have to really use your reason because you have so many different identities as a human being—in this case as an Indian, as a Hindu, as one who belongs to a certain class and has certain political views. The question is always, Which of these are primary identities? There's no way of avoiding that reasoning, so I spent a lot of time thinking about these issues between the ages of ten and fifteen or sixteen, when I became involved in politics myself and developed a clear view.

The third reason why I was affected by this murder, and why it was important to me, was that he told me, while my father was getting his car to take him to the hospital, that his wife had told him not to come to this area because it was troubled and because he belonged to a different community. But he had to come because there was nothing to eat at home. So even though he knew there was danger, he had to risk it for the sake of the family because they had nothing to eat. So when a job was offered, he came, and on his way to the job he was knifed. He died in hospital.

It became clear to me that these unfreedoms are related to each other. The unfreedom that comes from economic poverty generates an unfreedom of life and liberty in cases such as Kader Mia's, because he was forced to seek work in most dangerous circumstances. If you look at some of Sebastião Salgado's moving photographs of people working in dreadful mines or in other dreadful surroundings, you will see that they are being forced to accept their lack of liberty because of economic penury. It has become very clear in my mind that unfreedoms of different kinds are linked to each other. My last book, *Development as Freedom*, is really an attempt to put all that together.

WACHTEL There's one other event from your childhood that also seems formative. You had a severe case of palate cancer that was treated by doctors at radiation levels that would now be considered lethal. One critic suggests that this may have left you with a certain skepticism about current wisdom and perhaps even an inveterate optimism about problems that seem to be insurmountable. What effect do you think it had?

SEN Well, it changed me quite a bit. I was eighteen when I was diagnosed with cancer. I felt a lump in my palate. I was staying in a YMCA hostel at that time. My neighbour two doors down was a medical student, so I asked if he would have a look at it. I've always been a hypochondriac, I guess. He said it was probably nothing, but that there was a kind of carcinoma that looks a bit like that. He got me some books from the library, and I persuaded myself that I had squamous cell carcinoma. I self-diagnosed. I didn't have much money so I went to the outpatient department in a large Calcutta hospital, and of course they looked at it and said it was nothing to worry about. Then I went to the cancer hospital, which had just opened, and they did a biopsy. It turned out that I did have squamous cell carcinoma, grade two, as they pointed out. They gave me a dose of radiation which was more than eight thousand rads, which people don't get now. But Hiroshima had only happened seven years earlier, and people did not know the long-term effects of radiation. I nearly died of it, in fact. Later on, at the Adenbrooks Hospital in Cambridge, they did a calculation and figured that my chances of pulling through, even without the radiation—given the nature of the cancer—was about 15 percent, and with the radiation it was probably less than half of that. So I was lucky, and that gave me some optimism. As the years unfolded I remember celebrating one year, two years and then, my God, five years. That was wonderful.

I've always believed in science. I'm very much against nuclear bombs, but I also recognize that I was, after all, cured by nuclear energy, rather than being killed by it. I think it also gave my life a certain urgency in the days when I wasn't certain whether I would pull through. It also made me, on the whole, more optimistic than I had any reason to be.

WACHTEL In terms of optimism, you have brought a moral philosophy, questions about quality of life, to economics, which is typically about numbers and money, GNP and markets. In fact, you co-edited a book called *The Quality of Life*. How do you determine what quality of life is?

SEN I began with the premise that quality of life is the ability to do the things that you value. Then my co-editor, the classical philosopher Martha Nussbaum, pointed out that there is a clear connection with Aristotelian thinking. For me, the notion of quality of life came primarily from extending some writings of Adam Smith, John Stuart Mill and Karl Marx, who had all talked about freedom being important and other things being important only as a means to an end. But the real origin, I think, is Aristotle, who was concerned with the kind of life you can lead. So I was riding on the earlier work of people with strong Aristotelian influences. Aristotle had a contemporary in India called Kautilya, who wrote the first book on economics—*Arthashastra*—which was really about governance but also discussed economics, including famine and the connection between purchasing power and starvation. He didn't see quite as clearly as Aristotle the connection between the quality of life and the means to an end. Aristotle is a much clearer thinker and a much finer philosopher than Kautilya was. Kautilya was in many ways a finer governance person because he had much to say about preventing corruption and keeping checks and balances—very insightful.

But it was useful for me to compare the perspectives of different people at that time. I was also very interested in Buddhism at some stages in my life, although I've never really been religious. There are some early writings in Buddhist literature about deprivation, quality of life and so forth. After all, Buddha left his home to seek enlightenment. Indeed, Buddha *means* enlightenment, and this is what he attained after seeing three deprivations of quality of life. One day he saw a dead person leaving: that was the end of life. Then he asked himself why we have to die. The second day he saw a person who was extraordinarily old, totally debilitated, unable to do anything for himself, and Buddha asked himself why we must suffer the deprivation of old age and the deprivation of the quality of life that goes with it. On the third day he saw an extremely ill person, and saw how that caused suffering. The deprivation of quality of life was a very big part of all ancient thinking, but I think Aristotle was the best of the theorists.

WACHTEL But it hasn't necessarily been part of the thinking of modern economists. You introduced into the United Nations Human Development Index elements of quality of life beyond income, such as longevity, health care and education. In a sense these are the questions of the Buddha.

SEN Yes, that's right. The Human Development Report was started by one of my closest friends, a great Pakistani economist who, alas, died two years ago—Mahbub ul Haq. We were students together at Cambridge and he has been a lifelong friend. When he started it, I told him that he was carrying on Buddha's work. Human development has actually figured in economics a lot, if you think about it—William Petty in the seventeenth century and then, in the eighteenth century, Adam Smith and Mill and Marx. In contemporary economics it has become a bit more technocratized perhaps, but there were still quite a few economists writing about human development—I was by no means first in any way. But what was important at that stage was, first of all, to develop theory at a pure and uncompromising level, one that professional colleagues could not ignore. And at the same time—and this is the second thing I was attempting with Mahbub ul Haq and the Human Development Report—to link the Human Development Index up with the way assessment of development takes place in the world. The Human Development Index is, of course, a very crude index which I helped Mahbub to construct, to get in one real number. But the main glory of the Human Development Report is the variety of information it gives about education, health care, deprivation of various kinds and inequality. Even though I was the author, in some ways, of the Human Development Index, I tried to persuade Mahbub not to use it. I told him that it's vulgar to use just one number. If you want to know something about the quality of life in a country, you don't expect an answer like twenty-three; you expect a much more complex answer. But Mahbub was persuaded that since there was such a concentration on GNP, you had to have one aggregate index if there was to be any chance of defeating the dominance of GNP. I remember one occasion, just before the first report, when he rang me up and I told him that the Human Development Index, which he wanted me to do, would be a very vulgar marker. He was angry and hung up. Then he rang me back and asked me to do a Human Development Index that would have the same level of crudity, the same level of vulgarity, as the GNP—except better. So that was what I did.

WACHTEL One of the things that your index revealed was that African Americans have lower life expectancy than people in China or Sri Lanka, or in the Indian state of Kerala. If you went strictly with GNP, information like that would never emerge. That's an astounding statistic.

SEN It is. Doctors have been interested in that issue for some time; there have been articles in the *Journal of the American Medical Association* as well as the *New England Journal of Medicine* on that subject. I think the comparisons they did were primarily with particularly deprived areas—there was one famous study comparing Harlem with some poorer countries. But my thesis was that while these countries do have deprivation, to some extent there is a bigger pattern of deprivation where African Americans are concerned. This was astonishing, and I published my findings in *Scientific American* in the early nineties, showing that African Americans have a lower chance of surviving to old age than do Chinese, Sri Lankans and Keralans, for example. To some extent the gap has actually widened for African Americans, even though life expectancy increases elsewhere, in India in particular, have been faster. Now there are several regions in India where people have higher life expectancy than African Americans have.

WACHTEL How does this happen?

SEN I think the deprivational issues have not been addressed. America has paid a very heavy price for not having medical insurance. It's appalling to me that a country as rich as the United States doesn't have medical insurance. Forty-four or forty-five million people have no medical insurance. The states I'm looking at in India—Kerala, of course, the most, but many others—have some form of guaranteed medical care. It may not be of very high quality, but sometimes you don't need such a high quality of care.

There is a prevailing myth that says African Americans have high mortality because of violence. There's even a bit of nasty moralism in this, indicating that they bring it on themselves by being involved in violence and so on. That's why, in the Scientific American paper, I also looked at women, and at those above the age of violence, that is, over thirty-five. You get the same pattern. You can see that the differentiation between white and black is still very sharp between thirty-five and fifty-five, as a group. The statistics I was looking at in the early nineties indicated that black women between the ages of thirty-five and fifty-five had 2.9 times the mortality rate of white women. Even after correcting for income—which explains some of it—you still have more than twice the rate of mortality amongst blacks. So there is real deprivation there. There are a number of factors, and I might someday do a bit more on that—the particular contribution of race, the particular contribution of low income, the particular contribution of lack of medical care—what statisticians call co-variants, factors that link with each other and consolidate each other's effect and make each factor more significant. Looking at the situation in this way requires a kind of concentration on issues which, to some extent, economists have been too shy to tackle. I entered into it with a determination to answer some questions that had been bothering me since I had cancer. Mortality had been a big factor in my life.

WACHTEL You raise a difficult dilemma in the introduction to your book The Quality of Life. In trying to ascertain what is most important to thriving, should we look at the local traditions of the country or region under consideration, or should we instead seek some more universal standard of good living, which, as you say, has "the promise of a greater power to stand up for those whom tradition has oppressed or marginalized"? How do you decide what constitutes quality of life?

SEN Well, I tend to be quite prejudiced on that issue. I'm very much a universalist. There are cultural differences, of course, but I think ultimately—and here I take a cue from Aristotle—the very basic demands we have are much more uniform than the rather refined ways we have of meeting them. We may be interested in surviving, in being happy, in being entertained, in being educated, but the form of education varies, the food that we have varies, shelters vary. But the desire to be sheltered is the same, even though the houses, say, those in Japan and those in the United States, are often totally different. So I think I'd say that at a very basic level there is much more commonality, and the local differences are not that great. That's the first point to make. Second, I think we are also much more adaptable. We sometimes don't recognize how quickly we adapt.

If you think about Indian food now, very often you think of chili as a major ingredient. Now, chili was unknown in India until the Portuguese brought it there four hundred years ago. But Indians took to chili like fish to water and it suddenly became very important in Indian cooking, just as the English have taken to Indian food. Everywhere you go in the U.K., the British Tourist Board describes curry as authentic native fare. I was also quite amused to read in the Telegraph of an Englishwoman describing how totally English she was by saying that she's as English as daffodils or chicken tikka masala.

So it indicates how much the culture of another country can enter and become a part of your own. I think we learn a great deal of adaptability from each other. And quite a lot of what is made out to be a big thing in a local culture is very often a reassertion of a small part of that identity. All cultures have a great deal of variety, and then some ideologue comes along and decides what will be important—often in the form of religion.

I've recently been reading a book by a man called Sayed Mustafa Ali, a very good Bengali writer, who went to Afghanistan in the thirties. He wrote about that country and its prevailing debates. It's quite extraordinary: the views varied from very radical to conservative. The only view that's missing is that of the Taliban, the totally monolithic religious one. But somehow, if that had become the Afghan view, the authentic Afghan view, how could you interfere, how could you require that girls not be prevented from going to school? After all, they could say that's not a part of our Afghan civilization. The Afghan reformers of the thirties were very keen on things like education; they were not transplanted from abroad. Once one takes into account the variety within a culture, the pluralities within a culture, as well as our adaptability and the fact that often, at a deeper level, we have a lot of common desires and needs, it is a much less difficult problem than it is made out to be.

WACHTEL How do you transcend the government, the politics? How do you cut through and persuade the people in power that these things are possible?

SEN Ultimately, the main force that we have against traditional conservatism is democracy, because if somebody asks how could you interfere in a country's tradition, the answer is surely that it's not for you but for the population at large. You can't prevent people from re-examining a question just because it was claimed to be their past tradition—even if it had been, and quite often it wasn't. Just because something is claimed to be a tradition, it doesn't mean that they can't say, "Look, we want to walk away from that." If there is democracy, then along with that goes the ability to decide, vote, cast a ballot. It also includes a desire to participate, to debate and be involved in discussions with others.

I decided very early in my life never to become an official advisor to the government. I often write about governing policy, but I put my work in the public domain. I've been very lucky in living in three democracies in my life, namely, India, Britain and America. In each case, I could discuss my arguments and urge the government to listen to me, and since I've never had difficulty publishing what I write, the facts will always come out through the public media. I'm a great believer in democracy, whether we're influencing the government or participating in popular discussion, or changing matters of values and gender equity, for example, which have become major considerations in India, mainly through public discussion. It would have been unthinkable twenty years ago that people would talk about how to make one-third of parliamentarians women, which is one of the proposed acts on the table of the Indian parliament now. All of that is a result of public discussion, I think.

WACHTEL You've raised the question of women. In *Development as Freedom*, you say that "it is difficult to desire what one cannot imagine as a possibility." That statement seems to affect women more than anyone. You've been doing work on women for forty years and have come up with the astounding statistic of a hundred million missing women.

SEN That's so. It's one of the things that I got involved in when I was in school in Shantiniketan. We ran a night school, some of us. It became clear, even when I was fourteen or fifteen, how much harder it was for girls to go to school—not necessarily because families were opposed to it but because the girls often had a role in the family, looking after younger children, for example. I always thought that it was very important to consider the gender issue. Then, when I was working on mortality statistics, it became clear to me that there would have to be thirty million more Indian women alive if the differential had been the same as in sub-Saharan Africa, for example. Sub-Saharan Africa, of course, has a higher mortality rate than India—much higher—but there is no gender difference. Assuming that the average gender difference was the same as in India, but the differential was as it is in sub-Saharan Africa, then there would have been thirty million more Indian women and forty-two million more Chinese women alive. That was my first calculation. That gets you near a hundred million very easily.

WACHTEL In other words, in some societies, even though women outnumber men, the women were dying early?

SEN Yes. Quite often very early indeed. Basically, I think women have a biological advantage over men in survival, rather than a purely sociological advantage, as some people have claimed. Female fetuses have a higher chance of survival than male fetuses do. Much higher. For every 109 boys who are conceived, there are one hundred female fetuses. By the time they are born, the figure drops to about 105 males. But by the time you live life through, there are about 105 or 106 females compared with a hundred males. This is a reversal, because women have higher survival rates than men. Now, of course, with sex-selective abortion and gender bias—in Asia in particular, and most effectively in China—the statistics have changed. In India it's illegal, by the way, so it's much more difficult to have a sex-selective abortion, but it does happen. Now the number of male births has gone up, to 115, 125. That differential is quite striking because if there are, say, in Canada and the United States or Europe, 105 women to a hundred men, in China there are 94 women to a hundred men. In India, 93, in Pakistan, 91 women to a hundred men. Bangladesh, 94.

WACHTEL And that's where you get your hundred million missing women—by calculating the number of women who would have lived if they had been treated the same as men, with as much care and attention when young.

SEN Yes, the reason is differential neglect. There may be some infanticide, and that always makes dramatic news in the newspaper, but newspapers tend to ignore the non-dramatic story of neglect. What you're looking at is dreadful neglect. One of the studies I did was on hospitalization in Bombay. I was looking at the admission of boys and girls and trying to find out how ill they were at the time they were admitted. What I used as criteria were primarily when they died, how soon they died and so on. It turned out that you had to be much more ill, if you were a girl, for the family to bring you to the hospital—these are free hospitals—than if you were a boy. So at that level, neglect, rather than infanticide, is what you're looking at. I think infanticide in China is also exaggerated. The numbers reflect real neglect, and neglect is a very powerful weapon, especially when dealing with infants and small children.

To some extent, this continues throughout a woman's life. The remedy, of course, is women's empowerment through education, through employment. You can see immediately that the gender bias in mortality disappears with education and economic independence. You also see the fertility rate going down. People are worried about overpopulation. One of the interesting things to look at is that the lives most battered by constant bearing and rearing of children are those of young women.

Anything that increases the voice and decision-making power of young women tends to reduce the fertility rate.

Thus you find intercountry comparisons, but the most convincing is the interstate comparison and, even more convincing, the interdistrict comparisons in India, where there are more than three hundred districts. It turned out, on the basis of some fairly detailed statistical work, that the two strongest influences in explaining the fertility differential are, first of all, female education, and second, female employment— gainful employment. Between them, they explain more than 80 percent of the variation. Almost nothing else is needed to explain it. So women's empowerment is a factor. On the one hand, women are treated as patients. On the other hand, with education, employment, empowerment, women are treated as agents. The connection with women's agency and women's role as all-suffering patients is a close one. Quite a lot of the book *Development as Freedom* links the patient role with the agent role. And in the case of women it's particularly important, and not just for the future of women. One of the great things is that along with women's education comes a reduction of child mortality generally, for both boys and girls, along with a reduction of gender bias in mortality.

WACHTEL You suggest combining the extensive use of markets with the development of social opportunities. How can you achieve this balance, especially since greed and self-interest are seen as the engines of capitalism? How do you attain a balance that will establish the kind of priorities needed for social development?

SEN There are two interesting things about the market. One is that it gives people opportunities to enter a market, to do something if you are qualified to enter it. The qualification is very important. If you don't have any means of entering a market because you don't have any capital or available credit, you can't set up a business. Therefore, it's very important, in order to expand the market opportunities, to have microcredit facilities if it's a rural area, and to have land reform, so that you have a bit of an asset in the form of land to be able to enter the market. Because the market mostly helps those who help themselves, you have to have the ability to help yourself with a certain amount of capital. That's the first thing.

Second, the market is a very potent instrument in expanding income opportunities. But you need to bear in mind that there will be people who will not find employment. There will be people who will be poor. Technology will change and some people will be shoved to the wall, and then you need a social security system—you need guaranteed protection of various kinds. So democracy is a very good way of exerting pressure for social security. And you need basic education, just as you need credit, but you also need education to be able to enter contemporary trade and economic operations. For that, literacy is very important. In China, for example, one of the things that's been very little understood is the extent to which the Chinese post-reform success draws on China's pre-reform achievements in expanding basic education and health care. That gave empowerment to a whole section of people who would not otherwise have found it easy to enter the market. I think India's neglect of basic education, which is very slowly reforming, has cost the country dearly. People point out, quite often rightly, that India suffered from the fact that the markets were not welcome. That's true. That changed, of course, but there was also the fact that with a largely illiterate population, opportunity is still limited. For every university-educated person in China, there are six people in India who are university educated. That makes it very easy for India to enter the high-tech industries like IT or the Internet, in which Indians have made a killing. A lot of people earn their income from high-tech—millions. Yet there are many more millions who are completely excluded—socially excluded—from it.

WACHTEL Because their literacy rate is so much lower.

SEN Yes, and so in order to make the market a success, what is needed is not so much to restrain the market but, quite the contrary, to make the market vigorous, to make it easy for people to enter the market through education, land reform and micro-credit. And the market needs to provide protection—social security, democracy, famine prevention and other kinds of social protection. Embedding market freedoms along with other freedoms balances these things. So it's really this broader view that we have to pursue. That's the line that I have been trying to pursue.

WACHTEL And is it possible to pursue, given the power of multinational corporations?

SEN Yes, I think so. Multinationals are powerful, but so are people. Multinationals are very often powerful because they deal with a handful of civil servants or top government leaders who are not responsible to the people. For them, it's much easier to placate the multinationals. But once you get a democratic force and some rabble-rousing politicians who are prepared to protest, you can change things. Democracy is a very good tool to deal with the excesses of multinationals. Quite often multinationals do good. Quite often they do bad. And it's possible for democratic participatory politics to intervene in an appropriate way.

WACHTEL You're a humanist economist, which is sometimes regarded as a contradiction in terms, and, in fact, there are apparently people who think there are two Amartya Sens. Since winning the Nobel Prize, you've had a lentil dessert named after you—the Nobel Amartya. You're discussed in Amit Chaudhuri's novel *A New World*. Given that you have this public profile, as well, which Amartya Sen is in the ascendant?

SEN Well, I don't see any particular contradictions. It's true that I've spent a lot of time doing rather mathematical work in social choice theory, but that's quite closely related to what we've been discussing. After all, social choice theory had its origin in the European Enlightenment. It was the French mathematicians in the 1880s who developed this theory; many of them, like Condorcet, were strongly involved in the French Enlightenment. They were concerned with the question that if people take over, as they thought would happen with the French Revolution, how would they run a country, since different people have different views. How could you have a coherent society? In some ways, whether you're dealing with mathematical democratic politics or whether you're dealing with the mathematical measurement of poverty and inequality, which are all aggregate measures, you're asking questions that are motivated by popular participation. So even though the Nobel Prize was a result of my technical work, I think that work linked quite closely with issues of poverty and suffering. Basically, democracy—popular involvement—is the connection between social choice theory, including its mathematical exercise, and work on famine, hunger, development, the prevention of deprivation and violence, and identity conflicts. All these are, in my mind, closely integrated.

WACHTEL Do you think that your receiving the Nobel Prize means that there is now more of a concern for values in development?

SEN Perhaps, but not so much because of me. A lot of people have been writing about these things. One thing that has embarrassed me quite often is having work attributed to me that has been done by lots of people together. Even from school days, my classmates used to complain that I always shouted the most, and maybe it's my shout that caused some people to hear, but a lot of us have been working on similar problems, in different parts of the world. In some ways, the attention was easier to get via technical economic work, which I was much more involved in. But as a proud economist, I would dispute the view that economists tend to be neglectful of human concerns. I think we're quite a proud profession, and most economists, right from the beginning, from William Petty and Adam Smith and David Ricardo and Karl Marx and John Stuart Mill, have been very involved with human beings. That is our tradition.

September 2000

GLORIA STEINEM

From undercover Playboy bunny to the founding editor and sustaining presence of Ms. magazine, Gloria Steinem is a feminist icon, a journalist and activist who helped transform modern society and its view of women. The title of Steinem's 1983 collection of essays captures her spirit: *Outrageous Acts and Everyday Rebellions.* She's been hailed as continuing a tradition of vindicating the rights of women that goes back as far as Mary Wollstonecraft. Social critic and editor Deirdre English wrote that Steinem "is one of the few figures of twentieth-century feminism who are sure to go down in history, not only for her own achievements but also for her emblematic being." She came to represent women's liberation, the acceptable face of feminism, the "smart" blonde, an indefatigable speaker, a phenomenon.

Gloria Steinem was born in Toledo, Ohio, in 1934. She had a troubled childhood—her parents divorced, her mother was mentally ill—but she managed to win a scholarship to Smith College. After graduation, she studied and travelled in India for two years. Then, in 1960, she started working as a journalist in New York City.

She co-founded *New York* magazine in 1968, and wrote its political column. In 1972, she produced the first issue of *Ms.* magazine. She was its editor for seventeen years, and she remains associated with it today as consulting editor, co-owner and frequent columnist. Her most recent book is a collection of essays called *Moving Beyond Words* (1993).

Gloria Steinem has said that life after fifty, or sixty, is "another country." Indeed, she says that, if anything, she's now more radical than ever. At the same time, she surprised her fans when she married, at age sixty-six, the South African businessman David Bale (father of actor Christian). Given that one of her first breakthrough stories was an exposé of Playboy bunnies, there's a certain irony in the fact that she was inducted into the American Society of Magazine Editors' Hall of Fame the same year (1998) as Hugh Hefner of *Playboy*.

The story goes that when the first woman astronaut went into space, her mother, standing on the ground, declared, "God bless Gloria Steinem." An inspiration to so many, Steinem herself observed that "the imagination of change has to always precede the reality of change."

WACHTEL The First Wave of feminism was embedded in the suffragist movement, the vote for women. What do you think triggered the Second Wave?

STEINEM In a way, it was a similar impulse, because the First Wave was very much part of the abolitionist movement against slavery. Many white women and black women very clearly saw the parallel. It was a bit ironic to imagine that black women could be free for one reason and not the other. Similarly, the Second Wave of feminism followed the civil rights movement. The idea of freedom is contagious, and the caste systems of sex and race are so intertwined that they really can't be uprooted except together.

WACHTEL Is there a way in which it was related to the war?

STEINEM There are many different impulses and reasons besides women's reproductive role, though I think that is the most anthropologically deep one. There was also the Second World War, after which women were encouraged—or forced—to go back to the suburbs, get out of the workforce, leave their jobs to returning veterans. But they had had the experience of being self-supporting, so the restrictions of the fifties created a great deal of discontent. You can see that in Betty Friedan's book *The Feminine Mystique*. And also the Vietnam War was very important because young men were rebelling against being drafted in order to play their masculine role. Many women—even more women than men—were opposed to the Vietnam War. In some profound way, they felt that if men didn't play their role of going off and killing or getting killed in order to be masculine, we didn't have to play our feminine role, either. So there were many women who got politicized within the peace movement, just as we did within the civil rights movement. Yet, even in those very idealistic movements, they could still see that women were doing the mimeographing—there's a dated word—and getting the coffee and doing service work more than making the decisions. So out of that idealism and politicization also came an understanding that there needed to be an autonomous women's movement in order to create true equality, even within those idealistic movements.

WACHTEL I hadn't realized that women were more opposed to the Vietnam War than men.

STEINEM Yes, by far. Earlier and much more so. That's not unusual, actually, because women are much more skeptical about violence as a means of solving problems, partly because we just haven't been raised with our masculinity to prove. It isn't that we're smarter. We just haven't been so brainwashed into the value of violence and aggression, and that's partly because women are the main objects of violence and we know it doesn't change our minds.

WACHTEL Why does feminism come in waves, as in First Wave, Second Wave? Is it comparable to any other movement in that regard?

STEINEM I don't believe there are immutable laws of movements—it depends what you and I and everybody else does every day—but it does seem to be the case that movements surge forward, then go through a period of assimilation, dissipation perhaps, and then surge forward again. Gerda Lerner, a wonderful historian, always says that no movement has a lasting impact unless it lasts a hundred years. I think this longer view helps; then we can recognize stages.

WACHTEL Your own radicalization came about through stories that you heard at a meeting on abortion laws, in the late sixties. But I'd like to go back, just for a moment, to an earlier turning point, and that was the time that you spent in India in the 1950s, just after graduating from Smith College. Can you talk about how you were affected by your experience there?

STEINEM It had an enormous transformative effect on me, so much so that I didn't realize it till I was far enough away to look back. For one thing, it was the first time I had lived in a non-Western country, and it gave me a glimpse of how the majority of the world lives. For another, India had just gone through its own revolution of independence, and had a very strong Gandhian movement still, so there were many examples of transformative change with a minimum of violence—and the tactical lessons on how to make that happen.

Ironically, I didn't realize at the time that the women's movement in India had been the model for Gandhi in many ways. It, too—as so often happens—had been written out of history. Thoreau was seen much more as a model for Gandhi than the entire Indian women's movement. In the late seventies, I went back to visit a friend and colleague in India and we said to ourselves, Gandhi is such a wonderful tactical example for women around the world that we should look through his letters and publish what would be useful to women's movements. Then we interviewed one of the older women who had worked with him, and she listened to us with great patience and finally said, "Well, of course his lessons are useful to women's movements. We taught him everything he knew." In India, there had been a huge women's movement, as there was in most countries of the world, in the late 1800s and well into the 1900s. They espoused non-violent methods, because those were the methods women were comfortable with, to fight child marriage and *suttee*—that is, the burning of widows—and many other ills, and it was partly those tactics that Gandhi had learned from.

WACHTEL When you were in India you became involved with the Radical Humanists. What were they about? How did they influence you?

STEINEM They were mostly people who had been Communists before the Hitler-Stalin Pact and who were very, very committed to social justice. But it was not just the pact that made such a difference to people who had been Communists in India, but also that the Communist Party turned its support to the British Raj as an ally of Russia, and thus opposed the Indian Independence Movement. So, ironically, their disillusionment with Communism—as something that was more dominated from another country than organic to their own—came from feeling betrayed by its support of the British. So they took what they considered the highest ideals of Marxism, anarchism and social justice in general, and translated them into their own group, called the Radical Humanists. They were a really wonderful group of people who lived in different places all over India, and so became a kind of lifeline and safety net for me as I travelled, as well as a group to whose conferences I went.

WACHTEL You also travelled yourself in southern India during the caste riots, as a member of a peacemaking team. I've seen photographs of you in a sari and darkened hair.

STEINEM That was probably just my hair as it really was. Anyway, I was travelling through southern India and, quite by accident, came into a district called Ramnad at a time when there were very tragic and widespread caste riots. The whole area had been cordoned off and isolated by the national government in New Delhi in an effort to keep the riots from spreading. There was a group I was going to see that had been started by Vinobe Bhair, a land-reform movement that was trying to persuade landowners to give a portion of their land to the landless. From their modest little headquarters in a village, they sent out teams of people to walk through the villages in the riot area, to try to bring people together, to talk, to help put an end to the violence by at least explaining what really was happening, as opposed to the rumours, which were even worse than the reality. When I arrived, they had no more women left to go on the next team—they needed at least one woman, so women in the villages would also come to the meetings—and they asked me to go. I said, "Don't you think it'd be a little odd to send someone who's not even from India?" And they said, "You won't be any more odd than someone from New Delhi." So I walked through the villages for a week or so, with this team of two, sometimes three or four. It was unforgettable. I don't even know how to express it. The villagers were our only source of accommodation and food. Just sitting there, by the light of lanterns, listening to people begin to calm their fears by sharing them, learning the truth—it's a kind of transformation that I think can only happen in a small group, where everyone can speak. It's maybe the most transformative unit, whether it's twelve-step groups, or speaking-bitterness groups in the Chinese Revolution, or consciousness-raising groups in the women's movement. So it was an incredible process.

In retrospect, I realize it had an enormous impact, because in a way that's what I have continued to do for the rest of my life. Of course, we don't walk from village to village in this country—we take a plane or a Greyhound bus or something—but in a way, that's what organizers in social justice movements do everywhere.

WACHTEL Why do you think you felt so at home in India?

STEINEM I really don't know. One reason might be that it's big and diverse, in the same way that my country is. It's very open and accepting, unlike many European cultures, so if you're really interested, they're delighted to share with you or include you. Some of it was also personal to me. As a little girl, I had gone to Theosophical meetings because both of my grandmothers and my mother belonged to this group, which was an important philosophical and theological force in the late 1800s and well into the 1900s. In fact, many cities may still have Theosophical Lodges. Krishnamurti and Madame Blavatsky were names that people might associate with it. Their school of thought was heavily influenced by Indian thought, by Hinduism. So I used to sit in those meetings with my colouring book, which was called "Lotus Leaves for the Young," and I guess I absorbed something. I know that when I was in college, I was sufficiently drawn to India to do what was then considered to be an oddball thing: I took a course on India, taught by a woman named Vera Michaels Dean, a wonderful woman. But other things went into my going to India, too. For instance, I was engaged and trying not to get married. So going very far away seemed like a refuge. Everything in our lives is mixed.

But from the moment I arrived there, I felt at home. It was a detriment to my writing of fellowship reports, because you have to maintain your outside view in order to do that. Pretty soon, everything seemed perfectly logical to me, so it became harder for me to write from a Western perspective. Someone in Calcutta looked at the Hindu Book of Life, where you can look up your astrological future, almost minute by minute, and told me that I had been a Bengali in a previous life and must have done something really unfortunate to have been reborn in the United States! In any case, I really did feel at home. If I were to live permanently in any other country, it would either be India or South Africa; it would definitely not be in Europe.

WACHTEL Your grandmother, your father's mother, was an early feminist, part of the first wave. She was president of a turn-of-the-century women's suffrage group, a representative of the 1908 International Council of Women, and she marched for the vote. How aware were you, when you were growing up, of her achievements?

STEINEM Not at all. She died when I was a small child, but even at that, I heard only about some of her accomplishments—that she was a wonderful woman who had four sons, a great educator who founded the first vocational high school in Toledo. I heard great praise of her, but not the suffragist part. Years later I was sitting in an editorial meeting at Ms. magazine, and we discovered that each of us had a feminist ancestor in our families. The family didn't talk about that part of her life, because the feminist part was unacceptable. Not out of any malevolence, but either because it didn't seem important or was too rebellious. So it wasn't until a feminist historian in Toledo wrote a monograph on

my grandmother that I realized how much she had done in the suffragist movement.

For instance, my family had told me that she was elected to the school
board, but they didn't tell me she was the first woman ever elected. It
wasn't even a time when women had the vote nationally, only locally,
and she had been elected on a coalition ticket with the socialists and the
anarchists. She got elected by organizing women to go to the polls
together, because women were being kept from voting by what we would
now call sexual harassment, by gangs of men and boys who taunted and
threatened them if they approached the polls individually.

WACHTEL So you wouldn't have known of her because she died when
you were young. What's also interesting when you hear these stories is
that your grandmother didn't seem to have been able to help her
daughter-in-law, your mother, towards a life of her own.

STEINEM You're right, and I don't quite understand that, because my
mother, who was the inheritor of the vote and many of the fruits of the
suffragist movement, really continued to feel responsible for everything
in a very traditional way. Though she was a pioneering newspaper
reporter, she gave up her professional aspirations long before I was
born. I came to the conclusion—I don't know whether it's right or
not—that my grandmother, like many in her generation, was a feminist
in public life but not in private life. She didn't change the power structure of her household, and therefore came across to my mother as
someone who was just a superwoman, who could do it all. Clearly, we
still have that problem. Most women have two jobs, one inside the
home and one outside the home, and we haven't yet got to the place
where women—a critical mass of women, anyway—feel they have a
right to say, "Wait a minute, men have to be raising babies and little
children as much as women do." We also have to demand child care
and other structural changes if women are not to have an impossible
double burden.

WACHTEL You've written about your childhood: the instability, the
isolation, and above all, the difficulty of caring for a mother who was
mentally ill, because after your parents separated, your sister, who is

nine years older, went away to school and you were left with the role of caregiver, forced to become your own mother's mother. As you've described her, your mother was a loving, intelligent, terrorized woman. How did you make sense, through those years, of your mother's problems and of your life with her?

STEINEM You know, children accept what they see. I had never known her any other way. I think it was harder for my older sister, who had known her as a competent, well, professional person. I never did, so I just accepted it. If it hadn't been for my sister's refusal to accept her illness, my mother would never have ended up in a mental hospital, which eventually did help her enormously, but only after she'd already been incapacitated for a very long time—twenty years. She should have been helped much, much earlier.

WACHTEL Even your schooling was erratic. You never attended for more than a few months at a time and sometimes not at all, so your mother was your tutor as well as your guardian. What view of the world did you absorb through her, or perhaps despite her?

STEINEM She wasn't a tutor, except in the sense of scaring off truant officers with a teaching certificate she had, which turned out to be for something like college calculus. But she was a tutor by example, because she loved to read. There were many disparate books around, at least in the summer—otherwise we were living in a house trailer—and I could pick and choose from bushels of books, because my father, who was an antique dealer, would buy a whole library in order to get two first editions to sell. Mostly I learned from her love of books, and her attitude towards the world. She was philosophically inclined, and inclined towards a belief that things could be better. She gave me a sense of connection between me and the rest of the country. She was always telling stories about the Depression and how poor we had been and what a difference Roosevelt had made. Just the word *Roosevelt* would make tears come to her eyes, because she was so grateful for what she viewed as his getting us out of the Depression. So government seemed kind of intimate to me. Somebody in officialdom saw to it that she didn't have to live on potato peelings or make coats out of blankets. These were the kind of stories she told. I learned from her by example, but not usually from her conscious tutelage.

WACHTEL It surprises me when you say that you learned from her that things could be better, because I would have thought living with her during those years, from the age of ten to seventeen, would have been so difficult, and more hopeless than optimistic.

STEINEM It was hopeless frequently and—I don't know—frightening. The feeling in the pit of your stomach, the fear of not knowing what you would find when you went home. I think a lot of kids grow up with this, because their parents are alcoholics or ill or violent. There's a sense of not knowing what's going to happen. But I was young and I always knew somehow that I would grow out of it; that is, you know at some primitive level that you are going to live longer than your parent, so some day this is going to end. I think that makes a difference. It's the endlessness of bad things that makes it very hard. And also, in some sense—then, and for years and years afterwards—the very fact of how bad it was made me an optimist, because I kept thinking, Well, nothing can ever be as bad again.

WACHTEL It's certainly the response of a good survivor.

STEINEM I do think it gave me a kind of survivor's conceit. I remember reading about—and it was another thing that my mother made sure I knew about, which I'm grateful for—the concentration camps in Europe. I remember thinking against all logic that if I had been in one of those camps, I somehow would have survived. The problem is that it gave me great confidence, the feeling that I could handle whatever came, unrealistic as it might be. What it didn't do was make me think that I could shape what was coming. I learned how to respond but not how to initiate.

WACHTEL Although I remember reading somewhere that when you read Louisa May Alcott and various other kids' books, your fantasies were of the rescuer rather than the one rescued.

STEINEM That's true. I don't know why, except maybe because I was my mother's caretaker and just saw myself as a caretaker. I don't know how much is character and how much is situation. I was totally in love with Louisa May Alcott as a writer, not just of her children's or young people's books but also of her adult novels and short stories, which I read whether I could understand them or not. I used to fantasize endlessly about her coming back to life and what I would show her, what she would like to see first, what would surprise her. It was my favourite long-running fantasy. I was maybe eight or nine.

WACHTEL What did you respond to in her writings?

STEINEM Little Women was the first thing I read, and like generations and generations of young girls, I responded to a community of women, a female community, in which everything was represented—fun, learning, fear about the war—everything was there. They were having a hard time economically, but they helped others who were worse off. They had differences, they fought, but they loved each other and their mother, and they had hopes of something better after the war. I used to read it over every year.

WACHTEL Until what age?

STEINEM I don't know, maybe eleven or twelve, something like that. I read early because I learned to read early; there was nothing else to do, so I learned. So I must have read it every year for five or six years at least. Oddly, for part of that time I was reading Gone with the Wind every year, too. I also read Aunt Jo's Scrapbag and a novel called Work, which is quite a dark novel of the Civil War era and very feminist because much of it is about what women will be in the future—all by Louisa May Alcott.

WACHTEL When you wrote about your mother after her death, you did it with great poignancy in an essay called "Ruth's Song—Because She Could Not Sing It." What's striking in the essay is the lack of resentment you express towards her—only anger at a world that allowed her to drift in her own illness. But I understand that you weren't able to reread that piece for two years. Why not?

STEINEM It's hard to explain. It's as if there's some journey from head to heart, and your head knows things before you are ready to absorb them emotionally. So even though I wrote it, I didn't feel it as deeply as I did later when I read it. It was as if I was holding off part of the emotional impact in order to write it, and then that impact came later. Also, when I was writing it, I had the illusion that it was about my mother. Only later on did I realize that it was also about me.

WACHTEL In what way?

STEINEM When we write about our parents, it's not totally about our parents. It's about what we experienced and felt and our view of them and what our life was like with our parents. I'd protected myself, I think, in the intellectual process of writing it, and then it started to come home to me more. While she was alive, I was probably with-holding some part of myself so I wouldn't be overcome, so I could continue to function. But once she was gone, I allowed myself to real-ize the tragedy of her life, the loss of who she could have been. It was safe to realize it then, or safer. I think this happens a lot in different ways. I have several friends who were very badly abused—sexually—by a parent, and while the parent was alive, they either didn't remem-ber it at all or only remembered the reportorial details. Only after the parent was dead and they were safe could they fully realize and inter-nalize what had happened. Well, my situation was a little like that, although the danger I felt from my mother was only as someone who had to be taken care of, never her aggression or meanness. Only after that was gone, I think, did I get myself out of functioning mode, hav-ing to function and therefore withholding some feelings and realiza-tions in order to function.

WACHTEL As I mentioned earlier, you came to the women's move-ment in your mid-thirties, after attending an abortion speak-out in 1969. Until that time you preferred to call yourself a humanist, rather than a feminist. What changed?

STEINEM I came to understand what feminism really was. It's hard to get yourself back into that state of mind, but I think that I identified it with an admirable movement that wasn't mine—that is, women in the suburbs who were saying, "There must be more to life than this, I have a college degree, I have a right to be part of the workforce," which was the kind of "feminine mystique" beginnings of the movement. On the other hand, I had always been in the work force and was still having a tough time, so it didn't seem to relate to me. Also, I was usually the only woman in a group of male writers, so I was in that "only-Jew-in-the-club" place, which is not a good place to be because it requires some self-hatred. But it's a place a lot of us have been because you think that your only chance of getting anywhere is separating yourself from your group, and becoming part of the dominant group. People at New York magazine would say to me, "You write like a man," and I would say, "Oh, thank you." It's a state of mind. I guess I was trying, optimistically, to skip to humanism, which is to skip over the equalizing of power. I see women who still, understandably, want to do this: let's not talk about feminism, let's just talk about humanism. But if two groups that are unequal come together, they come together in a hierarchy. You have to individually raise up your group to the same level so you can come together at some time in the future. Humanism also has a completely different tradition, which has a little to do with women's equality but not a lot. Historically, it has more to do with believing in people instead of God. In the early seventies, I remember going to some big rally where I was supposed to speak, somewhere in Texas, and there were pickets outside with big signs saying that I was a humanist. I thought, How nice! Then I discovered that this was the beginning of the Moral Majority. For them, being a humanist was the worst thing, a very bad thing indeed. It meant you didn't believe in God.

WACHTEL What was your first act as a feminist, or with a feminist consciousness?

STEINEM I think there were lots of things that I did with a feminist consciousness, but not yet in an admitted way. It's the difference between your head and your heart again. Most of my good friends were women; I was a freelance writer in New York; I was part of a small underground of women writers because there were so few of us, and when a new one came to New York, I would give her the names of receptive editors and try to help her. These were all feminist acts. Or writing about the Playboy Club and discovering, even though my editors suggested that I write a funny, ascerbic piece, that I identified with the Bunnies and not with my editors. These were acts that weren't conscious, just a kind of inchoate will: not to be humiliated; not to see other women humiliated; to try to support other women where I could. But I didn't see it as political. I guess I saw women's position as inevitable, just something that we had to deal with. The realization that it was political came, for me, with going to that abortion hearing.

WACHTEL   And then putting your name on a public petition.

STEINEM   Yes, because I, too, had had an abortion when I was twenty-two, and had just left this country to go to London on the way to India. It was a very difficult experience. Not having the abortion, but trying to get the abortion was incredibly depressing, hair-raising, traumatic, all of those things. So, when I went to cover an abortion hearing here in the late sixties, and heard women telling the truth about having abortions, it was just cataclysmic for me. I had never shared this experience, certainly not in public and hardly at all even in private. It was the first time I had ever heard women talking about something that only happened to women, and taking it seriously. And so I began to think, Wait a minute, statistically one in three, or one in four, women at some time in their lives need an abortion. If that was true, why was it illegal, and why were we risking our lives and being sexually exploited and God knows what to get an illegal abortion? I started to question the fact that women's position was inevitable or immutable. I realized that it was political, just like the position of the races was political. It came from trying to control women's bodies as the means of reproduction, just like it came from trying to control certain races as a source of cheap labour.

WACHTEL   It's almost thirty years since you began publishing *Ms.* magazine, ensuring the use of the term *Ms.* and creating the only mass-circulation feminist magazine in America's history. The first issue sold out its run of three hundred thousand in a week or so—I remember going to buy it. When you look back at those early issues of *Ms.* magazine—the themes, the problems—what do you see?

STEINEM   I see themes that are really not different, but just at a point where the naming of the problem and the diagnosing of the problem was revolutionary in itself. Now we're considering remedies for the problems, although there are still things being named. The process is still going on. In a deep sense, the themes are not so different.

In that first issue, there was a piece called "Welfare Is a Woman's Issue." At that point, welfare was viewed as a racial issue. Somehow, it had escaped notice that just about everybody on welfare were women and kids, and more of them were white than black—although it was disproportionately mothers of colour. We're still fighting this battle. Now we're trying to get economic credit for caregiving, to attribute an economic value to caregiving, whether it is taking care of kids or invalids or AIDS patients or older parents, so that it has a value and can be deducted from your income tax. If you're too poor to pay income tax, you could get it as a refund, which would help to substitute for welfare. This is in the interest of such a wide spectrum of people that I think it's politically feasible. It would benefit anybody who is caretaking, whether they are middle-class or male or female. So there's an example of a theme that was being named in the first issue, and still continues in a more sophisticated, deep, complex way.

WACHTEL As co-founder and editor, you were closely involved with the magazine for seventeen years and you remain associated with it as a consulting editor and columnist. Apart from the fact that the magazine doesn't carry ads any more and has become a bimonthly, have any of the preoccupations changed?

STEINEM I think we've gone from naming to solving, or trying to solve. This is a great oversimplification, because all things have to go on at once, but, for instance, we've gone from rediscovering out-of-print dead women writers to publishing more and more new living talent. In the first issue there were unpublished works by Sylvia Plath and Virginia Woolf, which was wonderful, but now we're more likely to discover new unpublished authors. A huge outburst of creativity has been going on for a couple of decades now: women filmmakers and artists and rock bands and poets and poetry slams. That's a little journey in itself: from poets writing in their isolated and secret way, to young women with rings in their navels and purple hair standing up at poetry slams and just doing it. *Ms.* had a cover story just a couple of months ago about a woman who excels at poetry slams. So it's not as if it's totally different in terms of theme, but the forms that it takes are very different. I think it's important to say this for a different reason, which is that when we—golden oldies—look at younger women, we sometimes miss their feminist work in its full impact because we think it's going to come in the same form that ours did. We who benefited from consciousness-raising groups wonder where the young women are, but we're forgetting about Lilith Fair or the fact that Ani Di Franco's lyrics may have exactly the same intense meaning for many young women who hear them together in the audience—something we could only do in small groups in our living rooms. I also think it's easier to be humorous now because we're not fighting so hard against ridicule and to be taken seriously. In the beginning we also felt we had to put everything in every issue, because our critics said the magazine couldn't possibly last more than six months. Now the editors are a little more relaxed and realize that there's more room for humour and art and fun and sensuousness—and also that we have a right to all these experiences.

WACHTEL You mentioned earlier the historian Gerda Lerner's remark that real movements last a hundred years so that it's important to look at them in stages. So, what is—where is—feminism now?

STEINEM That's a hard question, because it's like describing the universe and giving two examples. It's wherever it is for the woman or man who's listening. But if you accumulate realities, you could say that in a way—and I hesitate to define; it's hard because you don't want to "define out" anyone—but I think that we've passed through the first big consciousness-raising stages on most kinds of themes, so that now we have a majority support for basic issues of equality. We've acquired a lot of tools—a lot of laws, a lot of experience, a critical mass of women in areas where women never were before—but we're still very far from completing even the old goals. Equal pay, of course, is the simplest one, but we're only closer to it, we haven't achieved it. Now we need to redefine work so that raising children is perceived as honourable and economically valuable work, whether done by women or by men. Because we were so occupied with trying to raise our daughters more like our sons, we are only now seeing how much we need to raise our sons more like our daughters—so that both males and females can be whole people. We did fight pretty successfully for the realization that women can do what men can do, but we're not far along with the idea that men can do what women can do.

WACHTEL Or want to do what women do.

STEINEM Well, if you want to have children, you have to be willing to spend some of your life taking care of them, whether you're a man or a woman. Most men are deprived of the experience of being close to their own children.

WACHTEL So when you say that the consciousness-raising stage is mostly accomplished, even if not all the goals have been—and goals come and go or get taken away and have to be fought over again—why do you think so many women are reluctant to call themselves feminists?

STEINEM One thing I should have mentioned in talking about the stage we're in is the very well-organized backlash against feminism, also against the civil-rights movement, the environmental movement, the gay and lesbian movement and all the social-justice movements. That backlash, which has been with us for fifteen or twenty years, has demonized many things: the word *liberal*, the word *feminist*, the phrase *affirmative action*. There's this crazy notion that feminism means man-hating. In the United States, more women self-identify as feminist than as Republican, but people don't compare it to that. The critics say, "If it isn't 100 percent or 80 percent of all women, then you've failed." I think the question is, "Compared to what?" The reality is that if you call yourself a feminist, you're talking not just about equal treatment for yourself but for all females of every race and group—and that is a very broad and deep revolution. I've always thought that we as women have two choices—either we're feminists or masochists, either we're full human beings or we're not. But in the short term, I can see that many women think there's punishment around the corner if they call themselves feminists, that it means they're going to be deprived of male companionship, or that it means you're anti-sex—which is so ironic because in the sixties and seventies, it used to mean that you were too pro-sex. It's all about keeping women from calling themselves feminists, and so from identifying with each other and acting together.

WACHTEL Certainly feminist politics has as many factions as any other movement or political activity, but is the concept of sisterhood still meaningful?

STEINEM Yes, I think it is. I think there's a much better understanding now that sisterhood must be defined by everyone within it, that white women or women with access to the media or writing can't be the only voices. But the fundamental experience of being a female human being in a male-dominant society includes some shared experience—in trying to be safe, in controlling your own reproductive life, your own life, period. So in the broad sense there is a sisterhood. It's just that it is now more diversely defined.

WACHTEL Is there a Third Wave of feminism?

STEINEM There is a self-named Third Wave, which I know annoys historians because the First Wave lasted more than a hundred years, and the Second Wave will, too—we're still in it, with probably seventy years to go. But people should have the right to name themselves, so these young women call themselves the Third Wave, and that's OK.

WACHTEL What shape does it take?

STEINEM The first shape that I saw was a group of mostly young female feminists, but male feminists too, who got together—a very diverse group, racially and ethnically—to help their constituency of young people and other "underserved communities," like poor communities, to register and vote. The United States makes it harder to do that than any democracy in the world. So they got on buses and went back and forth across the length of this country registering voters. That organization called the Third Wave has spread into many other activities. They have a foundation. They fund young women who are unable to pay for abortions; they give grants; they have a networking project in which they go out to many different communities around the country to see what is going on, and to identify groups that should be supported. All kinds of things. That's just one of dozens, maybe hundreds, of groups of young feminists.

WACHTEL Despite various setbacks, and no doubt feeling like you've had to reinvent the wheel, you've managed to stay very politically engaged. Is that hard?

STEINEM Yes, but it's harder not to. For instance, just by accident, I was speaking the morning after the last U.S. presidential election at Palm Beach County Community College. There were about nine hundred people at this lecture. The press hadn't figured out exactly what was happening yet. People started standing up and saying what they had experienced when they tried to vote and were either turned away completely, or ended up unable to vote for the candidate of their choice. People would tell their stories, and then six other people would say, "Oh, that happened to me, too!" Now, in that situation, who could resist passing around a sheet of yellow paper and writing down names and addresses so they can be reported to the proper place? That little act has ended up with me trying to help people testify before the Civil Rights Commission. Just yesterday, the report of the Civil Rights Commission, which was investigating the situation in Florida, was leaked by its right-wing members, who then said it was leaked by the other side. There's a war going on to try to disqualify the report, so that the— fraudulent at worst and inefficient at best—nature of the election won't be documented, so there won't be Congressional hearings. The act of giving a lecture leads to irresistible activities.

WACHTEL And you've been finding them irresistible for thirty years.

STEINEM Well, it's true, because if I don't do it, I always think: If I'd said this or done that, would it have made a difference?

WACHTEL I was surprised to read that initially you could barely speak in public.

STEINEM Yes, I was a true disaster.

WACHTEL How did you overcome that fear?

STEINEM Well, I've never fully overcome it. Depending on the degree of importance of the occasion, or opposition in the audience, or both, I still get nervous and my voice gets shaky—at least it's shaky to me, I don't know if other people can tell. My mouth gets dry. Each tooth seems to acquire a little sweater that I can't get my upper lip over. I sometimes think that if I were left to myself, I wouldn't continue speaking in public, but the truth is, after thirty years, I have come to realize that writing is no substitute for speaking, just like speaking is no substitute for writing. Something happens in a room when you're all together that just can't happen on the printed page. So I have come to value it very much and even sometimes to enjoy it—but it's still not natural to me.

WACHTEL What are the costs, if not the glories, of a public life?

STEINEM The most difficult one for me is that there come to be images of you out there that are actually independent of you—images with your name attached that can acquire more reality for other people than who you actually are. That's pretty upsetting. But I guess there's no way around it. If you play one game of Telephone, you realize how much a simple sentence can change in one room by going through twenty people. So any public act or statement is, as someone said, a joint project of the observer and the observed. It's not just what you do as a public person, but the whole life experience of the person who's observing you.

WACHTEL What kinds of images in particular?

STEINEM You can't exactly know, but about once every week or so, I'm confronted with a person who says some version of, "You're not as bad as everybody says." I think what they mean is that—and I feel this too sometimes about other women—if you are being a non-traditional person, refusing to play the usual role, then people think you must be aggressive, or tough, or humourless. I remember meeting Clare Boothe Luce, and there was this gentle little woman. I disagreed with her politically, but nonetheless she was very different from the person I imagined. Since there is no proper way for a female person to come to power—since we are still not convinced a female person should *have* power—then you can be criticized and resisted for almost any reason, even quite opposite qualities. I learned that from campaigning in Connecticut for a woman named Gloria Schaeffer, who was running for a statewide office. She was very gentle and ladylike and calm, and everybody said she would not be effective in politics because of those things. And then I would come back to New York and campaign for Bella

Abzug, who was running for the U.S. Senate, and everybody would say, "Oh, she's too aggressive and strong, and would not be effective in politics because of those things." Finally, I had to realize there was no right way to be—and that in itself is freeing. Then you think, Well, if there's no right way, then I might as well just be myself.

But it can be upsetting to be presented with a whole set of responses to something you didn't do. Here's a little example: Everywhere, even in books of quotations, I see, "A woman without a man is like a fish without a bicycle" as a quote attributed to me. I think it's funny, but I didn't coin that. A woman in Australia named Irina Dunn, a philosophy student, said that. She was reading a philosopher who said, "Man without God is like a fish without a bicycle," and so she adapted it and it's been out there ever since. I'm sure that I'll never overcome the impression that I coined that, which is also not fair to the woman who did.

WACHTEL I was thinking in terms of the images being out there. Is there even a burden in being beautiful?

STEINEM I think what all women tend to share is having our appearance be more a part of our identity than we would if we were male, and that's what we need to work on together. If you look the way society prescribes for women and you accomplish something, then you got there through men because of your looks; if you don't look the way society thinks you should and you do something, you got there because you couldn't get a man. It's disheartening either way. My version of it is disheartening because I sometimes feel that no matter how hard I work and how old I get, what I accomplish will be attributed to my appearance—and that's a bad feeling. It takes your heart out. I'm sixty-seven years old; I thought this would go away.

WACHTEL You've famously described life after fifty or sixty as "another country," and you were saying that age hasn't made you mellow. You speak of rage; in fact, you say you've become more radical with age. Do you still think so?

STEINEM Yes, I do. And I think this is a frequent experience for women, because most of us tend to reverse what is seen as the normal pattern—the male pattern—which is to be rebellious in youth and get more conservative with age. Women tend to be conservative in youth and get more rebellious with age. I've certainly found that to be true.

WACHTEL And they become more rebellious with age because—?

STEINEM Because you experience more of the problems. You won't be told you won't be hired because you're a woman any more, but twelve or fifteen years into it you still hit the glass ceiling or the sticky floor of the pink-collar ghetto and you begin to see men go past you. So that's radicalizing. Now you can make an equal marriage, which has taken thirty years of hard work in changing the laws, but when children are born, it gets unequal all over again. So a lot of the things that radicalize women happen as we get older—not to mention age itself, which is still a greater penalty for women than men.

WACHTEL But how do you think *you* are more radical with age?

STEINEM I don't think I used to see the real depth of what was wrong. I saw it on the surface, and I thought, Well, this is unjust, clearly, so if we just tell people about it, they'll want to fix it. Of course this is not true, because a lot of people are profiting from that injustice. It also goes much deeper than that. In the beginning, a lot of us didn't see the degree to which we had internalized our low estimation of women; that is, the degree of self-hatred and mutual low esteem that we needed to excise from ourselves. Nor did I quite see how political child-rearing was, and how much that needed to be done by men equally with women. I think what has helped me to become more radical is seeing the alternatives: looking at ancient, indigenous societies, the remnants of the oldest cultures on earth, whether it's native North American societies or the San or the Pygmy societies in Africa. I've been lucky enough to know more about these cultures, although just a tiny bit compared to what there is to know. You see what could be. If it was once like that for 95 percent of human history, it could be again. We don't want to and can't go backward, but we need to understand that hierarchy, nationalism, racism, sexual-caste systems didn't always exist. It gives you greater hope for the future. You also get more angry because you discover more things that actually were known and nobody told us. For instance, the whole state of Florida was governed for something like thirty years by Native Americans and freed or runaway slaves who fought off the government. Nobody ever told me that. Nobody ever told me that Mozart had an older sister named Nannerl, who, he said, was the talented one. This is the history that we now study, that we are only just learning and is exciting to learn, but it's infuriating not to have learned earlier.

WACHTEL It's very rare that we can actually identify people who've been instrumental in changing society, changing the face of society, the way that you have. I know you're going to say you didn't do it alone, but what do you feel is your greatest achievement?

STEINEM My greatest satisfaction is listening to people tell me how their lives have changed. We were discussing the downside of being a publicly identified person, but there is a great upside. Because I'm recognizable, people come and tell me things that really are intended for the entire movement, but I get the benefit of hearing the story because they know who I am. In terms of greatest accomplishment, I'm just not sure. I guess being a long-distance runner through the Second Wave, but I don't know what to attribute that to. It didn't feel like there was a choice. On the other hand, I do see a lot of people who did valuable things and then got broken or defeated by life and retreated. I feel both lucky and proud to have been able to continue.

WACHTEL I have to ask you this, because for the longest time you didn't feel that marriage was for you. In fact, you mentioned that when you graduated from college you went to India to avoid it. You got married in the fall of 2000, at age sixty-six, for the first time. What changed your mind?

STEINEM First of all, the marriage that wasn't for me is no longer the only form of marriage. If I had married when I was supposed to, I would have lost many, if not most, of my civil rights. I wouldn't have been able to use my own name, get a bank loan, have my own legal residence or credit. Marriage was originally designed for a person and a half, in Blackstone's common law, which both of our countries inherited. It's taken thirty years to change that. Not that I always thought about it in those terms; that's only part of it, because I also didn't feel as if I was formed enough to know who I wanted to spend the rest of my life with, nor did I think that marriage was the only way to live. It just didn't seem desirable or possible before. Personally, I also think what helped to prepare me for this change is that, for ten or more years, I was not in a relationship with a man, and was completely happy. I think we have to learn to be on our own before we can be together, to say no before we can say yes. Still, if you'd asked me last year at this time, I would have said, "Oh, I don't want to do that—that's just not possible. I support other people marrying, especially gay and lesbian people being able to marry, but it's not for me." But we met each other, David and I, and both of us seemed to have come out at the same place from different lives. I had been doing what I wasn't supposed to do as a woman, and he was definitely doing what he shouldn't do as a man, which was raising his three kids. We discovered we cared about the same things. We spent one entire month together, every minute, which neither of us had ever done before, even though we'd had very important relationships in our lives. Marriage seemed a way to be responsible for each other.

WACHTEL Yes, you mentioned that in the article in Ms. about the wedding. What does "being responsible" mean?

STEINEM It means that we're saying, "OK, no matter what happens, I'm in your corner. If a bad thing happens to you, I'm going to be there, and if you're in the hospital and you can't decide your medical treatment, I'll be there." It's a declaration of chosen family, which at some other stage of life we might have done in a different way. Maybe we would have bought a house together, but as it is, we each have a place to live and we live in both of them together. Or we might have had a child together, but at this point in our lives, this just seemed to make sense. Also, we were on our way to Oklahoma to the Cherokee National Reunion. David has friends who'd been married in an indigenous ceremony in South Africa, which is much more egalitarian, and so was the Cherokee ceremony. So it was a sort of harmonic convergence of us, the time, the ability to do this, the equality of the laws. We also wanted to recognize that these laws, although they're equal now, are not available to two women or two men, so we decided to refer to each other as partners, which seemed more universal, rather than husband and wife.

WACHTEL And politically correct, as we used to say in the old country.

STEINEM Well, maybe, in the sense that the opposite is politically incorrect.

WACHTEL So feminism has made marriage a more viable choice for independent women.

STEINEM I always said that would be the case. In the late sixties, people would tell me that feminism was the cause of divorce, and I would say, "No, unequal marriage is the cause of divorce." Feminism may make love possible for the first time. What looks like love from a little distance is often not love at all—it's dependence, or lack of choice. So love, in the sense of an equal, chosen, mutually pleasurable relationship, is made possible by feminism.

June 2001

JARED DIAMOND

A few years ago, when Jared Diamond won the Pulitzer Prize for Non-Fiction for his ambitious analysis of the past thirteen thousand years, *Guns, Germs and Steel: The Fates of Human Societies* (1997), I couldn't put my finger on exactly what he was. I assumed he was some kind of evolutionary biologist. Then I read that he teaches physiology at the UCLA School of Medicine, with a specialty in membranes. At the same time, he's an expert in bird ecology, studying bird fauna in New Guinea and other southwest Pacific islands. These are two completely unrelated fields, and only indirectly connected to his award-winning books—not only *Guns, Germs and Steel*, but also his earlier *The Third Chimpanzee: The Evolution and Future of the Human Animal* (1992). Diamond is also the recipient of the MacArthur "genius" award—a multiyear fellowship, no strings, to encourage innovative work.

Then I realized I wasn't alone. Anthropologist Mark Ridley describes Jared Diamond as a polymath, with a reputation for producing top-quality research papers at such a rate that "some suspect he is really a committee" [TLS]. Another critic termed *Guns,*

223

Germs and Steel an "epochal work. Diamond has written a summary of human history that can be accounted . . . as Darwinian in its authority" [Thomas Disch, *New Leader*]. When Diamond recently gave a lecture sponsored by the Harvard Museum of Natural History, he drew a crowd of almost a thousand people who gave his talk a standing ovation.

Jared Diamond was born in Boston in 1937. His father, a professor of pediatrics at Harvard, was famous for establishing the postwar blood bank program of the American Red Cross and for pioneering the use of transfusions for infants with blood incompatible with their mothers'. He died at the age of ninety-seven. Diamond's mother was a teacher, concert pianist and something of a language enthusiast. Diamond studied Latin and Greek at school; his mother then helped him learn German, and he later learned to read or speak Russian, French, Spanish, Finnish, Dutch, Italian, Neo-Melanesian and the New Guinea dialect Fore.

After Harvard and Cambridge, Jared Diamond began his career as a physiologist and then pursued a second career in bird ecology. For the last ten years or so—since *The Third Chimpanzee*—he's also been a popularizer in the best sense of the word, eager to reach a general audience. Hence the title of his 1997 book, *Why Is Sex Fun? The Evolution of Human Sexuality*. In his Pulitzer Prize–winning work, *Guns, Germs and Steel*, Diamond tackles the question why—as he put it—"Eurasians, especially peoples of Europe and eastern Asia, have spread around the globe, to dominate the modern world in wealth and power. . . . Why weren't Native Americans, Africans, and Aboriginal Australians the ones who conquered or exterminated Europeans and Asians?" Or, as the *Economist* irreverently headlined, "Geographical Determinism, [or] How white folks came to rule the world."

Diamond says that this problem has fascinated him for a long time, but it's only recently, through new advances in molecular biology, plant and animal genetics, biogeography, archaeology and linguistics, that he's able to attempt a new synthesis. And by finding his answers in geography and food production, Diamond is keen to dispel racist conclusions by pointing to "differences among continental environments, and not to biological differences among peoples themselves." Jared Diamond brings his knowledge of natural science to the questions of human history.

WACHTEL *Guns, Germs and Steel* is a wide-ranging look at the growth of human societies over the past thirteen thousand years. You draw from your knowledge of many disciplines—history, geography, evolutionary biology, anthropology, physiology—and you credit your parents with shaping your broad view of the world. How did your mother and father teach you to think outside one discipline?

DIAMOND It's not that they taught me explicitly. My mother had been a schoolteacher, but she was also an accomplished linguist and a concert pianist. My father was a physician. I had the good fortune to go to a small, excellent school in Boston, Massachusetts, where we had to take Latin for six years and were offered Greek for three years and had very good courses in history, all of which I loved. So I started out interested in many things, and I've been able to keep up my interest.

WACHTEL When you attended the Roxbury Latin School in Boston, what did you think that you might do later?

DIAMOND It was very simple, because my father was a physician. During my childhood, whenever people asked me what I wanted to do when I grew up, the answer was always that I wanted to be a doctor like my father. It wasn't until the spring of my senior year in college that I realized I wanted to do scientific research rather than become a doctor. And so at the last minute I changed course and decided not to go to medical school but instead to get a PhD.

WACHTEL But even though you had ambitions to be a doctor, there you were studying Latin and Greek and other languages. I understand your mother helped you learn German.

DIAMOND That's true. I figured I would be doing science for the rest of my life, and since I really loved languages and music and history, I decided to study history and classics and all the other stuff I was interested in. So I minimized my exposure to science, not only in school but also in university.

WACHTEL Your mother was a concert pianist and you're an accomplished musician yourself. Did you ever have to choose between science and music?

DIAMOND Yes, in a way. I was already sure that I wanted to be a scientist, but after I got my PhD in physiology in England and returned to the United States, the horrible realization that a scientist is expected to spend all his or her life working in one field gradually dawned on me. My field then was membrane physiology, which I enjoyed, but the idea of doing nothing except membrane physiology for the next forty-five years was horrible. So I looked around for a second career, and what I first considered was music because I loved Bach and I loved playing the organ. I also explored conducting and composing, but it turned out that I simply didn't have the talent, so I gave that up and remained an amateur musician, and instead went on into other areas of science and history.

WACHTEL You've also had a lifelong interest in birds. How did that develop?

DIAMOND That was simple. When I was seven years old, I looked out the window of our house in Boston and saw on the lawn an English sparrow, the most common rubbish bird in the United States. There was a bird book around, and I looked it up and decided that it was a chipping sparrow—which was absolutely wrong—but that first bird got me interested in birds, and I fortunately had third-grade and fifth-grade schoolteachers who were birdwatchers and got me hooked on birds. In the early 1960s, I began to study birds professionally in New Guinea, and I've been returning there ever since.

WACHTEL What fascinates you about birds and bird behaviour?

DIAMOND Lots of us are fascinated by birds because, for one thing, they can be identified. There are eight thousand species of them, and for those of us who like pigeonholing, birds can be pigeonholed. They're pretty. They sing and they can be recognized by sight. They're not like rats or bacteria, which distinguish each other by smell, a sense that we humans are hopeless at. Instead, birds recognize each other in the same way that we recognize each other, by sight and sound. Birds are the best understood of all animals, so in fact much of what we know about behaviour and evolutionary biology and biogeography has been learned from birds. And then, finally, there's New Guinea, where I study birds. New Guinea, I would say, is the most fascinating, wonderful place in the world. It has the world's most spectacular birds—birds of paradise—and a thousand tribes who speak different languages and were using stone tools until recently. So New Guinea is just a marvellous place to work.

WACHTEL You make a connection between a bird found in Australia and New Guinea, the bowerbird, and the animal origins of art. The male bowerbird creates an amazingly elaborate and decorative bower in order to entice a female to mate with him—but do you really think that human art has its roots in animal or bird behaviour?

DIAMOND Well, I would say that this is one root of human art. Humans do many complicated things that in the past had biological origins and today have gone far beyond their biological origins. But the fact is that male bowerbirds decorate their bowers in a complicated way. They choose objects of specific colours, depending upon the species. One species likes blue, another likes the combination of red and green, and they place the colours in particular places in order to seduce females. But God help the male that chooses the wrong colour, because he doesn't get any females. It's well known, of course, that there are human artists and musicians who exploit their talents to appeal to women or to men, but no one could say that the only function of human art is to seduce the opposite sex. We've gone far beyond that, but I wouldn't be surprised if, a million years ago, social reasons, including sexual reasons, were an element in the origins of human art, just as with bowerbirds.

WACHTEL You've said recently that emotionally you spend half your time in New Guinea. I understand it's a really attractive place in terms of birds and languages, but what does that mean for you?

DIAMOND Once you've been in New Guinea—in a New Guinea jungle—the rest of the world is just boring by comparison. There are all these birds, hundreds of bird species, most of which you hear and don't see. The jungle is a beautiful place. Initially, it's perhaps a dangerous, uncomfortable place, but once you get to know it, it's very safe. And there are wonderful people, really smart New Guineans who are walking encyclopedias of information about birds. They're in-your-face people who tell you what's on their mind, and if they don't like something, they get angry. They're also very different from each other. One-sixth of the world's languages are spoken in New Guinea—a thousand different languages. New Guinea is what most of the world was like before states and kingdoms started evolving; they didn't evolve in New Guinea. So New Guinea is a window into our past and it's just gorgeous.

WACHTEL Your time in New Guinea also stimulated some fresh ideas about language. The New Guineans speak a kind of lingua franca variation of English called Neo-Melanesian. You looked at other "creole" languages and discovered that the same grammatical features kept recurring. Why do you think this points to a link between animal communication and human language?

DIAMOND What I think it points to is a genetic background to human language. All animals have systems of communication based on songs, in the case of birds, or displays or smells. Proto-humans had their own systems of communication, as do modern chimpanzees and gorillas, involving gruntings and displays. With humans, the reason to suspect that there's a genetic basis for human language is that all humans have language. It's not the case that some humans have spoken language and some don't. We observe that when humans are forced to invent a language for themselves, all these independently invented languages are syntactically rather similar. These so-called creole languages—trade languages, plantation languages—arose independently all around the world, including in the U.S. South in the last century, where plantation languages arose spontaneously to let people of different backgrounds—Africans of different tribes—communicate with each other and with the plantation owners. All of these so-called creole languages are rather similar in their grammar. They have stripped-down prepositions, they lack most tenses, they lack plurals, but they do some very interesting, consistent things with their few prepositions and tenses, suggesting that all of these creole languages arise out of our hard-wired genetic programming.

WACHTEL So this connects to the Chomskian language revolution which posits that everyone is genetically hard-wired for language, regardless of which language they speak.

DIAMOND There's something of that. I would agree—and I think most linguists would agree—that there is a genetic basis to human language. What people argue about is the details, whether it's in particular cells in our brain, whether we have a gene for prepositions. But that there's some genetic basis for language I think is clear.

WACHTEL And does this genetic basis mean necessarily that there's a connection to animal languages or to evolution?

DIAMOND There's undoubtedly an evolutionary basis to language. Humans are not the first of the three million species now alive that communicate by voice. Vervet monkeys, for example, have a proto-language that has at least nine different words. Vervet monkeys have different grunts: there's a grunt that means "leopard" and a different grunt that means "snake" and another grunt that means "eagle" and one that means "strange monkey." What vervets lack is grammar. The only thing I would say that's unique about human language is grammar, the ability to combine words in particular ways to generate new meanings. Monkeys don't have that. Chimpanzees don't have it.

WACHTEL *Guns, Germs and Steel* was inspired by a conversation you had back in 1972 with a New Guinea politician named Yali. How did that conversation unfold?

DIAMOND When I went out to New Guinea in 1964, I was really naive. I knew that New Guineans had stone tools, not metal tools, that they were so-called primitive people. I was naive enough to think that they used stone tools because there was something primitive about their brains. But it took me literally half a day to discover that these were really smart people. So why is it that they ended up with stone tools while I, the dope who still can't find his way in the jungle or light a fire in the rain, came in there with steel tools and writing? This question was in the back of my mind, but in 1972, when I happened to be walking along the beach of an island in New Guinea, birdwatching, a local politician who was visiting there caught up with me and began asking me about this and that. We had a long conversation. Eventually, this politician, whose name was Yali, started asking me about the origins of New Guineans and the origin of the volcano on that particular island, and finally he turned to me and said, "Why is it that you white people came here with lots of cargo"—meaning material possessions—"while we black people didn't have any?" This was surely the most obvious question about the difference between New Guineans and Europeans. And yet, although it was the obvious question, I didn't have an intelligent answer to give him. I babbled something, but as soon as it came out of my mouth, I knew it was wrong. Yali's question kept coming back in my mind. Why these differences among the world's people, why these differences among Native Americans and Africans and Eurasians and Aboriginal Australians in the technology and writing and political systems that they evolved?

WACHTEL Why weren't they the ones who enslaved or exterminated the Europeans, rather than the other way around?

DIAMOND Exactly. Here I am, sitting in Los Angeles on land that five hundred years ago was populated entirely by Native Americans. Not a single European here. And if some visitor from outer space had come to the world ten thousand years ago and had been asked to predict whether now in Los Angeles there would be Europeans and Africans or whether now in Europe there would be Aboriginal Australians and Native Americans, with the last Europeans either exterminated or living on reservations somewhere up in the Pyrenees and Alps, the visitor from outer space might have been hard pressed to predict. So that really is the biggest question of human history in the last thirteen thousand years. Why is it that Eurasians rather than Aboriginal Australians or Africans ended up expanding around the world?

WACHTEL What kind of answers to Yali's question.did you hear from other scientists?

DIAMOND Most scientists at that time, and many scientists today, would say something like this—and I run into this all the time—educated people regularly say, when asked why is it that Europeans expanded to the New World and to Africa rather than Africans conquering Europe, that, "Well, um, uh, you know, I hate to say this, this isn't politically correct—is anybody listening?—but all right, let's face it, it's because Europeans are just smarter than those other people and, besides, those other people don't have the work ethic and the Judeo-Christian tradition and all that other stuff." This is the usual answer, the racist answer, even though there's not the slightest bit of evidence for any European genetic superiority. In fact, there's some evidence against it. But people fall back on this racist interpretation because differences among peoples are the most obvious fact of history and we've got to explain it to ourselves somehow. We see that people have different faces and hair colour, and so we assume that behind these faces and this hair lie different brains, although there's no evidence for it.

WACHTEL You're saying that ultimately the environment shaped the development of different civilizations, and this refutes explanations of biological difference among races. Are all other explanations inherently racist?

DIAMOND There are other explanations that invoke environmental differences and are not racist, but they are nevertheless incorrect. For example, some people will argue that the reason Europeans expanded over the world is that the cold climates of northern Europe forced them to be inventive—to invent housing, to invent clothing and other things. That's a possible explanation, but it proves to be wrong because all the significant inventions of the last thirteen thousand years were not made in Europe, least of all northern Europe, but in the eastern Mediterranean, in warmer climes. That's where agriculture began, that's where working with metal, writing and state political systems were invented and later spread to southern Europe. So, in fact, cold northern Europe was the embarrassing backwater of Eurasia until a thousand years ago.

WACHTEL Why do you think the concept of geography as a shaping force of societies fell out of favour among scientists for such a long time?

DIAMOND That's an interesting question. It fell out of favour in the late 1940s and early 1950s for a number of reasons. One reason is that people attempted to explain the course of world history in the early 1900s by invoking geography, but we simply didn't know enough then. That somewhat discredited geographic explanations, but shouldn't have. People attempted to explain the positions of the continents by invoking continental drift in the 1920s, and those efforts failed, but we didn't know enough about continental movements in the 1920s. Another part of this—and I think a big part—is that understanding the effects of geography involves knowing specific things about science. The effects of geography are mediated by differences between plant species and animal species in their genetics and chromosomes and behaviour and hybridization. Understanding the effects of geography involves understanding things about languages and archaeology, so scientific knowledge is required. But historians, for the most part, are not trained in the techniques, or methods, of the sciences. Finally, there's a feeling on the part of humanists that to acknowledge geographic influences is to deny the human spirit, to deny free will. Humans would rather believe that we can do anything and that the environment has no effect. That's palpably nonsense. Of course the environment has some effect. The problem is just to figure out what the effects are. These are the reasons for this unfortunately ignorant prejudice against the importance of geography.

WACHTEL One of the things that you state right at the outset is that you think New Guineans, if anything, may be *more* intelligent than Europeans, in spite of their primitive technologies. Why is that?

DIAMOND That is simply my experience, my perception of them. I have to say that, of all the sentences in my book *Guns, Germs and Steel*, the sentence that gets Americans, Europeans and Japanese angriest is my suggesting that New Guineans might be smarter than all of them. It's perfectly OK to sit down and have lengthy, dispassionate discussions as to whether Africans are genetically inferior to Europeans, but to suggest that New Guineans might be superior to Europeans—that's off limits. It simply strikes me, talking to New Guineans, that on average—there are big variations, but on average—New Guineans are more alert, more curious, quicker to learn, more talkative and more inquisitive than the average American or European or Japanese. New Guineans may have some slight genetic advantage because of natural selection in New Guinea. In New Guinea only the smarter people survive. Whereas in the last eight thousand years in agricultural areas of Eurasia, the people who survived were not those who were necessarily smarter but were instead those who had resistance to infectious diseases. Or is it just that New Guineans grow up not watching television and playing computer games, so there's a lot more stimulation in childhood? Maybe New Guineans don't have any genetic advantage. They obviously have an enormous developmental advantage over most American and Japanese and European children, but I can't prove that New Guineans are, on average, slightly smarter than Americans. All I can say is they come across a little smarter on the average.

WACHTEL In terms of addressing your question "Why did Europeans and Asians always triumph in their historical conquests of other populations?", some continents were inhabited by humans long before others. Why didn't the head start of Africans, for example, result in a society that would dominate a latecomer like Europe?

DIAMOND Africa is the continent where humans evolved. People have been in Africa for six million years, and it wasn't until about two million years ago that humans expanded out of Africa to Asia and Europe. So if a head start means anything, Africans had an enormous advantage. The explanation for Africans not profiting by this head start is that, as of thirteen thousand years ago, there was a level playing field. By this I mean that Africans had expanded out of Africa to Europe and Asia, and everybody throughout the world lived in a hunter-gatherer society with roughly similar levels of social complexity and technology. In short, there was a new ball game, as we would say. What gave the advantage in the new ball game was that in some parts of the world there were wild plant and animal species lending themselves to domestication. Only a few wild plants and animals can be domesticated to form crops and livestock. Those parts of the world where there were wild sheep, goats, cows and pigs, and wheat, barley and rice, are the areas that got a head start on agriculture. And having got a head start on agriculture, they then got a head start on the population explosion, on technology, including military technology, on developing writing and state systems. So those parts of the world where agriculture arose ten thousand years ago, where there was wild wheat and sheep and so on, ended up with the populations that expanded and conquered other peoples.

WACHTEL   And you've fixed the date at around thirteen thousand years ago because that's the end of the last ice age. Is that what created the level playing field?

DIAMOND   That's correct. Until the end of the last ice age, thirteen thousand years ago, everybody everywhere in the world was a hunter-gatherer. In fact, the first people that one would call farmers, settling down and getting a major part of their nutrition from crops and domestic animals instead of wild plants and animals, began about 8500 BC in the Fertile Crescent, that area of the eastern Mediterranean that runs through modern Iraq and Iran, Turkey, Syria, Lebanon and Jordan. Around the same time, or pretty soon thereafter, farming began in China and then it began in, of course, my beloved New Guinea and in the southeastern United States, Mexico, the Andes, the Sahel region of Africa, in Ethiopia and tropical West Africa. But those are the only nine places in the world—nine rather small places—where farming arose. From those nine homelands of agriculture, the practice spread out everywhere in the world. So, for example, here I'm sitting in California, which is the most fertile land in the United States, the centre of American farmland, but agriculture never arose spontaneously in California, nor did agriculture ever arise spontaneously in Saskatchewan or Alberta or Manitoba, the wheat belt of Canada, simply because there were not the wild species—wild wheats, wild sheep and goats—that could be domesticated there.

WACHTEL It had to wait for a European conquest to bring it over.

DIAMOND That's right. Once the grains and livestock arrived with the Europeans, it became obvious that the Canadian plains were great for growing wheat and California was great for growing avocados and tomatoes. But they had to be brought in from the outside.

WACHTEL Your book *Guns, Germs and Steel* shows how Eurasia developed most quickly and created the richest and most technologically advanced society. How do you define Eurasia?

DIAMOND I define Eurasia as the whole continent of what we consider Europe and Asia.

WACHTEL Does that definition embrace too much? For instance, do you think of India and Indonesia as part of Asia? Because in large measure they were colonized, rather than the other way around.

DIAMOND Yes and no. Once one says that the populations of the Eurasian continent had an advantage, then, as you say, one has another question. Why, within the Eurasian continent, was it Europeans rather than the people of the Fertile Crescent or the Chinese or the people of the Indian subcontinent who expanded over the world? That's a very challenging question because, again, Europeans were the backwater of Eurasian civilization until about AD 1000. Why is it that the people of the Fertile Crescent, who invented agriculture and writing and the alphabet, among other things, didn't parlay their head start? Or the Chinese, for that matter, who led the world in technology and almost everything else of significance until about the year 1400 or 1430? Why was it Europeans, rather than these advanced societies, who spread over the world? That's a separate question.

WACHTEL And how do you answer that?

DIAMOND Briefly, it's that there are geographic factors. The Fertile Crescent, for example, while it had natural advantages of wild plant and animal species that could be domesticated, lost its head start because it had the disadvantage of environmental fragility—dry lands that rather

quickly became deforested and salinized. The Fertile Crescent committed ecological suicide, and today the term Fertile Crescent is a bad joke.
Iraq used to lead the world in agriculture; today it is one of the most
unproductive areas of the world in agriculture because it's just such
fragile land. China had the geographic disadvantage of being just too
easily unified, unlike Europe, which is divided by mountain ranges and
rivers and peninsulas and islands. China is not geographically divided,
and so China was unified in 221 BC and has been unified most of the
time since. Europe has never been unified. Europeans are still struggling to unify Europe and they can't bring it off. Unity, you might think,
is an advantage, but it can also be a disadvantage because a dictator with
bad ideas can ruin things over a large area. That's what happened in
China in the 1400s, and it's what happened in China thirty years ago
when a few unwise people at the head of the educational system basically shut down the education system for one billion Chinese. In
Europe, because it's disunified, no one idiot can do things that have
consequences for all of Europe.

WACHTEL What about the fact that India, Indonesia and the Philippines, which were part of that original Eurasia, were themselves colonized and didn't eventually take over the world? They ended up being on
the losing side of the ledger.

DIAMOND The Indian subcontinent had technological and other
advantages over Europe fifteen hundred years ago. Friends of mine in
India tell me that a key feature that held things back was the development of a rigid caste system, which meant that people within a caste
married and communicated with each other but not between castes.
That impeded technological development because, for example, the
metalworkers were not in the same caste and therefore not in communication with the politicians. But why did the caste system develop in India
and not elsewhere? I can guess at geographic reasons behind that—the
environmental diversity, the biogeographic diversity of the Indian subcontinent—but that's another book. As for Indonesia and the Philippines, as tropical countries they have disadvantages compared to

temperate countries. Tropical countries have big public health problems. Germs live there all year round. The best public health measure is a cold winter that kills off germs. So tropical countries everywhere have crippling public health problems compared to temperate zone countries. But tropical countries also have less productive agriculture. Those are the two main reasons—public health and lower agricultural productivity—why all tropical countries have been disadvantaged. But it's also instructive, because in the last thirty years, those tropical countries that targeted this disadvantage and have invested in public health—Taiwan, Hong Kong, Mauritius, Malaysia, Singapore—have solved their problems and have become rich, the so-called tigers of Asia.

WACHTEL It's interesting because germs, in a sense, ended up being a hidden weapon of conquest.

DIAMOND That's right. Germs are a two-edged sword. Those nasty germs of infectious diseases evolved in Eurasia: smallpox, measles, tuberculosis, flu, et cetera. One has to ask why is it that Europeans brought all these nasty germs that wiped out most Native Americans, but Native Americans did not have nasty germs to give back to the Europeans. We've learned, within the last twenty years, thanks to studies of DNA and molecular biology, that these infectious diseases of humans came to us from the infectious diseases of our domestic animals. But most domestic animals were in Eurasia, not in the New World. So Eurasians evolved nasty diseases like smallpox and got infected by them, but simultaneously evolved both genetic and antibody immunity to these same diseases. That's why I refer to these diseases as a two-edged sword. When Eurasians arrived in the New World with smallpox and measles, most of the Eurasians survived the epidemics, but most Native Americans—95 percent of them—died from the Eurasian diseases, leaving only 5 percent of Native Americans to fight it out on the battlefield with the colonizers.

WACHTEL That's an astonishing statistic.

DIAMOND In Canada, for example, in the late nineteenth century, when the transcontinental railroad was being built through Saskatchewan, many Native Canadians experienced their first intense contact with outsiders, including the outsiders' diseases. It's documented that the Native population of Saskatchewan was dying at the rate of 10 percent per year—isn't that an incredibly high death rate?—due especially to tuberculosis, because they had no prior exposure to Eurasian diseases.

WACHTEL You portray an extraordinary scene of how a group of 169 Spanish soldiers, led by Pizarro, defeated an Incan army of eighty thousand in Peru in 1532. Why was this such a decisive moment in modern history?

DIAMOND The battle of Cajamarca in Peru in 1532 was a decisive moment in world history because this was the first encounter between the foreguard of the most powerful state of Europe then—Spain—and the most powerful empire of the New World. If any New World people had been able to resist Europeans, it would have been the Inca empire, this enormous, highly centralized, super-efficient empire of Native Americans. But, in fact, it was all over within ten minutes, when Pizarro's Spaniards, with horses and steel swords and armour, encountered the army of the Inca emperor Atahuallpa, an army of eighty thousand. Within ten minutes, the Spaniards had killed with their swords something like seven thousand of Atahuallpa's soldiers and porters without a single Spaniard getting injured. The Spaniards captured Atahuallpa, whom they then proceeded to hold for ransom for eight months. So the Spaniards, in effect, decapitated the Inca empire. They took over the empire, and that battle became not only important but emblematic, symbolic, because of the advantages the Spaniards had in that first battle: steel swords and armour, horses, and then smallpox—which had preceded the battle and already wiped out half the Incas, including the previous two emperors. The battle of Cajamarca was both significant in its own right and a symbol of all the other battles by which the Spaniards and other Europeans conquered the Incas and other Native North American societies.

WACHTEL It's another one of these astounding statistics—the idea that 169 Spanish soldiers, a thousand miles away from any Spanish support, in a foreign place, could defeat an army of eighty thousand in an environment where they belong, where they know everything. How did they do it?

DIAMOND It's utterly incredible. If you were to give me a time machine that could dial any place in the past and I could dial it once, I would dial Cajamarca, 1532, to see that battle. The Spaniards themselves were scared out of their wits when, on the previous night, they saw the campfires of those eighty thousand soldiers. Eyewitness accounts the Spaniards left there said, "We were so scared that we were urinating in our trousers out of sheer terror at the sight." But the Spaniards had horses, against which foot soldiers are helpless, and steel armour and swords that could slice their adversaries apart, whereas the Incas had only stone and wooden weapons. And then there was the psychological impact. The Incas were terrified by the sight of horses. In fact, most of the Incas in that first battle didn't even raise their weapons against the Spaniards. Later, when the Incas got used to horses, they did raise their weapons, but even then, people without metal armour, without metal tools, just got mowed down by people with steel swords and spears on horseback.

WACHTEL One of your more surprising observations about the battle is how essential literacy was to Pizarro's victory, even though he was himself illiterate. Why did the Spaniards' ability to read and write make such a difference in combat?

DIAMOND It made a difference because written reports coming back to Spain from the New World were important in two ways. These written reports included maps—very detailed directions of how to sail from Europe to Mexico and then how to get from Mexico to Panama and beyond. That was a huge advantage for the Spaniards. The second important factor was the detailed written reports from Mexico about the precious goods that were discovered among the Aztecs. These reports motivated other Europeans to go out, particularly when Pizarro defeated the Incas and sent back reports to Europe saying that the Inca emperor, Atahuallpa, had ransomed himself by taking a room about thirty-two feet long and twenty feet high and eighteen feet across and filling that room to the ceiling with gold and silver. When that report got back to Europe, some three months later, hundreds and then thousands of Europeans streamed to the New World to get rich. If all those other Europeans hadn't come in, maybe the Incas could have organized themselves and thrown out the 169 Spaniards. But by then, streams of Spaniards were coming to Peru to consolidate Spanish sovereignty.

WACHTEL You show how important food production is to the growth of any society. The Mayans and the Incas were sophisticated food producers. Why did the Europeans have such an advantage over them?

DIAMOND It's true that the Mayans and Incas and Aztecs and Native Americans in eastern North America were very sophisticated food producers, and many of the foods that we eat today—corn, potatoes, tomatoes, chili peppers, et cetera—are native to America. But Native American agriculture was about half as productive as Eurasian agriculture because it didn't involve broadcast sowing. That is to say, they didn't take a sack full of wheat seed and throw it across a field. Instead, Native Americans planted corn kernels one by one. They planted mixed gardens of corn, beans and squash, instead of broadcast sowing, and they didn't have the animal-drawn plows that Europeans had. So Europeans—Eurasians—could just till more land and their agriculture was about twice as productive as New World agriculture. Eurasian herding was far more productive because the only big domestic animal in the New World was the llama, and it was confined to the Andes. That meant that Native Americans outside of the Andes did not have domestic animals as sources of protein. They were protein-limited, whereas Eurasian societies had cows, sheep, goats, pigs, horses and reindeer, donkeys, yak, water buffalo, banteng and camels—animals that were sources of protein and pulled plows and served as cavalry in war and later pulled wheel transport.

WACHTEL The spread of crops in the Fertile Crescent, from west to east, was very rapid. And you seem to have had a geographic revelation on the importance of latitude in building empires. Why was Eurasia's east–west axis so crucial to its growth?

DIAMOND Insofar as there was any one eureka moment in my work on this book, it was when I realized the importance of Eurasia's east–west axis. If you picture a map of the world and look at the shapes of the continents, you can see that Eurasia is long from east to west and narrow from north to south. North and South America, on the other hand, are long from north to south and narrow from east to west, as is Africa. You might say, "So what, who cares about that?" But that was very important in geography, because a crop or domestic animal can spread east–west at the same latitude, always encountering exactly the same day length and sunlight and similar climate and diseases. So the spread of crops and animals east and west in Eurasia was rapid. The Romans were eating Chinese crops and the Chinese were eating European crops. The spread was rapid in Eurasia, but the spread of crops and animals was slow in the New World down that north–south axis. Corn, for example, couldn't get very far north from Mexico before there was a difference in latitude, day length and temperature. So it takes something like four or five thousand years from the domestication of corn to a time when Native Americans developed varieties of corn that you could grow in northeastern North America and southern Canada. The llama and the potato of the Andes never spread north through the hot isthmus of Panama to Mexico, and conversely the turkey of Mexico never spread south to the Andes. In Africa, the domestic animals of Eurasia took something like eight thousand years to spread down the north–south axis. So the north–south axis of the Americas and Africa meant very slow diffusion of crops and animals and the human technology associated with them. Whereas the much more rapid spread within the Eurasian continent meant that things invented or domesticated in one part of Eurasia spread rapidly to other parts and enriched the productivity in the crop and animal base of those other areas.

WACHTEL Writing appeared quite late in human evolution. Why do you see it as strongly linked to food production?

DIAMOND Writing is linked to food production in that there's a fact and then an explanation. The only societies that developed writing were food-producing societies. As far as we know, writing was invented independently only in the Fertile Crescent, China and Mexico, and maybe in Egypt; from those places it then spread. But in all of these places, writing arose in food-producing societies. The probable explanation is that writing requires full-time scribes. It requires records and it requires people who spend all their time keeping records. As far as we can tell, the earliest writing was used to keep tax records for kings, but you get kings and taxes only in agricultural societies where there's something to tax—sheep and goats and wheat. And then you need tax collectors and bureaucrats who are going to develop and use writing.

WACHTEL Though even where writing was developed, few people in society ever got near it.

DIAMOND That's correct. In the Fertile Crescent, only a small fraction of society was literate—the tax collectors and bureaucrats. Similarly, in Mexico, among the societies of the Maya and Vera Cruz, the first uses of writing that we know about were for royal propaganda, putting up big stones and monuments and saying, "I am the great king who defeated my rival next door and carved him into little pieces and took over his state." So writing in Mexico, as in the Fertile Crescent, was associated with the needs of kings and a complex society that had been agricultural for thousands of years.

WACHTEL You tell the story of Sequoyah, a Cherokee Indian, who in 1820 invented his own written language by taking English letters and then using them as symbols for Cherokee syllables. He couldn't read or write English, but he devised a syllabary that taught his people how to read. Why hadn't the Cherokee people created a written language centuries earlier?

DIAMOND The Cherokee people hadn't produced a written language for the same reason that no other Native Americans in North America developed a written language. In the southeastern United States, densely populated agricultural societies—the so-called Mississippian mound-builders—began to explode around AD 1000. Remember: in the Old World, first there was an explosion of densely populated agricultural societies, about 6000 BC, and then, three thousand years later, writing developed. Since this population explosion took place in the New World around AD 1000, you might expect that three thousand years later, in AD

4000, Native Americans in eastern North America would have developed writing. But they were not allowed the leisure. Unfortunately, Europeans arrived in 1492, putting an end to the independent trajectory of Native American societies in eastern North America. So, in short, the Cherokees and other eastern North American Indians would eventually have developed writing, but it would have taken them a couple of thousand years, just as in China and the Fertile Crescent.

WACHTEL So the winners are always the farmers. The hunter-gatherers of the world have inexorably been colonized or vanquished by farming societies. Why couldn't they have developed their own food production?

DIAMOND In most cases, hunter-gatherers were not given the opportunity to develop their food production. Some hunter-gatherers did. After all, all those people who did develop farming originated as hunter-gatherers. The first hunter-gatherers who became farmers in the Fertile Crescent and China and Mexico spread very quickly, taking advantage of their greatly increased population densities and their superior technology, including military technology and their nasty germs, to wipe out the hunter-gatherers. That's, of course, what happened in North America, in California. There were dense populations of hunter-gatherers here in California, but the California Indians never got the chance to adopt agriculture from Europeans, nor, in fact, from Native Americans in Arizona and New Mexico. Arizonan Native American agriculture did not cross the desert of southeastern California. And when Europeans arrived with their crops, they also arrived with their guns and diseases, and did not sit down and peacefully teach Native Americans to become farmers and to govern themselves.

WACHTEL You also provide the example of the Phaistos Disc, a clay disc from Crete, imprinted with 241 signs and letters. This disc was made in 1700 BC, which you say makes it by far the earliest printed "document." Why did it take another three millennia or so for printing to spread to the Gutenberg press?

DIAMOND The Phaistos Disc is a circle of baked clay, maybe about eight inches in diameter, that was discovered buried in the grounds of a

Cretan palace. Somebody realized these marks on the disk were not scratched by hand but had been printed, stamped by pre-made printing blocks. It is the first printed document we know of. But printing in ancient Crete died out after 1700 BC and didn't come back until it was reinvented in China and then mass-produced by Gutenberg. Printing didn't take off in Crete because there wasn't a demand for it. In 1700 BC, the only people who could write in Crete, anyway, were the king's tax collectors, but there's no great advantage to having this beautiful set of printed punches when there's not a large population that can use it or read it. So Cretan printing died out, as did writing itself in Crete and Greece, around 1200 BC. Writing came back to Greece with the alphabet about 800 BC, but it wasn't until the population increase in China and then in Europe that there were enough princes and bureaucrats—and enough people ready to read—that there was a demand for printing.

WACHTEL It's not just the invention, then—there has to be a need or a society's capacity to utilize the invention.

DIAMOND That's right. Another nice example is what people consider the greatest invention of the greatest inventor of all time, Thomas Edison. The phonograph was a mechanical device for recording sound. No such device existed until Thomas Edison got the idea. And there was no demand, initially—nobody was interested in it. Edison just liked to tinker, and to him it was a challenge. So he invented this phonograph and then he had to figure out what it was good for. He was disdainful of the idea of using it to record music; rather, he thought it could record the last words of dying people or teach sounds to the blind. And for twenty years, Edison objected to using the phonograph to record music, until people finally convinced him that it was worthwhile. The phonograph is a perfect example of something that was invented not because it was needed but just because somebody, Edison in this case, liked to tinker, and eventually somebody else figured out what it was good for.

WACHTEL That's an illustration of your line that invention is the mother of necessity.

DIAMOND That's right. For example, the physicists who invented the transistor about forty years ago and won a Nobel Prize for it didn't invent the transistor because they had been building radios and were sick and tired of big, clumsy vacuum tubes that broke down. No, they were tinkering. They had these theoretical ideas and they produced the transistor. But it was the Japanese who used the transistor and then redesigned the electronics industry. When I was growing up in the 1950s, I built a radio with vacuum tubes because the American electronics industries had such an investment in vacuum tubes that they didn't want to have anything to do with transistors.

WACHTEL So then you have economic protectionism limiting the capacity for invention.

DIAMOND Yes, and there are other examples of that. Gas street lighting was widespread in Britain in the late 1800s, and when electric lighting came in, there were strong objections to introducing it because British towns had already invested in gas lighting and they were going to lose their money if electric lighting became widespread. So many British towns tried to obstruct the development of electric lighting.

WACHTEL So why was Renaissance Europe ready to make use of "the millennium's best invention"—I'm using your words here—while Minoan Crete was not?

DIAMOND Renaissance Europe wasn't a small island like Crete. It was a chunk of a continent with lots of people who by then were relatively affluent and were trading and could read. So that's part of it. But Renaissance Europe, unlike Crete, consisted of two thousand principalities. If one of those princes could develop anything that would give him an advantage over another of the princes, then that prince was in a position to conquer his neighbour. And so, for example, when somebody in Renaissance Europe acquired the idea of gunpowder and guns from China in the 1300s, which let Prince Number One defeat Prince Number Two with guns, the other princes were pretty quickly scrambling for guns. Some princes said that guns were disgusting, we want nothing of them, and you can imagine what happened—their principalities were either wiped out or the princes who objected to guns changed their minds and adopted them. So the competition between two thousand different European societies was a great stimulus to technology.

In general, throughout world history, the military has been a big consumer of technology. In the early 1900s cars were introduced into the United States and Canada, but they were just a toy of the rich. Then, in the First World War, when the military needed to bring troops to the battle lines, the military realized that trucks were better than horses, so the military developed and invested heavily in trucks. After the end of the First World War, those trucks became available for civilian use. Similarly, airplanes were just a toy for daredevils until the First World War. Throughout history, the military has been a stimulus for the development of technology. That's not to say that I'm cheering for wars as a way to advance technology. It's simply that we have this tragedy that much technology has arisen from the most awful backgrounds, namely wars.

WACHTEL I think you're very careful not to cheer for anything that you describe. Even with societies that have become conquerors, in your analysis, I don't get the sense that you're necessarily championing these victors.

DIAMOND Absolutely not. I emphasize that I'm explaining *why* Europeans have conquered the rest of the world, not that Europeans deserved to have conquered the rest of the world because of their putative superiority. I say very clearly that in describing history, and trying to understand history, I'm not justifying it. I'm simply trying to understand it in the same way that, for example, my wife, who is a clinical psychologist and deals with rape victims and victims of genocide, is interested in genocide and rape. This is not because she wants to cheer on rapists and those who commit genocide, but because she wants to understand how these awful things have happened so as to prevent their ever happening again. Similarly, my goal in understanding world history is to understand why some people conquered and did absolutely awful things to other people, to understand how these bad things happened so we can prevent them happening again, and to dispel the idea that history has anything to do with racist explanations such as the genetic superiority of Europeans.

WACHTEL Today we have instant global exchange of information, we have freer trade and an increasingly universal culture. Will geographical differences among continents have much influence on the twenty-first century?

DIAMOND Yes—more than ever. If you look around the world today, we've got radio and telephones and the Internet. This morning I sent messages to Australia and to England. Does that mean that geography is irrelevant? Absolutely not. In the modern world, there are big geographic influences on rich countries and poor countries. In the modern world, tropical countries tend to be poor, temperate countries tend to be rich. Japan, Korea and Malaysia acquired agriculture from China, one of the first centres of world agriculture, as did Europe and then Canada and the United States from the Fertile Crescent. These temperate countries still have the economic and political lead in the world today. In fact, people say that economic differences in the modern world are increasing rather than getting smaller. Geography still plays a big role, but that doesn't mean that countries with geographic disadvantages should tell all their people to commit suicide because it's hopeless. Instead, once you can recognize your geographic disadvantages, then you know what to target to solve these disadvantages. That's what, as I mentioned, Mauritius and Hong Kong and Taiwan did. They recognized their geographic disadvantages, like their public health disadvantages, they went out and solved them, and their economies have now formed into First World economies as a result.

WACHTEL At the conclusion of *Guns, Germs and Steel*, you argue that the study of history should become more scientific. There are so many loose cannons in history—wars, powerful individuals like Hitler and Napoleon, sudden events like September 11th—how can history be made predictable?

DIAMOND History can be made predictable, just like many other sciences that have loose cannons can be made predictable. Similarly with geology. A local glacier can melt or a lake can give way and there's a loose cannon in evolutionary biology. An asteroid crashes into the earth and there go the dinosaurs. That's a loose cannon. One can make generalizations about geology and astronomy and evolutionary biology in the same way one can make generalizations about history. On September 10 I could not have predicted that the stock market would be way down on September 12, but on September 10 I could have predicted that the leading stock markets, on April 22 of the year 2002, would be those of New York, Tokyo, London and Frankfurt, not the stock markets of the capitals of Paraguay and the Congo. There are some generalizations that one can make from history, although there are also loose cannons and unpredictable events.

WACHTEL Do you get flak from historians for poaching on their territory?

DIAMOND It's not that I get flak; I get a lack of interest from historians. The interest in my book has been from everybody except historians: scientists, linguists, archaeologists, economists. That's because historians are trained to study the history of one country for decades—so you get a late-eighteenth-century Dutch historian and God forbid that that person study sixteenth-century Dutch history or eighteenth-century French history. But there are groups of historians who are interested in these bigger questions of history, long-term history. Economic historians, environmental historians and a group called "world historians" have been very interested in the big questions. To me it seems a tragedy, a double tragedy, that the majority of historians are afraid of, or shy away from, these big questions of history. It's a double tragedy because historians are the people who could tell us most about history, but they have copped out on this biggest question of history: Why is it that Europeans rather than Aboriginal Australians spread around the world? Historians gave up on the question, in reality, because it's a really difficult question for the tools of historians. Because historians gave up, people have fallen back on the racist interpretations. But the other tragedy is that it's meant that historians have opted out of dealing with the most interesting, difficult, important questions of history—these questions of long-term history. Now, these questions are being poached or encroached on by other people—anthropologists, archaeologists, linguists, geneticists—people other than historians. Historians are at risk of losing the most interesting and important part of their subject matter to other disciplines. I hope that in the future historians will learn more of these disciplines, which are so necessary for understanding the big questions of history, as well as the techniques of the historical sciences, fields such as astronomy and evolutionary biology, that have successfully dealt with these historical problems—fields that have loose cannons, just as history does.

WACHTEL From your analysis of the last thirteen thousand years, what do you want readers to learn so they can make improvements during the next fifty?

DIAMOND The most important thing that I would like people to learn is that the differences among us are not racial. The most important lesson we can learn is that all people have similar capacities. It's just a matter of environment that some ended up differently, and if today they are given equal opportunity, they can move forward. It's in all our interests to see to it that everybody is given an equal opportunity. Then all peoples can make their own way, and not be a burden on other parts of society.

April 2002

OLIVER SACKS

Oliver Sacks is simply one of my favourite people. He's a humanist
neurologist known to be as much metaphysician as physician. An
artist friend of mine once said she wished she had a neurological
disorder just so she could get to meet him. His combination of
intelligence, compassion and enthusiasm is irresistible to me. I'd
follow him anywhere—including, a few years ago, to *The Island of
the Colorblind*, as his 1997 book was called. It was a unique mix of
clinical description, travel writing, history, even a prehistory in its
exploration of botany and Sacks's own passion for ferns and
cycads. He pursued this further in *Oaxaca Journal* (2002).

But Sacks is probably best known as the author of his wonderfully titled collection of clinical tales, *The Man Who Mistook His Wife
for a Hat* (1985), and *Awakenings* (1973), his account of his treatment
of patients who'd suffered from a sleeping sickness epidemic dating from the First World War, and who were briefly brought back
to life in the late sixties. It was made into a movie with Robin
Williams playing the shy neurologist; Sacks was pleased with the
film.

For me, it's Sacks's 1995 collection, *An Anthropologist on Mars: Seven Paradoxical Tales* that best illustrates his particular territory where biology and biography intersect. These case histories—from a surgeon with Tourette's syndrome, to an autistic woman with a PhD in animal behaviour, to a blind masseur who suddenly regains his sight—make up some of the best, most moving stories—fiction or non-fiction—that I've read in years. Oliver Sacks is an unusual and, in some ways, an old-fashioned man, harking back to a nineteenth-century humanist tradition. He was born in 1933 in London, England, and raised in a house filled with books; he studied at Oxford, loves music and has a great belief in its therapeutic value.

I first met him in 1994 in Toronto. We talked about his cases, his earlier work and enthusiasms. Explaining his choice of specialty, he said that "the brain is the most interesting, complex and wonderful object in the universe, and it's a wonderfully exciting thing to study and be in contact with. I have nothing against kidneys and hearts and lungs . . . [but] the brain is you, not just biologically or genetically, it has all your experiences, it's you. The notion of a physical object which is also you fascinates me above everything else."

He also talked about his sense of remove—remove and sympathy. "Sometimes," he said, "I feel I'm not participating fully in life, that I'm a describer. Or that the detached, describing part of me is always there." Recently, Sacks turned to his own early life as his subject, exploring his childhood via his passion for chemistry in a book called *Uncle Tungsten: Memories of a Chemical Boyhood* (2001). When we spoke this time, he was even more open and candid, reflecting on the beginnings of his own original mind.

———————————

WACHTEL The house that you grew up in London in the 1930s and 1940s sounds like a child's dream home, especially before the war. Can you describe it for me?

SACKS Yes. It was a magical house to me, although I think it might have seemed a large, awkward Edwardian house to anyone else. It was a big corner house, built around 1902. It had lots and lots of rooms, not only for the immediate family but for various people who lived in. In those days, in the thirties, there would have been a nanny and a nurse, a cook–housekeeper and a chauffeur, a gardener and so forth. There were also special rooms where the patients came in. Both my parents were physicians, and they had their surgery—their office—in the house. And there were lots of odd rooms, in which things like knitting machines or sports equipment were housed. There was a library, which I loved, that was full of books and games. And a tiny, mysterious cupboard under the stairs that no one else was small enough to get into and I used to imagine was the entrance to another world. There was a great attic. The house had a complex roof with eaves and gables, and I used to imagine that it was a giant crystal—I was interested in crystals. And lots of music in the house. We had two pianos and one of my brothers played the flute and the other played the clarinet. There was a lot of coming and going.

WACHTEL And lots of people staying—relatives and friends.

SACKS Yes, a huge number of relatives. My mother was one of eighteen children, and our uncles and aunts came. One aunt would come from Palestine, as it was then, and another one from Cheshire, as it still is. Another aunt and her husband came for a while from Germany, where they'd escaped just in time, just after Kristallnacht. In 1940, when I was home very briefly during the Blitz, there was a Flemish couple who were refugees and who had just made it on one of the last boats from Dunkirk. So there were always lots and lots of people in the house.

WACHTEL Not only was it a family home, but as you said, it was where your parents—both of whom were doctors—saw many of their patients. What was that like, growing up with their work so much a part of the household?

SACKS Family life and my parents' professional lives were very close because their patients came into our home. I wasn't allowed into the surgery, although I was fascinated by it. I would occasionally see a strange violet light coming from under the door; this was the ultraviolet light being used. My mother was a surgeon and an obstetrician, and I would see all sorts of strange and disconcerting instruments. Later, I sometimes felt that the patients were intrusive and that the house was not fully ours. I certainly felt that when there were political—mostly Zionist—meetings in the house. I would hear people shouting and banging the table downstairs and coming upstairs to look for the lavatory and barging into my little room. I've had a hatred of all political meetings and all political impulses ever since then, because I thought of them as noisy and quarrelsome and because people would barge into my room. It was probably a very unfair feeling.

WACHTEL Although probably an apt and perspicacious description of political meetings generally.

SACKS I do remember going out with my father on some of his house calls. I loved that, but I rather resented the patients coming in. It was very common, in that era, that doctors would have surgeries in their own houses. Sometimes there was a different entrance for the patients, but there wasn't in our house.

WACHTEL Your father was born in Lithuania, but he left with his family when he was only three or four. What kind of a person was he?

SACKS My father was very genial and outgoing and immensely sociable. I don't think he ever forgot anyone's name and he loved hearing the details of people's families. My mother was extremely shy and probably a little withdrawn socially, although very much at ease with her patients and her students. Later I heard all sorts of stories about her performing, particularly for her students.

WACHTEL You heard a story about your appearance in her class.

SACKS Yes. Many years later, I took my own first book to an editor at Faber's, which had published a book of my mother's before that. This editor said, "You know, we've met before." I said I didn't remember, that I'm not very good with faces. And she said, "No, you wouldn't remember." She told me that she had been one of my mother's students. My mother was lecturing her class on breast-feeding and said there was nothing difficult or embarrassing about it. She bent down and pulled out a little baby that had been concealed at the foot of her desk and breast-fed it in front of the class. The editor said this was in September 1933 and I was the infant. I think it is typical of my mother, in a way—shy almost to muteness in some situations but perfectly capable of breast-feeding a baby in front of fifty people. I think I'm rather similar. I can be absolutely mute sometimes at parties and yet quite outrageous in front of a thousand people.

WACHTEL What precipitates the performer in you?

SACKS Well, I'm a storyteller and a demonstrator, as well, as I think my mother was. And it has to be something outside myself, or something to do with teaching or curiosity. Now, for example, I've taken again to carrying around a little spectroscope, as I did when I was a boy. A spectroscope analyzes light into all its different colours and shows the particular wavelengths of different atoms which are excited. When I started writing about being a boy with a spectroscope, I had to get another spectroscope and, as it were, become that boy again. A few months ago, I was gazing into a local bar which had neon lights and sodium lights and all sorts of fluorescent lights. Obviously the people inside were rather bewildered and upset at someone looking at them, as they thought, through a mysterious, tiny instrument. So I went into the bar and showed everyone the spectroscope and had them all look through it, and in ten minutes I had them all talking about spectroscopy instead of sex.

There was an eclipse about a year ago—a lunar eclipse—and I ran out with my nice twenty-times telescope. I wanted to draw everyone's attention. I saw a quarrel going on in the parking lot opposite me. I think some woman felt she had been overcharged and I went up to the two of them and said, "Look, stop quarrelling for a moment. There is a wonderful eclipse. Here is a telescope. Look at it. You will never see such an eclipse again and you can continue your quarrel afterwards." They were so taken aback that this is exactly what they did, and they were filled with wonder for a while. Then as soon as I went away, I heard the quarrel being resumed. I think there was something like this in my mother.

The demonstration, the teaching, the sharing of enthusiasm takes one out of the enclosed, solipsistic, frightened mode.

WACHTEL She shared a lot with you, from what you describe in your book *Uncle Tungsten*, in terms of responding to so many of your questions and pointing things out even as she was running the household and being a doctor and doing all these other things.

SACKS I think she often forgot how young I was. As a boy I adored metals of all sorts, and she once showed me that when tin or zinc were bent they emitted a strange noise. It's called the "cry" of tin or zinc. I asked her what the noise was from, and she said it was due to deformation of the crystal structure, forgetting I was five. I couldn't possibly have understood her. Later, in a way that distressed me a good deal, she would sometimes bring home stillborn fetuses—she was also a professor of anatomy—and demonstrate the anatomy to me and want me to dissect them with her. I found that rather grisly; it may be a reason why I have disliked anatomy ever since.

I think she hoped I would follow in her footsteps and be an anatomist surgeon. Her enthusiasm would take over, as when she breast-fed me in front of the class. I think she didn't have enough empathy for what an eleven-year-old feels when he sees a human fetus and is asked to dissect it. That shocked me—it was a little premature.

WACHTEL There was another instance you describe, when you were fourteen and she arranged for you to dissect an actual female cadaver, a girl who was also fourteen.

SACKS She'd asked a colleague to introduce me to this. I can almost see the yellow oilskin in which the cadavers were wrapped to keep them from drying out, and smell the formalin and mortification. The corpse that had been selected for me was, in fact, a girl of my own age. I wondered what she'd died from and what had happened. But I didn't ask. In a way I'm glad I didn't ask. I had to try to think of the cadaver as just tissues, but I think it scared the hell out of me.

WACHTEL And you didn't say anything? I mean, you spent a month dissecting—

SACKS No, I've never been able to say anything for myself. I hated evacuation—it was a very bad time—but I didn't say anything. I find it very difficult to say anything for myself, although I find it very easy to speak up for my patients or for my students.

WACHTEL Do you understand why?

SACKS I don't quite understand why. I think I have to work that out with my analyst.

WACHTEL You describe how difficult that dissection was for you. You've even speculated about your problems engaging with warm, living human beings because of the trauma.

SACKS Well, it was certainly quite a shock to see someone my own age in that state. I think connecting may have been made more difficult generally by the experience of having been evacuated. Many people of my generation have spoken of this, how after a traumatic evacuation experience, there are difficulties in bonding and belonging, which can be lifelong. These problems are not absolute, but I think a special effort often has to be made. Certainly, dissecting a corpse too early didn't help.

WACHTEL Let's talk a little about this evacuation experience. When you were six years old, you and your brother, who was five years older than you, were sent to school in the countryside because children were being evacuated out of London.

SACKS Yes, parents were put under a lot of pressure to evacuate children. Literally millions were evacuated. Sometimes it worked out well. My brother Michael and I were sent to Braefield, a school that had been set up by a schoolmaster from Michael's previous school in London. The schoolmaster was apparently a fairly decent man then, but I think he became deranged when he had absolute power in this strange boarding school in the Midlands, and a very unpleasant, sadistic streak came out. There was a great deal of beating. I don't know that the term *abuse* existed then, but in retrospect one would have to say it was a very abusive environment. We were all beaten for tiny infractions and sometimes apparently for nothing at all—for the love of it, or for his love of it. Food was very short and parcels were looted and there was a lot of bullying. Almost all the other kids at the school complained. My brother and I never complained—we've always had difficulty with that sort of thing. Finally the school was closed down and I came back to London in 1943. I was ten years old, and almost immediately I fell in love with chemistry and science, greatly inspired by two uncles of mine. Science seemed to promise a realm of clarity and order and control and predictability, infinitely far from what I was then seeing as the capricious and dangerous and terrifying world of people, at least of people like the headmaster.

WACHTEL But even at Braefield you were attracted to numbers and particularly to prime numbers. There seemed to be a security, a refuge, in numbers.

SACKS Oh, absolutely. One needed a refuge, and it had to be a mental refuge, in a way. I especially loved prime numbers because they were indivisible, they couldn't be broken down. I felt I was being broken down all the while. But 317 is 317. It has a wonderful, incorruptible, steely individuality. Can't be cowed, can't be broken. But besides the moral character of autonomy, I was fascinated that there should be prime numbers, and I wondered if there was any logic or pattern to them. I used to make enormous charts of prime numbers up to ten thousand. Did it make sense? Was there any mysterious determination of these numbers? I never found any, but I think in a way this was an intellectual precursor to my later love of the periodic table and the way in which all the elements and their numbers were related with a clear, beautiful determination.

WACHTEL While you were still at Braefield, one of your respites was visiting an aunt who also introduced you to numbers.

SACKS I've written about this aunt, my Auntie Len, in earlier books, in *A Leg to Stand On*. She had founded a school in Cheshire for delicate children, which at that time meant mostly poor children with asthma, tuberculosis, maybe autism. I wanted to be at her school, but I was not a delicate child, although I often wished I had been. She loved botany, and all the kids had gardens. She would sometimes take me into the woods, and she showed me the spirals on pine cones and the florets on sunflowers, how they formed a certain numerical series—one–two–three, five–eight–thirteen and so forth—each number being the sum of the two before. She showed me how arithmetic was built into this. She used to say God thinks in numbers. Numbers are the way the world is put together.

WACHTEL What did you make of that, given you were starting to doubt the existence of God around that time?

SACKS I was, indeed. I became very doubtful, I think too early, of a personal God. I don't know what my parents actually believed, but in practice ours was a fairly orthodox household and there were a lot of lovely, lyrical rituals. I used to love watching my mother light the Sabbath candles on Friday afternoon. The Sabbath is welcomed in as a bride, and I would imagine the Sabbath, the peace of God, as a cosmic event, the peace of God settling on different star systems all over the universe. But when I was sent away, which broke some of the trust or the bond between my parents and myself, I turned against the ultimate parental figure up in the sky, and from that time, I never have had any sense of a personal God. On the other hand, God as nature, God as order, I think can inspire a mystical or religious feeling. A God who thinks in numbers—what some philosophers have called a divine mathematics—came in its place.

WACHTEL I love the way you describe how you tested the existence of God.

SACKS Yes, in my seventh year, while I was at Braefield, I said I wanted evidence. "OK, God, listen to me. I'm going to plant two rows of radishes. I want You to bless one—or curse one, at least—to ensure that it grows differently." And of course they grew the same, so I said, "OK, You failed the test. No God." Perhaps many of us get disillusioned or lose faith at one point or another. I'm sorry it happened to me so young. Despite this, for years after, in the synagogue and at home, I loved the lyrical passages in the Bible. I was very conscious of the beauty of a lot of prayer, a lot of religious language. One had to think in terms of heaven and hell. I was fascinated by the biblical figures, although deeply disturbed, as I think many children are, by the near sacrifice of

Isaac. What got into Abraham? I think that's a very terrifying part of the Bible, and not unnaturally, it inspired an entire book by Kierkegaard.

WACHTEL You say you're not quite sure what your parents believed, but they practised a certain orthodoxy.

SACKS They kept a kosher house. They went to synagogue. They observed the festivals. My father loved Jewish food. His patients would feed him when he made house calls in the East End of London. My father was a man of enormous build and he became huge in later life from his love of Jewish food. But what did they actually believe? I don't know how much belief, in fact, enters into being Jewish. It may be that obedience and practice and the Law, following the Law, halachah, is sufficient. There's certainly very little sense of an afterlife, of heaven or hell. The religious life is entirely to be lived here. I don't know what they believed. I sometimes don't know what I believe.

WACHTEL You've described yourself as "an old Jewish atheist, whatever that means."

SACKS Whatever that means.

WACHTEL What does that mean to you?

SACKS On the one hand, I have no sense, and possibly never have had any sense, of an agency, a personal God, a paternal, law-giving God in the sky. On the other hand, I'm very conscious of coming from a Jewish culture, from a culture of curiosity and questioning and debate, which is characteristically Jewish. I sometimes wonder whether my love of footnotes has something to do with the Talmud—my father adored the Talmud—which consists of a central text with commentaries on it and then commentaries on the commentaries and commentaries on the secondary commentaries. The idea of the Law is very central in Jewish religion and sometimes takes on an almost mystical form, where the Law is seen as a beautiful woman who will perhaps reveal a tiny bit of herself to the student. The very word *revealed* or *revelation* goes along with that image. Nature, for me, somehow becomes equated with the Law, and specifically with the periodic table, this wonderful organization of the elements that entranced me as a child and still absolutely entrances me so that—

WACHTEL You're reaching into your pocket and pulling a periodic table out of your wallet.

SACKS I've kept one in my wallet for fifty-five years. I've somehow equated this with the tablets of the Law. I imagine Mendeleev, who invented it, as a sort of Moses bringing down the periodic tablets of the law.

WACHTEL Except there are a lot more than ten.

SACKS That's right. But this sense of cosmic law feels like a Jewish concept, in a way.

WACHTEL One of your other enthusiasms is swimming—you used to go swimming with your father, as well as going along on his house calls.

SACKS Oh, he loved swimming. He'd been quite a swimming champ when he was younger and he got all of us, all four of his sons, into the water when we were a few weeks old. Swimming is instinctive at that age. I used to love swimming with him. I think we all did. At first, as a kid, I obviously couldn't keep up with him, though I think from about twelve or so I began to match his strokes.

WACHTEL And you still swim two hours a day.

SACKS I still swim every morning, if I can. My father couldn't walk much past the age of ninety. He had very bad arthritis in his knees. But we would wheel him to a pool and tip him in and he'd take off like a porpoise. He swam till his dying day. His father had also been a good swimmer and apparently would always wear his yarmulke, his skullcap, in the water. On my father's side, there's a long history of loving swimming. I think there's almost a mystical feeling about the buoyant, transparent, supportive medium of water. It becomes a spiritual as well as a physical necessity and actually I do, as it were, a certain amount of my writing in the water because sometimes when I'm swimming, sentences and paragraphs and images start swimming through me, and then I come out dripping and try to get these ideas onto paper before I forget them. I adore swimming.

WACHTEL Does it still remind you of your father?

SACKS I think so. Yes.

WACHTEL How would you describe your relationship with him?

SACKS It was not as intense and charged or as ambivalent as my relationship with my mother, whom I passionately loved but was also rather afraid of and sometimes almost hated—at least when I was pushed into things I didn't want to do. There was almost too much identification with her. I think with my father it was probably easier and lighter, very much a relationship of doing things together, whether it was going on house calls or occasionally enjoying a cigar together. I share his love of Havanas. He also had a motorcycle and I had motorcycles. But I don't know how much real, close conversation there ever was with my father. It was more of an active relationship.

WACHTEL I've read that you still look for father figures.

SACKS Oh, well, I think we all look for father figures. Probably I'm much, much too old to do so now—a father figure for me would have to be ninety or so. Although, of course, a father figure can be younger than oneself. In turn, I find people look to me as a father figure or an uncle figure. I think I'm going to give up the term *father figure* and use *uncle figure* instead.

WACHTEL You describe W. H. Auden and another Russian scientist, A. R. Luria, as having been father figures for you.

SACKS Yes. For many years I would perhaps unconsciously seek and respond to, as it were, the wise old men, the Magi, the father figures, the authorities, whether they were in art, like Auden, or in science. I still enjoy special meetings. In fact, just two weeks ago I had lunch with Saul Bellow and then a couple of days later, I had dinner with Studs Terkel— two wonderful octogenarians, so different. Yes, and I think I have a certain filial love for both of them.

WACHTEL When you were a small boy, you developed what you describe as a love affair with chemistry. Where did that passionate interest come from?

SACKS It goes back to before the war. My brothers would sometimes do kitchen chemistry in the house. They'd pour some vinegar on chalk and it would bubble and a heavy vapour would come off which would then douse a candle. I didn't understand about carbon dioxide, but I could see something strange and invisible came off. Or they'd pour ammonia on red cabbage, which would then go through all sorts of strange colour changes and become bright green. But when I came back to London, I met my mother's older brother, Uncle Dave, who manufactured incandescent bulbs with tungsten filaments and who had a firm called Tungstalite. I remember visiting him in his factory and his laboratories. He was a born teacher as well as many other things, and he probably enjoyed the eagerness of his little nephew. Uncle Dave's enthusiasm for chemistry and metallurgy and mineralogy was immense and I think got strongly into me. He would even give me little bars of tungsten. He also had a great interest in the history of chemistry and the biographies of chemists. So science was presented to me as being a human endeavour, as having a very human face. There were stories about Scheele, the great Swedish chemist, who identified tungsten as an element in the 1780s. I think I thought of my uncle as a sort of Scheele figure, as an eighteenth-century figure, and this made me want to do eighteenth-century chemistry, so to speak.

WACHTEL What would that mean?

SACKS Well, it did mean not looking at current textbooks, but rather finding out the old ways of doing things, or being told them, and then trying things out. He showed me how to smelt various tungsten ores— tungsten occurs in different minerals—to obtain the metal, precisely as had been done in the 1780s. And later I wanted to do this for myself. Something like a dozen different metals were discovered in the eighteenth century and this entranced me. I wanted to repeat all the experiments and get in, as it were, to chemistry at its beginning. There was a great chemist called Cannizzaro who said that sometimes he would try to put his students back to the time of Lavoisier in the eighteenth century so they could feel the full impact of Lavoisier's revolution. He wondered whether the student needed to live through all the stages of a science, of chemistry. I started with my Uncle Tungsten, but there was another uncle, my Uncle Abie, who was a physics uncle. Both of them were very interested in light, which may have come from their father— my grandfather—the father of the eighteen children.

WACHTEL On your mother's side.

SACKS On my mother's side. I never knew him because he was born 164 years ago and died decades before I was born. I'm the youngest of almost the youngest. But he was an unusual man, equally drawn to the spiritual and the physical, a deeply religious man, but also a good amateur mathematician and inventor. He invented safety lamps for miners as well as street lamps, and had a special interest in light. And I think this was transmitted to at least two of his sons. With Uncle Dave— Uncle Tungsten—it was incandescence, it was hot light. With Uncle Abie it was cold light, fluorescence. And I was equally drawn to both.

WACHTEL Your parents encouraged you to set up a little laboratory.

SACKS Oh, yes, they were really very supportive. There was a back room that had once been used as a laundry room. As I mentioned earlier, the house had innumerable rooms, some of which were disused. The old laundry room had running water in the sink, and windows and cupboards, so I set up quite an elaborate laboratory. My uncles gave me things, and I spent all my pocket money on chemicals. At that time you could buy anything: a ten-year-old could buy potassium cyanide or thallium salts or explosive things. I did have a few explosions and eruptions of noxious gases and sometimes I had to run out to the lawn at the back, which rapidly developed charred patches.

WACHTEL You managed to singe your brother's eyebrows.

SACKS Indeed. There was a great sheet of flame once from hydrogen which caught fire. But Marcus was very tolerant. He grew the eyebrows back. I was lucky that I wasn't hurt or didn't really hurt anyone else. But I also think I learned prudence and responsibility. Maybe you have to have actual contact with dangerous things to learn this. You can't have this now. Chemistry sets nowadays have got baking soda and vinegar and chalk—it's like the kitchen chemistry one does when one is six. It's not real chemistry any more. You can't really see these lovely transformations. My little lab doubled as a darkroom—it was such fun, such an adventure. A lot of the books from earlier centuries convey this. Two of my favourite books were both 1860-ish books. One was called *Chemical Recreations* and the other was called *The Play Book of Metals*. Later, when I came to do science at school, I didn't like it nearly as much. There wasn't the freedom. There wasn't the sense of play and adventure. It had all become more fixed and formulaic and exam-oriented.

WACHTEL You say that you sought the special dangers of chemistry as a way of dealing with your own fears, "that by care and vigilance and prudence one could learn to control or find a way through the hazardous world." Were you conscious of that aspect of what you were doing at the time?

SACKS I don't know whether I was conscious or not. But in retrospect, I suspect that this is what goes on. Looking back fifty years, there's a danger of hindsight, of trying to retroject feelings and insights that a boy wouldn't have. Much of what I did was just done instinctively, impelled by some drive I couldn't explain or understand. Whether it was the drive to science or occasionally the drive to mischief of one sort or another—like the time I imprisoned our favourite dog, a dachshund, in the coal bin where she almost died in the winter of 1940. I think this was an indirect cry for help, a way of saying to my parents, "Get me out of my coal bin."

WACHTEL Because you were imprisoned at this school.

SACKS Yes, I suspect that this is so. But I don't know that a child can interpret his own behaviours or interests too much.

WACHTEL You describe a curious incident that happened when you were twelve. You were under a favourite table, that provided a kind of protection—

SACKS Oh, this was the Morrison table—that was another freaky thing. A lot of houses had these immensely strong iron tables, the notion being that even if the house collapsed, one would be saved from being crushed by the masonry. I loved this table. I think I regarded it as a protector, and I would make a nest under it. If there was an air raid, the whole family would go underneath it. But after one air raid, my parents were rather startled, when I emerged, to see a strange, bald circle on my scalp. They were very perplexed. They wondered if it could be ringworm, and the next day they had a skin specialist look at me. I felt he was probably looking right through me, and he pulled out a hair or two and looked at it under a microscope. Then he said it was *dermatitis artefacta*, which meant that I had done this myself. I blushed a deep crimson. But why I did it was never clear to me and it was not actually discussed with my parents, although it was obviously symptomatic behaviour of some sort.

WACHTEL It was around this time that you first went to the Science Museum and saw the periodic table. You became fascinated—

SACKS Ecstasy.

WACHTEL Ecstasy. Beyond fascination.

SACKS I was twelve then, and I'd already gathered quite a bit of chemical knowledge. I'd seen many of the elements and their compounds. I knew that elements belonged in families: let's say, chlorine and bromine and iodine were similar, and sodium and potassium were similar. I saw the table, with its wonderful scheme whereby all the elements are shown in relation to one another and have a mysterious pattern of recurrence, so that every eighth element, at least to begin with, seemed to echo the properties of the element before it. This struck me as the most beautiful thing I'd ever seen, the most economical, the most elegant. All of the elements, all of the building blocks of the universe, fell into an order. They fell into a natural order, an order partly determined, as my aunt used to say, by numbers. It was the numerical quality of recurrence that so fascinated me, the fact that if you arranged the elements by increasing atomic weight, you would get this wonderful cycling. Although why this should be so was utterly unknown to me, as it was utterly unknown to Mendeleev when he'd made the table in 1869. There was a huge mystery here—I want to say like the Trinity, but I don't know why I want to say that.

WACHTEL It's equal time. You said the tablets before.

SACKS The sense of the mysterious and of some profound fundamental law that must determine all of these recurrences was, I think, very strong. The periodic table was beautiful but, as it were, there was more to it than met the eye. Or one wondered what made it so. It was fifty years before an actual explanation of the periodic table came out; this required a completely new idea of atoms as being complex and as having nuclei and electrons and special numbers of electrons whirling round them. In the case of tungsten there are seventy-four electrons whirling around the nucleus. This is not arbitrary. Tungsten couldn't be anything else, say, except Element 74. And the seventy-four electrons are arranged in particular ways that give tungsten its physical and chemical properties, and so somehow then, as earlier it had been with plants, the numbers and actuality came together for me.

WACHTEL As a student of science you read about the findings and thoughts of the collectors and explorers, but you yourself are something of a collector. You collect not only prime numbers but mineral samples and coins and stamps and bus tickets.

SACKS Bus tickets. Oh, yes.

WACHTEL Bus tickets that you organize by their chemical elements.

SACKS Oh, I love these bus tickets. At the time I collected them, bus tickets were oblongs of coloured cardboard with one or two letters and one or two or three numbers. Early on, I got an o16 and an S32, which were my initials but also the symbols for oxygen and sulfur, with their atomic weights. I finally got bus tickets for all the elements with their atomic weights. I love these: in one cubic inch I felt I had an epitome of the whole world. All the building blocks of the universe.

WACHTEL Do you know what the impulse is behind your collecting?

SACKS It's the impulse to understand. It's the impulse to synthesize. I don't know that I am a real collector. I like books, but I have an awful habit of scribbling in the margins, so I don't want the books to be too fine. I have nothing which a real collector would want, you know. In a sense, I live surrounded by rubbish, but it's wonderful rubbish.

WACHTEL And it's rubbish that you've collected.

SACKS Well, the bus tickets were a finite collection. There was a point at which I'd completed it. I had elements 1 to 92 and that was that. I had the universe. It was complete. Although I then started wondering, well, why stop at 92? Are there elements beyond 92? But that's another story. So I think, in a way, this is somewhat different from collecting. I think this is perhaps more like completing a crossword puzzle or solving a problem, and in a sense I got there. With things like stamps, there's no end. I love stamps with pictures of islands on them, and I think I did a lot of vicarious travel with my stamp album. Strange stamps. I rather like the anomalies on stamps. I remember a very odd stamp which, it was said, at a certain angle showed the face of the murdered Archduke Ferdinand, whose assassination started the First World War. I was never quite sure whether I saw that or not, but the idea of a secret face in a stamp intrigued me. Perhaps there is the notion everywhere of a secret. I don't think I'm a collector as such, but I want to worm my way into a secret and, as it were, to see the lady of the Law more and more revealed.

WACHTEL As you entered your teen years, you moved away from chemistry and, in fact, you've referred to this change as "The End of the Affair." Why do you think your passion for chemistry diminished?

SACKS I don't know. Some of it may just have been the end of childhood. I think, with all of us, there is some point where the heightened, mysterious, mythical, magical world of childhood gets fainter. Wordsworth wrote about this and how the freshness and glory vanish in the light of common day. He also wondered about the shades of the prison house which, for him, were school. I think doing science at school partly destroyed my interest in science, in chemistry, because what had been private and secret and playful and adventurous became fixed and competitive and public and prosaic. It wasn't a holy thing any more. But then, of course, I was becoming an adolescent and the sense of the organic was happening. Hair was sprouting all over me. I started to have strange stirrings in my loins, and I think the human and the biological world were beginning to excite and distract me more. I remember there was a great hunger for the personal, although maybe indirectly. This partly took the form of a hunger for music. I had to have music, especially Mozart. Music called to me and moved me and made me want to howl. There was a beauty and wonder quite different from the scientific, mathematical one. The physical sciences were no longer enough. I think there was also a message, in a way, from my parents: "Well, OK, you're fourteen, you're a big boy now. You've had your bar mitzvah, you've grown up. Time for play is over. You're going to be a medical student. You're going to follow the family business," which ultimately I did.

WACHTEL Your three older brothers had also studied medicine.

SACKS Yes, although in a rather strange sort of way. I also think that the kind of chemistry I loved was descriptive, naturalistic, nineteenth-century chemistry. It was very sensuous for me—the colours and the textures and the smells and all the transformations. And chemistry, although I loved numbers, was becoming too mathematical, almost a part of physics and quantum theory. I think I'm basically a naturalist at heart, an observer-describer-naturalist-novelist, and perhaps I had the feeling—although this certainly wasn't something I could articulate at the time—that biology and medicine were still at a relatively primitive level where an observer-describer-collector-systematizer-synthesizer could feel at home. It had not become too recondite and abstract, as chemistry had become. So in a way I wanted to be an eighteenth- or nineteenth-century chemist, but that didn't make sense in the middle of the twentieth century.

WACHTEL You still carry the periodic table. Do you still dream about it?

SACKS Oh, yes. I often think of the periodic table. I dream of it. I love the licence plates of cars, especially in New York. I see UVW, and I think uranium, vanadium, tungsten. It's especially nice if they have their atomic weights or their atomic numbers. I like to see a U-92, a Y-39, a W-74. I often have strange chemical dreams. I was very close to two friends, Jonathan Miller, whom you know, and Eric Korn, and we, the three musketeers, become the three iron metals. We became iron, nickel and cobalt.

WACHTEL Which are you?

SACKS I'm usually iron. In one of my strange dreams, the grid of New York becomes conflated with the grid of the periodic table, and I always end up at the junction at Sixth Street and Sixth Avenue and the buildings there have a strange look, which I realize is a tungsten-y look. Now, tungsten, in fact, is in Period Six and Group Six, as it's called. I should add that there's actually no such junction in New York. It's only part of my dream New York. For me, the periodic table was the first revelation, I think, of the beauty of Law and infinite depth of determination and reality, of simplicity, in a way, and economy. Fifty-five years later, I haven't seen anything better. The genome may be going in that direction, but that's much more complicated and arbitrary. Nothing is arbitrary in this way in the physical sciences. Things are either necessary or impossible. You're not in the world of contingency and variation, which are, of course, the great wonders of biology. It's a simpler world.

WACHTEL In many ways, your memoir, Uncle Tungsten, seems to have been the story of your childhood search for order and stability in the world. Where do you find it now?

SACKS Well, I have friends and relationships which seem to have fidelity and stability. I love my patients and the clinical work and I love looking at the mechanisms of the brain and the mind. And until recently, I've had a very nice feeling of the solidity of the buildings and the streets around me. Now, like everyone, since September 11th—

WACHTEL You live in New York.

SACKS Yes, and the fabric of my security has been shaken and I think some rather deep sense of instability has emerged. Doris Lessing once made a comment on one of my books, Awakenings. She said it shows what a knife edge we live on. Now, in general, I don't think we live on a knife edge. It's true one might be killed, something might happen. But I think there's a certain reassuring solidity about the body. It's different from the solidity of tungsten; the solidity of the body and the organism, its adaptability and flexibility and resiliency, its many fallback mechanisms. It's the resilience of health that is different—it's the wonder of the organic. On the whole, people's characters are relatively stable. Interests endure and enlarge. In a sense, the stability of life itself, its constancy and growth, as well as the adventure and the risk, this is now my support.

November 2001

JANE JACOBS

Jane Jacobs is variously known as the guru of cities, an urban legend—"part analyst, part activist, part prophet." In the more than forty years since the publication of her groundbreaking book, *The Death and Life of Great American Cities* (1961), her influence has been extraordinary—not only on architects, community workers and planners but also on Nobel Prize–winning economists and ecologists. As one critic recently put it, "Jacobs's influence confirms that books matter. It isn't easy to cite another writer who has had a comparable impact in our time." A couple of years ago, she won the top American award for urban planning, the Vincent Scully Prize. This in itself was unusual, not only because she regularly vilifies planners, but also because with the exception of the Order of Canada and a few other prizes, she typically turns down awards—some thirty honorary degrees, including one from Harvard. Jacobs herself wasn't interested in finishing university—she went to Columbia for just two years.

Her editor, Jason Epstein, puts her among a handful of innovators—Rachel Carson, Julia Child, Betty Friedan, Martin Luther

King Jr., Dr. Benjamin Spock—who gave their fellow citizens "the confidence to challenge the life-denying follies of their times." On Canada Day 2002, she was named one of Ten Canadians Who Made a Difference by *Maclean's* magazine. Finally (one of my favourites), the *New York Times Magazine* included her in its hallmark list of "Irritating Women"—women who through the centuries have "tugged at history's sleeve and wouldn't let go"—from the medieval abbess and composer Hildegard of Bingen through the eighteenth-century feminist thinker Mary Wollstonecraft, concluding with Jane Jacobs.

Jane Jacobs was born in Scranton, Pennsylvania, in 1916. Her father was a family physician and her mother a schoolteacher and nurse. She knew from an early age that she wanted to be a writer. She also realized—from about third grade—that school wasn't a place of intellectual interest for her. After high school, she worked for the local paper and attended business school to pick up stenographic skills so she could earn a living. At eighteen, she moved to New York City and held a variety of jobs, both clerical and as an editor and writer. It was while she was working for *Architectural Forum* that she began the series of articles that became *The Death and Life of Great American Cities*.

The originality of her approach is the way she uses direct observation. As she captioned her illustrations in the table of contents, "The scenes that illustrate this book are all about us. For illustrations, please look closely at real cities. While you are looking, you might as well also listen, linger and think about what you see."

In the late 1960s, Jane Jacobs helped save her neighbourhood, New York's Greenwich Village, from destruction. In 1968, she moved to Toronto with her husband and their two draft-age sons and a daughter. Almost immediately, she was engaged in stopping the Spadina Expressway from cutting through her new neighbourhood in the Annex.

It's not often that I meet someone in studio and then have the opportunity—then pursue the opportunity—to see them again over a cup of tea. Some years ago, that happened with Jane Jacobs. We were talking about a book she'd put together about her aunt who was a pioneer teacher in Alaska. We didn't want the conversation to end, so a few days later I went to see Jacobs and her husband of forty-two years, a retired architect. (He died later that year, in 1996.) They were direct, warm and fun to talk to.

Jacobs still lives in that large comfortable house in Toronto's Annex. When I went to see her last summer for this conversation, it took a little longer for her to come to the door, pushing her walker, but she is as intellectually agile and engaged as ever. At one point, I got up to switch off her new refrigerator so the hum wouldn't interfere with the recording. She insisted on watching how it was done, saying, "I take my learning where I can find it."

Her most recent books are *Systems of Survival* (1994) and *The Nature of Economies* (2000).

WACHTEL You wrote your 1961 book *The Death and Life of Great American Cities* when you were living in New York. You said, "Most of the material for these musings was at my front door." In your case, I think the front door was, and still is, more than a metaphor. What did that connection to the life of the street mean to you?

JACOBS I knew what was going on and how interesting it was. What it meant to me was being in the middle of things—not off in some abstract way or, thank goodness, not up above it, with everybody being little ants down below and me being God.

WACHTEL You lived down on Hudson Street in Greenwich Village or, I guess, technically the West Village, whose "daily ballet," as you call it, you document in your book. What was your own front door actually like?

JACOBS Well, it had two steps up from the street to the threshold of the wooden door. It had an electric outlet up above it for a light. We put that in very soon after we moved there, but we never did get the light in.

WACHTEL You got the house in 1947, and initially the ground floor was a store and you lived on the upper floors.

JACOBS Yes. There was a candy store, which had been closed down and abandoned on the ground floor. At that time there were actually two front doors, one of them into the candy store and the other one into a narrow hallway with a stairway that led to the living quarters up above.

WACHTEL That image of the view from the front door neatly captures your own special qualities as a thinker and a writer because it's open, it's curious, it's down-to-earth. You're famous for helping us look at familiar things in a new way. I think one critic said your books are principally about what one could see if one opened one's eyes. How did you come by that attitude, do you think, to be so observant or naturally inquisitive?

JACOBS I don't know. I don't myself think that I'm unusual in that way. These are things that anyone can see. So let's put it the other way. How come I wasn't closed off from it? I think that, in many cases, people don't see what is in front of their eyes because they've been told what they should be seeing.

WACHTEL How does that happen?

JACOBS A couple of weeks ago, I finished writing an introduction to one of Mark Twain's books, *The Innocents Abroad*, which is being reissued by the Modern Library. One thing I was struck by in reading it was how much Twain emphasized that what he was trying to do was tell readers what they might see if they looked with their own eyes. He inveighed at great length against guidebooks and people who believed the guidebooks instead of what they were seeing. So this is an old problem. I suppose it comes from people wanting to be correct and not trusting themselves, fearing they'd seem like uneducated country bumpkins in his day, if they told what they saw and how it struck them. I don't remember ever being forced to wear those sorts of blinders when I was a child. Children *do* report what they see, if they're not pooh-poohed and are listened to respectfully. Grown-ups usually hear something interesting. That's a way of encouraging people to look with their own eyes.

WACHTEL Tell me about that childhood. What are your earliest memories of your household, of your neighbourhood in Scranton, Pennsylvania?

JACOBS When I was four years old, we moved to the house that I remember best, where I lived till I was eighteen. But my earliest memories, of course, are before four years of age, in a different house, and on the sidewalk in front of that house. In our household we had four children. One of them at that time was a baby, but there were three who were older. We had two vehicles that my mother called velocipedes, really tricycles. I learned to get out early to stake my claim on one of the velocipedes. Another memory is of my father, who was a doctor. He had one of the earliest automobiles in the neighbourhood. Automobiles have never seemed glamorous to me because, after all, they were just a workaday thing. He needed it to make his calls, but sometimes he would take my mother and my brother and me with him. I saw quite a bit of Scranton that way. One thing I saw was what we called the "built-down" houses. Scranton was a coal-mining city, and although there were laws about leaving columns of rock in the mines to support the ground up above, the robber baron companies would sometimes "rob the pillars." They would take out these supports for their coal, and then the ground would cave in above them. If there were houses above, the houses caved down into a hole. That's why we called them "built-down" houses.

WACHTEL So would people still try to live in them?

JACOBS Yes, people were still living in them. The worst danger was that sometimes the gas pipes broke and then people would be asphyxiated, or else there would be an explosion. Who needs terrorists when you've got robber barons?

WACHTEL Your original home at 1712 Monroe—the one that you moved to when you were four—is one of the three addresses to which you've dedicated one of your more recent books, Systems of Survival, along with the Greenwich Village address on Hudson and this one in Toronto. What made that first house special for you?

JACOBS Well, a place where you live from the time you're four years old until you're eighteen is your childhood home, really. I loved the house. It's still there. I visited it not long ago.

WACHTEL What was the atmosphere like in your home? Were there lots of conversations or debates?

JACOBS It was a cheerful place. We did a lot of talking. My father worked long, long hours as a doctor, at first making house calls. Later on, he kept long office hours, including evening hours because that's often when people could come. In the morning, he would get his newspaper, the *Public Ledger*, a Philadelphia paper, and stand it up in a wire contrivance that he had. But he didn't shut himself off with this newspaper—he was always reading nuggets to us from it. He had favourite columnists. I remember the name of one of them—Jay House—and he would say, "Let's see what Jay is saying today." Then he'd tell us if there was anything interesting.

WACHTEL Your father grew up on a farm in Virginia. What was he like? How would you describe him?

JACOBS Well, he was intellectually very curious, bright and independent. In some ways he was like a detective. He was locally very famous as a diagnostician, and a good diagnostician is a sort of detective. I loved to hear his stories about how he found out this and that. He had all kinds of patients, and he would tell us about them, so my two brothers and my sister and I got quite a picture of Scranton as a great mosaic.

WACHTEL You've said that you owe your intellectual independence to your father. How was that?

JACOBS Being a good diagnostician, he had to use his own eyes and ears, and his reason. He was also a good listener. My first job, after I got out of high school, was at the local newspaper. Fortunately that was right across the street from his office downtown. It was a morning newspaper, so my hours were from early afternoon until as late as need be. I liked that, working in the evening and at night and sleeping late in the morning. When I finished, I would go across the street to his office. Sometimes there were still a few people in the waiting room. Sometimes he would be reading his medical journals because everybody had left. Then, we would talk, and I would go home with him.

WACHTEL What would you talk about?

JACOBS If he was seeing any patients, he would tell me about that. I would tell him about what had happened at the newspaper. Or we would talk about things in general. Sometimes I asked him weighty questions like, What is the purpose of life?

WACHTEL What did he say?

JACOBS Actually, we were sitting on our front porch when we got into that conversation and he said, "Look at that tree, that oak tree." He pointed to the tree in our yard, and he said, "What is its purpose? It's alive."

I made of the answer that the purpose of life is to live, and so I told him that's what I thought. He said, "Yes, that tree has a great push to live—any healthy, living thing does."

WACHTEL Your mother was a schoolteacher and nurse who lived to be 101. From your letters to her, many of which have now been published, you seem to have had a wonderful relationship. Tell me about her.

JACOBS When I was an adolescent, I didn't have such a good relationship with her because she was brought up in a small town in Victorian times, and the result was what you might imagine. She read a lot and had many interesting stories to tell about her small town, but she was, in that Victorian way, quite prissy, and particularly about anything to do with sex. She was also very conservative politically, much more so than my father, who was open-minded and curious and more imaginative. So I would get into arguments with her, or I would feel I had to shut up about things that I really would have liked to talk to her about. Later on, I learned that there were all kinds of things we could talk about. There were still some things that were taboo, but I came to appreciate her more and more for the things we could discuss. She was sensible and loyal, a real reservoir of knowledge.

WACHTEL What kinds of values do you think she instilled in you?

JACOBS She was a very compassionate person. She had been a nurse in Philadelphia—that's where she and my father met, while he was a resident in the same hospital. Most of the child patients that she had were from very poor areas of Philadelphia and she would tell me how limited their lives were. She felt sorry about that. One of the things she hated, by the way, was freak shows, which in those days accompanied every fair or circus that came to town. She hated them because she felt that unfortunate people shouldn't be looked at that way. I've never been to a freak show in my life. Another thing I've never done is drink pink lemonade, which she told me to avoid because it was made by putting a dirty red necktie into the lemonade and squeezing it until the dye came out. I suppose, in the early 1900s in Philadelphia, before the Pure Food and Drugs legislation came in, in 1906, there were all kinds of dreadful chemical adulterations. To this day, I can't drink pink lemonade.

WACHTEL Both your parents grew up in the country, but you've said that they were both delighted to live in a city, that they found cities a superior place to live.

JACOBS Father often told us what a hard life farming was. He didn't romanticize it at all, and we knew very graphically how difficult it was. The farm he grew up on in Virginia was the kind of farm that is much romanticized today. It was a general-purpose family farm, about two hundred acres, which is enough to make a living from but not so big that you needed hired help. Among other things, they raised a kind of Scottish cattle called Black Galloways, and we had a skin of one of these that had been tanned and was on the floor under the stairs, where there was a nice nook with a bookcase. We always called it the "buffalo skin," we children, but it was a Black Galloway skin.

In the city, they liked the house that we lived in, the same as I did, and they enjoyed the people in the city. They had a lot of interest in how the city ran and what was there. They were public-spirited people. I think they appreciated the libraries and the various other amenities.

WACHTEL Sounds like you were thinking about cities from a very early age. In fourth grade, you questioned your geography lesson. When the teacher said that cities were located near a waterfall, you said you didn't believe this because mines were what was going on in Scranton. How were you so attuned to this?

JACOBS I loved going downtown, from the earliest I remember. I found it very interesting and exciting. In fact, I liked going to the dentist because it gave me a chance to go downtown.

Scranton had a very nice downtown, with an interesting array of stores—it was the city for quite a large catchment area. The high school I went to was downtown. The public reference library, which is a beautiful building and had a very good librarian—which is even more important—was downtown. My father had his office downtown. There was a courthouse and a courthouse square in the middle of things, with a statue of John Mitchell, an organizer of one of the earliest mine unions. For a city to put up a statue of a union organizer in its main square was quite unusual. The miners' children from a neighbourhood near ours would, on a certain day in the year, be excused so they could march in the John Mitchell Day parade, a big event in Scranton. I once asked one of these classmates who John Mitchell was, and she said he was the greatest man in the world. When I worked on the newspaper, the guild had just organized a local; it was the third newspaper in the whole United States to be organized. So Scranton was quite progressive in these ways.

WACHTEL You've said that you grew up with the idea that you could do anything. Was that unusual for a young woman in those days?

JACOBS No, it was not—it was quite common. These things ebb and flow. There had been a successful women's suffrage movement, which was followed by the notion that women were equal to men and could do anything. In the Girl Scouts troop that my sister and I belonged to, we had all sorts of merit badges, not just child care and being a hostess and those sorts of things, but for astronomy and tree finding and making things. All of this was part of a liberating ideology for women. We were lucky we grew up in an island of hope for women. I think that nowadays people don't realize how different that was from the way women were treated and thought of during the Depression and after the war. There was a real going backwards; it was reflected in the Girl Scouts and in the magazines for girls, as well as in society in general.

WACHTEL Both your parents were in helping professions. Were you inclined or encouraged towards that kind of social service yourself?

JACOBS No, I wasn't, and they didn't try to influence me as to what I should do, apart from one thing. My father told all four of us that it was a very good thing to know what you wanted to do and to work towards that goal, but you also ought to have something that was always in demand and was easy to get a job at, to fall back on. He said parents used to give their daughters dowries, but that it was much better to give them an education.

WACHTEL You weren't that crazy about education, though. I read that you learned a lot in grades one and two, but by grade three you were reading books under the desk for yourself. You had a restless mind, I think. What were you hungry for?

JACOBS Well, to tell you the truth, I thought that most of my teachers were rather stupid. They believed a lot of nonsense. I was always trying to educate them, so we would get into conflicts sometimes. In those days, classrooms were much more regimented than they are now. For hours we would sit there doing this or that and we wouldn't be allowed to talk unless we were asked a question. I had quite a few misapprehensions of one sort or another, and one misapprehension I had, when I was silent for all this time—which I never was at home—was a fear that I couldn't talk any more, that I didn't have a voice any more. So I developed what you might call a little tic. I would make a little noise in my throat, a little voiced noise, just to be sure I could still talk. My parents asked me one day why I did that. I didn't tell them because I had a feeling that if I did, it would open up the whole subject of how my teachers and I were at outs a good deal.

WACHTEL You were expelled in grade three. What did you do?

JACOBS Well, one night we'd been talking at home and my father told us in the course of the conversation that it was very foolish for children to make promises that they would do something for their whole life— that a promise was a very serious thing and you should never make one unless you were quite sure you could carry it out. It so happened that the next day in school a man came and spoke to us about care of the teeth. And at the end of this talk, he asked everybody to promise to brush their teeth every night and morning all their life, and to raise our hand to promise. I said to my classmates not to do this. They were putting up their hands and pulling them down. When we got back into the classroom, the teacher said she was mortified by our behaviour and what did we think we were doing? Some of the children said that Jane had told them not to raise their hands. So she wormed the story out and I told her that, no, that was a bad thing to do. She decided that the way to deal with this was to get me to make this promise, but all she got from me was an argument. So, at her wits' end, she expelled me.

WACHTEL From early childhood, you've carried on conversations with people like Benjamin Franklin or Thomas Jefferson. Not your ordinary imaginary companions. What need do you think this dialogue came from?

JACOBS I think a lot of children do that.

WACHTEL Benjamin Franklin?

JACOBS Yes, or whoever they choose to talk to.

WACHTEL What do you think this sort of dialogue satisfied in you?

JACOBS I mentioned I liked to try to educate my schoolteachers. Well, I was trying to educate, believe it or not, Benjamin Franklin or Jefferson, in the sense that they didn't know about a lot of the things that we would pass by on the street because they were born too soon. And they were curious about these things, so in a way I was testing out how much I knew about these things.

WACHTEL So it would heighten your own sense of observation because you would have to pay attention to details in order to explain it to somebody who hadn't seen it, couldn't see it.

JACOBS Yes, and since I went on the same routes all the time—to school, or I went to the store for my mother or to where we got the streetcar—if you walk the same route a great many times, it gets boring, so this was an entertainment for me, too.

WACHTEL You went to business school after high school, following your father's dictum to equip yourself with a skill to fall back on, and you worked as a stenographer. But you've said that all along you wanted to be a writer. What kind of writing appealed to you?

JACOBS I didn't know, but I began, like many children, writing verses and having fun with rhyming words and that sort of thing. I suppose it was because I liked to read so much.

WACHTEL You made your first trip to New York when you were twelve, in 1928, and you've described some of your impressions of that visit— lunchtime on Wall Street and so on. What was the most exciting thing about that experience?

JACOBS The number of people and how fast everything was happening. This was before the stock market crash and the Depression, so I was getting a glimpse of New York during its great boom time. I'm always glad I saw it at that point.

WACHTEL Did you know then that you wanted to live and work in New York?

JACOBS Yes, it appealed to me then. My sister, who was six years older than me, had gone to New York as soon as she graduated from college. So that pretty well settled it—I could go and join her.

WACHTEL When you were eighteen, you did join your sister in New York. You've described hunting for work and exploring the city in the process—the different neighbourhoods that actually became material for you when you came to write articles for *Vogue* or the *Herald Tribune*. You couldn't have known at the time that these explorations were part of a larger project for you, an investigation into the life of the city and the life of cities. What were you after, back then?

JACOBS It just interested me. I was drifting. I didn't have any great plan, and I don't, to this day. Insofar as I had any plan, it was just to pursue what interested me. Now, my husband's father had an idea about this. The advice he gave my husband when he was a boy was to get interested in something and study and work at it. He said that if you do that, you're likely to do well at it, and if you do well at it, you're likely to find somebody who'll pay you to do it. That was his career advice, and that's pretty much what I have always done. I think it's actually quite realistic advice. I think people who can work at something that really interests them, and that they're enthusiastic about, are much happier than people who take a job because it runs in their family or it's a big money-maker or it seems safe.

WACHTEL It was while you were working for *Architectural Forum* that you began what has become your most famous book, *The Death and Life of Great American Cities*. You've described a moment of awakening when you visited a new housing development in Philadelphia designed by a celebrated planner. Can you talk about that moment, that revelation?

JACOBS Yes. The chief planner of Philadelphia was showing me around. First we walked down a street that was just crammed with people, mostly black people, walking on the sidewalks and sitting on the stoops and leaning out of the windows. I think he was taking me on this street to show me what he regarded as a bad part of the city, to contrast it with what he was going to show me next. I liked this street—people were using it and enjoying it and enjoying each other. Then we went over to the parallel street that had just undergone urban renewal. It was filled with very sterile housing projects. The planner was very proud of it, and he urged me to stand at a certain spot to see what a great vista it had. I thought the whole thing was extremely boring—there was nobody on the street. All the time we were there, which was too long for me, I saw only one little boy. He was kicking a tire in the gutter. The planner told me that they were progressing to the next street over, where we had come from, which he obviously regarded as disgraceful. I said that all the people were over there, that there were no people here, and what did he think of that? What he obviously would have liked was groups of people standing and admiring the vistas that he had created. You could see that nothing else mattered to him. So I realized that not only did he and the people he directed not know how to make an interesting or a humane street, but they didn't even notice such things and didn't care. People sometimes ask me if I wrote this book to educate planners. My reply is always no, because I thought they were hopeless.

WACHTEL Your first book started as a series of articles and then turned into something much bigger. What happened?

JACOBS I was lobbying the editors of the magazine I worked for to allow me to do a series of four articles on topics like "The Uses of Sidewalks." I realized that if they were to be a series, they had to have a certain coherence. Since it was a monthly magazine and we were always scrambling to get it out on time, it would mean that I would need to be forgiven for not contributing for several issues until I got all four articles written.

WACHTEL Then, how did it go from being articles about sidewalks?

JACOBS I didn't end up writing them as articles. By chance I had given a talk at Harvard that attracted some attention, and one of the editors of *Fortune*, William H. White, asked me, because of that, to write an article about downtowns for *Fortune*. It was to be longer than any article I had ever written. I didn't think I could do it—they wanted twenty-five hundred words. All of our articles in *Architectural Forum* were much shorter. Then somebody else who had become interested in the *Fortune* article— this is the kind of thing that can happen in big cities—a man from the Rockefeller Foundation, invited me to a meeting with others from the Foundation. They were interested in cities and wanted to know if there was any way they could help me. Imagine, this is like having a fairy godmother descend on you.

Well, I began to think about it, and when I went back and saw the Rockefeller Foundation man, I said that I'd been thinking it over and what I wanted to do was write a book. All along, they had been hoping I would come to that conclusion. So I got a grant from them that would support me for a year.

WACHTEL But then it took two years.

JACOBS Then it took two years. At the end of the first year, I called up this Rockefeller man and said I wasn't done yet. He said, "Tell me something: Is the book turning out to be the way you planned it in the first place?" I said, "No, not at all, because I want to write about a lot of things that I didn't know I wanted to write about when I began." I thought to myself, That's the truth, but they're not going to like it—it sounds so scatterbrained. On the contrary. He said that was good, that's what they had hoped would happen.

WACHTEL What directions did it take that you didn't expect?

JACOBS I'd been to some new urbanist conferences and I didn't think they understood anything about the nature of cities. They plan the centre of a city as if it were a shopping centre, even though they talk about it being for people to come to on foot. I think that they leave out the notion of time. This was one of the things I discovered: time is terribly important in cities. Whether an area improves over time or whether it deteriorates, there are lots of lessons that are perfectly obvious that, to this day, I don't think planners—even the most trendy ones—are learning.

Then I wrote my next book, The Economy of Cities. In a way, that's the most important book I've written, I think, because I did discover some things that are really central to city economies and that I still think are not enough appreciated. One problem I noted was that economists and others love to say that what I'm describing is old-fashioned. One of the major criticisms I get from economists and from city planners is that I think small businesses are important. What I was thinking about, of course, was time, and where do large businesses come from originally? How do things start? The general idea at the time I wrote The Economy of Cities was that small businesses were an old-fashioned thing that were no longer of any importance. It's only a few years ago that it became the accepted new wisdom—which is true—that most of the jobs added in an economy are added in small businesses, not from growth in already large businesses.

WACHTEL At the time when you first published The Death and Life of Great American Cities, you had to defend the title, and in fact the British publishers felt that it wouldn't be understood. But why was that construction—Death first and then Life—so important for you? Were you confident that life was possible?

JACOBS Yes. If it was "Life and Death," it would look as if that's where cities were heading. I didn't think that. That's why I put Life second.

WACHTEL Near the end of that book, you say in thirty years' time things are going to be worse. Do you think that's happened? Are things worse now than when you wrote the book?

JACOBS In some ways they're worse and in some ways better. The things that are worse I don't think are so much focused or anchored in cities as they are in our North American culture as a whole.

WACHTEL What kinds of things?

JACOBS Just think about general current events. Think how many of our important institutions are failing us. Look what's happening to accounting, which we've counted on for centuries to tell us honestly the situation in businesses large and small. In countries where there has not been a tradition of financial accountability, and they don't track how various organizations and institutions are doing, where they're failing and where they're not, there are often very bad consequences. It's a great accomplishment in this civilization that we have a way of keeping count of things, and knowing where we are—keeping businesses honest, in that sense. Well, look what's happening. The scandals unfold daily in the papers and that's a very serious thing for cities, since they are the centre of so much of our economy.

Consider the family, the nuclear family. On the whole, I think we have to admit it's a great failure. When there's anywhere from a third to a half of marriages ending in divorce, that should give people pause. When both parents, working as hard as they can, cannot make enough money to pay a month's rent, that's pretty sad. Something is wrong there.

WACHTEL So how have things improved?

JACOBS Well, I think that things are getting better for cities in that there's not the great ruthless wiping away of their most interesting areas that took place in the past. Terrible things were happening when I wrote *Death and Life*, so that's an improvement. However, I think the urban sprawl outside of cities has gotten much worse. I think there's been a great loss of community of all kinds, mostly in the suburbs.

WACHTEL *The Death and Life of Great American Cities* is considered one of the most important books to be written on American urban life. "One of those rare books," as someone wrote, "that not only changed the way people think but actually changed the world that we live in." You're not an urban planner. You're not an economist. And in fact, although you took some classes at Columbia, you were never really interested in a degree. What advantage do you think your lack of formal training has given you?

JACOBS Well, I can give you an actual instance. When I got the grant to start writing this book, some people involved in the joint urban studies program at Harvard and at M.I.T. invited me up there because they wanted to talk to me. They had it all figured out—how I should use that grant, how I should use my time. They had decided what they wanted done and they were treating me as if I was a graduate student. What they actually wanted me to do was make up a questionnaire and give it to people in some middle-income sterile project somewhere, to find out what they didn't like. Then I was to make tables of it. They had it all worked out, what I should do. So I listened to them and remained polite, but I couldn't wait to get out of there. I felt so liberated when I left. I thought, Wouldn't it be awful if my career depended on these dopes, and I was obliged to do what they wanted? That's what would have happened if I had been trapped in a university.

WACHTEL In the foreword to the new edition of *The Death and Life of Great American Cities*, you say that obviously this book exerted "an influence on me and lured me into my subsequent life's work." How so?

JACOBS Doing this first book made me wonder about why some cities seem to succeed, in the sense that they don't wither away—that old idea that the purpose of life is to live—and they manage to succeed in continuing to live. I was aware of this because Scranton, like many settlements that depend on a mine or a particular commodity, did fail eventually. Everything changes, and no specialty lasts forever. I began wondering about that. What was different about the cities that didn't die but kept on finding new things to do? Some of these cities are very old and some of them are not, so I also thought there must be various processes that can be seen through time. Again, time was very important. That's how I got to writing my next book, *The Economy of Cities*. Then, the next logical thing was looking at how cities affect the outside world, how they affect each other and how they affect their hinterlands. That became *Cities and the Wealth of Nations*, and that's when I made the discovery that city regions were different from any other kinds of regions. Then I got interested in the sort of moral assumptions that regulate all this, and I wrote *Systems of Survival*, which led to my latest book, *The Nature of Economies*. And that's about cities and economies as part of nature. We are part of nature, after all.

WACHTEL It's interesting that you would take that approach in *The Nature of Economies* since you seem to have favoured cities over nature in your other writings. Is it because it's a different look at nature?

JACOBS Yes. I make the point that nature always wins. There are things you can do that work and things you can do that are unnatural and won't work.

WACHTEL One theme in your work is the interconnectedness of things, and one of the ways you get at that is through language itself. You point out that language follows a natural, unpredictable pattern, and in that way it's almost a model of evolution. It makes itself up as it goes along, I think is how you put it. Has the analogy with language been useful for you?

JACOBS I don't know whether *useful* is the right word. It just helps me clarify the fact that things start somewhere and then they grow and evolve. Language is all made up of process. That's what interests me—processes.

WACHTEL One aspect of process is a kind of diversity, whether it's in neighbourhoods or cities or the larger organizations that you've explored. As you say, specialization at the expense of diversity is unwholesome for both economies and ecosystems. Why is there such a drive for specialization? What is the resistance to diversity?

JACOBS It's one of those wrong-headed things that's become part of conventional learning. Adam Smith thought that specialization was wonderful and he mixed up a lot of things. He thought of it as division of labour among nations, and since he thought division of labour was good, then division of labour among nations must be good, too. Adam Smith was very good at using his own eyes and noticing what was happening, but when he got abstract like that, it became another way of playing at words and that's not very useful. Division of labour is very good in a pin factory, so it must be good in the world in general. No, then it becomes ideological, and we have to be very wary about that. Specialization was put on a pedestal as a great piece of wisdom, but in fact every specialty you can think of betrays the place that specialized it sooner or later.

WACHTEL For instance?

JACOBS Another place does it cheaper, better, or the thing grows obsolete.

WACHTEL When you talk about the relationship between economies and nature, you say it's not a matter of imitating nature but of using the same universal principles that the rest of nature does. How do you get at that?

JACOBS Well, development is a natural process. The earth itself has developed over time. At one time it was barren and had no life.

WACHTEL What about entropy? That's something that happens in nature, too.

JACOBS Yes, and probably what you mean is that everything's going to run down because of it. Well, maybe and maybe not. Most of the recent thought about the cosmos is that it doesn't run down. Certainly, things that have become disorganized don't reorganize themselves. If you throw a pack of cards on the floor, it doesn't put itself in order. I shouldn't even mention this because I don't know enough astronomy, but what I understand is that there are different zones in the universe and one of them is a zone where things are drawn in and made very dense—black holes. Eventually they explode or scatter into widespread matter, and then the cycle begins again, with matter getting into clumps as suns and planets. It's long been recognized that matter can't be made and it can't be destroyed. People know that, but they don't take it seriously enough. If it's true at all, then entropy does not destroy.

WACHTEL In the sixties, you were living on Hudson Street in New York, raising your family with your architect husband, around the time you were writing The Death and Life of Great American Cities. You became deeply involved at that time with your neighbourhood, your street, the city, the country, and you were forced—I think of it as forced—to become an activist. Was that kind of political engagement at all natural to you?

JACOBS No, it really wasn't. I wanted to be learning things and writing. I resented that I had to stop and devote myself to fighting what was basically an absurdity that had been foisted on me and my neighbours.

WACHTEL There was an urban renewal project in your neighbourhood.

JACOBS Yes. And the city officials who did it didn't know what they were doing. For that matter, neither did the federal officials. About the same time, they were trying to drive an eight-lane highway through where SoHo is now in New York. That's about the most successful part of the city. They didn't know what they were doing at all. They thought they were very smart about real estate; they weren't. Always be prepared to think that experts are stupid. They often are.

WACHTEL You were also part of a larger movement at the time. You marched on the Pentagon. And you were arrested with Susan Sontag and Allen Ginsberg during anti-draft demonstrations in New York. You've been charged with riot, inciting to riot, criminal mischief, and obstructing government administration. How did it affect you to be out on the front lines like that?

JACOBS Well, as long as it couldn't be avoided, which it couldn't be if you were a responsible person, you had to fight. As long as you're doing it, you might as well decide to have a good time. Of course, what makes it a really good time is if you win.

The charges you mentioned were for my involvement in opposing the Lower Manhattan Expressway, which would have wiped out what was to become SoHo. It was worth doing. How did it affect me? I'll tell you a little story. At one point, I had to go to the courthouse because a judge was going to make a decision about whether to proceed with those four accusations, each of which carried a year in prison as a penalty. We're talking about a total of four years in prison. A judge had to rule on whether it seemed serious enough that I should go to trial or whether it was nonsense—and it was nonsense, I'll tell you. But I went to court. And the prosecutor made such a case of what a monster I was, and my own lawyer didn't seem very well prepared at all. The judge was really down on me. I could tell that I was, as the saying goes, getting the book thrown at me. Up until then, I hadn't really taken very seriously that something so dreadful would actually happen to me—and it didn't in the end, but I didn't know that that day. I went home after the hearing—

I didn't have to have bail—feeling pretty depressed about it. Scared, too. When I got home, the children were all in school and my husband was at work. I went inside and I sat down gloomily at the dining table, feeling pretty hopeless. I could practically hear those jail doors slamming behind me. The first person who came home was my son Ned. He threw his school books down on the table and asked how it went in court. I said, "Oh, all right, I guess." He sat down and said, "You know, for a woman of fifty-three, you lead a very exciting life." And all of a sudden I felt about a thousand percent better.

WACHTEL In 1968, you left the United States for Toronto in protest against the Vietnam War and also to avoid the draft for your sons. This was serendipitous, certainly for Toronto and I think for you as well. You described your new home shortly after as "the most hopeful and healthy city in North America, still unmangled and still with options." What did you value most then in Toronto?

JACOBS In comparison to what was happening in U.S. cities at the time, Toronto wasn't being treated as if it were an occupied country with a conquering power knocking its people around. People weren't being treated as if they were guinea pigs. Another thing I admired was that when something was a failure in Canada, they didn't keep repeating it.

WACHTEL Like what?

JACOBS There were some very bad public housing projects, because Canadians had fallen for the same baloney as the Americans—great big projects where people were sorted out. They're still plaguing Toronto, a lot of these projects, but they had at least stopped building them. They also were closing down their federal Department of Housing, which was doing very bad things.

WACHTEL You mean by creating these kinds of public housing projects?

JACOBS And also putting highways through the city. We had to fight the Spadina Expressway.

WACHTEL Wasn't that ironic? You'd just finished fighting a highway in New York and then you come up here and it's a perfectly analogous situation.

JACOBS But it wasn't as hard to fight up here. For one thing, there wasn't as much federal money thrown at it. A lot of people think that our cities can be rescued if you can only get enough federal money, but money alone isn't the answer. The right things have to be done with the money.

WACHTEL And what are the right things?

JACOBS It depends on each city totally. Cities need different things at different times. I despair sometimes how, when the right things are done, they're soon forgotten. For example, when David Crombie was mayor in the seventies, affordable housing, public housing, was built in an entirely new and different way as infill housing, knit into neighbourhoods. Right down at the end of our block here, we have infill housing, where the subway wiped out a strip of older housing. It was a great success and it was also an economical way to create housing. Big developers with deep pockets aren't interested in small sites, and yet there are a lot of them and they add up. They also knit up the neighbourhood where they're built. So we knew how to do it. But while we were really becoming expert at this new way of looking at housing, the suburbs were going in the opposite direction. People weren't learning from the city of Toronto. About that time, the money dried up. So now I worry that when money becomes available for infill housing again, people will have forgotten what a decent and economical approach it was. People from all over the world used to come and tour Toronto to see this infill public housing.

WACHTEL When you came to Canada with your family, you decided you were immigrants, not exiles. Why was that important to you?

JACOBS We wanted to be a part of where we were. If you've come from somewhere else, that's being an immigrant. Being an exile is having it fixed in your mind that you've just come to a place as a stop-gap measure. One thing we realized when we were outside the U.S. was that Americans don't really think that any place outside of America is as real as America. We didn't, either, when we lived there, but we saw this as soon as we were outside of the United States and committed to a different place. It's a strange kind of egotism—which extends to one's country—that no place else could be as important, and if not as important, it's not quite as real.

WACHTEL You became a Canadian citizen in 1974, which in those days meant giving up your American citizenship. Given that your family was old-stock American, was that hard for you?

JACOBS No. I wanted to be here and felt very lucky that there was a country next door that I could come to. I didn't have the kind of attachment to America that gave me identity. I had some identity of my own. It didn't depend on my being an American. I was just as real when I was in Canada.

WACHTEL You soon had an effect on the city of Toronto, but how do you feel you, in turn, have been shaped by life in Toronto and in Canada?

JACOBS It's a much more civil place, and not as cruel a place as America, and I like this. Sometimes it's a little too much. For instance, sometimes in Canada and Toronto, you feel, when you're talking to somebody, as if you're talking to a pillow, that they will not actually say what they think. But on the whole, the civility and politeness is a really nice thing. While I have in this interview accused various people of being stupid, I don't do it to people's faces as much as I would have in New York.

WACHTEL When you say "less cruel," what do you mean?

JACOBS Well, I have to amend that. With our current provincial government, and with the one in Alberta, and the one doing all kinds of cruel things in British Columbia, I won't say that Canada is so much less cruel. There are a lot of really mean-spirited people in Canada. These provincial governments I've just mentioned are really mean-spirited. It's a funny thing. In New York, if you were in a battle and got the good words from somebody in government—nice compliments and things for your side—you began to shudder, because one side always got the good words and the other side got the good deed. That was the politically sensible thing, you see, to try to placate both sides. Now, for all its civility, that's something that Canadian politicians just never seemed to have learned, at least provincial ones. They are terrible towards the school system and at the same time they say the meanest things they can think of about it. They're not even giving the side that they're hurting the good words. So that's rather cruel, for the sake of cruelty. There are very resentful people running what I think of now as the Northern Alliance of provincial warlords. Very resentful people. They're getting their jollies out of kicking people—children or communities or the school system. And they seem to be under the belief that people my age are sitting around by choice in doctors' offices using public money. Malingerers. So maybe under all this civility there was a lot of resentment that is only coming out now. It's unfortunate.

WACHTEL To go back to the city itself, as a kind of literary metaphor, the city was traditionally a golden place, and the notion of the city as a focus of corruption and evil is, as you point out, a relatively recent one. Is there a model of a golden city in your mind?

JACOBS No, there isn't. Every city I know of has problems and has made mistakes. But as long as it's alive, and as long as its young people are attached to it and will still work at it, there's always hope and there's always the possibility of becoming better.

The world is full of people with plans to do things that they're very interested in, and very creative about. This includes people who are writing plays or painting pictures, people who are designing buildings or inventing things. What excites me is the aggregate of all those live, active people and the things they're trying to do.

WACHTEL Your first book was in part fuelled by anger. What angers you most today?

JACOBS One thing that angers me is the way most foreign aid is delivered, especially to the poorest countries. I think it's pretty well known now that most of the African countries that have gotten aid are worse off now than they were twenty years ago. That's not a politically popular or correct thing to say because it sounds as if I don't think they should receive any more aid. What I'm saying is, it has to be done differently. It's become conventional for countries that have contributed to that aid that's turned out to be minus and hurtful—actually hurtful, in many cases—to blame the International Monetary Fund or the World Bank.

Well, they're culpable, all right, for doing things wrong, but Canada's culpable, too. A lot of Canada's foreign aid is what is called "tied" foreign aid. The countries that receive it don't have a choice, really, of what they're getting. Perhaps it's certain kinds of engineering expertise for building dams, or certain other products. That's what Canada's contributing, and it's really for the benefit of the Canadian economy. It's a way of getting taxpayers to subsidize our own industries or services or products under the much more palatable-sounding foreign aid. The first priority is not at all the well-being of the country getting tied aid.

WACHTEL What do you think of the resurgence in activism that's being played out at these international globalization conferences?

JACOBS I'm glad to see it. I'm glad to see that people are caring about the world and not just thinking, Oh, that's far away and it doesn't affect me.

WACHTEL What's the view like now, from your home on Albany Avenue? What do you observe around you?

JACOBS I'm often amazed at how peaceful it is. And how lucky I am. And what a rare thing it is to live such a charmed kind of life. I don't want to be a parasite on the Earth. So much has been given to me—a nice house, space, lovely neighbours. I don't take it for granted.

WACHTEL What discoveries do you still make, just outside your door?

JACOBS I've discovered that I'm very envious of the people who skateboard and have in-line skates. I was a very enthusiastic rollerskater as a small child, but we didn't have skates that were nearly that wonderful. I just wish I could be on those skateboards or wearing in-line skates now. I was an enthusiastic cyclist and so I'm envious of the people who can still bicycle, but I don't feel I missed that. So I watch what people use to move around and there's plenty to see that's new. Who would think that the wheel could still have so many inventions left?

June 2002

UMBERTO ECO

In Italy, they call Umberto Eco "the Pavarotti of Semiotics," but he is more widely known as the man who wrote *The Name of the Rose* (1980, English trans. 1983)—a medieval detective story that became a runaway best-seller.

Umberto Eco was born in 1932 and grew up in a small town in northern Italy during the fascist period of Mussolini. He was the first in his family to attend university, going into medieval studies and writing his doctoral dissertation on the aesthetics of Thomas Aquinas. But this is how Eco writes about him, beginning an essay in honour of the seventh centenary of his death: "The worst thing that happened to Thomas Aquinas in the course of his career was not his death, on March 7, 1274, in Fossanova, when he was barely forty-nine, and, fat as he was, the monks were unable to carry his body down the stairs." No, the disaster that ruined his life befell him in 1323 when he was made into a saint. "These are nasty mishaps, like receiving the Nobel Prize, being admitted to the Académie française, winning an Oscar. You become like the *Mona*

Lisa: a cliché. It's the moment when the big arsonist is appointed Fire Chief."

That essay, "In Praise of St. Thomas," is from a book called *Travels in Hyperreality* (1986). In other words, even before Umberto Eco became a popular novelist, he was already an entertainer, a purveyor of fine ideas in accessible packages, a witty columnist and essayist, and an interpreter of popular culture. One of the earliest exponents of modern semiotics, he teaches it at the University of Bologna. Semiotics, he says, means he's "continuously trying to find the meaning of things under the text."

Umberto Eco is fluent in five languages. He has a huge personal library; in fact, he's had to move twice because the walls of his apartments were collapsing. The English writer Anthony Burgess once said of Eco, "No man should know so much." His novels reveal his fascination with history, philosophy, scientific theory, theology, cooking, occultism, astronomy, Renaissance warfare and so on.

What's amazing, perhaps, is just how successful these heavily laden novels are. *The Name of the Rose* has sold ten million copies in twenty-four languages. It was made into a movie with Sean Connery—a film which, incidentally, Eco hated. When Eco's second novel, *Foucault's Pendulum*, was published in 1988 (English trans. 1989), four hundred thousand copies were sold in Italy in its first two months. He has since come out with a novel about a seventeenth-century shipwreck near the Fiji Islands, *The Island of the Day Before* (1994, English trans. 1995), and most recently, *Baudolino* (2000, English trans. 2002), a fantastic medieval adventure about an Italian peasant with a talent for learning languages and telling lies. At the same time, Eco is the author of some forty non-fiction titles, including *Serendipities: Language and Lunacy* (1998).

WACHTEL In the essay, "The Miracle of San Baudolino," from your collection *How to Travel with a Salmon*, you described how, as a boy, you wanted to buy a certain novel because it was your "only hope of narrative and hence of reality." How is narrative your connection to reality?

ECO Your question is very difficult to answer. At this moment there are many persons—a semanticist, a neurologist, a psychologist—trying to answer it. Our way of facing reality, of understanding things, perceiving things, is narratively structured. To know what a tree is doesn't mean looking in a book to determine its nature. In order for a child to acquire knowledge of what a tree is, he has to learn a story. Once upon a time there was a seed. The seed was put in the earth. And then it grew up into a tree. Once you have the story of that tree, you have understood what a tree is. Today, those who work in artificial intelligence understand that in order to give a computer the ability to understand words, it's not enough to say "Man is a rational animal" or "Water is a transparent liquid." You have to express it in an elementary narrative way. In this sense, we are narrative animals; we grow up in narrations. Our mothers tell us stories, but not just stories like "Little Red Riding Hood." They are explaining the world to us in the form of stories. In my childhood, reading books and novels was a way to understand the world. When you have a curious and unusual experience, you try to understand what happened to you. When you try to put it in a narrative way, you find the cause, the effect, what really happened. When you are able to tell the story of what happened to you, you have finally understood what did happen.

WACHTEL You have an image of yourself pedalling across the village, going to the shop where they sold this book. Did you have a desire for story even then? Did you know what it was that you were after?

ECO I was writing stories by that time. My career as a storyteller started at the age of seven or eight. Then it stopped when I was about fifteen and started again when I was forty-eight. I remember when I was a child that I took a notebook and printed the title page in capital letters. Then I made a summary. Then I drew all the illustrations, every four or five pages. Then I started the first chapter. Then I stopped. So I was, at the time, the author of a lot of unfinished novels. I had the good taste to stop, rather like those who write poems between the ages of sixteen and twenty. The smart people throw them away and the silly people publish them.

WACHTEL But to look at the moment when you were in your forties, when you undertook fiction writing again and published *The Name of the Rose*. Why at that point did you turn to fiction?

ECO There are many explanations. I have another story to tell you. One day a friend of mine—a journalist working for a magazine—came to see me and told me that her editor had decided to ask some people who were not writers—sociologists, politicians—to write short detective stories that would be published every week. I said no, that I had never thought of writing a novel because I seem to be unable to write dialogue. Then, as a joke, I said that if I really had to write a detective story, it will be five hundred pages long and it will take place in a medieval monastery. She said no, it wouldn't do. I went home. I remember very clearly that morning: I went home and I said, why not? And I started taking notes about it all. This is the only serious evidence I can produce. Probably there was something turning in my unconscious. I had reached the point where I had all the things that I wanted. I had my university chair. I had published a lot of books, translated in many languages. Probably I needed a new challenge. There is another explanation I sometimes give in interviews, because in interviews you have to invent answers. When my kids were little, I told them a lot of stories. As soon as they became adults, I had to find a new and wider audience. I'd probably reached that certain age where I wanted to start something new. Now, there are gentlemen who, at that point, would escape with a ballerina to the southern islands, which is more expensive.

Probably there was another reason: all my scholarly books are narratively structured. In each of them, I tell the story of my research. In a sense I have always written novels, so at a certain point I decided to shift towards pure narrativity. I think I've always had this narrative impulse. I am a good joke-teller, I like to tell stories. For instance, in the last chapter of *Foucault's Pendulum*, where the boy plays the trumpet in the cemetery—it was something that really happened to me. Well, I told that story infinite times to friends, to girls I wanted to seduce, and I discovered that, step by step, I was performing it better—better and better. So when I decided to write *Foucault's Pendulum*, that was one of the images that became important. And finally I had to write down that story, which I had told so many times. So I was a plainclothes narrator. I did it privately without writing, but I had an impulse, a narrative impulse. Once I started, it seemed very natural to me.

WACHTEL Tell me about your family. I read that you developed your delight in the absurd from your grandmother's peculiar sense of humour.

ECO Yes, that's true, and from my cultural background as well. My maternal grandmother was a woman of little education. She went to school for five years only, but she was hungry for books. She was a born reader. She subscribed to a circulating library, so she always had books with her and she gave them to me. She read all kinds of books, from Balzac to minor popular writers of the era. I absorbed this taste for reading and for imagining narratives. On the other side, my paternal grandfather was a typographer. He died when I was five or six, so I have few memories of him, but at the end of his life, when he retired, he bound books. After he died there were a lot of books in his house that weren't picked up but were stored in a big, big box in the cellar of our home. At the age of ten, I discovered this collection of nineteenth-century books. I spent years reading this mine of narrative information, from Alexandre Dumas to Jules Verne. So through two of my grandparents, I absorbed everything that helped me, at the age of nearly fifty, to become a narrator.

WACHTEL Your father was an accountant, but you've described him as an intense reader also. What kind of influence on you did he have?

ECO He was an intense reader in his youth, but as an adult he only read one or two books per year. My mother read a little more. But at home we didn't have a library. Now I have fifty thousand books—thirty thousand in my apartment in Milano, ten thousand in the countryside and another ten thousand or so in my flat in Bologna, and in my little *pied-à-terre* in Paris, so I am up to fifty thousand. I have a problem with shelves—I was obliged to change apartments many times because they were collapsing. But in my youth, I didn't have shelves of books around me. The dozen or so my family owned were inside a closet, and some of them were considered too dangerous for a young person. They were erotic stories.

WACHTEL You were the first in your family to go to university, but your father wanted you to become a lawyer. What happened?

ECO You know that Agnelli, the owner of Fiat, is called l'*Avvocato*, the Lawyer, because virtually everybody has a degree in jurisprudence even though they don't necessarily make law their profession. It's a sign of having reached a certain social position to be an *avvocato*. So when I told my father that I wanted to do philosophy, he was terrified. He came to me every day with stories like that of a friend's cousin who studied philosophy and now was starving and obliged to wake up every morning at five o'clock to go by train to teach in a village. But in the end, he set me free to choose. My father died pretty early, at the age of sixty-five, but he saw that, having studied philosophy, I could write in an important newspaper and publish books. I had already become a public person, having studied philosophy, and I was not starving. Less than a year before his death, I published my book *Opera aperta* (*The Open Work*), and our greatest poet, Montale, who was then a Nobel Prize–winner, reviewed it in the most important Italian newspaper—with some objection—but he, Montale, reviewed my book, and my father was extremely delighted. And then he died. So I paid my debt for his permission to follow my wish.

WACHTEL That was forty years ago, in 1962. To go back for a moment, you grew up in a small town in northern Italy before, during and after the fascist regime of the Second World War. You once said that all the important and dramatic events of your life happened during your childhood. What was it like growing up at the time?

ECO Well, there was the war and it was the only time in my life when I was at risk of being killed. During my childhood, I witnessed great historical events. Shooting in the streets. At the age of thirteen, I learned that an atomic bomb was dropped on Hiroshima. I learned about the concentration camps and saw the first photographs that came from the camps. So really, I had a very dramatic childhood, which has become my private memorial repository, and you can see, in my novels, that I always pick up elements from that time. I lived the experience of a young man under a dictatorship, without knowing it. I discovered that I lived under a dictatorship only at the end of the regime. Then I discovered that there was something else in the world. It was a strange experience—very important in order to grow up with certain clear ideas. I was educated to an idea of heroism, of the beauty of death. That's why I'm a pacifist now.

WACHTEL Do you remember that moment of realization, that the dictatorship you'd been living under was not the only way to be?

ECO Yes. It was one morning when we were already living in the countryside because the city was bombed. We were living in the house of an uncle of mine who was mildly fascist because he was a hero of the First World War. He had lost one eye, part of an arm. And so, as is usually the case, fascism honoured him, gave him a cross. One morning he woke me up and said, "Umberto, you don't know what happened. Mussolini has been deposed." We turned on the radio and we learned, first of all, that the Duce, the man who looked as eternal as a force of nature, was kicked out, reduced to human dimensions. My mother told me to go out to see if there were newspapers, and when I went to the newsstand, there were not the usual newspapers I was accustomed to, but new newspapers with new titles. Each of them had a bill signed by the Christian Democrat Party, Communist Party, Liberal Party, Socialist Party, saying we have recovered our freedom. So for the first time, I read the word *freedom*. Then I learned that several political parties could exist. Since it was impossible that they were born overnight, that morning I understood that they had been somewhere, clandestine. Step by step, I realized that there was a different world, about which I knew nothing. Since I was bright, I began to understand a lot of other things, putting together old stories. The story of another uncle who went to my family to protest against fascism, and my father and mother told him not to shout. So, step by step, I put all those things together and it was a full immersion. I became a freedom expert in one week.

WACHTEL *Freedom* is a word that comes up quite a lot in your work and your speech, and I wonder if it goes back to that realization.

ECO Yes, to this epiphany. Epiphany.

WACHTEL I was also thinking of an article you once wrote called "Ur-Fascism." You have a great line where you say that, as a boy, you realized that "freedom of speech means freedom from rhetoric." What did you understand by that?

ECO The speeches of Mussolini and every page I read in my school books were full of rhetoric. I tell a story in *Foucault's Pendulum*—and this is another true story—where the parties arrive in the small town and the chief of the party appears, shows up at the balcony to celebrate the victory, and suddenly all the crowd becomes silent in order to hear the words of the winner. I expected a speech like one of Mussolini's, and instead he said, "My friends, after so many sacrifices, we are here. Long life to freedom." And he stopped. I saw this as an absolute absence of rhetoric. In fact, he had little more to say than that they were there. It was beautiful. It was a great discovery, one that probably influenced my entire life. Even in my private affairs, I have tried to demonstrate love, not to spell it aloud.

WACHTEL You've always maintained a European intellectual's right and duty to comment on politics. Do you feel a greater urgency to do that now?

ECO No, I think that it is a characteristic of European intellectuals. In France, in Germany, in Spain, when one is a poet, a novelist, a philosopher, one always feels compelled to express political ideas. It is not the same in America or Great Britain. Recently I tried to find the reason why, and I was told that in Europe the universities, from the beginning, were in the centre of the city. In England, Oxford and Cambridge were out in the countryside, not in London. In America, the campus is out of the city. In Anglo-Saxon countries, the intellectual life is always—from the spatial point of view, from an architectural point of view—separated from the city, while in the rest of Europe, it was inside the city. That certainly establishes different relations between town and gown, between the intellectuals and the city, and politics and the state. So it is an ethnic feature.

WACHTEL But more recently you've been warning about the rise of fascism.

ECO In recent years, there have been certain new phenomena in my country that led me to believe that my duty was to take a position, to say something. Maybe tomorrow, if the situation is more quiet, I will concern myself with something else. There have been times when I have been involved, in earlier years. In the sixties, I was among the founders of the committee for nuclear disarmament. I have often been involved in political activities, but I am not a political professional and I don't have any interest in becoming a parliamentary deputy or a minister. It's not my job. I would do it very badly. But every time it was needed, I gave witness.

WACHTEL You talk about the liberation in the forties as your first introduction to popular culture, when American G Is introduced you to comic books. How did you get from there to, say, Thomas Aquinas and then back again?

ECO I didn't go from comics to Aquinas, but from Aquinas to comic books. That's different. Even under fascism, the only domain in which there was a certain freedom was the domain of popular culture. Until the moment Italy declared war on the United States in '42, we were publishing Mickey Mouse and Flash Gordon. Some people were listening to jazz. We were watching American movies. So there was a taste for a certain popular culture when I was very young. Obviously, after the war it became more important. It became an ideology, if you want a symbol of another civilization. Because I was a young Catholic, St. Thomas Aquinas belonged to my culture. High culture seemed, in the beginning, to be something separate. I gradually understood that they were two aspects of the same civilization. In order to explain high culture, or avant-garde art, you have to also understand popular culture and vice versa. I found semiotics to be a good framework for studying both aspects of the same culture. The real turning point for me was the Beatles. They were pop culture, if you want, but I knew the history of music very well. When Cathy Berberian, the great singer, sang the Beatles as if they were Purcell, everybody discovered that Purcell was already there in the Beatles' songs.

At the time, I remember that Henri Bousseur, a Belgian musician of the avant-garde like Boulez or Stockhausen, said—apropos the Beatles—that they were working for us. He meant they were producing a new musical sensitivity in the young so that, at a certain moment, they would also understand us. I told him yes, but you are also working for them. And this really happened. In the middle of the sixties, there was a new interaction and merging in various aspects of culture so that today, it's pretty difficult to keep with the old distinctions of highbrow, middle-brow, low-brow. It's very uncertain. The same happened with pop art in America after artists such as Roy Lichtenstein and Claes Oldenburg.

WACHTEL There's a tendency now, in intellectual circles, to be very critical of popular culture, especially television, for playing to the lowest common denominator.

ECO Let's distinguish between pop culture and trash. Trash is a human tendency to ugliness that you can find in both pop culture and in high culture. There are, at this moment, three or four great comedians in Italy whom I consider geniuses and great artists. They are pop culture, because when they perform there are ten thousand people, mainly the young, in the audience. They are pop artists, but great artists. And then there is the trash. There is a lot of trash also among my fellow philosophers or novelists. The fact that most television is leaning toward trash production is due to a lot of commercial industrial needs, and probably it will become worse and worse. It's the same for the Internet. The fact that probably 50 percent of those using the Internet use it for sex and for chatting about sex is an infelicitous side effect, but it doesn't mean that the Internet is in itself pornographic.

WACHTEL A recent collection of your essays, called Five Moral Pieces, includes reflections on war, on the press and on fascism, and, despite the variety of themes, they're all, as you put it, ethical in nature, preoccupied with "what we ought to do, what we ought not to do, and what we must not do at any cost." Can you talk about what it means to you, as a self-described secularist, to be moral?

ECO Well, I developed this theme in an exchange of letters with Cardinal Martini, the Archbishop of Milano, who is also a biblical scholar. I was reacting to a question posited by Cardinal Martini, who asked, "How is it possible for a person with no faith to have a moral life?" I tried to say that there are basic, universal situations linked to our bodies—to speak, to eat, to sleep. If you analyze these universals, you recognize you wouldn't be offended by those activities. At the same time, you recognize that you shouldn't offend "the other" in those activities because you need the other. You need his glance, his recognition. Even the torturer needs respect or devotion on the part of the tortured; otherwise, he couldn't enjoy his sadistic activity. Because of this profound need we have for the other's recognition, we are drawn to respect in the other what we want to be respected in us. That is the essential core of every ethics.

WACHTEL Is this a form of the Golden Rule? Do unto others as you would have them do unto you?

ECO Well, if not golden, then silver. I have tried to base the principles of a lay ethics on a natural reality like our corporeality and the idea that we instinctively know that we have a soul (or something that serves as such), only by virtue of the presence of others.

WACHTEL You received a strongly Catholic education until you were twenty-two. As you describe it, your secular point of view was hard won, and you always wonder whether some of your moral convictions don't still depend on religious impressions you received early in your life.

ECO Certainly. Everything depends on the first impressions we received in our life. James Joyce also abandoned deep faith but remained profoundly shaped by his religious formation. You are formed by those things. You remain a Christian or a Catholic even though you don't believe in God. That's the point.

WACHTEL Your new novel, *Baudolino*, takes place in a very different world from the monastic setting of *The Name of the Rose*. It's a picaresque adventure, set amidst the political turbulence of the twelfth century, but

I'd like to begin with one of the significant images in the book: unicorns. You've said that you're not sure that they don't really exist. Where or how do unicorns exist for you?

ECO Well, for me they exist in the third world of literature and the imagination and sometimes they can be more alive and more realistic than real reality. My novel *Baudolino* is exactly about that, about people who invent, who imagine possible worlds, but then they believe in them so strongly, so staunchly, that they discover these worlds. You know that Marco Polo met unicorns.

WACHTEL Tell me about that.

ECO Marco Polo, during his trip to China, or perhaps coming back and passing through Java, said that he had seen unicorns. But since he was an honest man, he said that they were not white, but rather very ugly, and they don't give the impression of a love for virgins. Marco Polo said the unicorn chased them. What he had seen was a rhinoceros. But he was unable to conceive of and describe an unknown animal, so he had to use the only model he had in mind, and that was the unicorn.

WACHTEL Because the rhinoceros has a horn on the top of its head—

ECO Yes. But since he was an honest journalist, I'm sure they are not exactly like the legend says.

WACHTEL The legend of the unicorn inspires the hero of your new novel when he's a boy and then much later.

ECO Yes, but I also used all the monsters of the medieval bestiary, which, by the way, are not only medieval—they start in the Hellenistic period. There are a lot of texts. So for centuries and centuries, those monsters were as real as kangaroos for us. I think that most of the people in our world have not seen real kangaroos. But we can think of kangaroos, believing that they are real. Before Western explorers began their travels, they had an idea of the Far East, of a mysterious country where these monsters really existed, mixed up with real animals like lions and giraffes. In my book I have the skiapod, this marvellous monster with a single leg with which he can run at enormous speed and shade himself from the sun. And I have invoked other kinds of monsters, too. I enjoyed making them come alive. We have images sculpted in the cathedrals and in many miniatures in which we see the unicorn lying down with his foot above his head. But how did he move his leg? That was a problem. Where was his penis? Those are real problems I tried to solve in my story because I wanted these wonderful creatures to live a real life.

WACHTEL Of course, if we go back to the Greek, you get things like the manticore and the basilisk. Do you remember first encountering these fabulous creatures yourself in books or stories or images in art?

ECO Many of them I probably discovered during my childhood. But then, as a university student, I worked on the Middle Ages from a philosophical point of view, and I devoured all the material about civilizations of that period. Many of those monsters I saw on the facades of Roman abbeys like Vezelay or Moissac, so I feel comfortable with them. I've known them for a long time.

WACHTEL Why do you think we need creatures like the unicorn in our lives?

ECO There are many reasons. The question could be rephrased: Why do we need fairy tales? Why do people go to see *Spider-Man* now? The impulse and the desire to fly is eternal in human beings. If you hate somebody, the idea that, with a stroke of your finger, you can fling him twenty metres is a profound desire in us. We satisfy it with fairy tales. But monsters like unicorns were important in Greek culture and in the Middle Ages because they have symbolic value; they were not considered in themselves. I think that many monsters were invented just in order to prove a moral truth or some biblical allegory. Or people attributed to normal animals habits that they didn't have just in order to make them into symbolical machinery. For instance, the lion was told to erase its footprints with its tail in order to escape the hunters. In that sense, he was a symbol for Jesus Christ, who erased the sins of mankind. So I think that first they thought of the possibility of an allegorical mystical signification, and then they invented characteristics in order to make the animal signify something.

WACHTEL Fabulous creatures like these from myth and legend, while more obscure today, were part of the popular consciousness in the

Middle Ages. The medieval world was the fictional setting of your first novel, *The Name of the Rose*, and now you've returned to it in your new novel, *Baudolino*. Tell me about this Baudolino. He is a natural story-teller. He's a poet. He's a creator of fiction, a creator of reality.

ECO He's a novelist.

WACHTEL Exactly, and how much of you is in this aspect of his charac-ter—that playfulness, that inventiveness?

ECO Well, much of me and much of every other narrator, so it's not so strictly autobiographical.

WACHTEL You have Baudolino coming from your own birthplace in northern Italy, Alessandria, and, as you say in the novel, he actually wit-nesses the creation of the city in 1168. You draw on local lore here, with Baudolino's father as the mythical character who saves the city from Barbarossa's siege through a trick with a cow. What's the story here?

ECO Well, the story is real in the sense that it comes more or less from that time. Barbarossa was besieging the newborn city of Alessandria. The city was built up in a hurry, but it resisted pretty well and Bar-barossa spent more than one year on the siege. He wanted to escape, but he had to save face. In the city, they were in a terrible, miserable sit-uation, but then the old peasant Gagliardo had an idea. He had a cow that was starving, as was everybody in the city. The townspeople picked up all the grain they could and filled up the cow with this grain. Then Gagliardo took the cow outside the walls and, as expected, the cow was captured by Barbarossa's soldiers, who opened the belly of the cow and found it full of grain. So Gagliardo was brought to Barbarossa. Bar-barossa asked how he could have so much grain that he would give it to the cow. Gagliardo said that they had many cows inside, so they ate meat and gave the grain to the cows. So Barbarossa had an official pre-text to leave, because the siege would take too much time, and that's how Gagliardo saved the city. That is the legend. I made Gagliardo the father of Baudolino.

WACHTEL So this was a way of exploring your own roots. To what degree were you interested in doing that?

ECO When aging, you return to your origins; it's a normal attitude. I also was fascinated by the character of my countrymen—typically skeptical, ironical and not rhetorical. Baudolino, in fact, was born more as a language than as a character. I started writing the first ten pages of the book in an invented language, what could have been a legendary northern Italian language at that time, but we don't have documents about it, so I was very free to invent it. I invented it by using all my memories of my local dialect. And so, through that language, I was obliged to accept its psychology and, step by step, the character took shape. So I didn't start from the idea of a given character who I then made speak. On the contrary, first I made an anonymous voice speak and then I found the character.

WACHTEL One of Baudolino's gifts is that he picks up languages easily and can speak like a native after hearing just a little bit. So he is a marvellous linguistic vehicle for you in the story.

ECO Yes. That was a miserable trick on my part, since I was thinking of a person who travelled from Italy to Greece and to the Far East. I did this in order to avoid the typical Hollywood movie situation in which everybody speaks English. I gave Baudolino this gift of language to help him travel through different countries with ease and interact with everybody. This is an allusion to the apostolic gift—earlier I had written about a search for universal language. This idea amalgamated with other elements of the narration, but it was born, frankly speaking, just as a trick.

WACHTEL But in what way did your local dialect—or the people of your region—create a kind of temperament for you? You've said that it's the source of your own temperament.

ECO Thirty years ago, I wrote a small article about my city. It was a review of a book about the history of Alessandria. You know that all young intellectuals living in a provincial city want first thing to escape and go to a big city. I did so at the age of eighteen. I lived in Torino and then in Milano and, in a way, I abandoned my city. But gradually, as I wrote about Alessandria, I realized that many aspects of my character— as a writer, as a thinker, as a person—were largely influenced by those roots. For instance, we were, I discovered, anti-rhetorical. It seemed that St. Francis of Assisi passed through Alessandria and converted a wolf. But St. Francis supposedly converted a wolf in Gubbio, in central Italy. OK. Probably he converted many wolves in his lifetime. But Gubbio traded on that legend, and the people of Alessandria forgot it. They were unable to generate a myth.

The only pope born in Alessandria was a known nepotist—he put his nephews in positions of power. Alessandria had a flourishing Jewish community but was unable to create a ghetto. They are so anti-rhetorical, they cannot even be racist. You need a certain faith to be racist. That's why they are very skeptical. Their first reaction to every event is that maybe they don't believe in it. Let's check. Once a certain person offered me a lot of money to create a cultural foundation. I went to talk to a lawyer, but then I started smelling something rotten. I abandoned the project. I was right—they were rascals. But my first reaction—and only after a while I discovered it was due to my origins—was that whenever somebody comes to you offering money, first call the police. Don't trust them. That's typical of my area. And so Baudolino is a little like this.

But you know, the decision to write this story came by mysterious and tortured ways. I started musing about the great fakes in history and I remembered immediately one of the greatest of all was the famous letter of Prester John, which described a fantastic kingdom in the Far East so vividly that many, many people went there. For centuries, they looked for this kingdom. At this point, I realized that the letter of Prester John was forged, probably in the time of Frederick I, known as Barbarossa, which is also more or less when my native city was founded, in order to resist the invasion of Barbarossa. Then I had the idea that I could return to my roots and tell the story of my city, of my people, and at the same time, I could tell the story of Prester John's kingdom. All I needed was to invent a little liar able to produce that forgery with the spirit, the character, the typical skeptical attitude of the people of my land. So, at the same time, I paid a tribute to my roots and a tribute to Utopia.

WACHTEL   And the little liar is Baudolino.

ECO   Yes, I am responsible for this idea, because many characters in the book say, "Baudolino, you are a liar." But Baudolino is not really a liar, if you consider that a liar is lying about the present or the past. Baudolino is lying about the future, which is more exciting.

WACHTEL That does give it a different twist. Because the real and the invented and the relationship between the two, between truth and fiction or falsehood, is a theme that you've explored in your critical writings. Here you mix historical fact—I mean, characters and events—with your own fabrications. So the line is thoroughly blurred.

ECO Not only that, but I make Baudolino forge a lot of documents—letters, ideas—that really existed or were accepted. I mean, when Baudolino invents tricky solutions for Frederick Barbarossa in order to solve a political situation, in my novel I make it the invention of Baudolino. But in real life, it was a historical fact.

WACHTEL Your novel *Baudolino* focuses on a quest with real historical meaning—a search for the kingdom of Prester John. Who was Prester John?

ECO This letter I mentioned, which was produced in the middle of the twelfth century, described this immense kingdom full of camels, elephants, lions and exotic monsters, with rivers full of milk and honey, buildings in ivory and precious stones. A land of marvels, governed by a king who was called Priest John. But mysterious—why a priest? Why John? The idea was that, in the era of the Crusades, beyond the Saracen lands, there was an older Christian kingdom where the identity between priesthood and imperial power coincided, while in the West the emperor was fighting continuously with the pope. This idea had a political impact because it gave a reason to go towards the east and then towards Africa, beyond the land of the Muslim. It provided a justification for the Western penetration of those lands, because they would have to be conjoined to reach the other Christian kingdom. During the twelfth, thirteenth and fourteenth centuries, the legend grew, because during all that time, the letter was translated into other languages and continued to circulate. The rumours about Prester John moved the kingdom from the Far East to Africa. And in the Renaissance, the Portuguese exploration of Africa and, in a sense, the first act of colonization, was made under the standard of Prester John. They wanted to find the Prester John kingdom. And they found it. They found Abyssinia and Ethiopia, which was a Christian kingdom inside Africa. Not so splendid and not so rich, not so glorious as the one described by Prester John—Prater Giovanni. That was when the myth became a real thing.

So you see, this was a strange document. We don't know whether it was produced for the pleasure of imagining a new world, like every utopian dream, or for real political purposes. In any case, it had an enormous impact on Western politics towards Africa and Asia. And the letter is full of contradictions. It seems to be written by a man having visions. That's why I had my character create it under the impulse of some drug. The letter is very mysterious, but that gives it its charm, and the fascination it produced. That's the kingdom of Prester John.

WACHTEL That earthly paradise is attractive to many different characters in the novel for many different reasons—spiritual or romantic, political or material. What do you think was the most compelling aspect of the Prester John legend?

ECO The fascination of the Western world for the East starts very early in the Hellenistic period. Think of Alexander the Great, who goes east to Afghanistan and beyond. And then came stories about the marvellous travels of Alexander, who met monsters and so on. This is long before Prester John. So this dream of the new world, of the lands beyond, was typical of the era. The same dream brought Colombus to the discovery of America and it lasted until Cook, with the discovery of Australia, because people went to look for the Terra Incognita. It was only at the moment in which every place of the world was discovered that all the legends stopped. We don't have unexplored new worlds on this planet. That's why Kennedy invited young people to go to the conquest of stars, because we have lost a place for Utopia. The charm of Prester John was the charm of every description of another land. That propelled people to explore the whole world. It was only in the nineteenth century, the world being already known, that in a sense the Utopia became—instead of geographical—temporal, historical. Marx. We have to create a different society, a communist society. Now it has been proved that that also didn't work, and that creates an element of crisis for all of us. We have no more new worlds to dream of.

WACHTEL In the realm of the fantastic beings that we talked about earlier, these creatures of myth and legend that Baudolino and his men encounter on their quest for the kingdom of Prester John, there are a lot of surprises. For instance, however freakish in appearance, the community is astonishingly tolerant. In fact, they seem blind to each other's physical differences.

ECO Yes, instead they are mentally, theologically, racist. They are so different from each other, but they are unable to see the difference. For them, to have one leg or two legs or three legs, it's the same. But on theological points, they are ready to kill each other.

WACHTEL Tell me what that's about, because they debate endlessly.

ECO Racism has not only to do with skin colour, it has also to do with ideas, ways of thinking. And so there can be a theological racism, which is more terrible than the physical one. But then, you have not yet mentioned the principal element in *Baudolino*—although I would not like to speak about it because I want to leave my reader the final surprise—the love story with Hypatia.

WACHTEL I would not forget. It's my next question.

ECO I fell in love with that girl in writing the story, because she has a beautiful mind. Such a simple love is possible for Baudolino. I never had a similar experience, but I could have if I had met someone with as beautiful a mind as Hypatia's.

WACHTEL When you say these characters are racist, is this a different model—to have theological debate be the source of difference between people?

ECO Even in our modern world, massacres are not necessarily due to ethnic difference, but to mental difference. Think of all the persecutions and massacres by Stalin. They were not based on ethnic elements, but on the expulsion of the heretic. Think of all the stories of heresies through the centuries. The heretics are brought to the stake, not because of an ethnic difference but because of a mental difference. Fights among fundamentalisms are not always based on ethnic ideas.

They can have religious, ideological, political reasons. If you want, I admit to a meaning in my story, which usually I refuse to do. I tried to invent a community in which there were no ethnic discriminations, but only mental, ideological, theological discriminations. It is the least fantastic story in my novel, the most realistic one.

WACHTEL In the medieval environment, the time of the Crusades seems so brutal and corrupt and violent and torn by division—

ECO Like in our time. Don't exaggerate. More witches were burned after the Renaissance. Their persecution is more typical of modern times than of medieval. They were killing each other, yes, with gusto. But it happens also today.

WACHTEL Do you feel protective of the Middle Ages because it's your territory?

ECO Well, yes, but the Middle Ages has been so misunderstood, first of all, because it didn't exist. How can you define, with a single word, one thousand years? The Middle Ages was an invention of modern historians. Ten centuries between the fall of the Roman Empire and the discovery of America—an era of great technological invention, philosophical development, literary greatness.

WACHTEL You're a medievalist, I know. I remember, years ago, hearing you talk about *The Name of the Rose*. When you were asked why the first hundred or so pages are so difficult, and make such demands on the reader, you said that it took you a lot of work to write it, and so the reader should have to work hard, too.

ECO Yes, the reader has to pay a certain price in order to enter a new world. Otherwise it's too easy. I remember there were certain books that played an important role in my life. For instance, Dr. *Faustus*, by Thomas Mann: from the age of twenty to the age of twenty-five, I started it three times without finishing it. Finally I had the courage to cross a certain threshold and I enjoyed it and it was an important book to me. I believe that readers have to be respected—they don't want anything free.

WACHTEL When you gave the Norton Lectures at Harvard, which were collected in a book of essays called Six Walks in the Fictional Woods, you talked about "the model reader." What is the model reader?

ECO I have written a lot in my scholarly books about what other authors speak of as the ideal reader. For certain authors—let's say, the authors of dime novels, of pornographic novels—the reader already exists, is there, like the target of advertising. I want to sell to house-wives, I want to sell only to bachelors, I want to sell only . . . And so these novels are conceived for a specific, pre-existing target: to please young girls, to please old gentlemen, to please people obsessed with sex. A serious author, on the contrary, doesn't look to a pre-existing readership; he or she wants to create that. And all the instructions for becoming this model reader are included in the book. The reader who arrives at the end of the book, having had a satisfactory experience, has become the model reader of that book. Take Proust. Could he have conceived of a pre-existing reader able to accept some thousand pages about private memories? Probably not. He built it up, step by step, and you enter Proust and gradually you become what he wanted you to be. That's what I mean by model reader. You don't need any external evi-dence to say what the model reader of this book should be. It's the book that tells you that. The model reader of Finnegans Wake is different from the model reader of Balzac, but you can play both roles, if you want. One of the experiences of literature is that you can become different kinds of model readers according to the author you are read-ing. And sometimes you can't. There are a lot of very important, mar-vellous books of which I am not the model reader, and so they remain closed to me.

WACHTEL Such as?

ECO This changes through the years. There are books that look repul-sive to you at the age of twenty, and then suddenly, at the age of forty, you discover that you are ready to enter this world and accept the seduc-tion of the book, of the text. The author is a ghostly entity; the only real entity is the text.

WACHTEL Forty years ago, in your book The Open Work, you anticipated the interactive relationship between the reader and the text and the emphasis on interpretation and openness—the possibilities of interpretation. More recently, I read that you said that the rights of the interpreters have been overstressed. Is there a risk of interpretation going too far?

ECO Yes. I am very happy and proud when somebody says that, in '62, I anticipated this trend with The Open Work. Probably this is true. I was at that time following, day by day, the experiences of certain musicians, like Berlioz, Boulez and Stockhausen, who were making new compositions that could be performed and enjoyed in different ways. It was the right moment for starting to think about this theory of the openness of the work of art. But notice that the title of my book was The Open Work. There was openness on one side concerning a precise object that cannot be erased or cancelled. In the last few years, when I say that the rights of the interpreter have been overemphasized, I mean that certain critics tend to forget that they are dealing with a precise text, and the text imposes certain limits. My position is that the interpretation can go ad infinitum, but it doesn't mean that every interpretation is a good one. A text is a choice. Today, you see there are critics who say that with the new hypertextual techniques, with the Internet, you can collaborate collectively to make different novels out of an existing novel. So once you have arrived at the point where Little Red Riding Hood meets the wolf, you can change the story and not have the wolf devouring the grandmother. That's true. It can be a good exercise for improving creativity, but it has nothing to do with the nature of a text. When you read War and Peace, if you participate passionately with the story, you would prefer that Natasha doesn't go with that miserable Anatole and remains faithful to Prince Andrei, and you would prefer that Prince Andrei not die. But he dies, and she goes. One of the great experiences in literature is that you are continuously looking at possible different trends of the story, but you are obliged to accept fate—destiny—such as it is. You cannot interpret War and Peace in the sense that Prince Andrei was something else. No, you are confronted with a sort of a terrestrial image of God's will or destiny. You have to accept it. So it is a dialectic, an interaction between you and your drives, your compulsion, your will to interpret the book in different ways, and the real existence of a text, which is something finished. You have to interact with a certain fidelity.

WACHTEL There's a kind of anarchy—potential anarchy—in semiotics. If something can mean almost anything, then how do we agree on common meanings to communicate?

ECO In this case, the text becomes a pretext for your fancies, for your daydreaming. We do it frequently with books. It's not forbidden. It happens to me when I go to a concert; after the first five minutes of being excited by a certain melody, I start thinking of my personal affairs. I'm using the musical composition as a pretext. But I am also a flute player. A bad one, but a flute player. When I play, I cannot escape this way; I have to interpret what is written. I know that I can keep a note a little-little longer to make some variations, but I cannot play one note instead of another. I cannot go beyond certain limits imposed by the text. The same composition can be interpreted by ten interpreters in ten different ways, and that is the open side. But there is a certain point beyond which you are no longer playing a composition, but rather taking it as a pretext and improvising. I can improvise. A good jazz man can pick up a Beethoven theme and go. A jam session is another form of art, very respectable and very creative, but it is not the way you should interpret Beethoven. So I always make a distinction between interpretation and the use of a text. I can use a text even to take pages to wrap prosciutto or salmon. It is a use for a text.

WACHTEL Now, earlier you said that what matters is the text, and that the author is less important, is a ghost. What do you mean when you say that?

ECO When you read The Iliad, you have The Iliad before your eyes. You don't have an image of Homer, who is dead, and who was probably not the author of The Iliad anyway. So you have nothing to ask Homer. You have to ask the text, and the only Homer you see is the one who has written this text, this model author. The dialectic is between the model reader and the model author. For me, it is absolutely irrelevant, for example, whether Proust was a homosexual or not. What is relevant is that Baron de Charlus was, and Proust was enormously perceptive in describing the Baron de Charlus. That is the homosexuality I am interested in when reading *La recherche*. The private homosexuality of Proust is a biological accident for which I am not responsible and in which I'm not interested. I am a good reader of biographies, and that is another story. I can be interested in the private life of Proust, as I can be interested in the private life of Winston Churchill. It is another kind of interest.

WACHTEL As a critic, you've addressed yourself to problems of perception, of decoding, deciphering, interpreting. How do *you* want to be read?

ECO I think that, as a theoretician, as a semiotician, as an academic, I can develop a lot of theories about interpretation. As an author of novels, I know that my texts are a message in a bottle. So it can happen that somebody reads me in an absolutely idiosyncratic way, refusing to play the game of the author, who is the authorized interpreter of these texts. I can simply tell somebody, "No, you were wrong, because you say that in my book something happened that in fact didn't happen." But that's the most I can do. For the rest, I must set the readers free. It happens that sometimes they find in my books things that I didn't have any idea were there, but since I believe that the text is more powerful than its author, sometimes the responses of the reader have helped me to discover that there was something that I didn't suspect in my text. I must say, "Oh yes, it's true, it's there." That's all. I've made an analysis of different interpretations of my novels. I take various examples in which sometimes the readers found things that I was obliged to recognize were there. Some of the time, they clearly misunderstood—not my book, but the normal sense of the words. It's a message in a bottle. I have always said that the author should die after having finished the novel. It's only the publisher that insists on your survival because they expect the next book.

WACHTEL Have you changed as a reader? Do you find you read any differently now, at this point in your life, in this new century?

ECO Yes. For instance, since I started writing novels myself, I am unable to read contemporary literature. I feel biased. I am not without prejudice. So I carefully avoid writing about contemporary literature. I don't understand how certain novelists can write about other people's novels or how certain poets can write about the poetry of other poets.

WACHTEL Do you miss reading fiction?

ECO No, I read something else, like the history of literature in the seventeenth, eighteenth and nineteenth centuries, or the first half of the last century. There is still enough to read. At any rate, I'm frequently obliged to read contemporary literature anyway, but I don't feel that I'm in an unbiased position. If they write differently from me, I am not interested; if they write the same, I am irritated; if they write better than me, I am more and more irritated. So I don't feel honest reading my contemporaries.

WACHTEL What's your attraction to the detective novel—the mysterious death, the murder?

ECO Detective stories are a secular transfiguration of an eternal religious, metaphysical problem. Whodunnit? Who is the guilty one—or the virtuous one, depending on the way you see the world? If the world is a mess, who is the guilty one? So the detective story transports the form, in the framework of an acceptable and recognizable dimension. We are in London, we are in New York. A man has been assassinated, killed—that's all. But transporting those manageable dimensions is the great metaphysical question. *Oedipus Rex* was a detective story, so even at the origins of our unconscious life, if Freud is right, there is a detective story.

WACHTEL There is a coda to the novel *Baudolino*, in which we return to the question of truth and lies. And Niketas, the historian to whom Baudolino has been telling his story, must decide what is true or not. Is Niketas a real person?

ECO Yes. He has written three volumes, among other things, on the history of the emperors of Constantinople, and in the third part of his chronicle, he described the siege of Constantinople. Everything that happens in my story was narrated in great part by Niketas. I had also the chronicles from the point of view of the Crusaders, but Niketas was a real character. It was interesting to me to write so much of the book as a dialogue between Niketas and Baudolino. Niketas, being a historian, is not sure that Baudolino is a reliable witness. You never know if what Baudolino says is true or not. Not even Niketas knows.

WACHTEL Does it satisfy a skeptic such as yourself to tell a story with so many tall tales?

ECO Well, I hope that my readers will be as skeptical as I am and not take me too seriously.

WACHTEL I read that you've chosen for your epitaph a quotation from the seventeenth-century poet Tommaso Campanella: "Wait, wait. I cannot." What is that about?

ECO It's the last two lines of a utopian book describing an ideal republic. The book is written as a dialogue between a passenger and another person and, at the end, one says, "Wait, wait. I cannot, I cannot." It's a very curious way of ending the dialogue. I don't know why, but I thought it would be very beautiful as an epitaph. Also because the best one seems to have been used by Thomas Hobbes on his grave: "This is the philosopher's stone."

WACHTEL How do you relate to the idea of "Wait, wait" and "I cannot"?

ECO I think that will probably be my last thought. I'm not sure. I've not been there. Let me try it—then I'll tell you.

May 2002/November 1995

MARY DOUGLAS

In 1949, Mary Douglas, a student at the influential Oxford Institute of Social Anthropology, went to what was then the Belgian Congo to do fieldwork among the Lele. Not long after she returned to England, she said she had discovered in herself "a prejudice against piecemeal explanations." That approach has marked her work ever since.

As one critic put it, "Mary Douglas is not an anthropologist's anthropologist. Her mind is too curious and too wild. Her work is about boundaries and markers, about purity, ambiguity and pollution, which is all very proper, but she herself traverses the boundaries dangerously." He went on to say that "The special genius of Mary Douglas, in every sense of the word *genius*, makes her into the academic equivalent of one of her most striking examples: the Pangolin, a scaly anteater, poised between categories."

Mary Douglas has consistently been a system-builder, a constructor, a believer in the ability of the social sciences to make sense of how we live. She links the exotic with the apparently ordinary, venturing into the fields of economics, ecology, theology, nutritional studies and consumer theory. She sees ritual as central to our social systems—from the exotic to the everyday, from the observed to the overlooked, such as setting a table or bringing chocolates as a hostess gift.

Her 1966 classic, *Purity and Danger*, is "an analysis of concepts of pollution and taboo." In it, she writes, "As a social animal, man is a ritual animal. . . . It is not too much to say that ritual is more important to society than words are to thought. For it is very possible to know something and then find words for it. But it is impossible to have social relations without symbolic acts."

In 1993, Mary Douglas returned to her interest in the Old Testament, a subject she had alluded to in *Purity and Danger*. She published *In the Wilderness: The Doctrine of Defilement in the Book of Numbers* (1993) and then *Leviticus as Literature* (2000). She says that her attitude towards the Bible was shaped by her training at Oxford. "Our researches were framed by an interest in the moral construction of the universe and the nature of belief." *Times Literary Supplement* critic Gabriel Josipovici observed: "The Bible [has] long been of interest to anthropologists; what [is] new in Professor Douglas' work [is] the combination of respect for the text, a training in Oxford anthropology and a human warmth and empathy which are uniquely hers."

I went to see Mary Douglas at her home in North London, just after her eightieth birthday. (She was born in 1921.) When I arrived, she was helping out a young textile student from Belgium, who had come to see the unusual raffia pictures and pillows that she had brought back from the Congo. Raffia was an important part of the Lele economy. In the living room, there were books of photographs, artifacts and texts, dating from her fieldwork more than fifty years ago. After lunch, which she later referred to as yet another sort of ritual, we talked in her upstairs study.

WACHTEL You began your career as an ethnographer with fieldwork in Africa, but you're also an observer of the culture around you and you have a particular eye for the details of human behaviour that we take for granted and which reveal so much about how our lives are organized. Were you always such an acute observer? Always curious?

DOUGLAS We were brought up by my grandmother, and she had a very regular, highly organized household. Afterwards that always seemed very interesting to me. Why do we have to change our sheets on Mondays? Everything was very fixed, and so the ordinarily curious child would question this practice. My grandmother would claim to be flummoxed by these questions because—"Well, why not, we've got to change them once a week"—and she didn't know that I wanted her to say, "Well, it's a convention, dear." She hadn't come round to that way of thinking about it, but I was trying to discover whether there were reasons or whether there were just conventions underlying it.

WACHTEL So the Sunday roast would become Monday's cold meat and Tuesday's shepherd pie.

DOUGLAS Yes, that's right. And if there was any left on Wednesday, we'd have rissoles. Or perhaps rissoles were sometimes substituted for shepherd's pie.

WACHTEL You were born in Italy in 1921, almost by chance, because your parents were travelling to England on leave from a colonial posting to Burma. What are your memories of early childhood?

DOUGLAS I have a strong and romantic feeling about Burma. I'd love to go back and see it, but I left at the age of five. At that time it was thought to be very dangerous for white children to be left in the tropics after the age of five. There was one girl we knew who was left till she was seven, and everyone thought that was risking things.

WACHTEL Do you remember much from Burma in those very early years?

DOUGLAS No, but I've got a lot of photographs to supplement my memory.

WACHTEL Your family was Roman Catholic, which set you apart from the mainstream in England. Did you have a religious upbringing?

DOUGLAS My family wasn't entirely Roman Catholic, but there was a Roman Catholic member of our family in each generation. My grandfather was an Irish Catholic married to a Protestant, and he brought up his children as Catholics and sent them to Catholic schools. So my mother was a Catholic, convent-educated, and when she found out she was dying she handed us over to the nuns. In fact, my grandmother had sent us to Catholic Sunday School and had taught us our catechism, although she was a very staunch Protestant. She did it out of a great sense of duty.

WACHTEL Were you aware of seeing the world through a particular lens?

DOUGLAS I think the 1920s and '30s for Catholics in England was a very sectarian time. They were on the defensive against Protestants and other unbelievers. And yes, being a Catholic did make a difference. There were foes outside, adversaries that one had to contend with.

WACHTEL Another dramatic change came when you were twelve. You've mentioned that your mother died, and your father then retired early from colonial service. At that point you were sent to a boarding school, to the Sacred Heart Convent in Roehampton. How did you adjust to that environment?

DOUGLAS I loved it. I always enjoyed being at school. I think I must have had an especially privileged position. My parents were away and the nuns felt obliged to pay special attention to us because we were "grass orphans," my sister, Pat, and I. Pat was only three when she was sent home to be with me. My parents felt that I would be lonely without someone, since I was only five. So poor Pat was sacrificed for my well-being. I was a tremendously bossy child and I think I made it very difficult for her. But I was always happy at school, probably because it was privileged for me.

WACHTEL Privileged?

DOUGLAS Yes. The nuns said, at first, "This child's mother is abroad"; second, "This child's mother is dying"; third, "This child's mother has died"—and so they all spoiled me and gave me advantages and favours, privileges. I loved it.

WACHTEL How did your education at the Sacred Heart prepare you intellectually or spiritually or temperamentally for what came after?

DOUGLAS It gave me a tremendous loyalty. First of all, it gave me loyalty to whoever was in charge, coupled with a sense of how precarious authority was, and how it needed to be backed up by us, the children. So I felt very committed to the kind of hierarchical structures I was used to, which put me out of tune, certainly, with more libertarian and nonconformist and agnostic and rationalist friends that I made later. Very much out of tune. But then, the nuns gave us a sense that we were lucky, we were chosen. So it was a matter of pride, as well, and therefore of intellectual independence.

WACHTEL So there was a somewhat peculiar combination of authority and intellectual independence—on the face of it, it sounds at odds.

DOUGLAS No, it's the opposite. Authority was backing us, and we knew we had a responsibility to carry out what was right, independent of the world, which is other people.

WACHTEL But there was a respect for the institution.

DOUGLAS I had a deep respect for institutions; I still have. I think institutions are in real trouble. And this puts me very much against the grain of the counterculture in sociology and social sciences, because there's been this long tradition, since before my generation, of thinking of the individual as being suppressed by institutions. I had grown up to think of institutions as places that promote intellectual freedom. They enable the individual to reach their full potential, which I think is right.

WACHTEL Were your ambitions unusual? When you were growing up, were young women encouraged to develop themselves or to seek a career?

DOUGLAS That's the other thing. I think I also owe that to the nuns, because they were all independent women who left the world and came to educate us in religion and live dedicated lives. So it seemed natural for us to go on and do what we could, but we were very badly prepared for it, in fact.

WACHTEL How so?

DOUGLAS Well, when I got to Oxford—and I think it must have been touch-and-go that I got in at all—I met girls my age who had been at high schools, as they called them then, and they were absolutely competent in mathematics, for example, and good at languages, none of which I was, not even Latin. It was a complete struggle just to keep up when I first got to university. I hadn't ever had to work before, in the sense of really working.

WACHTEL At one time you considered sociology at the London School of Economics, but the nuns discouraged you. Was it sociology that was too radical or was it the LSE that was too radical?

DOUGLAS I don't think really it was that. They just didn't know what the LSE was; they didn't know what sociology was. All they knew was Oxford. And all they really knew about Oxford was history. But I didn't want to do history—or couldn't, because I wasn't good enough—and I wanted to do something sociological. Then they heard about this thing called PPE.

WACHTEL PPE is politics, philosophy and economics, which is what you did at Oxford. Did you have any particular role models?

DOUGLAS No, I didn't. But neither did I feel aware of the kind of obstacles there were to women having an independent career. I had no consciousness of it at all. But I had that extreme shyness and readiness to be self-effacing, typical of the time and my convent-school training. It was very bad for me. It didn't do anything to help at all.

WACHTEL Making yourself invisible.

DOUGLAS Yes.

WACHTEL In what sorts of instances?

DOUGLAS I would never have dreamed of stepping in and taking charge. I never thought myself sufficiently good to do that. Even when I published, it was ages before I thought my books might be good. I published *Purity and Danger*, which has never been out of print and has done so interestingly well, but when I completed the text, I just didn't know who might be interested in reading it. I'm amazed actually to realize how out of touch I was with my own colleagues.

WACHTEL You've said that it was your war service at the Colonial Office that made you an anthropologist.

DOUGLAS That's quite true. I'd never heard of anthropology, so I couldn't have done it before. But in the war everyone was mobilized for work, and you could be mobilized into almost anything you chose. With my having a background in the British Raj and feeling competent and confident about travel and other people—foreigners—as soon as I met anthropologists I knew that I wanted to be one. I met Raymond Firth then; he was working in the Colonial Office, which was very depleted because its young people were out on war service. So Raymond gave up his academic career for a year. And I met some others. I met Bill Stannet and Phyllis Kaberry, and I read quite a lot. I was absolutely thrilled. I thought anthropology was a marvellous topic. I still do.

WACHTEL What was it that attracted you so much?

DOUGLAS I'm not sure. It seemed obvious. Let me think what I read. I'd done three years of PPE by that time, and it was very dry and very academic and very abstract. But when I read Audrey Richards's wonderful book, *Land, Labour and Diet in Northern Rhodesia*, I could see a woman getting into the homes and learning from the other women what they were doing and what the task was about—cooking and who to cook for, and how to present your food, and then all the hardships: the men going out to work in the mines, and having to run the village on their own. Audrey Richards's empathy for them was amazing, but so were her measurements and the figures that she collected. I was absolutely bowled over by the kind of openings that her work suggested for things one might enquire into in a completely different way. And then I read Evans-Pritchard on the Nuer, and I realized there was a really intellectual way of approaching the whole subject.

WACHTEL An intellectual way of approaching it. How so?

DOUGLAS His three books on the Nuer, starting with their environment, were impressively abstract and at the same time detailed: which tribe lived where and what the relationships to the others were. Evans-Pritchard put it all on charts and diagrams so that you could see that he was either right or wrong. Any Nuer could come along and tell him he was wrong. It was all up front and yet very intellectual. It was the same for his analysis of their politics and their fighting, and his ideas about law and family and kinship. Again and again, the data was all there, beautifully presented; he had it all organized, and the background fitted together. The same for religion. It was a tour de force, really. I don't think anything has been done quite like that again.

WACHTEL Can you say what particularly engaged you? Was it the idea of going out and collecting these stories or was it the intellectual construct that you could make from them?

DOUGLAS Hard to say. Certainly I never thought of them as stories. It was an intellectual attraction, but it was also the action, that you went out and had to do something—meet people and talk to them and engage them and find out what they were thinking. That was attractive, too.

WACHTEL You studied at the Oxford Institute of Social Anthropology, which was a very lively place in that post-war period and home to a number of influential scholars. Can you describe the atmosphere there and the institute's prevailing approach to social anthropology?

DOUGLAS It was very exciting. There was an enemy to attack, an enemy called "ethnology," which is something the Germans did before World War I. But in my time it was old-fashioned, rudely called "conjectural history," which meant you weren't particularly interested in the people; you were interested in bows and arrows, or knives or hut size—anything—and you made little maps about where different objects came from, but the people weren't anywhere in it. It got very complicated as they tried to find these circles of culture exchange across the world. We had an Egyptian with us who said, "We're very happy to find that Perry (in our university in London) had found that all world civilization came out of Egypt." That was the main question of ethnology: Where did it all come from? Whereas we were asking a new kind of question: How did people live, what were they like, how did they manage? It was much more in keeping with the politics and economics that I'd read, and more sociological and contemporary. We traded books and libraries for much more action and a more humane approach.

We were looking at how the minds of people in other societies work, and indeed we discovered that they work the same way as ours. There was a whole argument with the French, particularly with Lévy-Bruhl, about something called "primitive mentality." A lot of people still assume that "primitives" have a different mentality, different mental equipment from us. This was the view to attack; this idea was the enemy. So we analyzed their cosmos, that is, the way that they built their universe, and their ideas of the world and of justice and of the person, and how that fitted in with the way they lived. That was the main project, and it felt completely new and exciting.

WACHTEL   And to show that it's not so different from our own?

DOUGLAS   And to show that if we were there we'd be pleased to be there. You know, it wasn't at all as it had been presented to us. These people weren't a lot of automatons with the rigid hand of culture holding them down and no individual able to think at all. On the contrary, they were live, thinking, interacting individuals, with their thoughts collectively working out some kind of scheme for the universe and for justifying their morals and their behaviour to each other.

WACHTEL   Was this inspired by some sort of post-war egalitarianism or democratic spirit?

DOUGLAS   I think so. It came directly from France, from Durkheim's and Mauss's work on primitive religion and classification. The theory was already there; we had to do all the fieldwork, to qualify and modify and extend the idea of how the mind works. It isn't an intellectual, isolated thing: the brain is in the body and the body's in the world, and there are other people there, and if you are thinking, it's in interaction with other people and not an isolated thing. That battle is still on, by the way.

WACHTEL   Who are the enemies?

DOUGLAS   Oh, individualists in psychology, economics. They all assume one kind of person, unspecified, but mostly a rational-choice kind of person, with no culture around them and no other people to respond to or be responsible to, or for. There's a tremendous challenge still. We haven't won at all. But that's how we started and I'm dismayed to see that many people in anthropology aren't very interested in it now. It's an old-fashioned idea that belongs to the fifties.

WACHTEL You originally wanted to do your ethnographic fieldwork in Italy or Greece, but you were persuaded instead to go to Africa. Why Africa?

DOUGLAS Because I could get funds, first. And second, or perhaps first, because all my teachers had been to Africa, and so they knew that there was a big theoretical field of questions that had to be answered, and comparisons that needed to be made. If a student goes to a field where nobody has studied at all, you really have very little to cut your teeth on. We had to see whether our material matched anybody else's and we had to know a lot in order to write at all, because if something had been said before, it wasn't very interesting and it wouldn't get published.

WACHTEL Mid-twentieth-century British anthropology was very African-centred. Was that because it was accessible and safely colonized at that particular time?

DOUGLAS Yes. We got our money from the Research and Development Council and they had a big investment in Africa. Polynesia belonged to Australia, and American Indians to America. India was feasible, but most of it had been done by Indians. So Africa was the obvious place, really. For theoretical purposes, I'm so glad I went there.

WACHTEL You particularly wanted to research a matrilineal society. Why was that?

DOUGLAS Well, it is very intriguing. It's a society in which women are no better off than in any other society, but a man traces his kinship through women. So the woman is the link and the man relates to his mother's brother rather than to his father. That's the main point about matriliny. Matriliny is nothing to do with matriarchy. It means that a man inherits from his mother's brother and his own legacy goes to his sister's sons. These societies produce interesting theoretical problems that need a lot of work. In fact, I regret very much that nobody has worked on those problems in the Congo since I was there, because I would like to see how what I discovered about matriliny fits in with other matrilineal peoples. For instance, if the system is patrilineal, the men stay at home and the women go to their husband's village. But with matriliny you often have a rule that the man goes to live with the wife's parents. Then every village is inhabited by male strangers, which makes a different kind of village. It is more fragile. Tremendous effort has to be made to keep the village together and also to bring back sons who've gone away. But the sons leave and the sister's sons are there, you see, but they weren't born there. So that kind of village structure has all sorts of political implications. And I still want to see whether other people who had variants of that structure were reacting differently. However, kinship studies went out of fashion and it just wasn't done.

WACHTEL Why was it important for you to study a matrilineal society at the time?

DOUGLAS You had to choose a problem, and I'd heard that the most interesting kinship problems would come out of matrilineal societies. The other attraction of this particular area was that it was polyandrous—a woman could have several husbands.

WACHTEL Although you point out—and I think this is crucial—a matrilineal society and even polyandry doesn't necessarily mean that women have power.

DOUGLAS Not at all. They had no power. They were pawns in the game. I didn't know that when I first went there.

WACHTEL You were very determined to go into the field. In fact, you sold your mother's fur coat to raise the fare to go to a conference in Brussels, which resulted in your working in the former Belgian Congo. As a woman, were you discouraged from going?

DOUGLAS Not at all. On the contrary, there was a lot of kindness and help, and especially from Tervuren, the big Africa museum in Brussels, which has connections to the Congo.

WACHTEL Your teacher, Evans-Pritchard, warned that you'd better not get sick or else other women might not be able to do fieldwork.

DOUGLAS Yes. That's right. "Don't do silly things," he said, "don't take stupid risks."

WACHTEL Because you'd spoil it for other women anthropologists?

DOUGLAS Yes. But he didn't encourage only me; he encouraged a lot of women students.

WACHTEL In 1949 you began your fieldwork among the Lele people in what was then the Belgian Congo, in Central Africa. What was that experience like for you?

DOUGLAS Very, very intense. I had never lived so intensively before.

WACHTEL On your own.

DOUGLAS Yes. I had to just take decisions on the spot, where to go, what to accept when people offered me things. I couldn't write home for advice. I was generously received at the mission station in Basongo when I first arrived, and I had to learn something of the language. It was hard—I'm very bad at languages. After some weeks, the nuns found me a cook; I couldn't go without a cook. This cook, Makum, was a clever chap, a wonderful support at all times, and a great personal friend. He recruited another servant and the two of them, although they were very young, took charge of me.

We went to the nearest village, recommended by the missionaries, where there was a hut that I could live in, but Makum didn't like it there at all. First of all, it wasn't one of the villages that his own village was related to, so that was a problem for him. But my biggest problem was that I couldn't get out of the village. We were too near the administrative station, and everybody was afraid that if anything happened to me—if I twisted my ankle in the bush or anything—they'd be gunned down or get into real trouble, neither of which would have happened. They kept me in the village all the time. I couldn't get out to see their fields, or the forest, or the river, or anything; I couldn't see them working. So Makum said, "This is no good. Come on, we go to my village." In his village everything was completely different. First of all, it was a very small village; secondly, I came in as a relative, a sort of aunt to Makum, whom they knew well. I lived in a tent for a bit, but they quickly converted a big hut for me. I felt completely at home. They let me do anything, go anywhere, and I could make friends much better. So those were the kinds of decisions I had to take and it did me a world of good. In a small village like that, everybody knows where you are and what you're saying and what you're doing. That's what makes it so intense.

WACHTEL How did your work among the Lele people change your ideas, or inspire you?

DOUGLAS It's changed everything I've ever done. They're marvellous people—very subtle and intellectual and full of gaiety and laughter and fun—but they're absolutely shackled by their fear of each other's sorcery. And so I became deeply interested in how people can make life hell for each other, by accusing them or making them fear that they will be accused of causing every kind of illness that happens. If anybody has a cough or a cold: Who is the sorcerer who has done this? How do you get him? Make him confess? Hurt him? So that has been a kind of mission, to understand what I call "sectarianism." It was a very egalitarian village society.

When I was in Paris recently, Pierre Bourdieu, the French sociologist and anthropologist [who died in 2002], said he had read my book about the Lele and he thought that their society was a little Utopia. That is the exact opposite of how I felt about it, but I could see where he got that impression. The principles of their constitution were worked out explicitly in order to cut out envy, which they felt was the cause of sorcery. I'm glad that he admired them for that. He saw from what I had recorded that they didn't allow any kind of accumulation, everything had to be distributed, nobody could be richer than anybody else in case people got jealous of them. If a man had a special talent, like drumming or carving, he could do it and be the carver or the drummer for the village, but as soon as he trained an apprentice who became as good a drummer or carver as he was, he was forced to retire, because you can't have two masters in the same village. The old one would be jealous of the young one. They tried to make these kinds of constitutional arrangements so that people couldn't be harmfully jealous of each other. It was a great preoccupation, very impressive, but it didn't work.

WACHTEL And why do you call this sectarianism? In what way?

DOUGLAS Well, sectarian in the sense that they were a closed community. They put barricades around their houses so you couldn't see in. They feared the outsider; they dreaded the outsider. They thought the outsider was going to bring them danger and trouble. I think that's very sectarian—black and white, insiders and outsiders.

WACHTEL And the egalitarianism?

DOUGLAS Sects are mostly egalitarian. In fact, they are, very strongly. They have to have all sorts of extra rules to make egalitarianism work, like the Lele did. So that's given me one of my big interests, studying sectarianism. Also, they didn't have ancestor cults, unlike in West Africa, Nigeria and parts of the Sudan, where ancestors are so important for religion. For the Lele, ancestors were dangerous rather than helpful. You really tried to keep on their good side. They couldn't do much for you, but they could harm you. There's a lot of danger and harm in this cosmos. I felt very sad about it.

WACHTEL I'd like to talk for a moment about that exotic creature the pangolin—the scaly anteater. Can you describe the pangolin and its importance to the Lele and to your research?

DOUGLAS I wish I'd been there longer and had learned the language better. But the system was one of little cult groups, which you had to be initiated into. There was a special group of people initiated into the pangolin cult. Only they could eat the pangolin, and they had to. I was interested in the foods they could and couldn't eat, the animal foods. They told me about an animal that lives in the trees, that has scales like a fish but is a mammal. So when they caught one, they showed it to me and I took photographs. It curls up in a ball. When it sees a hunter, instead of running away rudely, like most animals do—animals have no good manners—the pangolin would politely bow its head and then curl up into a small, modest ball. The hunter would wait until it had unrolled and then he'd knock it on the head and kill it. So the pangolin was a creature halfway between humans and animals. It was halfway between everything, between water and sky animals, living in the trees. If they caught a pangolin, they had to immediately hold up everything else and have no other cult ceremonies till they'd done the pangolin ceremony. And that was very secret. They carried the corpse of the pangolin around the village, like they carried the chief around the village when he visited them. In fact, they called the pangolin a chief. They would say that the pangolin had come to their village, as if he'd voluntarily walked in to be sacrificed. They would sing, "Now we enter the house of affliction, now we enter the house of affliction."

To my great chagrin, the day they were having a pangolin ceremony in our village, the missionaries called, very friendly and nice of them, to see if I was all right, but I wasn't able to find out what was happening. Anyway, it would have been difficult for a woman, and you need to be very, very fluent to be able to follow what's going on. I got it mostly from Makum afterwards. Whenever the village was short of food, the pangolin men would do a ceremony, and then the whole forest would soften up and they could hunt again properly. It was also a fertility thing. It brought babies to the village. Women conceived. They'd say, "Ah, the pangolin has come! Now we're going to have meat to eat and the mothers will conceive." So everything was going to be all right when the pangolin came. The Lele are capable of a great depth of spiritual interpretation.

WACHTEL   After your initial fieldwork, you said that you discovered in yourself a prejudice against piecemeal explanations. What did that mean for you? What were the implications?

DOUGLAS   It's not quite true that I discovered it in myself. That was the standard teaching of post-structural anthropology, so that Lévi-Strauss structuralism and the rest all required you to know what the whole structure was. Anthropology had taken that position long before; structuralism has very old roots. You have to know the whole system to know anything at all. It was something I had drummed into me in my studies. A piecemeal explanation is one in which you focus on the one object and ask, for example, why they are interested in pangolins. You would get very odd answers to such questions, and they'd be very superficial and unconnected with anything else. So what you have to ask is: What is their attitude to animals? How many kinds of animals do they recognize? How do they distinguish different kinds of animals? What you discover is that they classify animals of the above, which are birds—and squirrels count as birds because they live in the trees—and animals in the water—including pigs, because wild pigs live in the water. Then there are grassland and forest animals, and animals on and under the land. The fact that the pangolin crosses several of those big categories, being a mammal that lives in the water and in the above, as well as on the land, is very interesting. It distinguishes itself as a very strange animal.

WACHTEL Your best-known book, published in 1966, is *Purity and Danger: An Analysis of Concepts of Pollution and Taboo*. It arose out of your experience among the Lele, and like much of your work that followed, it crosses boundaries between different cultures and different disciplines. What made this investigation into pollution behaviour so central to your understanding of how we live?

DOUGLAS I was very, very excited about the thought that every culture probably had a wastepaper-basket category. I became obsessed by the idea of that which cannot be analyzed, or that which cannot be classified. What do they do with them? They can't classify everything. Classifications are man-made, and nature resists total classification. There must be so many cases that don't fit. So it was an extension of the training in non-piecemeal work and in classification. What do they do with the non-classifiables? What sort of waste bin do they use? I had a lot of fun with that sort of interest, and I particularly put it to work to understand impurity. Frankly, I don't really think it works very well now. That particular part—the unclassifiables—I haven't been able to do much with, whereas the kinds of classification remain a very fruitful source of ideas.

WACHTEL I was thinking about the anomalies, the things that can't be classified. You once described dirt as being "matter out of place." There's something very intriguing about this.

DOUGLAS Yes, that was it. This is what I call the wastepaper-basket aspect. You know, you've got to throw things away; some things just don't fit. I was sure that a psychological approach to disgust was wrong, inadequate, superficial, and that a classificatory, sociological approach to disgust would be more fruitful, would yield more results. Now, when I say "disgust," I mean the fact that hitherto the idea of impurity had been associated with feelings of abomination and disgust, particularly in the Bible, and I'm sure that that was just wrong. You have to take a classificatory approach to impurity—what is classifiable and what isn't. I thought that impurity could be identified everywhere as the unclassifiable. However, religious impurity gets more and more curious and rich the more I get into it, and it doesn't seem to work frightfully well like that. A lot of my colleagues went to town on this. I'm glad they didn't quote me particularly, but rather treated the idea that anomalies were always disgusting as their own idea. You see, the pangolin was anomalous, but it wasn't disgusting at all. It was venerable. Edmund Leach, in particular, really went to town on anomaly as a source of unease and disgust. I did say quite a lot about it in that book, but it wasn't the main point. The main point of the book was that you had to study impurity and purity—and all attitudes of this kind—sociologically. Taboo is a social response. It is cultural, and has to fit in with the rest of what they are doing—their actions—not something that goes on in the mind by itself or in the emotions. The emotions are there, but they might or might not be engaged attitudes to impurity. That part of the book hasn't really been taken up very much, so I've been writing about it ever since.

WACHTEL As you write in Purity and Danger, "We shall not expect to understand other people's ideas of contagion, sacred or secular, until we've confronted our own." And then in the book you relate the cult of the pangolin among the Lele to Jewish dietary laws in Leviticus and Deuteronomy. It's a connection that at first seems surprising.

DOUGLAS Well, it seemed to be the right thing, because whenever anybody talks about purity, they think about Leviticus and Deuteronomy. So I thought I'd found an explanation, in that the Levitical laws, which are the principal ones, are a way of sorting out the animals according to environment, very much like the Leles' air set of rules, and also the water and land sets of rules. The environment and the living beings are separated out. So I looked at the idea that has been accepted for the last two thousand years, that these creatures you couldn't eat were abominable, which is the normal translation, meaning horrible and disgusting. All the exegeses, all the kinds of interpretations of why they shouldn't be eaten, have started out from the idea that there's something abominable about these animals. It left biblical scholars scratching their heads and trying to think what was abominable about the camel, the hare and the rock badger.

WACHTEL Because they didn't have cloven hooves.

DOUGLAS Yes, and what was abominable about that? Anyway, I came back to it many years later, and tried to learn some Hebrew so I could challenge the biblical translations.

WACHTEL To stay back with *Purity and Danger*: the pangolin, as you pointed out, was not abominable, but you made comparisons between Jewish dietary laws and the way the Lele regarded the pangolin.

DOUGLAS But it wasn't just the way the Lele regarded the pangolin. It was one species in a whole series of animals—obviously not one animal, not piecemeal. The Lele classified a lot of animals; women could eat some, children could eat some, and pregnant women and young boys were distinguished by special diets. It was complex.

WACHTEL One of your purposes in *Purity and Danger* was to correct the prevailing assumptions about the role of ritual. In that book and also in *Natural Symbols*, which followed it, you stress the importance of ritual to social life. Why did you feel you had to make a case for that?

DOUGLAS Well, it was the 1960s, wasn't it? There was a big anti-ritual move on—rituals were thought to be meaningless. It's really a nonconformist Protestant idea against any established church; it's a position of revolt. Established churches have rituals. If we want to get more directed to God by ourselves, we don't need rituals. So you don't want all these priests and pastors, you can do it without them. You can have a direct interaction. Even though there was a very strong move against ritual at that time, I had to come out in favour of ritual, because I knew it made sense.

WACHTEL And that goes back to your own affinity for institutions?

DOUGLAS It's all of a piece, yes. I probably wouldn't have felt it was important if I hadn't felt very committed to the kind of upbringing I had.

WACHTEL You say that as social animals we are also ritual animals, and it's not too much to say that "ritual is more to society than words are to thought. For it is very possible to know something and then find words for it. But it is impossible to have social relations without symbolic acts." That really struck me, because I always think that words and thought are inextricable.

DOUGLAS I don't think it's right that words are everything. I think words are a bit overvalued in our civilization and that you can certainly have thoughts when you see rituals or when you're involved in rituals, without words.

WACHTEL But it's impossible to have social relations without symbolic acts?

DOUGLAS Yes, I think so. I don't think social relations go very far without symbolic acts.

WACHTEL Maybe I need to understand better what rituals are. When you say that as social animals we are ritual animals, what does that mean?

DOUGLAS It's because of our need to communicate. A ritual is something that's repeated, not merely a one-off gesture that might be just a signal. Rituals can be expected to happen again, and their meaning comes from having been done before and from the expectation that they will be done again. So they're part of a series that links the individual to past individuals and to other individuals. They confer meaning on ordinary actions by being specialized, ritual ones. There are ritual objects, too, like chocolates or flowers, which you give people. Rituals create the kind of avenues down which we walk and decorate the places in which we dance, as it were.

WACHTEL Do you think that these rituals need defending, too?

DOUGLAS I feel that people misunderstand their own ritual behaviour. They know they jolly well need to lay a table correctly, with the knives and forks on the correct side of the plate, but they don't recognize this as ritual. They take care of private rituals but despise similar rituals at a more elegant, a more esteemed level—like public rituals.

WACHTEL When *Purity and Danger* came out, were your ideas well received?

DOUGLAS The book got some very good reviews, but it didn't get into university courses for a long time. We sold about two hundred copies in the first two years, I think. And nobody talked to me about it. I needed more conversation in order to know what I'd said, so I wasn't able to explain it very well. I didn't teach it, so I didn't get questions back from the students.

WACHTEL In looking at your career, you mention that to some degree you were slighted by the British anthropologists because you'd gone to do your fieldwork in what had been a French colony and that the French weren't paying that much attention because you were writing in English. You were a woman, you were a Catholic, you were also raising a family; you were yourself somewhat marginal to institutions; you pursued very original ideas. Did you find yourself something of an outsider in the field?

DOUGLAS Nobody who works in a foreign milieu gets attention from their home country. Maurice Bloch, who wrote in English about French-speaking people in Madagascar, told me this. He couldn't sell his books in England or get people to give courses on them. It wasn't part of the syllabus structure. Yes, I felt very much an outsider.

WACHTEL Was that frustrating or was it an advantage in some way?

DOUGLAS Probably those things that are frustrating turn out to be advantages. You have to go on writing in order to explain what it is you have done.

WACHTEL In a review that you wrote of a biography of Margaret Mead, you observed that she was something of an outsider and that part of that had to do with her being a woman.

DOUGLAS Yes, I felt that very much about her. It wasn't a review I wrote—I think it was just a marked observation on her life. People like Robert Merton, and other people at Columbia, where she should have been teaching, thought of her as an oddball. And so she was, and I think she got odder and odder, and more and more original, because she didn't have to toe the line about anything. She stayed in that little flat just above the museum and was almost a freelance anthropologist, in my opinion. This did leave her freedom to experiment with all sorts of things, but it didn't give her the discipline of being in the mainstream. In my case it was a bit different. The mainstream itself dried up after 1968, so that now anthropology departments have hardly any teachers who know the kind of anthropology that I was brought up in.

WACHTEL But you were saying that if Mead, who showed such early brilliance, had been a man, she would have been snapped up by a major institution.

DOUGLAS I think so. Yes. They would have thought they had to, or she would have been a menace if they didn't have her on their side. Yes, she was obviously very bright, but she was also a very pushy person and determined to be in the front, and so they would have had to accept that, and it would have been easier if she had been a man.

WACHTEL I'd like to look at the range of your work through the years, the way in which you've tied together the exotic and the apparently ordinary, to try to understand how we live, by venturing into other disciplines such as economics, ecology, theology, nutritional studies, consumption theory. Why do you think you've been that eclectic in your approach?

DOUGLAS Well, there's a very straightforward answer. The anthropologist's career goes like this: doing fieldwork, doing it again in the same field, then doing a PhD. Then going back to somewhere near that field, or something similar, and then going back to that place again—back and forth in the same area, building up a whole collection, sending students there and collaborating with other people who are sending students into the region, and going to relevant conferences. Now, in my case, I had three children quite quickly, so I couldn't follow the usual career path. I find that most women whose lives include more than their work do what I did, which is to turn to philosophy or to library research that they can do without going into the field. But in my case there was an added complication: in 1961, when my children were still quite small, there was a civil war in the Belgian Congo and the whole field collapsed. My colleagues from Belgium were scattered; two went to different parts of America and one stayed in Brussels. Since there wasn't the possibility of regularly keeping in touch with the field, I had to turn to whatever I could do. I had the kind of freedom that Margaret

Mead had, to do what I liked, since nobody in Congolese research was especially asking me, "Come along, collaborate with me and we'll do this."

WACHTEL And how did you determine what you liked?

DOUGLAS I remember people were really surprised when I said I had to take a year off to do economics. My husband is an economist. I thought that describing, in a condensed way, the power of symbols, I could do well by studying money as an example, because economists have a wonderful compressed language about monetary behaviour—they talk about "liquidity" and "inflation" and "supply-side economics." I thought there would be some word or group of theories that would help me to understand the mutual confidence that money depends on. So I started to read economics, and I realized that economists are all writing from the production side; I was obviously interested in the wider behavioural side. Production is not so separate in the kinds of tribes I was talking about, because part of everybody's life is to be a producer and a consumer. Economic theory dichotomizes us as either consumers or producers, though we know that producers also consume. So I was very sure that to do economic anthropology I should be studying the theory of consumption, and I took a year off to do that. I loved it, I enjoyed it.

WACHTEL It would be difficult to touch on all the areas of daily life that you explore through your research—from shopping and choosing a doctor, or furniture, to environmental concerns and analyzing poverty and risk or consumption as a kind of ritual itself. But in each of these you find a social purpose; you stress that humanity is only possible within society. Why is that view so important to you?

DOUGLAS It seems, first of all, terribly obvious, and at the same time I keep seeing things written as if it wasn't true. So it's something that has to be corrected. And you're right: this is a central theme in my work.

WACHTEL You've applied anthropological insights to everyday behaviour in Western culture. For example: the rituals associated with eating—your investigations into English working-class food habits were especially revealing. What were some of your discoveries there?

DOUGLAS The kinds of things that came out of it are mostly method-ological, in the sense that we've discovered a way of measuring how much structure is put into a meal and who takes the trouble to create this. This was the American research that was published as *Food in the Social Order*. We started with four teams of anthropologists working in America, one among the Sioux Indians, one among North Carolina blacks, and one among Italian Americans in Philadelphia. There was also a study in Tennessee, but that one never worked out. They were applying the anthropological technique of not asking questions, but rather sitting around and eating the food, quietly noting the calendar and who was present. It was a very highly planned research project. The researcher eating the food was watching for what kind of rules there were about what goes with what. Imagine a family in which they just have potatoes, and only potatoes, every day, nothing else. That would be totally unstructured—only one variety and nothing done to it. But if they were celebrating Sunday separately, by having a bit of sauce, or if they were having fish on Fridays—that would be a bit of structure. You can add in all sorts of variations to make it more and more structured. If you can only have mint sauce with lamb and red currant jelly with chicken, and only mustard with beef, that's what structuring is. We were interested in what kind of rules they had about how the food could be served, because there's a lot of work to do to maintain those rules. You had to keep shopping and supplying. Where do people find the energy and power and intention? Where do they get the desire to put all that structure into simple eating? So that's what our research was.

We also wanted to measure structure, so we had a very good mathe-matician working on this. The measurements were going to be part of the set of comparisons we used later, but we never managed to go on with the work because the boss at the Russell Sage Foundation, Aaron Wildavsky, under whose aegis I started this work, was fired within six months of getting the job and we couldn't carry it through. (It wasn't anybody's fault, except those who fired him.) The idea was to work out ways of comparing the structures, because unless you can say how much structure there is *here* compared with *there*—and you would need very close comparisons—you can't really say much about structured-ness. It was a very specialized methodological thing, but fun.

WACHTEL You mentioned that you began learning Hebrew in your seventies. Are you now able to read the texts in the original?

DOUGLAS No, I can't read Hebrew fluently, but mercifully, thanks to the efforts of scholars, the Pentateuch—the whole of the first five books of Moses—have come out in the most wonderful array of commentaries, and several of them have the Hebrew text on one side and the English text on the other, with a whole lot of commentaries underneath it. So you can know enough to read, and after a bit, knowing the script, you get to know particular bits of the language, although I'm sunk when it comes to road signs in Israel. But certainly, knowing Hebrew was very important for analyzing the translation of abomination, for example. I'm still not quite happy about it, but I felt that the whole thing has been so misread—both Numbers and Leviticus, but especially Leviticus—by generations of Jewish scholars. The rabbis put far more emphasis on interpreting purity and the rules of purity and making them into rules of everyday life than they did on trying to understand the philosophy and the beautiful construction of the book itself. The emphasis on God's compassion and kindness and love is there in Leviticus. Christians always think the New Testament brought a religion of love and forgiveness, which is absolutely untrue. It's there in Leviticus, right in the very middle of the book. When you study certain words to see what went wrong with their translations, you can see what got us into the mess of saying that certain things God made are abominable. He couldn't have said that; it doesn't fit. If you accept that interpretation, then Leviticus is a book that is right out of line with the Psalms, and the rest of the Prophets is full of internal contradiction. It's been treated as a very peculiar book, but I don't think it is. I think it's absolutely straight down the middle of the Pentateuch. I'm quite tempted to go out on a limb and say that this is the book that Jesus was thinking of when he told the Pharisees and the scribes that they had it all wrong.

WACHTEL You wrote in the introduction to your book that "to study the book of Leviticus as an anthropologist has been a project very dear to my heart." Why is that?

DOUGLAS Partly because it's a complete book. This is quite tendentious. It's quite a dangerous proposition to make to a lot of Hebrew scholars, because they like to think of the different parts of the Pentateuch not as complete books—the Pentateuch is the book and these are the bits of it. But I think that compositionally it is a rounded and very beautiful piece. So it's a great joy to read it and to discover how elegantly and elaborately it's been composed. Also, I was able to go back to my own theories and fit them in better. I've had to completely revise my ideas about animal foods and forbidden foods in Leviticus.

WACHTEL Wasn't that in the back of your mind for thirty-five years, in a sense?

DOUGLAS No, not at all. I went back to it because I was invited to give some very prestigious lectures in Edinburgh—the Gifford Lectures—and they gave me three years' notice. If you're told to do something in three years' time, you spend hours and weeks thinking what on earth would be worthy. I thought I would put everything together. It would be the last big thing I would do, and it would be on the sociology of knowledge and the sociology of science—theories of mind—which come out of all the other work and fit it all together.

While I was thinking of what to do about those lectures, writing little headings and things, Catherine Sakenfeld at the Presbyterian Seminary in Princeton asked me to come and speak to her students. I was to discuss a certain passage in the Book of Numbers, about the people who find a corpse, someone murdered, in a field that doesn't belong to anybody. They have to find a red cow, sacrifice her, and make certain declarations. I had never read any of the Book of Numbers before, and when I read that, I realized I was way out of my depth. I had no clue what it was about and knew I would have to spend an awful lot of time to understand it. However, I had the anthropologist's confidence that what we could say about sacrifice would always be useful. But no, I found that I really couldn't say anything that the students didn't know already. It was shaming.

Somehow the Book of Numbers took hold of me as I began reading it. I gave the Gifford Lectures about it, and somebody said, "Look, you're reading the book straight, but you're not reading any of the commentaries on it, are you?" Anthropologists really don't want to look at the commentaries until after they get to know a thing. To my horror, when I read the commentaries, I found that the book was dismissed by some respected Bible scholars. Everybody was apologizing for, or else declaiming against, its lack of structure, its disorderliness, its chaotic constructions. Why was this here and not there? And particularly the ending: one scholar would chop off the ending here and another chop off that bit there. They were under the influence of "source criticism," which makes you less interested in what the book is about as a book, because you're not treating it as a whole. You're treating it as a series of archaeological stratifications in which different authors have added different things, and all your skills must go to finding out which author said what—all imaginary authors. I felt amazed that you could treat a sacred book in that way and not assume that it had been at some point put together with a purpose. Anthropologists would never dare say to an informant, "Look, let's cut out that last part and get to the really essential bits." But this was what was happening to Numbers. I found afterwards that it happens with a lot of archaic texts. In the 1880s there was a German professor of Sanskrit (Paul Deussen) who translated the Vedanta, the Indian myths. It was so full of repetitions that he tried to create a single thread by cutting out all the repetitions.

I was on to one of these big snags in interpretation. The anthropologist's proper task is to read the book, which I knew I was trying to do too quickly. When I read Numbers carefully, I said to myself, Why don't they like it? What's wrong with it? What the scholars didn't like was that there was a piece of law and it was interrupted by a narrative, about the people leaving Mount Sinai and going towards Jordan, and all their adventures in the desert. Then suddenly there'd be a break and the reader would be given a lot more laws, and then the story would be picked up again. There were a lot of repetitions. Anthropologists have got a tradition for reading that kind of thing: you look for the structure in it; you don't take it piecemeal. What I found—and I really feel very thrilled with the discovery—was that this ancient book had been composed in alternating sections, story–law, story–law, story–law, and arranged in a circle. Number 1 and number 7 are stories; number 1 starts a story and number 7 finishes it. Number 12 and number 2 are laws. The stories are odd numbers and the laws are even numbers. Very creepily consistent! You couldn't do it by hazard; you couldn't imagine it just happening. And so I discerned the classical ring composition, which I had known nothing about before I started. I had to learn to read synoptically—that is to say, you read it across, like you read a sonnet. You've got the rhymes in your head and when you hear the word again, you remember it and link it up with the previous line, and it's a regular pattern in your mind. You read it across, not longways. So people have been reading the Book of Numbers longways and it was meant to be read across. It comes out totally differently, very coherent and very elegant and very beautiful. But all the time I was doing it—and it took years and years and years—I kept worrying: supposing I fall down a drain or supposing I get run down by a bus, the Book of Numbers will never be analyzed. I thought it so important. And when I had finished working with Numbers, I knew I had to go back to Leviticus.

WACHTEL So having finished Numbers, you returned to Leviticus. Did you know that you were going to be revisionist, or that you would have to change?

DOUGLAS I knew then that I was already very revisionist, because I had done a major revision on the Book of Numbers. It's a very political book after all, not just a neutral set of laws. At that point I had to learn some Hebrew, because there were translations I really wanted to verify.

WACHTEL Is it possible to say how your view of Leviticus changed from when you used it to help you understand pollution and purities?

DOUGLAS Yes. You have to understand a little bit about the structure of the book and get into literary structures. This thing called "ring composition" is a well-known rhetorical form, in which the beginning is announced, and when you get to the middle you hear the beginning repeated and you know you've got to the middle. Then it starts going back again towards the beginning. So when you've got a ring, it's your job to see what kinds of parallels are being made by the writer between the beginning and the end.

When I went to work on Leviticus I had been helped by doing Numbers, with its story–law, story–law structure. When I looked at Leviticus, I thought that the Numbers structure couldn't apply at all, because with only two stories it couldn't be a principle of organization. Suddenly one day it occurred to me that perhaps it was, so I looked at the stories again. They're very punitive stories: the sons of Aaron get killed by fire and then the blasphemer gets stoned. I looked at their placing in the book. There are three parts to the book: two stories make a book of three parts. The first part is a ring; it's all about the sacrifice of animals and illnesses that need to have sacrifices done for atonement. It occurred to me that there *was* a structure—three uneven parts, getting smaller and smaller. The proportions of the book, divided by narratives of disaster, are the same as the proportions of the Tabernacle built by Moses in Exodus.

First there is a huge court of sacrifice where the altar is and where the animals are brought in for sacrifice. Then there's a door that only the priests are allowed to go through. In the book the first of the punitive stories is placed there. Only the priests go through that door into the sanctuary. The second part of the book is about where the priests can go in and the position of the lamp stand [menorah], the altar of incense and the altar of showbread—three pieces of furniture. It's all about the priests: what a priest is, who he can marry, what food he can eat, and so on. So then the second terrible story introduces the last part of the book, which is where in the plan of the Tabernacle you go through the last screen into the Holy of Holies. This is where the Ark of the Covenant rests, with two cherubim over it, and tremendous amounts of smoke going up so it's obscured. Inside it is the Book of the Testimony, the promise that God made to Israel to be their Lord. In the book of Leviticus the last and smallest section is all about God's covenant.

WACHTEL So rather than being a book about rules and prohibitions and abominations—

DOUGLAS It's a tremendous spiritual exercise. It's called a "mobile Tabernacle." You can carry it around. The real temple has been destroyed and you've got this book. It's like the stations of the cross in Catholicism. You don't need to be in any particular place, but you enter the Tabernacle, you go through the door, you can even see into the Holy of Holies. But apart from the consummate literary skills that are involved, it's a great joy and thrill to read, quite amazing. It draws on Genesis and the other books of the Pentateuch, and you have to use them to interpret it—it is about forgiveness and God's love. I really loved it. I miss it. I finished it and I miss it. I'm still writing about it.

WACHTEL Do you think that your work in social anthropology, and especially your research into the meaning of ritual and now more recently into the books of the Bible, has deepened your own religious commitment?

DOUGLAS Probably. I think I've been lucky to be able to pursue it like this.

WACHTEL You've had a long career as both a researcher and a teacher in England and the United States. What do you feel is your own greatest contribution to the field?

DOUGLAS I don't know, really. I think the idea of the human being as a social animal should be important, but I don't think anyone needs me to say it. Probably Leviticus.

April 2001

NOAM CHOMSKY

A world-famous linguist and dissident intellectual, described as a "latter-day Copernicus," Noam Chomsky has turned around the way we think about language, the media and political discourse. The most frequently quoted praise of Noam Chomsky is from the *New York Times Book Review*: "Judged in terms of the power, range, novelty and influence of his thought, Noam Chomsky is arguably the most important intellectual alive today." That last phrase appears on the dust jackets of his books, and is mentioned whenever reporters talk about his political activism.

The irony is that, for Chomsky, the *New York Times* is one of the major perpetrators of what he calls a "web of deceit," or "thought control in a democratic society." The story goes that Chomsky's dentist noticed that he'd been grinding his teeth. His wife observed that it wasn't happening at night when he was asleep. Eventually, he realized it was occurring every morning while he read the *New York Times*.

Noam Chomsky is an iconoclast and gadfly of power. He speaks for no particular ideology, and no party claims him. Despite his fierce critique of American foreign policy during the Cold War, he was no favourite of the Soviet Union. His works—even his scholarly writings on linguistics—were banned there. In Chomsky's view, the responsibility of intellectuals is to speak the truth and expose lies. He said that almost forty years ago and he believes it today.

The Oxford Companion to the English Language says that Chomsky is considered to be "the most influential figure in linguistics in the later twentieth century." In the late fifties and sixties, Chomsky argued that humans have an innate capacity to learn language, a kind of "deep grammar" that is bred in the bone, that's part of our genetic makeup. "A fundamental element of being human," he said, "is the ability to create language."

The impact of his work was so great that it's been dubbed the Chomskian Revolution. According to the citation indexes in the Arts and Humanities and in the Social Sciences, Chomsky is the most-cited living author, and he ranks eighth if you include living and dead writers, beating out Hegel and Cicero.

Noam Chomsky was born in 1928 in Philadelphia. Despite his age, he maintains a daunting schedule—travelling, lecturing, writing, dealing with the media, as well as teaching linguistics at M.I.T. He produces more than a book a year. I estimated sixty titles; he said he didn't know, he wasn't sure. The first was Syntactic Structure (1957); more recently, The Architecture of Language (2000) and 9-11 (2002).

After being relegated to the margins in the late seventies and eighties as far as mainstream media was concerned, Chomsky has found new audiences as a result of the activism surrounding globalization. For instance, in spring 2002, after the world forum in Porto Alegre, Brazil, he spoke in the United States to houses of three thousand and more. Chomsky feels he's witnessing the birth of an international movement which, he says, "the left has been dreaming about since its origins." When his volume of interviews about September 11th was published—denouncing the "war on terrorism"—it came out simultaneously in France, Japan, Taiwan, Italy, Australia, Portugal, Sweden, Greece, Brazil, Germany, the Netherlands and the U.S.

––––––––––––––

WACHTEL The picture that I have of you is of a man with a really tireless, dedicated and even ascetic life. A long time ago that's how Norman Mailer described you after sharing a jail cell briefly because of a Vietnam War protest. He used the word *ascetic*. How does that word sit with you?

CHOMSKY It's more or less accurate, I guess, although I do plenty of things that are quite self-indulgent, increasingly so, now that I have grandchildren.

WACHTEL Can you give me an example of your self-indulgence?

CHOMSKY Playing with my grandchildren, for example. That's the maximum self-indulgence.

WACHTEL I was waiting for something a little richer, you know.

CHOMSKY Richer? Well, you know, over the summer I go into total hermit-hood. I've discovered over the years that the only way I can survive my schedule from the beginning of September through the end of June is to disappear entirely over the summer and barely answer the telephone. I see a couple of old friends, and family comes by—that sort of thing—but my wife and I both work most of the day. We'll take off in the late afternoon and go swimming or sailing.

WACHTEL Even during the summer you work most of the day.

CHOMSKY Yes, most of the day.

WACHTEL You once said that it's likely that literature will forever give far deeper insight into what is sometimes called the "full human person" than any modes of scientific inquiry may hope to do. And yet, you rarely refer to works of the imagination. How have you been influenced by fiction?

CHOMSKY That's hard to say. I read a lot of fiction. I read a lot more when I was younger. I do actually refer to it now and then, but it creates one's sensibility in ways that are hard to explain. Understanding of people and what they do enriches one's intuition in particular ways I find hard to articulate.

WACHTEL When you read fiction, what do you turn to?

CHOMSKY I have fairly conservative tastes, usually nineteenth- and early twentieth-century literature. Sometimes modern things.

WACHTEL What books have influenced your beliefs?

CHOMSKY Too many to list or even sample, from childhood, when summer vacation in particular meant many delightful hours curled up in a chair working through the shelves of classics brought home from the local library. But perhaps I might mention one aspect that is rather personal. From childhood, every Friday evening was set aside for reading Hebrew classics with my father, including much of the great Yiddish literature translated into Hebrew (sometimes by the authors). One particular favourite, not as well known as he should be, was Mendele Mocher Sforim. And one great regret is that I haven't had time to revisit those early experiences, and savour them from the point of view of a life in retrospect rather than prospect. Someday, I hope.

WACHTEL I was struck by a remark of yours about how you'd always been resistant—consciously resistant—to allowing literature to influence your beliefs and attitudes.

CHOMSKY Insofar as I can. I'm not just referring to literature, but also to the visual arts, to documentaries, and so on. It's one thing to have your imagination stimulated and heightened, it's another thing to find the truth. Literature has always had a great impact on me. However, I try to base conclusions not on personal convictions and attitudes, but on evidence that is independently available—with what success, others can judge. I don't try to hide my beliefs and attitudes; in fact I try to make them as prominent as possible—as everyone should, I think, to allow others to understand where they're coming from and to interpret what they say accordingly. But that is quite consistent with the attempt to keep what one privately thinks and feels from shaping conclusions about particular matters, as much as possible. One can't get out of one's skin, of course, but to the extent that self-awareness and self-criticism allow, I try to put to the side intuitive feelings, emotional reactions—perspectives that are not determined by the evidence itself. That's obviously an unattainable ideal, and I don't claim to achieve it, even to the extent that I try, but at least one ought to try. As a normative principle, I think it's a good one.

WACHTEL Do you think there are truths to be found in art, in literature?

CHOMSKY In my own professional work, I've always held, very insistently, that in the domains that are important for our lives, we generally learn a lot more about people from art and literature than from the most sophisticated work in the sciences, including my own special areas of interest, and probably always will. That shouldn't be a great surprise. It's only rather recently that even the core hard sciences have had much to contribute to practice in the various crafts.

WACHTEL I'd like to get at the origin of your sense of justice, your sympathy for the underdog.

CHOMSKY The origin? It comes from having grown up in the Depression, I suppose, and from early childhood memories of people coming to the door and trying to sell rags or apples or something like that. From travelling in a trolley car past a textile factory where women were on strike and watching a riot where police beat the strikers. Then there's experience that isn't immediate, the kind of experience that comes from reading, from film, from secondary sources, as well as personal experience. From another point of view, it comes out of the assumption that human beings have fundamental, intrinsic rights that are infringed upon in numerous ways, leading to sometimes grievous injustice, right before our eyes. This is a particular concern, to the extent that we ourselves—I myself—am involved in it. So I'm much more concerned about crimes committed, say, by the United States, where I have some grave responsibilities, than about the crimes of Genghis Khan. I can get upset about those, but I can't do much about them.

WACHTEL What effect do you think it had on you to grow up in a neighbourhood in Philadelphia that was pro-Nazi during the early days of the war?

CHOMSKY That was frightening. For a large part of my childhood, we

were the only Jewish family in a neighbourhood that was mainly German and Irish Catholic. Very anti-Semitic. Most of the kids went to
Catholic school. I should say that until I was well past the age of reason,
I had a visceral fear of Catholics and Catholic schools. It was hard to
overcome when I met people like, for example, the Berrigans, although
I knew it was irrational. The neighbourhood *was* pro-Nazi. This was the
1930s, and I recall celebrations when Paris fell. My brother and I knew
that we had particular routes that we could take—not others—to get to
the bus or to the store or wherever. I don't want to exaggerate this,
either. The anti-Semitism was real, but you could still play with the
neighbourhood kids. You just never knew what was going to happen
next, so there was a little wariness. But that was to some extent part of
the neighbourhood, always in the background. Of course, what was
happening in Europe was very frightening. I can remember listening to
Hitler's Nuremberg rallies, not really understanding my parents' reactions. By the time I was eight or nine, and able to understand what was
happening, watching one part of Europe after another fall to Hitlerism,
I was frightened. Especially when right around me I could see reso-
nances of it.

WACHTEL You say that your anarchist interests go way back to early
childhood. How did that come about? I find it hard to picture a young
kid having a grasp of or an affinity for anarchism.

CHOMSKY This was the 1930s, remember, which was a very lively,
exciting period with lots of political debate and discussion. Although
there was deep depression, there was lots of hope for the future. A large
part of my family was unemployed and working class. Nevertheless,
there was a sense of hopefulness and discussion and debate and work. I
grew up in the midst of that and became very much involved and interested in all these issues. By the time I was old enough to act on my own,
I was frequenting Fourth Avenue bookstores in New York, and picking
up anarchist literature in anarchist offices, talking to members or relatives who were involved in these movements and concerns. The Spanish
Civil War was one event that caught my interest enormously. The first
article I can remember writing was right after the fall of Barcelona, and

a year or two later I was handing out anarchist pamphlets and literature and thinking about what had happened and what it meant. Those interests and concerns simply never changed. My own greatest political involvement at that time was with what was then Palestine, what later became Israel.

This was the early 1940s. I grew up in a virtual ghetto, I suppose. My parents were in a primarily Jewish environment, a first-generation immigrant environment. They were both Hebrew teachers, and the important thing in their life was the revival of Hebrew culture and the cultural revival in Palestine. I read Hebrew literature with my father from childhood—nineteenth- and twentieth-century Hebrew literature, and older sources, of course. I spent my time in Hebrew school and later became a Hebrew teacher. All of this became very connected with my political interests. I was, at that time, committed to a wing of the Zionist movement that was still significant in the 1940s, one that was opposed to a Jewish state, though it was considered a live part of the Zionist movement and was concerned with the possibility of Arab–Jewish co-operation in a framework of co-operative socialist institutions. I never actually joined anything. I wasn't much of a joiner, and, while I was associated with the actual movements that were involved in these things, I could never join them because they were all either Stalinist or Trotskyist. I was already very anti-Leninist at that time—anti-Marxist, in fact. And so, while I agreed with them about lots of things, I could never really become a member. I lived on a kibbutz formed by those groups some years later for a brief period, and in fact thought of staying there, but joining was an impossibility because of my anarchist commitments.

WACHTEL These anarchist commitments go back to such a young age—writing about the fall of Barcelona for the school newspaper when you were ten, saying that your views haven't really changed that much since you were twelve or thirteen. Obviously they've gotten more sophisticated, but what does that say about you that your views would be so firmly fixed at such a young age?

CHOMSKY Maybe it means I'm obtuse. Or maybe it's a matter of see-

ing that something's right and just sticking to it and trying to understand. I think that these ideas are the right ideas. It seems to me that the
intellectual tradition that led to modern anarchism—and that includes,
incidentally, the mainstream of classical liberalism—is very much mis-
interpreted. By that I mean Adam Smith, Wilhelm von Humboldt, who
inspired John Stuart Mill—the libertarian side of Rousseau. Rousseau
is complex, but there is a libertarian side that developed into the classical liberal tradition, which was then seriously aborted, in my opinion,
by the rise of industrial capitalism. That tradition is a very valid one. It
leads to modern libertarian socialism or parts of the anarchist tradition,
and I think that it's basically a sense that human beings have a fundamental right to self-realization, to self-fulfillment under conditions of
freedom and voluntary association. The classical liberals like Humboldt were not individualists in the primitive style of Rousseau. As
Humboldt put it, he wanted to remove the fetters from human society
and to increase the bonds—these being bonds of voluntary self-
association. Classical liberalism in this form was sharply critical of
property values. So, for example, Humboldt argued again, the worker
who cultivates a garden is more its owner than the person who simply
enjoys the fruits of the other's labour but may technically own it. Adam
Smith's anti-capitalism derives from the same root. He recognized that
division of labour is ultimately intolerable because it will turn every
human being into something as stupid and ignorant as it is possible for
a creature to be, thereby undermining the essence of human nature,
which is the right to create freely and constructively under one's own
control and without external constraints. Out of this comes a concep-
tion of freedom and rights and social organization that challenges any
form of authority and domination, that asks it to justify itself. Sometimes such justifications can be given—maybe under contingent historical circumstances or maybe more deeply—but the burden of proof is
on the system of authority and domination. Quite typically, that burden
can't be met, in which case one will try to work with others to overcome
those structures of authority and domination and to increase positive
freedom, not simply in the sense of removal of, say, state controls but

freedom in the sense of forms of social organization that allow people to realize their potential, their need to be active and creative.

WACHTEL Have there been any societies where these ideals have been put into effect?

CHOMSKY In every society, to some extent. In our society, to some extent those ideals are realized; in other respects they're not. And what we seek, if we're honourable, is, in my opinion, to confront and remove the enormous ways these ideals are not met. Remove the fetters, create new social bonds, in Humboldt's terms.

WACHTEL In 1964 you made a decision to become an activist, to commit much of your life to political action. You were already a successful linguist. You had a family. Things were good. Have you ever looked back? Have you ever thought about the things that you had to give up?

CHOMSKY Oh, sure. Lots. As we've discussed, I didn't really change my views at that point, but I did decide that it was just intolerable—and intolerably self-indulgent—merely to take a passive role in the struggles that were then going on: signing petitions and sending money and showing up now and then at a meeting. I thought it was critically necessary to take a more active role and I was well aware of what that would mean. It's not the kind of thing where you can put a foot in the water and get it wet and then leave. You go in deeper and deeper. I knew that I would be following a course that would confront privilege and authority. My own views were highly critical but didn't have much of an effect when I expressed my opinions in small groups. It would become a larger and more damaging part of my life as I proceeded. I have no illusions about the nature of the intellectual community, with conformism, its techniques for marginalizing or trying to eliminate critical and independent thought. It's always been true; it remains true. I had a fair picture of where it was going and I was unhappy about it. I gave up lots of things but felt it was necessary. And there are many compensations, of course.

WACHTEL What sorts of things did you give up and what sorts of damage did you have to endure?

CHOMSKY I live in a world of constant lies, vilification, denunciation and marginalization. What I gave up was lots of free time to work on things that I find really exciting.

WACHTEL What pushed you over into that level of activism back then?

CHOMSKY It was a combination of what was happening in the civil-rights movement and the growing U.S. war in Vietnam, which by 1964 was very serious. I felt completely hopeless about it at the time. I recall that in 1964 there was virtually no opposition to the war, no organized or vocal opposition. In fact, that didn't develop until years later. It seemed highly unlikely to me that it would ever develop. What did develop a couple of years later came to me as a big surprise.

The early stages were by no means pleasant. In late 1966, there were a couple of hundred thousand American troops in South Vietnam, and the U.S. had been bombing North Vietnam regularly for a year and a half. Now, Boston, where I live, is quite a liberal city, maybe the most liberal city in the country. Yet it was virtually impossible in Boston to have a public, outdoor demonstration against the war. In 1966, even public meetings in churches were attacked, physically attacked. And that was considered right. There was no protest by the liberal community. On the contrary, there was protest *against* the people who were daring to question and criticize American state power and its exercise. That's pretty much what I expected. I also got involved very quickly in the resistance movement and anticipated that there would be unpleasant consequences, like, for example, years in jail. Which was not remote at that time.

WACHTEL You're sharply critical of American foreign policy everywhere in the world. I think that's probably even an understatement. I get the sense that it's not so much that the United States behaves badly, because you recognize that all countries act out of self-interest. You have said, "Violence, deceit and lawlessness are natural functions of the state, any state," and given that the United States is such a big and powerful state, it only follows that it will do all that in spades. But what really seems to enrage you is the hypocrisy of the American system, that it claims to take a high road. Is that right?

CHOMSKY The hypocrisy of the political leadership doesn't particularly enrage me. I just take that for granted. But what I do find enraging—I never get over this emotion, though I realize its impropriety—is the way in which the educated sectors behave in the manner of the commissar class. It's their deceit and distortion and subordination to power, their unwillingness to face the realities in front of them, which just promote an aesthetic or emotional point of view, that I find hardest to tolerate. Maybe because I live in those circles. I should understand that, objectively, that's their role, as much as it's the role of a person who wields state power to be deceitful, but the distinction is nevertheless there, emotionally.

WACHTEL By commissar class, you're referring to the intellectual world, the media? A world that you expect more from?

CHOMSKY I don't expect any more from them and I never did. I don't want to exaggerate. But in large parts of the media and in educated, respectable sectors rather generally, that strikes me as just appalling and intolerable. If you look back at history, to the earliest sources, this is the way it's always been. Take the Bible, the earliest literary source that we have, and consider the people who are now respected—the prophets. They were reviled then. They were imprisoned, driven into the desert and hated, in large part because of their moral teaching and because of their geopolitical analysis. A large part of what they gave is what we would today call political or geopolitical analysis. They warned of the consequences of policies that were being taken. The people who were honoured at that time were those whom we now call false prophets, and I think that there are good reasons for that. Obviously, pandering to power will lead to respect and authority and privilege. Condemnation of immorality, of the abuse of power, of the destructiveness for the general public of the use of power—such policies will lead to antagonism on the part of those who have the capacity to use violence or to organize the masses against people who question that authority. That's obvious, and the picture that you see in the Bible is one that replicates itself over and over again in every society, including ours.

WACHTEL I don't want to accuse you of presumption, but do you identify with the prophets in the Bible?

CHOMSKY No. I would say that this is true of every critical element in any society. I mention that because it's a classic example.

WACHTEL How does the media do what it does? As a target of your critiques, the hypocrisy of the media is a key subject. They claim to be gadflies, but you find that they work in a blinkered and complicit way. How do they do that, and how does it work so well?

CHOMSKY I should say, incidentally, that the media are not fundamentally different, in my opinion, from a substantial part of scholarship and intellectual opinion. The journals of opinion and the operations of those who call themselves public intellectuals are not very different from the media. The media are a lot easier to study because there's a ton of material and you can look at it systematically and it's there day by day. But what they bring out is not unique.

How does it work? They operate within a framework of assumptions and understanding that supports existing power structures that tend to exclude or downplay or sometimes totally eliminate or even lie about actions of domestic power—state and other powers—in our society. That means corporate, financial, state power—actions conducted by these power centres that are inhuman, violent and harmful to human values and human interests. These actions are marginalized and downplayed, and a picture of the world is presented that is conducive to, and that tends to justify, their authority and their actions. In fact, if the institutions didn't behave that way, they themselves would be undermined and replaced by others that do. So, for example, if the New York Times, let's say, started telling the truth about the world, including the truth about the exercise of domestic power, financial, corporate and state power, it would not exist for very long. It, after all, is a major corporation selling a product to other businesses. It relies on its relations to the state for a good bit of its function, and this would be gone. Also, if individuals who enter into the major media at high managerial positions—I include here cultural managers like editors and columnists—hadn't internalized those values, they wouldn't last very long. Now, it's not that the people are lying. I think they're being honest, for the most part, but they get where they are because they've internalized values that are supportive to power. I don't want to claim that it's monolithic. The *Boston Globe* just ran an op-ed of mine a couple of weeks ago. And I have had personal friends there among the top editors over the years.

It's a complicated country. A simple description of any complicated system is going to be misleading. We happen to have a highly effective doctrinal system and a very narrow ideological spectrum, but there are exceptions. Furthermore, it's widened over the years, in my opinion. So, for example, the media are considerably more open now, in my judgement, than they were, say, thirty years ago.

WACHTEL Why do you think that is so?

CHOMSKY I think it's because the country has changed, and when the country changes, its institutions change. The public is far more critical and far more dissident, by orders of magnitude, than it was thirty or thirty-five years ago. I mentioned a little while back that even in the mid-sixties, in a liberal city like Boston, public demonstrations on the Boston Common or even meetings in churches were attacked, often by students, incidentally, with the support of the media—liberal media— in this city. That's inconceivable today. In fact, the attitudes and perceptions and understanding of the general population have changed radically on a whole host of issues.

Let's take what is in some ways the most striking. The original sin of American society is what the founding fathers were honest enough to call the extermination of the Native population. People like John Quincy Adams were pretty appalled by this, at least in his later years, but in American culture this genocide was really not recognized until the 1960s. When I was growing up, we played Cowboys and Indians. We were the cowboys, and thought nothing of it. Until the 1960s, when a major cultural change took place in the United States, there was no recognition of the horrifying atrocities that led to our living where we are and doing what we do. The fact is that the American Industrial Revolution was based on the extermination or expulsion of the Native population in the United States and then the enslavement of masses of people—it was known in a certain sense, but it wasn't recognized as the major crime that it was. It's only since the 1960s that there has been—

even in scholarship, I should say—a recognition of the enormity of what happened to the Native population and a general willingness to at least try to come to terms in some ways with that extremely ugly aspect of our history. You could see it in 1992. It was assumed that the quincentennial would be a celebration of the discovery and liberation of the hemisphere. That didn't happen. Not at all. And it didn't happen because the public simply wouldn't tolerate it. Thirty years ago, that's exactly what it would have been.

That's one aspect of an improvement in moral values, of a cultural advance which is quite significant. It shows up in many other ways with regard to feminist issues, ecological issues, solidarity with Third-World peoples in many different respects. Multiculturalism is a case in point. As is the case with any popular movement, there's going to be a fringe that is unpleasant, ridiculous, maybe intolerable. But the main development is quite significant, I think, and it has affected the media, as well. So the kind of support for U.S. violence and terror that would have proceeded without question in the 1960s, while you might find it in short bursts today, would be open to criticism in a manner that was not true then.

WACHTEL What's come to be called the Chomskian Revolution in linguistics suggests that we're born with a linguistic silver spoon in our mouths, the capacity to acquire language—that nature has given us a head start on language. It also seems to go beyond language. It seems, at heart, a more democratic, a more optimistic view of humankind.

CHOMSKY That could come out of it. I don't want to push it too hard because when you get beyond language and some aspects of vision, real scientific knowledge begins to drop off very fast and we're back in the area where we started at the beginning, looking at literature and history and experience and intuition. But it can be used as the basis for a rather optimistic view and, indeed, was. If we go back to the Enlightenment again, these connections were, in fact, drawn. Humboldt and Rousseau, whom I mentioned earlier, developed an optimistic view of human nature, the idea that human nature is based on what was later called an instinct for freedom, a drive to be free of external constraints, to be creative and so on. And that, indeed, came from a basically Cartesian picture, which stated that the fundamental aspects of human nature, in particular human freedom, are simply beyond the range of any mechanism. At the core of human nature is what was called, as far back as the sixteenth century, "generative capacity," a capacity to create, to innovate, to construct from the resources of your own mind the principles on which your knowledge is based, and, in fact, to construct new thoughts, to express new thoughts. The idea that intelligence is a generative faculty in this sense goes back at least to the late sixteenth century, and was developed richly in the Cartesian revolution and later picked up by the Romantics in the Enlightenment. This notion of intelligence entered into political theory in a way that is rather natural, though by no means proven, as the belief that the core of human nature is this drive for self-fulfillment under the conditions of free action, undertaken by oneself and out of one's own volition. So from Humboldt's point of view, every person is at heart an artist. A craftsman, let's say, who acts under his or her own volition, is an artist. If the same craftsman does the same thing under external control, as Humboldt puts it, we may admire what he does, but we hate what he is.

WACHTEL You have a lot of faith in ordinary common sense—that people, if only they had all the information, would make the right decisions. And at the same time, you—probably more than most of us—have spent a lot of time scrutinizing international atrocities, being aware of what goes on in the world and looking at it when most of us, even if the information were available to us, don't really want, or are too preoccupied elsewhere with our daily lives, to pay that kind of attention.

CHOMSKY Well, how optimistic or pessimistic I am isn't really important. Suppose I were to believe that there's a 2 percent probability that people, if brought to see the actual facts of the world around them, would act in a moral and humane way. I would still devote myself to enhancing that 2 percent probability and seeing what can be done with it. Now, I happen to think it's a much greater percentage than that. I should say, incidentally, that this kind of optimism about people's capacity to act in decent, humane ways when they understand the realities is shared by people in power almost universally. If you look through history, or even today, you'll very rarely, if ever, see a statesman or a leader turn to the public and say, "Look, it would be in our interest to go slaughter those guys over there or to rob them or torture them or terrorize them, so let's do it." You never find that. What you do find is an elaborate set of rationalizations and excuses and quite elaborate constructions developed by intellectuals, which make it appear as if robbing them and torturing them and killing them is right and just. Well, why bother with that unless you're afraid, at some level of your consciousness, that if people know the truth they're not going to let you get away with it.

WACHTEL You've occasionally been chided for not coming up with enough positive alternatives, for not coming up with some revolutionary strategy to get at the root of the problems. How do you respond to that? Is that part of your job?

CHOMSKY Sure. First of all, I don't think that anybody, certainly not me, is smart enough to plan in any detail a perfect society or even to show in detail how a society based on more humane commitments and concern for human values would function. I think we can say a lot about what it would be like, but we can't spell it out in great detail. Furthermore, what it would be like is, I think, reasonably well understood and has been, in some ways, for centuries. We would like to see a society in which we overcome coercive institutions. Absolutist, unaccountable institutions should not be tolerated. In our time, that means primarily the financial and corporate centres that are basically totalitarian in character and now transnational in scale. It also means the state powers—and now larger-than-state powers—that respond to their interests. And the same is true for structures of authority and domination down to the level of the family. Those should be combatted and overcome. We should work for democratic control in communities, in workplaces over investment decisions, eliminating hierarchic relations and relations of dominance among people and states and ethnic groups. All of that's understandable. I think you can go on to describe in greater detail how freer and more democratic structures might function, but the real answers will come by experience and testing. You couldn't spell out in detail in the mid-eighteenth century how a parliamentary democracy might work. You had to try it. The general ideas could be there, but you had to try them and explore them and experiment with them. And the same is true of the expansion of freedom and democracy and justice today. As for revolutionary strategy, I've never heard of one. When I look over history, the only strategy I see is trying to educate yourself to help others become educated, to learn from others, to organize and, to the extent that organization proceeds, to take action to try to relieve injustice and to extend freedom. Now, that action can take many different forms. So just in my own life, I've been involved in things ranging from direct resistance, to giving talks or taking part in meetings. There are no further secrets, as far as I'm aware. The problem is one of dedicating oneself, to the extent you can, at least—nobody is a saint—to the tasks that have to be undertaken. And, you know, we can see what they are.

WACHTEL You used to draw parallels between the Soviet Union and the United States as two power blocs. The Soviet Union, as the dictatorship, resorted to violence to maintain control; the United States, as the democracy, relied more on propaganda. It hasn't been an unalloyed good, but what positive things do you see coming from the breakup of the Soviet Union?

CHOMSKY The elimination of Soviet tyranny is a major step for human freedom. In fact, in my view it's a great victory for socialism. Contrary to the propaganda of both of the great power blocs—the Western power bloc and the Eastern power bloc—the Soviet Union, from its first days when Lenin and Trotsky took power, was militantly anti-socialist in every respect. They immediately destroyed the socialist institutions and understood what they were doing. It was done on principle. The former Soviet Union, and most of Eastern Europe, quite predictably, in my opinion, is now being driven back to a Third-World level. To a large extent, that's what the Cold War was about. In an international society dominated by private capital and private power and its state manifestations, a large part of the world is just a service area—the South, the

Third World, the former colonial world—and no part of it is permitted to pursue an independent path. To a large extent, the Cold War was fought about that.

It really began in 1917 and 1918, as the better historians have noticed. The West, the more powerful combatant, won the war, meaning the rich and powerful sectors in the West won the war. The larger part of the population in the West lost the war, in fact. Eastern Europe, or large parts of it, is now returning to its Third-World origins, pretty much where it was in the early part of the twentieth century. That means a very serious decline, but it also means enrichment. Remember, a Third-World society has sectors of great wealth and privilege, and Eastern Europe does, as well. So take Russia: the economy's collapsing; people are suffering. UNESCO recently reported that there's an estimated half-million deaths a year in the former Soviet Union since 1989 that are a result of the collapse and the neo-liberal reforms that have been imposed on them. Yet they're selling more Mercedes-Benzes for $150,000 a shot in Moscow than they are in New York. The people who are buying them are often the old Communist Party leaders. That is what's sometimes called nomenclature capitalism. They're the victors of the Cold War, not the people of Russia. Large parts of Eastern Europe are returning to a Third-World service model. That offers new weapons against working people in the West. So multinationals like General Motors or Audi can find workers in Eastern Europe at a fraction of the cost of Western workers, who are now being called upon by the business press to abandon what are called their luxurious lifestyles and to become more competitive, meaning that they need to face the fact that it's easy to gain profits and power by exploiting much cheaper labour in the East. When General Motors moves over to, say, Poland, they insist on something like a 30 percent tariff protection, like Volkswagen does when it goes to the Czech Republic, because they don't believe in free markets. They believe in free markets for the poor, not for the rich. They believe in state power and protection for the rich. These are the consequences of the end of the Cold War, and they're not pretty. But one of the worst systems of tyranny in human history has been eliminated, and that offers all sorts of possibilities of liberation and a new scope for human spirit and human freedom.

WACHTEL You seem to have moved from being a voice at the margins, a gadfly, to becoming virtually a spokesman for a new left, thanks to the anti-globalization movement. What do you make of what's going on now?

CHOMSKY First, the term *anti-globalization* is misleading. The term *globalization* has been pre-empted by power centres to refer to their specific version of international integration, based on "free trade agreements" that the business press sometimes more accurately calls "free investment agreements." No one is anti-globalization, certainly not the left and workers' movements; international solidarity has always been among their central themes. The question is, What kind of globalization? In whose interest?

As for what's going on now, the movement concerned with globalization directed to the needs of people rather than investors and financial capital has become a powerful force. Its origins are in the South: in Brazil and India, for example, where very important popular movements developed years ago, opposing the neo-liberal version of globalization and seeking alternatives. In the past few years, they have been joined by significant sectors in the North, drawing from the substantial popular opposition to the forms of globalization instituted by private and state power—one reason for the very limited public disclosure. The meetings of the World Social Forum in Porto Alegre have brought together a very broad and diverse constituency, and might constitute the seeds of the kind of genuine international movement that has been a vision of the left and workers' movements from their modern origins. But although I've been speaking and writing about these issues for many years, and participate as much as I can, I'm not a spokesperson for this or any other movement—and participants, I'm sure, don't see me as such.

In specific response to your question, there was a time, forty years ago, when I felt very much like a "voice from the margins." It was hard not to feel that way when talks about, say, the Vietnam War, drew massive audiences of three or four people, and intense hostility. By the late 1960s that had changed, and in later years popular movements have extended substantially, not only in scale but in the range of issues that they address. I don't feel at the margins. In fact, on many central issues I suspect I'm rather close to substantial and often majority popular currents, which often diverge sharply from the elite attitudes and commitments. The growth of the popular globalization movements hasn't led to much change—for me, at least—in these respects. There have, however, been major changes in this respect since the September 11th atrocities, which were a kind of wake-up call for many people. Requests for talks, discussions and interviews escalated very quickly with the growth of interest and concern about many issues that had been pretty much off the agenda for most people.

WACHTEL Do you think these groups concerned with globalization can be an effective voice of dissent?

CHOMSKY More than dissent. Also development of constructive alternatives, which are badly needed, maybe even desperately needed if the species is to survive very long—a statement that is, unfortunately, no exaggeration.

WACHTEL There's a sense after the attacks of September 11th, the invasion of Afghanistan and the delineation of an "axis of evil" that the public discourse has become more polarized. What do you think?

CHOMSKY In some respects, yes. Intellectual discourse has followed a rather normal path in times of crisis, shifting towards greater subordination to power, sometimes with a kind of fanaticism. The general public, in contrast, has become more open-minded, concerned, engaged, in ways that cannot be characterized in simple terms.

WACHTEL How has your own life—the division of your own resources, in terms of activism, scholarship and family—been affected by the events of the last year or so?

CHOMSKY For many years, demands (in the "activist" domain, roughly) have been very intense, but since 9-11, they have gone into orbit. I must spend at least an hour a night just turning down invitations, with real regret, and scarcely a moment has been left unscheduled. There are only twenty-four hours in a day, so there are inevitably conflicts with family and professional engagements. What gives is personal life; there's no other choice.

June 2002/February 1994

Arthur C. Clarke

About a quarter of a century ago, when the president of M.I.T. was introducing Arthur C. Clarke, he said, "Our next speaker is the only person I know who can be unambiguously introduced by a four-digit number—2001." Though the date that he helped mythologize is past, Clarke is still actively engaged in speculating about our future—whether it's life on Mars or the danger of asteroid impacts. He remains committed to space travel. As he said recently, "The dinosaurs became extinct because they didn't have a space program." Clarke himself has been described as an "interplanetary treasure" for his visionary writings in both science and fiction.

His book 2001: *A Space Odyssey* (1968) sold more than three million copies. Altogether, the numbers are impressive: in the last half century, Clarke—now Sir Arthur—has published some eighty books that have sold more than seventy million copies. Described as the "colossus of science fiction," he's won every major writing prize, was named to the Aerospace Hall of Fame, and was even nominated for a Nobel Peace Prize.

Arthur C. Clarke was born in 1917 in Minehead, a small town on the sea, facing the Bristol Channel. The beach, that great crescent of sand from which he could see the coast of Wales, became his dream landscape—he sought it out on the Bay of Rainbows on the moon, and later on the south coast of Sri Lanka, where he's lived since 1956.

Clarke was brought up by his grandmother and aunt, while his parents struggled to make a living on a farm twenty miles inland. His father, a veteran of the First World War, died when Arthur was fourteen. By this time, Clarke was already writing fantastic stories for his school magazine, having developed an "addiction" for the pulp magazine *Amazing Stories*. When he couldn't afford to continue his schooling, he moved to London to take a job with the civil service. He shared a flat with two other science-fiction and space enthusiasts, and together they formed the British Interplanetary Society, of which he was "treasurer and general propagandist."

In 1941, Clarke volunteered for the Royal Air Force—what he later described as "the single most decisive act of my entire life." He became a pioneer in ground-control approach radar. In 1945, he wrote an article that envisioned communications satellites—a worldwide network orbiting the earth. It was one of his most extraordinary and accurate predictions. After the war, he studied math and physics at King's College in London and completed his degree in two years with top honours. His first book was non-fiction, *Interplanetary Flight*; it was published in 1950. A year later, his first novel, *The Sands of Mars*, came out. Because of his attachment to scientific rigour, Clarke is godfather to a generation of "hard science-fiction" writers, as opposed to *Star Wars*–style space fantasy. And he's written almost as many book of non-fiction as fiction.

In the mid-fifties, drawn by the warm climate and the sea— Clarke was an enthusiastic scuba diver—he moved to Ceylon, now Sri Lanka. In the 1960s, he contracted polio, and, although he recovered, for the past five years he's been mostly confined to a wheelchair as a result of post-polio syndrome. But Sir Arthur remains active and curious. Invoking his childhood enthusiasms, he's already composed his own epitaph: "He never grew up; but he never stopped growing."

A few years ago, he collected his essays in a book called *Greetings, Carbon-based Bipeds! Essays from 1934 to 1998* (1999). He talked to me by phone from his home in Colombo, Sri Lanka.

WACHTEL Can you describe where you are—the room, the house, the technology that you have there with you?

CLARKE I live in a suburb of Colombo, about a mile from the sea. I used to live by the sea, which I love, but unfortunately salt corrosion on my equipment drove me inland. I'm in a very big house, which belonged originally to the bishop of Colombo, and I share it with my Sri Lankan family—my Sinhalese partner, his Australian wife and their three delightful daughters; unfortunately, two of them are in Australia at college at the moment. My own room is a very big one; it's full of books and three computers, and my chihuahua, Pepsi, who guards my privacy.

WACHTEL Your name is associated with space and the stars, but your original inspiration was the sea. Can you talk about your early experience of the sea and how that shaped you?

CLARKE I was born within a few hundred yards of the sea, in Minehead, in Somerset, on the southwest coast of England. My childhood was spent near the sea, playing on the beach. That experience dominated my life, though perhaps I wasn't consciously aware of it until I went to London and joined the civil service in 1936. Later on, when skin-diving techniques were developed, I rediscovered the sea and went to Australia to do my book on the Great Barrier Reef. That was in 1954.

WACHTEL The beach seems to be imprinted on you. You write that "when I look at the ten-day-old moon through my telescope, the Bay of Rainbows [one of the most beautiful lunar formations] reminds me

irresistibly of Minehead—though on a scale a hundred times greater."
Minehead figures strongly in your imagination.

CLARKE Yes, it does. I wrote a very short story called "Transience,"
which is about a beach, but it takes place at three different times in history, in very primitive times, now, and in the future. The beach is
unchanged, but the human race has come and gone.

WACHTEL Can you describe the grip that the beach has on you?

CLARKE Well, it's subconscious, so I really can't. It may be the accident of where I was born. If I'd been born in the middle of a grass plain,
I might have had a totally different psyche.

WACHTEL In your 1978 collection, *The View from Serendip*, you write,
"For the last twenty years my life has been dominated by three Ss—
Space, Serendip, and the Sea." Serendip, of course, is one of the ancient
names of Ceylon. How did those three Ss—Space, Serendip and the
Sea—become connected for you?

CLARKE Well, it does seem like an accident, but the other reason I
became interested in the sea again was through my interest in space. I
realized when the new skin-diving techniques came along, I could
experience weightlessness, which is one of the characteristic phenomena of space travel. Even though I didn't go into space myself, I could
feel like a spaceman by diving underwater, which is just what I did. And
then, because I became interested in that experience—if only in London
swimming pools—I decided to go further afield to the world's greatest
coral formation, the Great Barrier Reef. On my way to Australia, by sea,
I stopped off in Colombo for one afternoon and met some of the local
divers. They suggested I come back, and that's what I did. That was how
the three things were linked together.

WACHTEL Did you realize then that coming back would mean coming
back and staying?

CLARKE No, I'm sure that when I came to Ceylon, as it was then in 1956,
I didn't dream that I would settle down here, but my partner, Mike Wilson, married one of the local beauties, and so this is where the show
ground to a halt. But the quick reason, which I often give when people ask
me why I've lived so long in Ceylon, is—thirty or forty English winters.

WACHTEL That you haven't had to live through.

CLARKE Exactly.

WACHTEL You've also said that, "While I cannot account for it, no place other than Ceylon is now wholly real to me," that other places are no longer quite convincing, that "their images are blurred around the edges." What makes Ceylon, or Sri Lanka, so real to you?

CLARKE Because it's a tropical country, there are extremes of sunlight, and I'm afraid other extremes as well, alas. But it resonates in my subconscious, and all my friends, and particularly my little chihuahua, are here now. All my books are here, too, and, of course, home is where the books are.

WACHTEL Is there something else about the place that has that kind of reality—because what you're describing now, one could make anywhere. Is there something particular about Sri Lanka?

CLARKE The variety, I think: animal life, human life, different people, different cultures. I was brought up in a rather uniform society—I don't think I saw a dark face until I was in my late teens. Now I seldom see a white one.

WACHTEL In terms of the sea, you've pointed out that the mask, the breathing tube and flippers of the modern skin diver were depicted by Leonardo da Vinci in his notebooks, that the sea had long been a place of mystery and magic. You say, "It is our great fortune to be born in the age that opened the door into the sea. Yet we have never really escaped from it." What do you mean by that?

CLARKE The sea is in our blood, almost literally: the composition of blood and the composition of sea water have many similarities, so perhaps there's a physiological reason for this.

WACHTEL You've written that "the world beneath the waves is beautiful but it's hopelessly limited, and the creatures who live there are crippled irremediably in mind and spirit. No fish can see the stars; but we will never be content until we have reached them."

CLARKE When I said that life in the sea is crippled, I meant that fish can't develop fire—and fire is the basis of all technology. That's one reason why the sea is limiting. However, there is such an extraordinary variety of creatures in the sea, such weird beasts, that I find it hard to imagine anything in space that's weirder than some of the things you see on the coral reef.

WACHTEL You've said that our destiny is in space. What shifted your gaze? What do you think first hooked you on space and technology?

CLARKE My first scientific interest was actually geology—I collected fossils. But round about 1930, probably through reading science fiction, I became more interested in space. I made my own little primitive telescopes and saw the moon and all that, and from then on my primary interest was space. I suspect the garish old pulp magazines—*Astounding Stories, Wonder Stories*—really inspired my imagination, with pictures of spaceships flying to other planets and weird creatures and all that sort of thing. At first I didn't realize that this was more than a theoretical interest. I didn't realize that space travel was actually possible, not just an idea in pulp magazines. In 1930–31 I read David Lasser's book, *The Conquest of Space*, which was the first book in English to give a serious account of the possibilities of space travel. I thought, Well, my goodness, this could be real—but I didn't think it would happen in my lifetime.

WACHTEL I was reading that as a kid you wired your bedroom for wake-up calls, you built wireless crystal sets, that you even created your own news flashes.

CLARKE I never actually broadcast anything, but I certainly had a crystal set and I used to listen to the BBC with earphones. That's a pleasure that this generation has lost.

I was able to do pretty much what I wanted. We lived on an isolated farm—our nearest neighbours were about a mile away.

WACHTEL There's a character in one of your books—a boy who spends a lot of time on his own. He's a bit lonely, he's a loner. Was there an element of that in your own childhood?

CLARKE I didn't feel lonely and I had many friends, but I also liked to get away by myself, with my books and magazines, and of course, particularly, my beloved Meccano set. I must have spent a large part of my childhood playing with Meccano, building all sorts of machines and strange devices.

WACHTEL What was it about the Meccano set that appealed to you so much?

CLARKE I obviously had a mechanically inclined imagination and it was wonderful to put all those beautifully coloured bits and pieces and gear wheels together. I feel rather sad that the generation that's growing up now doesn't know Meccano. They're stuck to the keyboards of their computers, and although the information technology is marvellous, it does tend to separate them from the real mechanical world of metals and gear wheels and all that. I'm worried that some of our young engineers will make some disastrous mistakes because things that work on the computer screen may not work so well in real life with real materials.

WACHTEL When you were twelve, you came across your first science fiction magazine and your life was "irrevocably changed." What made that March 1930 issue of Astounding so—astounding?

CLARKE I can still remember the cover very vividly. It showed a spaceship that looked like a giant glass conservatory. They don't build spaceships like that any more. But I can still remember some of those [serialized excerpts of] Brigands of the Moon. I refer to all this in my book Astounding Days, which is my science-fiction autobiography, a tribute to the old pulps.

WACHTEL It was through science fiction, especially the pulp magazines that were so popular then, that you learned of what you describe as the "multi-dimensional world." Can you say how it intrigued you?

CLARKE The science fiction of the pulp magazines covered all sorts of possibilities and even more impossibilities, and they did stretch my mind, although I was then more interested in the physical world than the biological world, which of course is now becoming more and more important. But the science fiction of the pulp magazines explored all sorts of possibilities in astronomy, space travel, dimensional travel, time travel and also biological possibilities—all sorts of monsters going back to Frankenstein. This stretched my imagination, and that's the beginning of all real progress.

WACHTEL Your early influences included some literary classics of the science-fiction genre, such as Jules Verne, Edgar Rice Burroughs and H. G. Wells. What makes a work of science fiction a classic?

CLARKE Some of these "classics" won't survive rereading now. But recently I read one which came out in the 1930s, The Time Stream, by John Taine, who was the American mathematician Eric Temple Bell, and I found to my great delight that it still held up fifty years later.

WACHTEL Can you generalize about the works that have influenced you most?

CLARKE In fiction, Edgar Rice Burroughs is a much underrated writer. He invented one of the best-known characters in the whole of fiction, Tarzan. His Mars stories are nothing like the real Mars, but tremendous people like Carl Sagan were turned on by Burroughs. I don't think I could reread him now, but he is certainly a very enjoyable writer, particularly when you're young. They say the golden age for reading science fiction is about twelve, which is when I first started reading it. Some might make it as high as fourteen or fifteen. Besides Burroughs there's H. G. Wells, particularly The War of the Worlds and The Time Machine. Recently I had the privilege of writing an introduction to those classics. I'm sorry I never met Wells; I would love to have done so. I have his autographed photograph looking at me from the wall at the moment. Also there's Olaf Stapledon, one of the greatest imaginations of all time, and I am happy to say that he is now being rediscovered. Last and First Men, a history of the human race in the next two thousand million years, is one of the greatest works of imagination ever published.

WACHTEL You found that one at the Minehead public library.

CLARKE Yes. I can still recall the actual shelf on which I saw Last and First Men, in 1931. I remember taking it back and then copying out the time scales. In that book he gave a series of time scales, like a sort of map of the past and present. Now was the centre of each of the lines and then he went into the past two thousand years for the first one, and AD 2000 in the second, with the birth of Christ in the middle. Then he extended them as he went through the book, and so the final one was, I think, ten million million years, both ways. In the very last scale, there's a dot in the centre: on the left-hand side the planets were created, and just a fraction of an inch away from it, the end of man occurs.

WACHTEL You were twenty-nine when you published your own first science-fiction novel, Prelude to Space. You were involved then with the British Interplanetary Society—you even dedicated a book to them. Who were they? What role did they play?

CLARKE The British Interplanetary Society was founded by Phil Cleator in 1933. He and a local group in Liverpool, including the well-known science-fiction writer Eric Frank Russell, formed the Society, and we science-fiction fans—premature space cadets—made contact with them. Eventually the centre of gravity moved to London and now the Society has its headquarters there. It's still going strong, on the South Bank. I had the privilege of visiting it recently on one of my very rare trips outside Sri Lanka.

WACHTEL Can you describe the enthusiasm of the Society at that time, its goals?

CLARKE We were sure that one day space travel would be possible, and we published a journal with our ideas and designs for spaceships— some of which, incidentally, still stand up pretty well. But of course we were a tiny minority and no one took us seriously. In fact, most people thought we were completely crazy.

WACHTEL You've described a debate you had with C. S. Lewis and J. R. R. Tolkien.

CLARKE Yes. I met Lewis in Oxford. I think it was the only time we met, and it was a very pleasant meeting. My correspondence with C. S. Lewis, which is very extensive, is being published by a small American press. I'm looking forward with some apprehension to rereading what I said to Lewis. We were on quite friendly terms. I knew his wife, the American poet Joy Gresham, much better because I met her every week at the science-fiction meeting in the London pub where we all gathered. Incidentally, at that first meeting with Lewis, in the East Gate, in Oxford, I didn't know who the guy with him was, and I didn't realize it was Tolkien until years later.

WACHTEL And what were the sides in the debate? Were they opposed to the idea or skeptical of the merits of space travel?

CLARKE I think Lewis hated the idea. He thought that God's quarantine regulations shouldn't be broken, and looking at the world today, I think he had a point.

WACHTEL Science fiction was an inspiration for both your creative writing and your scientific writing, and in fact you've credited science fiction with launching many a scientific career. I'd like to talk a little about the relationship between science—what we know or can find out about—and science fiction—what we imagine. You've pointed out that all the pioneers of astronautics were inspired by Jules Verne. Many of the American astronauts and Soviet cosmonauts were early fans of science fiction. Neil Armstrong dedicated a monograph "to Arthur"—to you. Can you talk about how the two disciplines relate to each other and perhaps fuel each other?

CLARKE I've always regarded science and science fiction as two sides of one coin. Science fiction can't live up to its name unless it is firmly based on science—otherwise it's fantasy. Now, I've nothing against fantasy—Tolkien's work is perhaps the best example. Fantasy is fine; I thoroughly enjoy it and I've written a few—very few—pieces of fantasy myself. But science fiction can only be valuable and realistic if it is based on a good knowledge of science. You don't have to be a scientist to write science fiction, but you must at least have some feel for science and some understanding of it.

At the same time, many top scientists have written science fiction. There's no doubt that science fiction has had a tremendous effect on scientific careers. The best example I've had of that recently is one I'm very proud of: Donna Shirley, the senior woman engineer in NASA who was in charge of the Mars Pathfinder program that sent back those wonderful images from the little rover that ran around and poked at the Martian rocks, sent me her delightful autobiography, In Managing Martians. In her book, she thanks me for turning her on to Mars as a small girl, when she read my novel The Sands of Mars, which was written almost half a century ago.

WACHTEL You've always been careful to point out that science-fiction writers seldom attempt prophecy, that you're more interested in extrapolation.

CLARKE Yes. There's a common fallacy that science-fiction writers try to describe the future. Occasionally they do, but more often they try—and I'm quoting my friend Ray Bradbury here—not to describe the future but to prevent it.

WACHTEL What does that mean for you, in terms of your own writing?

CLARKE Ray is really reflecting 1984 and Brave New World, which were both science-fiction attempts to prevent futures. They've succeeded rather well, in a way. In my own science fiction, I've always written about something that I thought could happen, but very often it was something that I hoped would not happen. One problem with writing about Utopias is that they're very dull, and so you try the anti-Utopia or the disaster. Giant man-eating plants or invasions from space are much more exciting themes for science fiction, which is why, particularly in Hollywood, it tends to be associated with disasters.

WACHTEL There does, however, seem to be an element of optimism in your writing, in the sense that perhaps human evolution can be aided by some interplanetary or intelligent life from afar. Is that something that you hope will happen—or won't happen?

CLARKE There's certainly an element of wishful thinking in some of my stories, particularly Childhood's End, where I hope that the aliens will come and save our bacon before we make a complete mess of the world. I'm afraid there's not much likelihood of that. But it's an idea that is being used more and more often. In the first alien-invasion stories, like The War of the Worlds, they're always hostile aliens, but lately we've had friendly aliens, as in E.T. But of course we don't know if aliens exist.

WACHTEL Even in your most famous work, 2001: A Space Odyssey, there is the sense that the alien may be not only benign but crucial in human evolution.

CLARKE The theory—the idea—in 2001 that our evolution was triggered by something in the past is very difficult to prove one way or the other. I don't think it's very likely; I think we're entirely homegrown creatures of this planet.

WACHTEL I was just thinking in terms of trying to prevent the future, as well as fantasizing or imagining how it might be.

CLARKE Of course, stories of anti-Utopias, particularly after the atomic war—*On the Beach* and that kind of thing—were attempts to scare people to behave properly. Whether that's a good idea, whether it'll work, is a question that only history will answer.

WACHTEL You've said that science fiction maps out possible futures, as well as a good many impossible ones, that it encourages "the cosmic viewpoint." How does that work? Can you talk about what cosmic viewpoint science fiction embraces?

CLARKE This began with Copernicus and Galileo, who realized that this world was only a tiny part of the whole universe. Perhaps a sense of humility is a good thing for any species, though it's not yet as well developed as it should be in ours.

WACHTEL You're saying that science fiction is virtually the only kind of writing that deals with real problems as well as with possibilities and what might happen to humanity?

CLARKE I think that science fiction deals with the whole of reality. So-called mainstream fiction dealing with adultery, or whatever, is only a tiny bit of the real universe, and the literary mandarins don't seem to recognize that. And incidentally, if I may blow my own trumpet, I'm delighted that my knighthood was for services to literature, which does imply that science fiction has been recognized as literature.

WACHTEL You don't like to make predictions—in fact, you prefer to call them forecasts—but your fiction and non-fiction have both been remarkably prescient, in terms of the first flight around the moon, the moon landings. Some of your other forecasts have been further from the mark, but in the preface to your latest collection of essays, *Greetings, Carbon-based Bipeds*, you say, "Often it has been more interesting to see where (and why) I went wrong, than where I happened to be right." Can you talk about how or why you have missed the mark?

CLARKE My main misses have been in timing. One can be quite sure that something will happen, but one's estimate tends to go wrong for two reasons: it's rather easy to exaggerate what might happen in the short term and then not realize how much more can happen in the longer term. My first stories about space flight were perhaps the reverse of that; I set them in a too distant future. 2001 is a classic example. When Stanley [Kubrick] and I wrote that in the mid-sixties, the moon landing was imminent. In the film we showed a big moon base and journeys to Jupiter and Saturn. At that time, back in the mid-sixties, there were plans to land on Mars in the 1980s! That seems hard to believe now, but it could have happened if it weren't for Vietnam, Watergate and a few other diversions. The point I'm trying to make is that you can never predict the future accurately, but that has to do with political rather than technological considerations.

WACHTEL I was wondering also about the HAL-like computer that can not only talk but read lips, plan, scheme, murder. Artificial intelligence seems quite far from that now.

CLARKE The one thing I thought was too far-fetched in 2001 was HAL lip-reading. Well, they now have lip-reading programs; they're not very accurate, but they do have computers that can get a fair degree of accuracy. I came across an interesting reference the other day. Paul MacCready, who built the first flying machine that you could actually fly by manpower—the Gossamer Condor—recently said that the most important phrase of the last century was, "I'm sorry, Dave, I can't do that."

WACHTEL That's HAL demonically disobeying at the end of the film. Why did MacCready say that was the most important phrase?

CLARKE Because that's what we're up against in the near future, and they won't do what we tell them to. I've just been sent a fascinating book from M.I.T. called *Robosapiens*, which is about the rise of robot intelligence. There's a general feeling that around 2020 we'll be second-class citizens on this planet.

WACHTEL You wrote in 1972 that one safe prediction about the twenty years that lay ahead was that we'd see at least one development or discovery which no one would have predicted. In retrospect, what would that be? What discoveries have most surprised you?

CLARKE The interesting ones have been inventions rather than discoveries. The most surprising invention was the microchip and what that's led to; it's revolutionized everything. And also the compact disc. The idea of having the entire encyclopedia in a little silver platter you can hold in the hand still seems incredible to me, and a good example of my well-known third law—that any sufficiently advanced technology is indistinguishable from magic. To me, the compact disc and the microchip are still magic. As far as discoveries are concerned, I'm hoping that there may be some more exciting discoveries in space. The gamma-ray bursters and the quasars and the extraordinary things the astronomers are turning up—no one would have believed they were possible. In fact, I'm rather worried about gamma-ray bursters, these tremendous bursts of energy, many millions of times more powerful than the sun. If any of them happen near us, we've had it!

WACHTEL Where are they occurring?

CLARKE Gamma-ray bursters are all over the universe. We're not quite sure what causes them—perhaps black holes colliding. The energy output from these things is absolutely colossal. It's possible that they've affected evolution by blasting the earth in the past and wiping out many forms of life. If it happens again, there's nothing we can do about it. The other danger from space that I've been much concerned with is asteroid impact. In fact, my novel The Hammer of God is all about that. Now there is a project, Space Guard, which I suggested should look for dangerous asteroids or comets and do something to divert them.

WACHTEL As we head into the next millennium, do you think we're in trouble as a civilization?

CLARKE We're in great trouble in many ways, not only from our own activities but because of pollution—that's the main problem. Global warming could be an issue, although there's still some debate as to whether that is happening or not. And sometime in the next century we're going to have several major impacts on the earth. We've had at least three in this century, luckily none of them near highly populated areas. We've been very lucky. But that's going to happen again some-time and no one knows when it will happen. That's why a Space Guard may be important.

WACHTEL Do you think we'll go back to the moon, to build the lunar colonies that you've envisioned there?

CLARKE I'm sure we'll be going back to the moon, but it won't be for quite a while. Maybe 2010 is too optimistic—2020 might be more probable.

WACHTEL In your novel *The Fountains of Paradise*, set in Sri Lanka, you imagined a space elevator reaching up to a stationary orbit, and now the discovery of a new carbon molecule would actually make the space elevator possible. You've talked about this nanotechnology as the real breakthrough that will open the gate to the universe. How? What effect would it have?

CLARKE Nanotechnology is already beginning to transform our world. Its aim was to do fantastic things with objects so small you can hardly see them—in fact, some are quite invisible. We'll be able to send small exploring robots round the universe, to send back information and tell us where we should go and places we'd better stay away from. And there'll be nano-robots roaming around in our bloodstreams probably in another decade or so, looking for nasty germs and zapping them. Nanotechnology is the great technology of the future; it's linked, of course, with genetic technology, which is the other great frontier.

WACHTEL Are you hopeful about genetic technology? It seems to be something that causes uneasiness as well.

CLARKE Genetic technology, by which I mean the ability to modify future generations of animals and of course human beings, is an awesome responsibility, and obviously, like all great scientific developments—well, look right back to fire, at all the damage that fire has done, but civilization would be impossible without it. I hope that the debate on genetic engineering will lead to guidelines being laid down and that people will adhere to these guidelines for the benefit of future generations.

WACHTEL There's been recent discussion, even at the U.S. government level, about the impact of nanotechnology on society, that human civilization could be changed or even replaced in some way by technology. Do you have any concerns about that?

CLARKE One of the important things of the future is the development of artificial intelligence, which will depend on nanotechnology to some extent. You might say that the current generation of computers depends on micro-technology and the microchip, which will soon be the nanochip. The general feeling is that artificial intelligence will reach the level of human intelligence around about 2020, but the question arises: Will these machines, these intelligent machines, be conscious entities? Will they be able to say with Descartes, "I think, therefore I am," or will they say, "I think, therefore I am, I think."

WACHTEL Or, "I think because you've programmed me to think."

CLARKE Exactly.

WACHTEL Do you really think artificial intelligence will be at a par with human intelligence by 2020? That's scarcely a couple of decades away.

CLARKE That's a guess. People have tried to extrapolate the rate of progress of computing power, which may not be the same as intelligence, but I think there's general agreement that sometime in the coming century it will reach our level. Then there's no reason to suppose it shouldn't go on to heights we can't imagine, but it depends on what you mean by intelligence, which is obviously more than mere processing power.

WACHTEL And when you say that the microchip will become the nanochip, do you mean that the microchip will seem like an elephant compared to the size of a nanochip?

CLARKE Yes, although already we're faced with limits; they are getting down to the molecular and atomic level and it's impossible to get smaller than that. I remember people, fifty years ago, saying that such a creation might be the size of a house, and then it eventually came down to the size of the human brain. Perhaps ultimately you could have a brain equivalent to the size of a walnut. I think you'll still be able to see it.

WACHTEL Your work draws on a sense of wonder that's essential to science fiction. It's not just hard science, although it's technologically accurate insofar as possible. You've said of your own 2001: A Space Odyssey that it poses metaphysical, philosophical, even religious questions. How would you describe your own sense of religion or spirituality, of humanity's place in the universe?

CLARKE I think any intelligent person must have a feeling of awe at the size and scale—and perhaps even more, the complexity—of the universe, particularly the biological kingdom, even though we know only a very small part of the biological world, just that of this planet. One of the great questions is whether there are biologies elsewhere, on Mars or on other planets. But I don't have any religious feelings and in fact I'm very opposed to religion, given the appalling atrocities and crimes committed in its name. But I sometimes like to think of myself as Buddhist, because of its peaceful nature.

WACHTEL One of your best-known stories, "The Nine Billion Names of God," seems to take a rather ironic view of religion, until its surprise ending, and another well-known story, "The Star," also touches on the idea of some higher order.

CLARKE Yes, the mystery of the universe, and whether there is any greater power behind the universe. Incidentally, I sent "The Nine Billion Names of God" to the Dalai Lama and I got a very nice note from him saying that he enjoyed it. "The Star" is about a Jesuit astrophysicist—many astrophysicists are Jesuits, by the way; I know this because some of them are good friends of mine—who discovers that the star of Bethlehem was a nova that destroyed a wonderful civilization, and he has to go back to the Vatican with the news. Another Catholic friend of mine—in fact, the head of a Roman Catholic university—said, "You know, you underestimate us Jesuits; we would have loved to have gone back to the Vatican with that news."

WACHTEL Do you understand why these questions grip you?

CLARKE It's because they deal with that wonder of the universe, which indeed 2001 does. My favourite story is "The Transit of Earth," which is the last moments of the first man on Mars. It's already set in the past, because it takes place in 1984, but it was written in 1970, soon after the Apollo program finished, when there were serious plans to be on Mars by the 1980s. And in 1984 something very interesting happens on Mars. If you look at the sun, you see the earth crossing the face of the sun as a small black dot. So the story is about the feelings of a man, you know, seeing his home planet in the crossing of the face of the sun and knowing that he'll die soon afterwards. There'll be another transit of earth in 2084—a strange coincidence, a hundred years later—and I'm sure that by then there will be men and women on Mars.

My favourite novel, I think, is *The Songs of Distant Earth*, because it has many emotional associations and it's set on a planet which to some extent is a version of Sri Lanka or perhaps an idealized Sri Lanka.

WACHTEL In an essay on the dangers of prophecy, you distinguish between "failures of nerve" and "failures of imagination," and as you say, "It is highly instructive, and stimulating to the imagination, to make a list of the inventions and discoveries that have not been anticipated—and those that have." You give examples of unexpected discoveries, such as X-rays and nuclear energy, radio and TV. What can we learn from this?

CLARKE I think the lesson is that the universe is a mechanism for providing continual surprises to the human mind. We can never outguess nature—or God, if you like. There's always something new and wonderful beyond the horizon, which of course is a very good thing. It would be sad if we discovered everything and knew everything. What would be the point of living after that?

WACHTEL You go on to ask, "Now what can we expect or imagine?"

CLARKE The point is that I can't imagine what is unimaginable, but I'm sure there are some big revolutions ahead. The one I'm particularly interested in—and a lot of my friends would laugh at me about this—is the energy revolution, with the reports of new sources of energy that started ten years ago. There was the cold-fusion brouhaha that was laughed out of court, and a couple of scientists, Pons and Fleischmann, who said they'd generate energy almost at room temperature. And there's a big debate still going on as to whether we can, in fact, tap new sources of energy. If this is the case—and I hope it may be—it will be the biggest technological and, indeed, political revolution, because it'll change the whole face of the world and it'll be the end of the oil age.

WACHTEL You, of course, are credited with predicting, or at least anticipating, the communications satellite. In 1945, you proposed a trio of earth satellites to provide a worldwide system of radio and television communications, and you realized that a global communications system would make possible a new global culture. What do you make of that global culture now?

CLARKE Well, there's certainly lots of it—bits of it—that I don't like and I see horrible things on TV, but it has, indeed, made a global culture and established not only the global village but I hope soon the global family of man. And it's changed the geopolitical situation: we now have an age of transparency. You can't hide things that are happening anywhere. Cameramen can go in with a small mobile set and send their pictures straight to their home studio and then back to the local people. No one can stop that. Censorship is still possible to some extent, but the worst excesses of the past are gone. The world is much more transparent and open than it was, and that is one of the results of the communications satellite.

WACHTEL And then, of course, more than thirty years after conceiving of the geosynchronous satellite, the only privately owned earth satellite station in the world was installed at your home in Sri Lanka.

CLARKE That's true. That was back in the late seventies. I don't even have a satellite dish now, incidentally, because I can get everything I need through fibre optics, which is another extraordinary revolution. Who would have dreamed that a piece of glass the size of a hair could carry hundreds of television programs and millions of audio programs? That's a fantastic technological revolution, like the microchip and the CD-ROM, which we spoke of earlier.

WACHTEL The usual view is that technology is alienating, that it can even dehumanize us, but you've taken the opposite position. You say that technology wisely used gives us time to think and gives us an unlimited number of subjects to think about.

CLARKE Yes, I do get annoyed at these anti-technology people. Technology is civilization. You can't have civilization without technology. Admittedly, you could have technology without civilization, but I hope we aren't headed that way. Technology begins, I would say, with clothes; then the discovery of fire, the taming of fire. Everything we depend on is some form of technology.

WACHTEL So you say technology is what made us human, because of the beginning of fire, because of everything that came from that?

CLARKE That's right, though perhaps the most important technology of all is speech, followed by writing and then printing. These are the technologies that make civilization possible.

WACHTEL Why do you call speech a technology?

CLARKE Well, that's a debatable point—whether there's a construct, whether it could happen—but grammar is a kind of technology, vocabularies and grammar. I think you could call it a technology.

WACHTEL Alien intelligence has been an enduring theme in science fiction, in print and on screen. Much of your own work turns on our desire to know about other civilizations, or features visitations from other life forms, as in "The Star" or *Childhood's End* or *Rendez-vous with Rama*. We seem to long for signs and for contact. Why do you think that is?

CLARKE I guess it's the feeling of loneliness. It would be sad if we're the only intelligence in the whole universe. On the other hand, some people might think it's exhilarating that there's all that universe out there for us to discover and perhaps exploit and colonize, as we've colonized this world, often to the detriment of its other inhabitants.

WACHTEL You write in *Rendez-vous with Rama*, "the long-hoped-for, long-feared encounter had come at last." Why that tense mix of hope and fear?

CLARKE Because we don't really know what is out there. Is it going to be E.T. or Darth Vader? These are two extremes, you might say, of the alien idea that the various media have invented. H. G. Wells was probably the first to portray the really destructive, evil alien invaders from space, and although there have been a few friendly visitors, the alien ones are much more exciting.

WACHTEL You've often said that you'd like to see proof of life elsewhere, preferably intelligent. Do you really think we will make contact with an alien intelligence?

CLARKE I feel almost sure that one day we will discover other life and other intelligences in the universe. At this very moment we're getting some remarkable images from Mars. A set of three images has come through, and one looks exactly like a collection of fir trees in an icefield, and it's hard to see what they are except trees. I'm still waiting for a serious discussion of this image. There's another extraordinary thing that looks like a giant serpent, like one of the sand worms in the movie *Dune*, precisely like them. It's probably a collapsed lava tube, but it's certainly intriguing. There's also a weird thing that we call a "dalmatian"; it's a series of black and white spots—probably snow melting on a sand dune. But it has very sharp edges and looks like some enormous organism. It stops abruptly. Why is that? Anyone can look at these images on the various Mars Web sites.

WACHTEL As we've talked about, one of your themes in 2001, in *Childhood's End*, is human evolution through contact with an alien intelligence. Is that something you believe?

CLARKE If we do contact alien intelligences, any scenario is possible. They may be hostile, in which case we've probably had it; they may be benevolent and try to help us, and that might not necessarily be a good thing either. We might lose the world if things become too easy, if we learn too much without our own efforts. Or they might even be completely neutral and not give a damn, any more than we worry about the other life forms on our planet—although I'm happy to say that we are becoming more concerned with our fellow creatures.

WACHTEL In one of your essays, "A Choice of Futures," you say that if there isn't any other intelligence in the universe, it would not only be surprising but it would confront us with an awesome responsibility. How so?

CLARKE Yes, that's right. If there's nothing else out there in this colossal universe, and we are the only intelligence, then it's up to us to preserve that intelligence and not let it destroy itself, as it sometimes seems in danger of doing. It is an awesome responsibility, and it's up to us. If we do survive our "childhood diseases," which affect us now, then we may go out and do something about this enormous and wonderful universe.

WACHTEL In a 1973 essay on Mars, "The Snows of Olympus," you wrote that "men need the mystery and romance of new horizons, almost as badly as they need food and shelter." And (elsewhere) "even if we could learn nothing in space that our instruments would not already tell us, we should go there just the same." Why do we need to know the mysteries of space?

CLARKE The first people who climbed Everest, when asked why they did it, replied, "Because it's there." That's become a cliché, but we are the exploring, inquisitive ape, and when we cease to wish to explore, we cease to be human.

WACHTEL You talked about the psychological appeal of space travel, that as soon as there's a general belief in its possibility, it affects humans' psychological outlook.

CLARKE Yes, it has happened, in fact. Space is part of human consciousness now. That began when the first images of the earth from space came in, and people realized emotionally as well as intellectually that we are living on one rather small, beautiful but fragile planet, "the third rock from the sun." Being able to see that beautiful and complex heritage in such detail now, particularly from the earth reconnaisance satellite, which you can tune into now, and you can see your own town or even your own house on your TV screen—I think that gives a sense of global unity, which was not possible in any other age.

WACHTEL Given that there are finite resources and so many needs on our planet, how can we justify spending billions on a space program?

CLARKE The billions that have been spent on the space program have come back many times. There are benefits in communications, in the meteorological satellites, which have saved hundreds of thousands of lives, and in the earth resources satellite that has shown us where our planet's resources are and has enabled us to monitor things like pollution. The money spent on space is one of the best investments we've ever made. An argument might be made about sending men to the moon. We see the use of space technology near earth's orbit, but why go on exploring space with human beings, at great expense? Well, that's a psychological question and I think the answer depends on human nature. You could argue either way. I think that we have to go on to explore space, and now they have found a very good practical reason: our earth is being blasted time and again by meteor and asteroid impacts, which have changed the course of civilization and, in fact, wiped out whole species, including the dinosaurs. That's going to happen again. So perhaps the biggest reason for going into space is to watch out for oncoming projectiles. If we don't go into space, sooner or later we will become extinct.

June 2000

HAROLD BLOOM

When I first talked to Harold Bloom, his unique combination of emotion and intellect triggered an enormous response from listeners. It was not long after he had published *The Western Canon* (1994), an impassioned defence of reading the classics. Initially, because of his reputation as a pugnacious reactionary, disdainful of new movements in contemporary literature, I had expected not to like him. Admire him, yes, but not warm to him. But he was so engaging, erudite and full of enthusiasms that I felt immediately drawn to him. Here was good company. He made me want to read more—more of his own criticism and more of the books he so clearly loves. And to talk to him again, when I came to do the special series *Original Minds*.

For the past thirty years, Harold Bloom has been—as the *New York Times* put it—"one of the world's most influential critic-scholar-theorists." The breadth (and speed) of his reading, as well as his amazingly retentive memory, are famous. He can recite Milton's *Paradise Lost* from beginning to end, most of Blake, Spenser's *The Faerie Queene*, Shakespeare and so on. He's published twenty-eight books and written introductions for some six hundred volumes of literary criticism.

"Everything about Harold Bloom is outsized," wrote one critic. (No wonder Shakespeare's Falstaff is a kind of alter ego to him.) So who more likely to survey *all* of Western literature and decide what's important, what constitutes the canon? And then to tackle his great love in the 768-page *Shakespeare: The Invention of the Human* (1998). Bloom remains astonishingly prolific. Often alternating literary analysis with works on religion—such as his unlikely bestseller *The Book of J* (1990), where he maintains that crucial passages in the Old Testament were written by a woman—Bloom came out with *Omens of Millennium: The Gnosis of Angels, Dreams, and Resurrection* (1996). Then *How to Read and Why* (2000), *Stories and Poems for Extremely Intelligent Children* (2001) and *Genius: A Mosaic of One Hundred Exemplary Creative Minds* (2002). Indicative of his celebrity, *Entertainment Weekly* noted that Bloom "may finally have attained blockbuster status" by signing "a rumored $1.2-million deal" for his book on genius and imaginative power.

At the same time, Bloom continues to teach at Yale and at New York University. This intellectual vigour is somewhat belied by his demeanour, which, while not exactly heavy, is marked by an undertow of sadness. But he was full of affection when we met at the CBC's New York studio for the first time (the previous interview had not been face to face, but studio to studio). I've drawn on some of that earlier conversation here to fill in his background.

WACHTEL You once said that there's no distinction between literature and life. I'd like to talk about that, about how literature became so much a part of your own life. Could we go back to your first discovery of English literature?

BLOOM I was raised in a Yiddish-speaking household in the East Bronx—I was born in 1930—and lived in a neighbourhood where only

Yiddish was spoken in the streets. To this day my English sounds a little odd, even though I was born in New York City, because I learned English by reading it and by guessing at the pronunciation.

WACHTEL Why did you have to guess at the pronunciation? Is this because you learned English before you went to school?

BLOOM I started teaching myself English and some other languages, but primarily English, when I was about four years old. I was an obsessive reader as a young child, for reasons that I don't altogether understand, but an absolutely obsessive reader, and of course I was already reading Yiddish and studying Hebrew, but I did not study any English or hear any English spoken until I went to kindergarten when I was five and a half—but by then I'd pretty much taught myself to read English.

WACHTEL Have you speculated about those obsessive reasons?

BLOOM I was the last of five children in a loving but very poor family. We lived in a confined space, though we lived I think amicably enough, my siblings and myself. I was much the smallest. I was also clearly the cleverest—none of the others, I believe, went beyond high school. Had I been born in an affluent household and been the kind of person that I clearly was from the beginning, I suppose I would still have been an incessant reader. My parents were proletarian and their parents were proletarian—my father was a garment worker, my mother a housewife, and my grandfather was a carpenter, I believe, in Russia-Poland—he was murdered by the Nazis. I eventually found out from talking to all the surviving relatives that there had been great-great-uncles who had been both Talmud scholars and Kabbalists, so there must be something that is inherited in this kind of an interest. When I was a very small child, for instance, any language that I learned to read—and this has been true throughout my life—I could read at a simply shocking speed. I don't read as quickly now, at the age of seventy, as I could when I was, say, twenty-five. Unless I force myself to slow down, and if I'm reading for information rather than aesthetic pleasure, I still read pretty much by turning the pages and taking in the whole page at once. And I have a scandalous memory, a frightening memory. Anything that has really moved me in prose or verse, I remember. I remember the poetry pretty much by heart and I can give a pretty accurate paraphrase, including a lot of quotations, of the prose. I guess I was a kind of freak.

WACHTEL Did you have an awareness of what you describe as a scandalous memory, and a certain freakishness, when you were young?

BLOOM No, no, I took it all absolutely for granted. After all, I led a very private existence; I was mostly with my siblings and my mother and father and a few school friends, and I didn't do particularly well in school. Our neighbourhood was so bad that one couldn't go to the public high school. I went by exam to the Bronx High School of Science, which was the worst possible place in the world for me because, then and now, I have no interest whatsoever in science and very little in mathematics. So I did rather poorly; I didn't finish quite at the rock bottom of the class, but I finished rather low. And I would never have gotten to be an undergraduate at Cornell or any other university, except that I took the New York State Regents exam and finished first in the state. It was one of those multiple-choice tests that was based upon very wide reading and, having read everything and remembered everything, I was bound to get a perfect score in it. On that basis Cornell gave me a fellowship, even though I'd never even applied to Cornell, and they admitted me as a freshman. Once I was at Cornell, I met remarkable teachers, including M. H. Abrams, a very distinguished romanticist who mentored me, and, though I've tried to reciprocate by mentoring young people, I don't think I've ever managed to do as much for anyone as Mike Abrams did for me. I owe Abrams a great deal.

I was a very shy and awkward person—I don't have many social graces now, but then I was painfully shy. I was so frightened at Cornell in my first year, I would keep very close to the wall when I walked down the hallways. It sounds almost morbid, though I don't think I was psychologically morbid. I felt so strange; it just seemed so bewildering to me. Then even more so when four years later, in 1951, I became a graduate student at Yale, where I found the atmosphere very mixed. I managed to avoid most of the teachers of the New-Critical, neo-Christian persuasion, which was the reigning orthodoxy then, except for one very remarkable man, William K. Wimsatt, and even though he and I fought like cats and dogs intellectually, he was someone with whom one could disagree. He was very Aristotelian and Roman Catholic. At Yale, as at Cornell, I found remarkable teachers.

WACHTEL Going back to pre-kindergarten or thereabouts, you learned English by sounding out the words of Blake's "Prophecies."

BLOOM When I was a little boy I fell madly in love with Blake. I was rather like Northrop Frye before me, and eventually he also became something of a mentor figure for me, though we didn't meet until I was teaching at Yale. I fell in love with Blake's poems, especially the long poems, even though I did not understand them. How could I possibly have understood them at the age of four and a half or five? But I memorized them; I used to read them night and day—in library editions. I didn't own an edition of my own until a few years later when I asked one of my older sisters to get me the Nonesuch edition of Blake, which was an extraordinary expense for her, but she kindly did it. So that was the second book I owned. The first book I ever owned—I still remember this because I saved my own money to buy it—was The Collected Poems of Hart Crane. To this day I'm madly in love with Hart Crane's poetry. I couldn't possibly have understood it then, just as I couldn't possibly have understood the Blake. I was just in love with the incantatory quality and the strangeness and the sound and the feel of it.

WACHTEL You were able to fall in love with great poetry that moved you before you could comprehend it.

BLOOM Who knows on what level one comprehends? The difference between canonical poetry, between, say, Shakespeare, Milton, Wordsworth, Spenser, Dante, Yeats, and inadequate poetry or less adequate poetry, or verse pretending to be poetry, or these days, God knows, the sorry stuff which is neither prose nor verse but pretending to be verse—all of this multiculturalist stuff here in the United States—the great difference in the end is that there are so many levels at which one could understand that perhaps one understands long before one can begin to understand. Probably one is understanding more than one knows at the beginning, and then at a later time one can practise a kind of exegesis upon it. I certainly found it very strange.

WACHTEL Do you know what is the pull of poetry? I know that as a child you read lots of prose as you worked your way through all the shelves of the local library, but do you understand the particular pull of the poetry you still favour?

BLOOM It's the sense of crossing—it's why I myself could never write a line of verse and never tried. It's crossing a threshold that seems guarded by demons. It's entering that realm that I think children through the ages have entered: a sense of a magical world, a world of heightened perceptions, a world where everything is wonder and speculation. I think the hieratic language, the metrical element in that, the deeper and darker rhythms that wind their way in and out of the metric—I think the whole extraordinary question of the deep relation between sound and sense has a profound enchantment. There is, of course, visionary prose, right down to *Finnegans Wake*—which in a deep sense, I suppose, could be regarded as prose poetry—which has very much the same effect. And there is also that miraculous translation, if it can be called a translation since it's so much a recreation in its own right, the King James version of the Bible, ultimately founded on the genius of two translators, Tyndale and Coverdale, both of whom were extraordinary writers of evocative prose.

WACHTEL You've been virtually haunted daily for sixty years by a stanza from a Hart Crane poem, "The Broken Tower." Crane is probably your favourite modern poet—

BLOOM

> And so it was I entered the broken world
> To trace the visionary company of love, its voice
> An instant in the wind (I know not whither hurled)
> But not for long to hold each desperate choice.

That must be the stanza.

WACHTEL Why has that particular piece of writing had such a grip on you?

BLOOM "The Broken Tower" is Crane's death poem, in effect. I first read it more than sixty years ago, when I was eight or nine. I'm not sure I fully understood what it meant when it first sang itself into my memory, but I think I must have intuited that it had a kind of Gnostic sensibility to it. "And so it was I entered the broken world"—a world evidently broken even as it was created. "To trace the visionary company of love"—trace, presumably, in every sense to draw it again, but also to track it, to try to find "the visionary company of love." I've loved that phrase for years. I used it as the title of a book I wrote in my late twenties, *The Visionary Company*, which was about English Romantic poetry. Many years later, when I was reading a beautiful fragment from a novel by Walter Pater—*Gaston de Latour*—there, in the first chapter, the young poet Gaston is taking his first communion; it's described as an outdoor scene on the lawn of the church. Pater writes that the young Gaston was never to forget that sense of the visionary company standing all about him. Crane, as I discovered later, was a deep reader of Pater, though nowhere in his letters or his books is there to be found a fragment of *Gaston de Latour*. He takes so much from Pater that there's every reason to believe that Pater is the source of that beautiful phrase, "the visionary company of love." But to go on with it, "its voice/An instant in the wind" means it's very difficult to hunt down. Then we come to that line—heartbreaking when you know Crane's life as well as his poetry—"But not for long to hold each desperate choice," because Crane, who was homoerotic and always in search of what he thought would be the true life partner, says later in the poem, "my long-scattered score/Of broken intervals." It's a wonderful multiple meaning because it means his poetry, and it means, of course, a kind of musical score that you write, where the intervals are not just diminished or augmented but broken, so it produces a jangling effect. He also means it in the sense of a sexual score, rather grimly: "my long-scattered score/Of broken intervals . . . and I, their sexton slave!" So it is a poem, in the end, about the poetic gift itself having been too strong for the human psyche—Hart Crane's psyche—that carries it. I still remember as quite a young boy being almost overcome by the extraordinary outburst when Crane cries out, "The bells, I say, the bells break down their tower,/And swing I know not where." That lingered in me for a very long time. As I say, I probably understood it intuitively long before I would have been capable of paraphrasing it.

WACHTEL It's Crane's death poem.

BLOOM It's his last considerable poem and it may very well be his death poem. He wrote it in Mexico City a few months before he died. It is, I think, his last substantial and completed poem, and his last great poem, it is fair to say. It's a poem he had very serious doubts about. The poem seems to express, among a good deal else, the anxiety that the poetic gift may be shattered and finished in him. It certainly wasn't, on the evidence of the poem. He sent off copies to a number of his poet-critic friends in the United States—Malcolm Cowley, Kenneth Burke, Ivor Winters and Allen Tate—but he didn't receive a reply from any of them; perhaps he didn't leave enough time for a reply. And I don't know that a reply would have helped him very much. He did, most probably, commit suicide. He leaped from the deck of the ship that was taking him back from his Guggenheim year in Mexico to New York City.

WACHTEL He was just thirty-two.

BLOOM Yes, he was thirty-two years and some months old, so he did not live to be thirty-three, the christological age. He does seem to me, in terms of his innate poetic powers—what might be called his natural gift as a poet—the most extraordinarily promising of all American poets ever. The poets that many would put ahead of him and that even I would entertain strongly as other candidates—Walt Whitman, Emily Dickinson, Robert Frost, T. S. Eliot, overwhelmingly Wallace Stevens—had those five died when they were just thirty-two years old, we would not think of them now as the great poets we do regard them, quite properly, as being. Crane just did not have enough time. He did not give himself enough time.

WACHTEL You have—as you say—"a scandalous memory" when it comes to poetry. And memorization is, for you, an important part of the process of appreciating work.

BLOOM I try to teach my students never just to memorize by rote, but to read poems aloud, both to themselves and to others, but especially to themselves in solitude. When it is read aloud, it can catch fire in you, if it is a poem that, as Samuel Taylor Coleridge would like to say, "finds you." If students are found by a particular poem, then I urge them to give it a chance to possess their memories so that they will come to possess it by memory.

WACHTEL And for you, in a way, whether a poem lives in your memory becomes a kind of touchstone for poetic quality. If it doesn't stick, then you find something lacking.

BLOOM I remember discussing the work of a poet—who shall be nameless—with another poet who is a good friend of both mine and the nameless poet, and asking if it bothered him that there were no memorable phrases. My poet friend said to me that the poet we were talking about couldn't care less, that he felt the whole question of writing in memorable phrases was almost beside the point. I was, and am, a little shocked by that. Memory, in terms not just of poetry but of imaginative literature and its apprehension, can scarcely be overemphasized. I've been reflecting on this for most of my seventy years and believe that we really can't think in the full sense of thinking without the work of memory, both active and beyond our awareness of the extent to which we rely upon memory. I argue quite passionately with my students, insisting that it's absolutely crucial that we read deeply and reread and remember the very best that has been thought and written. Without stocking our memory with the strongest works that have been written, we impoverish not just our memories but our ability to think for ourselves. I am deeply worried about the future of democracy in countries that are so profoundly dependent upon it and honoured by it and with it, as are the United States and Canada, because young people increasingly yield to screens of different kinds rather than read and reread really powerful books. I worry whether they will learn to think independently, whether they will be able to resist demagogues, whether they will learn to resist all those people, in the universities and sent out by the universities to the media—in the English-speaking world, in particular—who are, in effect, cheerleaders. This has become, for me, a kind of educational and cultural anxiety.

WACHTEL Are you ever surprised by the particular fragments or poems that do haunt you?

BLOOM Oh yes, because so frequently they come unbidden. There is a wonderful fragmentary lyric by the English poet-painter Isaac Rosenberg, who was killed in action on the Western Front in the First World War, which begins,

> A worm fed on the heart of Corinth,
> Babylon and Rome: not Paris raped tall Helen,
> but this incestuous worm.

And then he turns it into a sort of Blakean prophecy against what he fears is happening to England. I don't know why recently that has come popping into my head. I began the section on poetry in *How to Read and Why* with that wonderful lyric of A. E. Housman, "Into my heart an air that kills," because as I was sitting down, facing the problem that I face throughout the book, which is that I wanted as short a book as possible—a kind of primer, a sampler, and yet one had to choose from such an enormous wealth of material—suddenly, without my even thinking of it, it sang itself into me, "Into my heart an air that kills." Which is so wonderful because he means, of course, a tune, but he also means an air that you breathe and the notion of either the tune or the air that you breathe instead of giving you life, killing you, hurting you so much emotionally.

> Into my heart an air that kills
> From yon far country blows:
> What are those blue remembered hills,
> What spires, what farms are those?
>
> That is the land of lost content,
> I see it shining plain,
> The happy highways where I went
> And cannot come again.

That poem sang itself into my head when I was a small boy and I hadn't thought of it for many years. So even though it means I won't be organizing this section chronologically, somehow the poem seemed to me so perfect an epitome of a relatively simple but immensely plangent and powerful lyric that I decided I would start with it.

WACHTEL You've described poetry as "the crown of imaginative literature." You do favour it over prose fiction because, as you say, it's a prophetic mode. How so?

BLOOM There are, of course, great visionary novels like Emily Brontë's *Wuthering Heights*, and there are, obviously, astonishing visionary dramas. Shakespeare, of course, mostly writes in verse, though not always; he's the best prose writer as well as the best verse writer. *A Midsummer Night's Dream* and *The Tempest* must be pure instances of visionary drama. But by and large, although it is the foster child of prose romance, the novel has tended, even in visionary writers such as Dickens or Joyce, to have a strong element of social realism and a representation of everyday reality in it. Short stories, which are relatively modern—from the last two centuries and perfected just from Chekhov to the present day— tend quite frequently to have something of the visionary intensity that so many of the best poems have. But on the whole, if one thinks of the transcendental and extraordinary—to use that wonderful phrase from Ralph Waldo Emerson—in literature, one is going to find it more often in poetry than in narrative or meditative prose.

WACHTEL I want to talk a little about poetry and the spirit, because not only have you written a lifetime of criticism and appreciation but you've also addressed yourself to spiritual themes. These two pursuits seem closely related to you. Are they?

BLOOM Well, they certainly have been in the last decade. I seem to have, for a while, alternated books like *The Book of J* and *The American Religion* and *Omens of Millennium*, on the one hand, and books like *The Western Canon* and *Shakespeare: The Invention of the Human* and *How to Read and Why*, on the other. I seem to have gone back and forth between what could, in a very broad sense, however heretical on my part, still be considered religious or spiritual books and works that are still within what

I think is my tradition of literary criticism, which follows the work of Dr. Samuel Johnson and William Hazlitt and, to a lesser extent, Walter Pater and Oscar Wilde. I suppose I no longer see a real difference between what it is that I get from the major works of the literary imagination and what the religious ideas or texts, which more often than not are heretical, give me. They are Gnostic or hermetic, or at least visionary or mystical. I always do try, in writing, to distinguish between the two modes. I even tried to invent a category that I called "religious criticism," particularly in *The American Religion*, but it seems to be, of all my books, the most misunderstood and the most misused. It's curious. When I went out to Salt Lake City to give lectures and seminars on Joseph Smith, the prophet, seer and revelator who founded Mormonism, the people I got along best with, talking about questions of spirituality, were the intellectuals among the American Mormons. I find them fascinating, inventive, but they would not want their religion to be regarded as a heresy—no one within a heresy wants to be regarded as a heretic. They regard themselves, indeed, as the truest Christians, the truest disciples of Jesus Christ. And yet, though they don't like me to say this, they're not even monotheists. They believe in a plurality of gods; they're henotheists, as it were. So they are, in fact, a profound and fascinating heretical departure, historically considered, from the major traditions, first of Judaism and then of Christianity.

WACHTEL You've talked about the profound influence of Northrop Frye. You were just seventeen when you read his book on Blake, *Fearful Symmetry*.

BLOOM I was seventeen and a Cornell freshman. I've now written a foreword to a new printing of his other masterwork, *Anatomy of Criticism*, which I hope the shade of Norrie, if it came back, would not find irreverent. I remarked in the introduction, genially enough, that every time I came to Toronto to give a lecture, Norrie insisted upon introducing me, even if there were two lectures, two nights in a row. He would always want to do that. Old friends who are no longer teaching there but are still around, those wonderful scholar-critics Eleanor Cook and Jay MacPherson, will no doubt remember these occasions.

It was probably my obsession with William Blake, whom I started reading very young when I was reading Hart Crane, that brought me to Frye's work. I don't suppose I am a Blakean any more the way I was as a young scholar-teacher. In those days, it would have horrified me if somebody had asked what was the better poem, Pope's *The Dunciad* or Blake's "Jerusalem." I would have been quite shocked and said there's no question whatsoever: it's Blake's "Jerusalem." If somebody asked me now, I would say, rather sadly, well, I still love "Jerusalem" and still know it almost by heart, but I think that Pope's *The Dunciad* is the more powerful and accomplished achievement. I'm rather stunned that I have lived to say that. I remember that Norrie, every time he introduced me, would go to great pains to distinguish his United Church of Canada Platonic vision of literature, and of Blake in particular, from my Jewish Gnostic vision. Norrie did not like Gnosticism, and he once attributed what he least liked about my mature work to Gnosticism. We really parted company in 1973, when I published *The Anxiety of Influence* and sent it off to the great man in eager expectation of his liking it. He wrote me back a letter saying he didn't like it at all, that it was the natural consequence of my Gnosticism. Which was an odd sort of remark, but I think a very witty one and probably a deeply perceptive one also. He was, as we all know, a most remarkable reader.

WACHTEL Could you describe briefly what you wrote about Jewish Gnosticism in *Omens of Millennium*? We're familiar with agnosticism or not knowing, but could you say what you mean by Gnosticism?

BLOOM Gnosticism may or may not originally have been a Jewish phenomenon. The modern scholars of Gnosticism dispute the existence of a Gnostic religion. Certainly in the second century of the Common Era, there existed in Egypt, in Palestine—throughout the ancient world—an extraordinary heresy from the viewpoint either of normative Judaism or the normative Christianity of that time. It held that the Creation and the Fall were not separate events but were absolutely the same event. If you could explore its implications from the viewpoint of either normative Judaism or any traditional orthodox Christianity, it is a very shocking notion indeed. It also held that the best and oldest part of each one of us is no part of the Creation, is no part of nature, and is neither the body nor the soul and is certainly not the intellect. It is what was called the *pneuma*, or breath—sometimes they used for this notion the metaphor or trope of the "spark." This element, which is best and oldest in us, is a fragment of the original Godhead. Indeed, ancient Gnosticism and its various modern derivatives—and its many poetic affiliates through the ages—permeate what we call European Romanticism. One thinks of poets like Novalis and Rimbaud as being essentially Gnostic. Blake, with a difference, was essentially Gnostic. Perhaps Shelley. I think of Hart Crane very much as a Gnostic poet. I suppose I qualify as a Gnostic: I regard myself as profoundly religious in temperament but very heretical ever since I was a little boy. Indeed, I remember when I was bar mitzvahed getting into terrible quarrels with the rabbis who were counselling me and educating me, and I even had the satisfaction of having one of them denounce me in Yiddish as one of the *minim*, the ancient Hebraic term which is used in the Talmud for the earliest Jewish Gnostic heretics.

I suppose for me not to be even historical about it now, but just to be personal or experiential, it seems to me that there are two aspects of what I'm willing to call divinity, but one is split off from us, is in exile. One is in the interstellar spaces in some solar system, far beyond our own, and cannot hear our prayers or our cries or our hopes. He or She or It cannot be in touch with us and we cannot be in touch with Him or Her or It. And another part of divinity is, indeed, that *pneuma* or spark, which is so buried in the rock of the self, a kind of pure diamond down there in the mud and the muck, that you might perhaps, two or three times in a lifetime, in a moment of reverie or vision or sudden knowledge, be able to come into contact with it. Yet, somehow one knows it is there. Now, this is obviously not a mode of discourse which is acceptable to Protestants, Catholics, Islam or normative Judaism. But there are scholars, including the late Gershom Scholem, who was someone I knew rather well personally and who was a great influence on me, who have held that Gnosticism is indeed of Jewish origin and that the earliest kabbalah long precedes the medieval texts that we have and probably did exist among the ancient Jews.

WACHTEL Can you say when you have come in contact with your own "spark"? Has it been through reading, through poetry?

BLOOM I suppose it was first stirred in me through reading Blake so endlessly when I was a child and then becoming a Blake scholar. I wrote a book on Blake and then I wrote a commentary to David Erdman's definitive edition of Blake, a commentary which is still useful. I haven't looked at it for many years and probably wouldn't want to, because for me, at that time, Blake was scripture and I wrote it, I suppose, in the spirit of Rashi commenting on the Torah. I don't think that Blake is Torah any more, but then I don't think the Torah is Torah any more, either. I remember saying in some Harvard lectures back in 1987 that I thought that any distinction that scholars or churches or the public made between sacred and secular works of the imagination was finally more of a political distinction than it was a literary or intellectual distinction, and that to believe in the end that some texts are more sacred than others is, for me, as wrong as to believe that some places or spots are more holy than others. Blake said, very beautifully, "for everything that lives is holy," and he was quite right. I simply mean that I don't like to make distinctions between great works of the imagination, even if some of them are adopted as scripture and some are not. One has lots of precedent for this, of course, among the poets. William Butler Yeats regarded the poetic tradition as being essentially scriptural for him. And, of course, Yeats became a very complex kind of Gnostic and hermetist, though he carried it as far as occultism, where I don't quite follow him.

WACHTEL For you, literary criticism seems to have been a kind of calling; you say that you came to it very early and you've been utterly unswerving.

BLOOM I think that is the case. I remember when I was a small boy, I had a very nice uncle by marriage, a man named Sam Feldman, who owned a candy story out on Coney Island in Brooklyn. I was out there with him one day and he gave me some candy, and he said to me—I don't think I was more than eight at the time—"What are you going to be when you grow up, Harry?" and I said to him—we were speaking in Yiddish, of course—"I'm going to be a professor of poetry when I grow up." I had no idea really what that meant at all, though I had heard already that there were places called Harvard and Yale.

I thought of this in a strange and sad way many years later, in 1987 and 1988, when I was simultaneously Charles Eliot Norton professor of poetry at Harvard and still at my home base as professor of humanities at Yale. I was suddenly struck by Freud's great warning, "Beware of wanting anything too much."

WACHTEL Did you always realize that literary criticism was going to be your world? That you would be engaged not in writing novels or poems but always at the level of appreciating and analyzing?

BLOOM I started to read Dr. Johnson and Hazlitt when I was fairly young. I was reading them when I was a high school student and was absolutely enchanted by them, and I fell madly in love with Ruskin when I was about fifteen or sixteen, a year or two before I went up to Cornell. I knew that I didn't have a storytelling faculty in me. I tried it once; years later, in 1979, I wrote what I called "a Gnostic fantasy," The Flight to Lucifer. I wish I hadn't published it. It was all right to have composed it, but I shouldn't have published it. The prose was pretty good, but the story was totally dead; I haven't got an ability for prose fiction, and, as I say, verse for me is a threshold guarded by demons. I knew that I wanted to be some kind of a critical writer.

WACHTEL Is there a hierarchy? Do you feel at the very top is poetry and then fiction and then criticism? Do you conceive it that way at all?

BLOOM Well, I'm not quite sure how one establishes hierarchies. I do believe that literary criticism is either part of literature or it ought not to exist at all. Obviously, one is not and never will be Dr. Samuel Johnson or William Hazlitt, or Ruskin, or for that matter Northrop Frye. Quite clearly at their strongest, Johnson, Hazlitt, Ruskin, Walter Pater in the greatest essays and in Appreciations, Oscar Wilde in his extraordinary critical dialogues, Kenneth Burke at his very best, Frye at his very best—

these are aesthetic experiences. Johnson is certainly the best critic I have ever read in my life in any language I'm capable of reading. The greatest of The Lives of the Poets seem to me at least as extraordinary in their way as Rasselas, marvellous as it is, or as the great poem The Vanity of Human Wishes. I don't know about a hierarchy. I love poetry more than I love prose. I still, naturally, try to read every poem that reaches me. I guess it's an addiction.

WACHTEL The intensity of your personal response to particular works of literature seems to be the guiding principle for you in your critical assessment. Do your judgements always arise out of that intimate experience of reading?

BLOOM Yes, I'm afraid so. I know that this can be turned against me, but it does seem to me that first comes the aesthetic experience, the overwhelming shock that something is indeed intensely beautiful and exalted and sublime, and then comes love. One falls in love, and out of that love—out of that deep affection—comes the psychic energy and, I hope, something of the skill to understand it better and help explain it to others. As I say, this can be turned against me because, after all, it could be said, "Well, if you don't think Alice Walker is a remarkable writer it's because you have failed to love her work"; or "If you don't think Sylvia Plath was capable of writing a poem, it's because you have failed to love her work." I would find it very difficult to have a response to that, except to say, these don't seem to me to be aesthetic artifacts, they seem to be something else.

WACHTEL You've talked about how the importance of reading deeply is to augment one's own growing inner self, to make a proper use of one's own solitude, which, as you describe it, is ultimately to confront your own mortality.

BLOOM Well, what else can it be? One reaches one's sixties, one's friends start to die of one disease or another or one accident or another; it's difficult to maintain old friendships, it's very difficult to make new friendships; one tries to be benign, one tries not to be self-aggrandizing; one tries to avoid relationships which might be self-aggrandizing. I mean, all human beings are like this. Sometimes one succeeds, sometimes one fails. But in the end, one is alone. We are all of us alone. I'm told these days we have to consider ourselves as beings in society. Well, I pay my taxes and I desperately hope the Democrats can make a comeback in our wretched country, and I try to contribute as much as I can to every possible charity and so on, but in the end one knows one is alone, that one lives at the heart of a solitude, that we all live at the heart of a solitude, that we all have the consciousness of mortality.

WACHTEL I get a sense that this relationship, the solace that reading provides, is not just a function or a characteristic of advancing years but has been your connection to reading from even a young age.

BLOOM It's not just a way of cheering oneself up; it's not, I hope, a way of aggrandizing one's own ego—and I'm perpetually accused of that. Why that is, I can't altogether understand. I once asked Norrie Frye that, and he said, "Harold, you have a fierce personality and it gets into what you write. You're always going to be subject to that accusation." He added, "I've accused you of that myself." And he was right, he had accused me of that. It's pleasure in the end, but it's that intense kind of pleasure which has a painful element in it. Our solitude is a harsh thing. The Marxists tell me that the smallest human unit is two people. I think that's an idealism. I think we are in the end alone.

WACHTEL If reading isn't a solace, what is it?

BLOOM One is trapped in a perpetually growing inner self; it's a discipline for that growing inner self; it's an education for that growing inner self. It has a generous basis also, though I wouldn't want to put it on a societal basis necessarily. I don't know if it's a selfish activity in me. I've earned a perfectly good living. I cannot say that I was not also in it for the living and to support my children and my wife and myself. I've taught tens of thousands of students; some of them occasionally come back or send me a letter and let me know that something was communicated to them, that something in their spirit is a touch less lonely. I don't want to be sappy about this in any way. I get a lot of letters about *The Western Canon*. I throw out the nasty ones immediately, whether right-wing or left-wing or those which accuse me of racism or sexism or I don't know what kind of horror. But I get very touching letters from ordinary, common readers and some uncommon readers also, saying that I've helped send them back to a particular work, or I've helped send them back to reading, or that in some sense in some register I speak for them.

Gertrude Stein said so beautifully, and I'm never tired of quoting it, "One writes for oneself and for strangers." I think probably one reads for oneself and for strangers. Maybe in the end one even teaches for oneself and for strangers; certainly one is aware of the people in the room, certainly one gets to know their personalities, but there's a kind of despair in that also, because you can't ever really quite bridge that gap in teaching. Maybe there's an element of desperation in it, I don't know. Maybe there's some attempt to overcome one's personal limitations—which in my case are very thick indeed.

WACHTEL At one point in your life, you suffered from a spiritual crisis.

BLOOM I had a very bad time when I was, indeed, in a Dantesque middle of the journey. At thirty-five, I went through a terrible year. My wife and I and my sons went abroad because I had fallen into a very deep depression and I could not shake it. For a while I could not read. I couldn't even look at the sky. So we took a year off from Yale and went to England. Eventually, reading returned. Therapy did not work for me—not even with the very distinguished Freudian therapist I worked with at Yale, and then the not-at-all-distinguished therapist to whom he sent me in London. I found that reading Emerson probably did more for me. I read all of Freud again and again that year, but my interest in Freud was eventually subsumed by my interest in Shakespeare. I came to understand that what I had found in Freud was to be found much more powerfully in Shakespeare and that Shakespeare was Freud's true source, though he did not want to admit it. In The Western Canon, I wrote—only half mockingly—a Shakespearean reading of Freud, because I thought that was a lot more useful than any Freudian reading of Shakespeare.

But that year—in the middle of the journey, exactly thirty-five years ago, half a lifetime away—Emerson converted me to what might be called Emersonianism, which is self-reliance as a religion, not in the horrible business sense of Henry Ford but in that sense in which Emerson inspired Walt Whitman and Emily Dickinson and so many since. In the sense of what Emerson calls "the god within."

WACHTEL You said it was an excursion into a personal literary theory.

BLOOM Yes. Two summers later, in 1967, at about the time of my thirty-seventh birthday, I woke up from a terrible nightmare in which I felt that a giant winged being whom eventually I came to identify with Blake and his eagle's vision of the covering cherub—a mythological figure I had spent a long time discussing with Northrop Frye, since we were both fascinated by it—had been suffocating me. I gave a lecture called "The Covering Cherub, or Poetic Influence," at the Cornell Society for the Humanities a year or two after that, and eventually republished it, though it's a strange document, in a volume called *Poetics of Influence: New and Selected Criticism*.

But it was really the first draft of what became the initial chapter of *The Anxiety of Influence*, a chapter entitled "Clinamen," the Lucretian word for a swerve, a sudden movement of the atoms as they fall downwards. According to Lucretius, without that sudden swerve, or *clinamen*, there could be no fresh inception in the world, there could be no freedom—we would all be overdetermined or predetermined in every way. *The Anxiety of Influence* took me forever to write. I wrote that first draft in the summer of 1967, and it wasn't until January 1973 that I published the book. I suppose, though it's so long ago now, it was a watershed in my work. What books I had written before that—including a large book on Yeats published in 1970 and a collection of essays with a title evoked by Hart Crane, *The Ringers in the Tower*, published in 1971—were all like my earlier books on the Romantic poets. They suffered from what now seems to me a kind of idealism that hadn't yet deeply enough pondered what literary experience was. So I went through a phase that started in the summer of '67, writing a long book on Wallace Stevens and in the early 1980s publishing a book of essays called *Agon* and a shorter book called *The Breaking of the Vessels*, which was a kind of Gnostic parable of Creation.

And then I changed again. I went into a third phase, in which I became very conscious of the crisis in the teaching of literature in Anglo-American universities. I set myself very strongly against what I would call the countercultural element which has since become wholly dominant, whether they call it New Historicism or whether they—wrongly, I think—call it feminism. They also call it Marxism—though it has nothing to do with Marxism or cultural studies, which has largely replaced literary studies in our academies. In reaction to this, I started to edit a vast series of volumes for Chelsea House, anthologies of literary criticism in which I could write Johnsonian introductions for the common reader. Sometimes these are quite short, sometimes more extensive. I may have published almost a thousand of these. I have commercial motives, but so did Dr. Johnson. I quote my hero: "No man but a blockhead ever wrote, except for money." I think that's a very good motto.

But I have been concerned about this crisis in education, and I hope to write a book about it. Information is readily available to us, but where shall wisdom be found? That is the great biblical question, of course. The Hebrew Bible would say that the fear of God is the beginning of wisdom. But that is not the way I think I would want to answer it. I suppose in this third long phase of my work, both as a teacher and a writer, I have not addressed myself to academics, though I think a number of students do read me. Since I've turned my back on the academy—although some say it's hypocritical of me since I continue to teach both at Yale and New York University—I'm doing what I've always done, only now I try to write for the broadest possible audience because I have discovered, from people's reaction to my work when I go on the road in support of a book, as I did extensively with *How to Read and Why*, that the people who come to hear me and who talk to me don't like the way they were taught, if they were taught in the last third of the last century. They don't like the way they were taught "how to read and why," as it were, in English-speaking universities and colleges, and they feel that the study of literature has been politicized, and indeed replaced, by cultural studies.

WACHTEL You said something tantalizing that I want to pursue, which is that you would not answer the question "Where shall wisdom be found?" with the traditional biblical response.

BLOOM   That the fear of God is the beginning of wisdom. Yes.

WACHTEL   Do you know where you would begin?

BLOOM   Yes. In the works of William Shakespeare. Wisdom is to be found in the great writers. It is to be found in Shakespeare and Homer and Dante and Chaucer and overwhelmingly, of course, in Cervantes.

WACHTEL   You said in *Omens of Millennium* that knowing yourself, knowing Shakespeare and knowing God are three separate but closely related quests.

BLOOM   Yes, I think so. It would be Emersonian or Valentinian [second-century Gnostic, Valentinus] to say that you cannot know God without knowing yourself. And that indeed you cannot truly know yourself without knowing God. I'd always deliberately put off teaching and writing about Shakespeare because I felt that, of all the writers I had ever read, he was the most profound and much the best in any language I was able to read. I simply did not feel that I was ready to teach Shakespeare until I was in my early forties. I knew that I needed to grow up to it. When I finally felt that I was ready, I still didn't feel that I was intellectually and emotionally mature enough. Even now, I feel that I'm not mature or strong enough to fully read or teach or understand Shakespeare. I can still remember that one of the first public talks I gave about Shakespeare, at Queen's College here in New York City, was to an audience of mostly professional Shakespeareans from around the city who had gathered to hear me. They were rather startled by the way I was talking. It was the kind of thing that eventually became my book *Shakespeare: The Invention of the Human*, many years later. One of them, who was a very decent soul, came up to me afterwards and said that it troubled him that I talked about Shakespeare exactly the way he would talk about God. I looked at him in a perfectly cheerful way and I said, "Well, my dear fellow, that's fine as far as I'm concerned. It doesn't bother me to say that Shakespeare is God or that God is Shakespeare." He went away very troubled, shaking his head. I can't remember if he was normative Jewish or normative Christian, but he thought that I was either very wicked or facetious. But I don't think that what I said was either wicked or trivial.

WACHTEL   But the quests—the knowability of Shakespeare, the knowability of God and the knowability of yourself—are in some ways related?

BLOOM I think they are closely related. We're not, as it were, mixing up spiritual and literary considerations. I would say—not so much in my defence but quite cheerfully—that I would far rather mix up spiritual and aesthetic considerations than mix up political or social considerations with the aesthetic. I still think I can make aesthetic judgements which are quite different from spiritual judgements; thus, I spiritually loathe, despise and abominate the late Thomas Stearns Eliot, but I would have to admit aesthetically that "The Wasteland" is a great poem and that a great part of Eliot's earlier poetry, up to and including "The Wasteland," and "The Hollow Men" in 1925, is an extraordinary body of imaginative achievement, even though spiritually Eliot's religious and cultural criticism repels and infuriates me. It seems to me fascistic. And his literary criticism I've always disliked violently. I feel that if you turn it upside down you get something much closer to the truth about literature.

I have been reading and rereading recently the extraordinary confessions of St. Augustine, which I must admit spiritually appall me. They make me very unhappy indeed, but they are intellectually and even aesthetically extraordinary. Augustine is a great writer and a great spirit. I reread twice a year, and have every year of my mature life, Jonathan Swift's *A Tale of a Tub*, which I think after Shakespeare's prose is the best prose in the English language. But I cannot think of a book that infuriates me more or is more of an indictment of me, which is why I read it; I figure it is very good for me. It is, after all, a great satire against visionary enthusiasts, the people whom the great Swift calls "projectors." I don't think Swift would have liked me at all, or liked the way that I talk about literature or about life. But it's a great book by one of the greatest writers there is. And its aesthetic effect upon me, as well as Swift's intellectual effect, is enormous. But at the same time, as I say, it's profoundly antithetical to me and I find it in many ways repellent. So one can keep one's aesthetic judgements distinct from one's spiritual judgements, but I am sometimes aware that a different kind of value can come from the insights of an imaginative understanding—and in my case beyond that to a profound affinity—that illuminates certain writers for me, as they might otherwise not be illuminated. Though not Shakespeare. I remember one reviewer thought that I was bringing in, as he put it, "the dank crankeries of ancient heresies in order to illuminate Shakespeare." No. No. I think Shakespeare had some hermetist interests, but then he had interests in everything. Shakespeare is all-inclusive. Shakespeare is the container; everything else, including ourselves, are the things contained. It is not possible to overesteem or to overestimate the reach or the understanding of Shakespeare. I think Thomas Carlyle—to mention a great but almost forgotten name—was quite right. He said that if one were to choose the single quality in which Shakespeare is most outstanding, it would be excellence, the power of intellect, and let that include all the others. And I think Carlyle was right. Emerson said that Shakespeare wrote the text of modern life. Shakespeare is a miracle ultimately beyond my understanding, though I've done what I could with it. I seem, by my deliberate bardolatry, to have evoked a whole range of responses. The very distinguished critic Sir Frank Kermode was quoted by the New York Times—not exactly my favourite newspaper—as saying that Bloom's idea of Shakespeare's invention of the human is mere incense-burning. To which my only reply would be, "Well, if I'm going to burn incense to anyone or anything, I will very happily burn incense to Shakespeare."

WACHTEL You were saying earlier that you thought of Blake as a god.

BLOOM It seemed to me, when I was a young man, not so much that Blake was a god but that his writings were a kind of alternative scripture. Now—to use one of Northrop Frye's fine phrases, though he meant by it the whole form of romance in general—the secular scripture for me is The Complete Works of William Shakespeare. I mean this as an aesthetic statement also. In his rather wonderful book called James Joyce and the Making of Ulysses, Frank Budgen, who was a friend of Joyce's in Trieste—a painter, not a literary person—asked Joyce the desert island question: If you could have only one book if you were cast away, what would it be? Joyce replied magnificently—and this is verbatim—"I should like to answer, Dante, but I would have to take the Englishman because he is richer." One hears in that both a resentment on Joyce's part towards the precursor who filled him with anxiety—Shakespeare rather than Dante, who was not a source of anxiety—and also the Irishman's resentment of the ultimate Englishman, as it were. But I think Joyce is right: If I could have just the one book, it would have to be a complete Shakespeare. If there were a second book, I would have trouble. I suppose in the end I would have to choose the Hebrew Bible and settle for either Dante or Cervantes as the third, though that would be a difficult choice, too. I love Cervantes. I don't love Dante. But if one had to choose between the *Commedia* and *Don Quixote*, I guess I would simply say both. And then I would have all four books.

WACHTEL I want to talk for a moment about your book *The Western Canon*—I know we've been talking about it already, but more directly and even more simply back to basics, what is the canon? Why do we need it?

BLOOM There is no mystery about canons. A canon is a list. That's all. We need it because we *have* to read Shakespeare; we *have* to study Dante; we *have* to read Chaucer, Cervantes, the Bible, at least the King James Bible; we *have* to read certain authors; we *have* to read Proust, Tolstoy, Dickens, George Eliot and Jane Austen. It is inescapable that we have to read Joyce and Samuel Beckett. These are absolutely crucial writers. They provide an intellectual, dare I say a spiritual, value which has nothing to do with organized religion or the history of institutional belief. They remind us in every sense of re-minding us. They not only tell us things that we have forgotten but they tell us things we couldn't possibly know without them. And they reform our minds. They make our minds stronger; they make us more vital. They make us alive! You know, ten years ago I was much condemned for providing my own interpretation of the blessing in *The Book of J*. I said that when somebody blesses someone else in what is called the Old Testament, the Hebrew Bible, it always means one thing: it means *more life*. Cervantes and

Chaucer and Shakespeare and Dante—Shakespeare above all—provide one with the blessing of more life.

There is no set canon. There cannot be and there shouldn't be. I tried to make this very clear. But there are certain books that I really do feel we, all of us, should read as early as possible. What does education mean if it does not expose children and young people to Shakespeare and Cervantes and Dante? If Dante is too difficult, Shakespeare is universal. Shakespeare is the true multicultural author. He exists in all languages, he is put on the stage everywhere, everyone feels that they are represented by him on the stage. Cervantes is an absolutely universal author—almost Shakespearean in his power.

WACHTEL Why do you think *The Western Canon* came under attack not only from the left but also from the right?

BLOOM I certainly came under attack from the right. All the neoconservative journals—such as *Commentary* and the *American Mercury*, the *New Criterion* and the *National Review*—published harsh, angry reviews, denouncing me as a believer in art for art's sake and as somebody who doesn't believe that literature has a moral and religious basis. I've been condemned for saying that one does not read Shakespeare or even Dante for the moral or religious value of it. They have been just as savage in their way as the journalists and reviewers of the School of Resentment, the so-called left, have been on the other side. I have been very happy at getting it from both sides. It has been as much vindication, I believe, as the book could hope to have.

WACHTEL Why is the canon the venue for this kind of debate, or battle?

BLOOM I suppose it is because we are a rapidly collapsing society. It's the emancipation of selfishness. Some years ago, in testimony before either a Senate or a House committee, one of these Gingrichites actually said that not only should we cut off money for all illegitimate children whatsoever but we should again have a social stigma on illegitimacy! The function of the canon is to read Shakespeare and look at Edmund, the bastard in *King Lear*, look at the great bastard Faulconbridge—most magnificent creature—in *King John*. You wouldn't have these hideous moral imbeciles if they really could read Shakespeare, if they really had studied Shakespeare. I am firmly convinced of that.

WACHTEL You subtitle your book on Shakespeare *The Invention of the Human*. How has Shakespeare invented us?

BLOOM The subtitle of the book was somewhat tropological and after all, as a critic I am—or try to be—a faithful disciple of the greatest of all literary critics, Dr. Samuel Johnson. The great Johnson said that the essence of poetry was invention, by which he meant discovery in the deep sense, and so if Shakespeare is the essence of poetry, the essence of imaginative literature, then I'm just being Johnsonian in saying that the essence of Shakespeare is invention, and what he most profoundly and beautifully invents or reinvents is the idea of the human. But I also meant, rather more specifically, another sense in which I wasn't at all original. The London solicitor and literary critic—he was never an academic—with whom I used to correspond, the late Owen Barfield, wrote, among other fine works of criticism, a wonderful book called *Saving the Appearances*. Barfield wrote—and I may not have this quite verbatim but I have the gist of it—that it can embarrass us, it can almost humiliate us when we realize that what we like to feel are our own emotions are actually Shakespeare's thoughts. Now, that is pretty much what I'm trying to say when I write about Shakespeare as the inventor of human personality as we possess it now, that what we like to think of as our emotions are actually Shakespeare's thoughts. They are what Shakespeare has put down in language.

There's a certain aphorism of Nietzsche's that I think came to him out of his reading of *Hamlet* in particular. Nietzsche remarks, "That for which we can find words is something that is already dead in our hearts." He adds that there's always a kind of contempt in the act of speaking. I find that a dreadful insight, and of course one hopes it isn't completely true. That would mean that if any of us ever said to another, "I love you," he or she was actually speaking something that had already passed, not something alive in the heart

WACHTEL Surely it must not be true.

BLOOM Hamlet thought it was true, and I fear that Shakespeare finally believed it was true also. Certainly when Hamlet, in one of the great soliloquies, castigates himself for, like a whore, he says, unpacking his heart with words, you have exactly the Nietzschean insight. And, of course, Nietzsche has said so beautifully of him, "Let's not think about Hamlet as someone who fails to act or someone who thinks too much." I think that Nietzsche is responding to Coleridge when he says, quite rightly, that Hamlet thinks not too much but much too well, thinks so well that he thinks his way through to the truth, and all you can do with the truth, according to Nietzsche and according to Hamlet, is to die of it and with it and for it. You cannot live with it. Indeed, Nietzsche finally tells us that we possess literature, we possess art, because otherwise we would die of the truth. I suppose that's a restatement of unpacking one's heart with words or being able to say something only if, indeed, it is already dead in our hearts. I don't know that between Hamlet and Rosalind in As You Like It, and John Falstaff, my particular hero—of whom more in a moment—and Cleopatra in Antony and Cleopatra, with those four figures in particular and then with Iago in Othello and Macbeth—the great hero-villains—Edmund in King Lear and, of course, with the overwhelming figure of Lear himself—I don't know if in some sense Shakespeare has not, in fact, reinvented the human, if he has not changed our whole notion of what our personality is or is not capable of. Certainly, Falstaff and Hamlet in particular seem to define for me what is human.

WACHTEL To get back to Shakespeare's subscribing to that statement of Nietzsche's—that for which we can find words is something already dead in our hearts. You put the question in your book about Shakespeare and you say it remains urgent in its implications, whether Shakespeare is fundamentally a celebrant of life or nihilistic.

BLOOM He is both. He invented ambivalence, as we know it—what Freud was to call ambivalence. He invented Western nihilism, but he is also the most immense celebrant of life. Falstaff matches Alice, Chaucer's Wife of Bath, in that regard. She cries out, "For I have had my world as in my time." He cries out, "Sir Walter Blunt: there's honour for you! . . . I like not such grinning honour as Sir Walter hath: give me life." These are two immense vitalists. Shakespeare is at once a great vitalist and ultimately a nihilist beyond our understanding of what nihilism can be. As I read the great Shakespearean parts of the collaboration with Fletcher, in Shakespeare's last play, The Two Noble Kinsmen, or as I read The Tempest or as I tend to interpret Measure for Measure or the great tragedies or Timon of Athens, it is very difficult: this greatest of all vitalists, Shakespeare, is finally also a far greater nihilist than anyone who has come after him. I suppose we need terms that we have not got to describe Shakespeare accurately. I don't think Shakespeare can be accurately described. You can try to apprehend him in one way or another, but he is ultimately not just beyond our comprehension but beyond our apprehension, to use the distinction that Shakespeare invents in A Midsummer Night's Dream.

WACHTEL You identify with the vitalist. Your alter ego in Shakespeare is Falstaff.

BLOOM Sir John Falstaff who, however, ends in great sadness. Who ends totally rejected and heartbroken.

WACHTEL But the tragedy is that he is so full of life.

BLOOM It's as though I ought to turn to you, Eleanor, since, though I have loved you from afar until now, it's as though I were to say to you, "Thou hast damnable iteration, Eleanor, and art indeed able to corrupt a saint. Thou has done much harm upon me, Eleanor. May God forgive thee, Eleanor. Before I knew thee, I knew nothing and now to speak truly am I become little better than one of the wicked." That's magnificent. There can't be anything in literature better than that. And it's a mockery, of course, of all kinds of things, but what beats through the mockery, the parodistic excess of it, is Falstaff's extraordinary exuberance. He is, as Ben Jonson said of another matter, rammed with life. He's like Sancho Panza or like Panurge in Rabelais, and yet he transcends them. The only real equivalent I can find for him is Alice, the Wife of Bath, and she's perhaps a touch more sinister. We don't know, after all, what happened to her fourth husband—

WACHTEL You've said that it's hard to find a satisfactory production of

Shakespeare on stage, and you obviously prefer to read him.

BLOOM Well, I have distinguished antecedents. The great Goethe said that he would rather read Shakespeare than see him staged, though he did stage Shakespeare. Charles Lamb so despaired of seeing *King Lear* properly acted that he wondered why one would go to the theatre to see a travesty when one could stay home and read the play.

WACHTEL But at the same time, you were inspired by an early performance of Ralph Richardson as Falstaff.

BLOOM I was either fifteen or sixteen. It was here in New York City, the Old Vic in its prime, with Richardson, with Olivier and others. The matinee was the first part of *Henry IV* and the evening was the second part. I attended both. Sir Ralph Richardson. It was one of the extraordinary experiences of my life.

WACHTEL What was so remarkable about his performance?

BLOOM His Falstaff. If only it had been recorded. If only it had been put on tape. If only there were a film of it. He was Falstaff, but he was somehow the only possible Falstaff. He had seen through everything and yet would not abide, either in just mockery or despair. He surged with vitality. When he is resurrected on the battlefield after he plays dead, it was resurrection in the full sense. He just bounded up extraordinarily and cried out, "Embalm me." He was every kind of intelligence, every kind of vivacity, every kind of perception, every kind of energy, every kind of extraordinary mixture of immanence and transcendence at once. He was both transcendental and extraordinary, but he was so powerfully immanent on stage that he gave me a new sense of what presence could possibly mean as a concept. Indeed, it wasn't until years later that I remembered that the Hotspur in Part One was Laurence Olivier in his prime—his exuberant prime—and that astonishingly, with an incredible virtuosity, in the evening Olivier was Shallow. Amazing to see him go from the dashing last representative of a sort of cavalier's glory, of chivalry, of honour, to the fourth radish of Shallow in just a few hours.

WACHTEL Do you think it was because of the power of Richardson's performance, rather than the text, that Falstaff overtook you?

BLOOM No. I think I was already taken with the text and the commentaries on it, especially A. C. Bradley's marvellous essay "The Rejection of Falstaff," which is also an exaltation of Falstaff. Not the Falstaff that Sir William Empson once dismissed as a lovable old dear. Falstaff is no lovable old dear. I don't think I would want to have dinner with Sir John Falstaff. He would certainly pick my pocket and I might be very lucky indeed not to have a shiv put into my ribs. He's a very dangerous fellow, a professional highwayman. He's not someone you can morally trust. But then there are very great poets—François Villon, Arthur Rimbaud, Christopher Marlowe—whom you wouldn't want to have dinner with or be in the same room with at night. These were very dangerous human beings, great criminals as well as great poets. Falstaff is both a great triumph of the imagination and a very wicked fellow indeed, though not ever malevolent.

WACHTEL Do you understand why there are so many movie versions of Shakespeare nowadays?

BLOOM It's very curious. We live in the age of the screen—the television screen, the motion picture screen, alas, the computer screen, though I know the Internet is absolutely commercially necessary, that it makes available to people who otherwise couldn't afford it all sorts of potentially very useful material. It's just that I'm afraid that people who haven't had real educations could drown in the Internet, never learning to differentiate between one thing and another and just sinking into that great grey ocean of information and text. But it happens that we need not worry about three authors in particular, three authors who wrote in English and seem to translate marvellously to the screen—any kind of a screen. They are Shakespeare and Charles Dickens and Jane Austen. For reasons that I don't always fully understand, since they are three very different writers—though Austen is very affected by Shakespeare, and Dickens, though he wanted to prefer Ben Jonson, is also deeply affected by Shakespeare—they seem to lend themselves to screen presentation.

WACHTEL And you, in all your perversity, favour, of all the screen versions of Shakespeare, Kurosawa's Japanese—

BLOOM Yes, I'm afraid so. I had a debate one night on stage at the 92nd Street Y with Frank Kermode. We differ on many things, and we were debating Shakespeare and how he ought to be appreciated. Sir Frank found it very odd that I should prefer Kurosawa's *Throne of Blood*, his version of *Macbeth*, and *Ran*, his version of *Lear*, since he said there's no Shakespearean text there at all.

WACHTEL There's no English.

BLOOM There's no English. Yes. And I don't know Japanese. And yet I have seen both those films, *Throne of Blood* and *Ran*, four or five times each, and they're not only magnificent films but it seemed to me that Kurosawa caught the spirit of both *Macbeth* and *Lear* far better than any screen versions that I've ever seen of either work or, indeed, of most stage productions. Though I have seen some remarkable perform-ances—Ian McKellen's Macbeth was quite remarkable.

WACHTEL It's curious that Shakespeare, who is the centre of your *Western Canon*, is somehow so appreciated, loved, in the non-Western world.

BLOOM That's the greatness of Shakespeare. Students and professors from all over the world tell me of productions that they have attended of Shakespeare in the most extraordinary places—in Indonesia, in Bul-garia, in Nigeria, in all kinds of countries, where frequently the groundlings—as Shakespeare would have said—in the audience sometimes have trouble with their own language on stage and cer-tainly know no English and yet they are fascinated because they some-how feel that they are there on stage, that Shakespeare has understood them and put them on stage. It's an amazing phenomenon, and it quite clearly has nothing to do with cultural materialism or British imperialism or all those things that the postcolonialists in our univer-sities or the new historicists and all the other resenters—as I call them—obsess about. No. Shakespeare is the closest thing that we have to universal literary and human genius, and he is instantly appre-hended and, indeed, to an amazing degree, *comprehended* almost every-where. I still remember a learned Bulgarian friend, now a professor of English at the Hebrew University, who told me about a performance she had seen in Sofia of several of the great Shakespearean plays. She said that the audiences felt very passionately that this was, indeed, literature and life coming together, that this was, for them, absolutely natural, absolutely habitual.

WACHTEL You say somewhere that Hamlet is as frequently invoked as Christ—

BLOOM I would think that Hamlet is, in a sense, the secular Christ, or the intellectual's Christ. He seems to be almost as real a presence as Christ, though obviously I will shock many people by saying that and I do not mean impiety. I respect deeply held religious beliefs. But Hamlet has had an effect upon the world which is quite extraordinary. No more capacious, no more comprehensive consciousness has ever been represented than Hamlet's. It's a kind of miracle on Shakespeare's part that somehow Hamlet really has touched the infinite. I've always found the most astonishing critical judgement in the history of the English language is T. S. Eliot's amazing assertion that *Hamlet* was an aesthetic failure, whereas *Coriolanus* was a great aesthetic success. It strikes me as the height of perversity on Eliot's part, and could be saved only if Eliot intended it as an irony, though I fear he did not so intend it.

WACHTEL You followed up your massive work on Shakespeare with, as you say, an intentionally smaller book, the boldly titled *How to Read and Why*. You said recently that forty years ago you could never have imagined writing a book with that title. What happened? What made this book necessary?

BLOOM Well, two things. One, which I now try to de-emphasize as I tried to de-emphasize it in the book, is the reputation that I accumulated in regard to *The Western Canon*. It was almost as though certain people confused me with my late acquaintance Allan Bloom. I'm not a conservative; I'm certainly not a cultural conservative. I'm anything but a political or religious conservative. I'm an old-line socialist who, since the death of Norman Thomas, has voted for the Democratic candidates because I can't get a socialist candidate elected. But I do greatly fear George W. Bush. I like to call him the "least distinguished" graduate of Yale University in the three hundred years of that university.

But to get back to why this book was necessary now. I wrote *The Western Canon* and, to some extent, *Shakespeare: The Invention of the Human* partly to fill a need—somewhat defensive but not altogether so—for readers who had been neglected by what has happened to the study of literature in universities. But that wasn't the impetus for *How to Read and Why*. In the last two or three years, I have come to understand much better that the great enemy of reading all over the world is not the fashion for cultural studies that has replaced literary studies in the university. I deplore that, but I think it will pass like all fashions. No, the great danger is that we are in the age of information. We are in the age of the screen. We may soon be in the age of virtual reality. We are, alas, now entering the age of the e-book, which I passionately deplore because I think it's a terrible cultural regression. It was such an enormous advance to go from a scroll to a codex, the initial form of what we now regard as a printed and bound book. Now we are going back to the scroll: that's what a screen is. You can press buttons and one scroll will replace another scroll, but it's still a scroll.

The great enemy of reading today is the Internet. The great enemy of reading today is being on-line. A lot of people become angry when I say this. Some young people argue that they can't afford the books I want them to read. To that I have to bow in considerable humility. I'm properly chastened.

WACHTEL What about libraries?

BLOOM Unfortunately, I don't know how libraries are in Canada these days, but they're badly shortchanged in the United States. They're not even open every day of the week, as they should be. I owe everything to the New York Public Library. Without the New York Public Library of the 1930s, I would have had no chance: the Melrose Branch Public Library in the Bronx and then the Central Branch, the Fordham Road Library and finally the 42nd Street Library. Until I went off to Cornell, that's where I was educated. That gave me access to all the books there were. Libraries aren't like that any more. They're not properly financed. They're not kept open enough and too frequently they're just computer centres.

WACHTEL To some extent, that's what's happening in Canada as well.

BLOOM Yes, and that's what's behind *How to Read and Why*. I have a great fear of the screen. I'm not a Luddite—I know that the Internet is an international economic and commercial necessity, that this cannot be reversed. I know that the e-book is upon us. But I greatly fear its effect upon younger minds and younger readers, and I have deep concern about the future of the only reading that matters, which is close and deep rereading of the very greatest that has been thought and written. We need it. We need it desperately. I'm condemned for elitism, but I don't think this is elitism. This is being a democrat with a very small d as well as a large D. Democracy will survive only if we can think powerfully and well, only if we can remember the very strongest works. We need Shakespeare, and not just on the screen. Not just as images. We need Dante. Whether or not we need the Bible spiritually is up to the individual, but I would say with certainty that from a literary and aesthetic and intellectual point of view, we very much need it.

WACHTEL Do you read differently now from when you were young?

BLOOM Yes. I read with more sadness. One goes through a lot of sadness in one's life, both on one's own behalf and on behalf of loved ones and friends and others. I don't think I have the primal exuberance as a reader at the age of seventy that I had at the age of seven or eight or fifteen or twenty-five or even thirty-five. I probably am a better reader than I was even two or three years ago, in the sense that the more one knows, the more one's memory can bring to bear. It's very odd. Brain cells do wear out and quite frequently when I try to remember somebody's name—even that of an old friend—in order to introduce them to someone else, I can't remember it, which is very embarrassing. But I can remember every fictive name. I can remember every passage of poetry I've ever cared for. I can give you an account of any novel or short story I've read. Sometimes, indeed, I can quote it. So the stores of memory get greater and greater and one learns better how to use one's memory. I try to teach people—and I follow Shelley in this—that deep or authentic reading requires learning how to give up easier pleasures in favour of pleasures that are much more difficult. It is true that reading is a much more difficult pleasure for me than it was earlier in my life, and therefore, in a sense, it is a higher pleasure. But there was a kind of simple joy in reading, an exultant or ecstatic sense that reading brought me when I was young, that I don't get as often nowadays. There is, to that degree, a falling-off. I think it was John Ruskin who said quite wonderfully that old age is a shipwreck. At seventy, I read differently because I read and reread against the clock. I always ask myself, and I urge others to ask, Should I reread this rather than that? Should I read this for the first time rather than that? Because for reading, there never will be enough time. There never has been enough time. I've read all my life, but I have not read everything I want to have read.

WACHTEL I was going to ask you about that, because you're fond of quoting Mallarmé: "The flesh is sad. And I've read all the books." But you don't feel that you've read all the books?

BLOOM No, and I still have an appetite for them. Someone recently told me about a book I should have known about a long time ago, Richard Heinze's wonderful study of the *Aeneid*. It's just arrived in English translation and I've started to read it. I feel quite wonderful about having this on hand. And I've been rereading, for the first time in a number of years, *The Praise of Folly* by Erasmus, and I find that wonderfully invigorating.

WACHTEL You've always talked about reading as a way of finding out about your authentic self, and at the same getting outside yourself because you don't get a chance to live enough lives otherwise.

BLOOM Yes. We cannot live all lives.

WACHTEL Is part of the falling-off of the pleasure because you already know that authentic self? It's been discovered, so there isn't that part of the search left for you.

BLOOM No, I don't think it's that. The self is still undiscovered country. One is still going there, still finding it. I think I have the energy of response that I always had, but I get tired. The flesh gets weary.

WACHTEL You chose a beautiful line from one of your favourite modern poets, Wallace Stevens, for the epigraph to *How to Read and Why*.

BLOOM Yes.

The reader became the book;
and summer night
Was like the conscious being of the book.

That's very beautiful. I still experience that sense, a little brokenly, perhaps. But I'm glad I chose those lines as the book's epigraph. I hold by that, Eleanor.

October 2000/January 1995

ACKNOWLEDGEMENTS

Since my last selection of interviews, *More Writers & Company*, was published, I've had the opportunity to do a number of special series for radio—on India, Israel, Russia, Berlin, South Africa, Islam, and most recently, *Original Minds*. In every case, I've had the good fortune to collaborate with the indispensable founding producer of "Writers & Company," Sandra Rabinovitch. Working together so closely creates a kind of trust and understanding that one finds in only the best relationships. I feel both lucky and grateful.

I would also like to acknowledge the support and encouragement of Damiano Pietropaolo and Susan Feldman, and the dedication and generosity of the show's ongoing producer, Mary Stinson (here with respect to Oliver Sacks), of contributing producer Ian Pearson (for Jared Diamond and Amartya Sen), and the unfailing assistance and good humour of associate producer Nancy McIlveen. In the early stages of this project, I enjoyed conversations with the executive producer of "Ideas," Bernie Lucht.

My colleagues on "The Arts Today" have included Stephanie Conn, Jesse Wente, Sascha Hastings, Li Robbins, David Carroll and Lisa

Godfrey; they provide both stimulation and camaraderie. Linda Perry in New York and David Clifton in London have warmly welcomed both me and the guests.

A number of people have been invaluable in helping to transform radio interviews into this book. First, of course, the subjects themselves who agreed to have their conversations appear between these covers; I feel gratified that no one who was invited refused. Then my friend Carroll Klein who threw herself into the editing with such good will, optimism and expertise. I'm still not sure how she figured out *Pali* and *Prakit* from [unclear]. This is not to diminish the attentive transcribing of Susan Young and Hedy Muyssen.

I continue to be impressed by the loyalty and tact of my agent, Jackie Kaiser, and the enthusiasm of everyone at HarperCollins: David Kent, Iris Tupholme, and my editor Nicole Langlois.

I have been sustained in many ways by many people. Previously, I've simply expressed a blanket gratitude, but you all deserve to be named, if not implicated. I feel privileged to know Carol Shields; her generosity and courage and astuteness are awesome. Her friendship has given me so much pleasure and inspiration.

In recent years, I've experienced the unexpected gift, and have benefited enormously from the intelligence, wit and encouragement of Christina McCall.

To borrow (and invert) Tennessee Williams, I've always depended on the kindness of friends—chief among them Gayla Reid and Marta Braun, who will read whatever I write and catch egregious locutions like this one. As you well know, I owe you far more than I can say (and you can say it better anyway).

And I am grateful for all the varieties of help I receive from Marlene and Frank Cashman (& the Beautiful Boys + Ilana), Sharon Batt, Sherrill Cheda, Caroline Christie, Georgia Earls, Kath Farris, Beth Haddon, Avis Lang, Royce LaNier, Aidan McQuillan, Barbie Nichol, Don Shields, Lynn Smith, Audrey Thomas, Andy Wachtel, Jeannie Wexler, Trish Wilson, and Elizabeth Wood. I also want to thank the adhoc proofing crews, past and present, which include some of the above as well as Rita

West, Grant Harland, Sylvia Cymbalista, Marc Clapp + Sue Brandis, Matt Drayman, Beth Kaplan, Anne Russon, Rhea Tregebov and Sandy Wiseman.

In the last year, I've been made aware ever more acutely of the fragility of life. Consolation is hard won; there are the usual avenues—work, art, nature—but it is the constancy and affection of intimates, family, friends that see me through. I know of no adequate way to acknowledge that.

And I am deeply grateful to CBC Radio listeners who continue to communicate their responses to the program. You keep the show alive.

Eleanor Wachtel is a writer and broadcaster who has hosted CBC Radio's *Writers & Company* since its inception in 1990, and *The Arts Today* since 1996. In addition to her widely acclaimed books, *Writers & Company* and *More Writers & Company*, she contributed to the anthologies *Lost Classics* and *Dropped Threads*, and has co-authored and co-edited three other books. Wachtel received the 2002 Jack Award for her support of Canadian books and authors, and *Writers & Company* has twice received the CBC Award for Programming Excellence, in 1995 and 2003. Born and raised in Montreal, where she studied English literature at McGill University, Eleanor Wachtel lives in Toronto.